Expert Spring MVC and Web Flow

D1568144

Seth Ladd
with Darren Davison,
Steven Devijver and Colin Yates

Apress®

Expert Spring MVC and Web Flow

Copyright © 2006 by Seth Ladd, Darren Davison, Steven Devijver, and Colin Yates

ISBN-13 (pbk): 978-1-59059-584-8

ISBN-10 (pbk): 1-59059-584-X

Printed and bound in the United States of America 9 8 7 6 5 4 3 2 1

Lead Editor: Steve Anglin
Technical Reviewers: Rob Harrop, Keith Donald
Editorial Board: Steve Anglin, Dan Appleman, Ewan Buckingham, Gary Cornell, Jason Gilmore,
    Jonathan Hassell, James Huddleston, Chris Mills, Matthew Moodie, Dominic Shakeshaft,
    Jim Sumser, Matt Wade
Project Manager: Sofia Marchant
Copy Edit Manager: Nicole LeClerc
Copy Editor: Stephanie Provines
Assistant Production Director: Kari Brooks-Copony
Production Editor: Katie Stence
Compositor and Artist: Van Winkle Design Group
Proofreader: Nancy Sixsmith
Indexer: Broccoli Information Management
Cover Designer: Kurt Krames
Manufacturing Director: Tom Debolski

Distributed to the book trade worldwide by Springer-Verlag New York, Inc., 233 Spring Street, 6th Floor, New York, NY 10013. Phone 1-800-SPRINGER, fax 201-348-4505, e-mail orders-ny@springer-sbm.com, or visit http://www.springeronline.com.

For information on translations, please contact Apress directly at 2560 Ninth Street, Suite 219, Berkeley, CA 94710. Phone 510-549-5930, fax 510-549-5939, e-mail info@apress.com, or visit http://www.apress.com.

The source code for this book is available to readers at http://www.apress.com in the Source Code section.

To my father, who brought home
that old 1200-baud modem from work and
kick-started this crazy journey.
—Seth Ladd

To Mum and Dad, for always encouraging my curiosity.
And to my wife, Lisa, for being my wife.
—Darren Davison

For Beeky and the wriggler for putting up
with the late evenings, and Bruce and Jessie
for missing out on the walks.
—Colin Yates

For Filiz.
—Steven Devijver

To my wonderful wife, Keri,
and our little bundle of joy, Annabelle.
—Keith Donald

Contents at a Glance

Contents

About the Authors

 **SETH LADD** is a software engineer and professional Spring Framework trainer and mentor specializing in object-oriented and testable web applications. He started his own company building websites at age 17, but now enjoys having a real job. Currently working for Camber Corporation, Seth has built and deployed systems for NEC, Rochester Institute of Technology, Brivo Systems, and National Information Consortium. He has architected and developed enterprise applications in Java and C for both the server and remotely connected embedded devices. He enjoys speaking and teaching, and is a frequent presenter at local Java user groups and at corporate developer conferences. Seth is very thankful for living and working in Kailua, Hawaii, with his wife.

 **DARREN DAVISON** is a principal consultant for UPCO, specializing in J2EE and open source Java technologies. He has been involved with Spring since the summer of 2003, well before its 1.0 release, and he used the framework to underpin a global intranet site for an investment bank. Darren has previously worked for multinational manufacturing and engineering companies on e-business, infrastructure, and many web-based projects.

Away from work, Darren enjoys the never-ending journey of discovery that is GNU/Linux. When not in front of a computer screen, he likes reading and any form of live entertainment.

STEVEN DEVIJVER is an experienced Java developer who started developing J2EE applications in 2000. In 2003 he discovered the Spring Framework, and since then he has been one of its most enthusiastic users. Steven is a senior consultant at Interface21, teaching hundreds of students every year about the Spring Framework.

 **COLIN YATES** is a J2EE principal architect who specializes in web-based development. He has been a freelance consultant for the past three years and has worked in a number of environments, both structured and chaotic. Since graduating with a software engineering degree in 1997, he has held a number of positions, including development lead, principal systems engineer, mentor, and professional trainer. His principal skill set includes mentoring others, architecting complex problems into manageable solutions, and optimizing development processes.

Colin was first introduced to the Spring Framework in January 2003 by his mentors, Peter Den Haan and David Hewitt, and he has never looked back. After a couple of years using the Spring and Hibernate technology stack to good effect, in May 2005 he became one of the early adopters of Spring Web Flow, finally finding the missing item in the web development toolbox.

A self-confessed addict of the green bar that comes from following test-driven development and XP, Colin regularly frustrates new team members by introducing a continuous build environment.

When not hanging around the Spring support forums (http://forum.springframework.org), Colin can be found out walking with his wife and two dogs, practicing martial arts, attending his local church, or preparing for the arrival of his first child.

About the Technical Reviewers

■**KEITH DONALD** is a software consultant specializing in delivering customer-driven, enterprise-class Java applications. An experienced developer and mentor, Keith has built applications for customers spanning a diverse set of industries, including network management, information assurance, food services, education, and retail. He has extensive experience translating business requirements into technical solutions.

Keith has been involved with the Spring Framework as a user and core contributor since July 2003. He is the founder of the Spring Rich Client Project, an emerging module built on core Spring that substantially reduces the time and effort required to build a well-architected, enterprise-ready Java desktop application. He is also the colead of the Spring Web Flow module, a core Spring web offering that lets developers model business processes that span many screens in a logical manner.

Keith enjoys speaking and teaching on technical and business software-related topics, and has a career-oriented weblog where he frequently posts articles. Contact Keith at keith@interface21.com.

■**ROB HARROP** is a software consultant specializing in delivering high-performance, highly scalable enterprise applications. He is an experienced architect with a particular flair for understanding and solving complex design issues. With a thorough knowledge of both Java and .NET, Rob has successfully deployed projects across both platforms. He has extensive experience across a variety of sectors, in particular retail and government.

Rob has been a core developer of the Spring Framework since June 2004 and currently leads the JMX and AOP efforts. In addition to his work on the Spring core, Rob leads the Spring Modules project, which is working to provide Spring integration for a variety of popular useful open source tools. He cofounded UK-based software company Cake Solutions Limited in May 2001, having spent the previous two years working as the lead developer for a successful dot-com startup.

Rob is the author of five books, including *Pro Spring*, a widely acclaimed, comprehensive resource on the Spring Framework. He is a member of the JCP and is involved in the JSR-255 Expert Group for JMX 2.0.

Acknowledgments

A book is never written by the authors alone. It is the product of many people's expertise and hard work, time, and superhuman efforts. This book belongs to everyone who had a hand in producing it.

I'd like to first thank my wife, who has the patience of an angel. Her love and support has been monumental through this endeavor.

My coauthors deserve huge thanks, as they have added their unique and invaluable knowledge and insight to make this a stronger book than I could have ever produced alone. Thanks Darren, Steven, Keith, and Colin!

No one would be reading this book if it weren't for the talent and professionalism at Apress. Specifically, I owe my heartfelt appreciation to Sofia Marchant and Beckie Brand for coordinating the many moving parts and making sure the book is the best it can be. A huge shout-out is owed to Stephanie Provines, without whom we would have capitalized Spring MVC 12 different ways. Her attention to detail was impressive and extremely valued. I specifically want to thank Steve Anglin as well, for giving me this opportunity. And to all the people behind the scenes, I am forever indebted to you.

I had the pleasure of having Rob Harrop perform the technical review for the book. His advice was always accurate, helpful, and professional. Thank you, Rob, I was honored to have you as part of the team.

Thanks to Erwin Vervaet, Dan Leuck, and Colin Sampaleanu for their expert opinions while reviewing the book. Thanks to Kathleen Fitzgerald for the photo shoot. And finally, thanks to the Spring Framework developers and community, from whom I have learned an incredible amount about software development.

Seth Ladd

I thank Seth Ladd for the opportunity to coauthor this book and for writing this excellent book in the first place. I also thank Rob Harrop for sharing his insights of Spring Web MVC and for doing the technical review of this book. Many thanks to the core Spring developers for creating and constantly extending this amazing framework. Thanks also go to Erwin Vervaet and Keith Donald for creating Spring Web Flow. I also thank my family for supporting me. I especially thank my girlfriend, Filiz, for her support, for proofreading, and for the warmth and energy she gives to me. Thank you all.

Steven Devijver

CHAPTER 1

Introduction

I can still remember the time I first realized what the Spring Framework was and how it could help me. I was tasked with building a web application that will register new businesses with the local government, and being a Java shop this meant the standard set of frameworks at the time: Struts, JavaServer Pages (JSP), and Hibernate. Having built many applications with these technologies, we dove right into development.

When beginning a new application, I always want to improve a few things from the last product development cycle. This time around, it was time to get serious about two things, unit testing and good object-oriented design. Sure, I had written plenty of unit tests before, but I had never begun a project by writing tests first. And although I've been studying and developing with OOP for many years now, I continue to learn new techniques that help the design of the application retain sustainability in the face of change.

So, off we went developing the application, writing tests for the domain model, creating a service layer (a façade for the web layer to integrate with), and beginning the build-out of the Struts layer. Each layer in the system seemed to progress nicely, but that's exactly when we ran into trouble.

As integration between layers began, we noticed that it became harder and harder to write good tests for the system. The application was using the Service Locator pattern to integrate the service layer and the web layers together. This pattern was implemented using a static lookup, which proved impossible to change for our unit tests. The question soon became, "How do we integrate these components such that both writing tests and running in production is simple and efficient?"

Enter the Spring Framework.

More precisely, enter an introduction article about the Spring Framework, posted to TheServerSide (http://www.theserverside.com). The original article has since been updated: http://www.theserverside.com/articles/article.tss?l=SpringFramework. I still remember printing it out, stapling it together, and sitting back down to my desk to see what all the fuss was about. Could it really help me create easily testable applications? Could it really bring OOP back to web development? There was only one way to find out.

I passed the article off to the boss, and I still remember his Aha moment after reading it. We decided to go for it and use the framework to integrate the components through the new-fangled Dependency Injection. This led to easily testing the components, which led to better code, which led to happier clients. We then replaced our in-house Data Access Object (DAO) framework, one thing led to another, and we had a highly tested, full-blown Spring MVC application.

Of course, ripping out all of the Struts code and in-house cruft took time and energy, but we found we could do it in stages, lowering the risk of the integration. We made some mistakes and wrote lots of code, and in the end we had a better product—with a better design and a clear vision of how we wanted to write web applications from that point onward. In other words, we found what we were looking for in Spring MVC for our Java web applications.

My hope is that you can use this book to peer deeper into Spring MVC and learn new and interesting ways to use the framework to enhance your applications. We found that Spring MVC makes doing the right thing easier, and sometimes simply possible, and we hope you'll find as much joy using it as we do.

—Seth Ladd

Skipping Ahead

If you are the impatient type, you've probably skipped this chapter altogether and headed for the code. If you're still here, we have a recommendation for you. If you want to jump ahead and start with building a Spring MVC application, feel free to check out Chapter 4. There you will find elementary details on how to start building your first Spring MVC application.

We also recommend that you return to the previous chapters to learn about the theory and background of web application creation with Spring MVC. It will help to provide the context for the rest of the book.

How to View This Book

You should look at this book as your in-depth guide to the many features and functions of Spring MVC, including tips and tricks to get the most out of this flexible framework. This book also contains some best practices for developing well-designed and decoupled web applications.

This book is part guidebook, part tutorial, part web development manual. This book works best as a companion to *Pro Spring* by Rob Harrop and Jan Machacek (Apress, 2005), because it does not cover the Spring Framework in a general sense. It is dedicated to and focused on the best ways to write web applications using the Spring Framework and Spring MVC.

Roadmap

This book covers a lot of ground. Use this roadmap and chapter outline for a quick overview of what you will find inside and where.

- Chapter 1 is, well, this chapter you're reading now. It contains an overview of the book and its target audience, as well as where to go for more information and support.

- Chapter 2 is a refresher on the Spring Framework. If you are new to Spring, this can help paint the picture of why the framework exists and what problems it is trying to solve. Entire books are devoted to Spring, but this chapter can kick-start your discovery of the framework. If you are brand-new to the framework, you should purchase a full book on Spring, such as *Pro Spring*.

- Chapter 3 covers the architecture and design of typical Spring MVC applications. Light on code but heavy on design, this chapter presents details on the common layers found in web applications and some simple guidelines to build applications that take full advantage of the Spring Framework.

- Chapter 4 shows you the goods, with a jump start on Spring MVC. The impatient will find this a good starting point to get the feel of a real application. This chapter doesn't go into much detail, but it does take what you've learned from Chapter 3 to build some real functionality.

- Chapter 5 goes into detail about the real workhorse of Spring MVC: the `Dispatcher-erServlet`. In this chapter you'll find all the ancillary services that all web applications require and how they can be configured and extended. Services like multipart file upload support and Locale resolution are covered here.

- Chapter 6 outlines and explains all of the different `Controller` options found in the framework. `Controllers` are written by you to handle incoming web requests, much like servlets or Struts Actions. Spring MVC provides a rich menagerie of `Controllers` to help with many different use cases and requirements.

- Chapter 7 introduces the view layer. Here you will find a tour of how views are managed and how they are integrated into a full Spring MVC application. Darren Davison, committer on Spring's view technologies, contributed both Chapters 7 and 8.

- Chapter 8 builds upon its predecessor and informs you how to integrate the popular view technologies with Spring MVC. JSP, Velocity, FreeMarker, and XSLT are just a few of your options for rendering the view, all covered in this chapter.

- Chapter 9 covers the Validation Framework. It also introduces Valang, a new and exciting validation system to make writing custom validation rules quick and easy. Steven Devijver, the author of Valang and Spring Framework committer, contributed Chapter 9.

- Chapter 10 provides examples of and discussion on testing your Spring MVC applications, including Spring's handy mocks and stubs for the Servlet API. We take the view that testing should be quick and painless, so we use a combination of simple unit tests and mock objects to write tests that run inside your IDE (and outside of your container).

- Chapters 11 and 12 cover the cutting-edge Spring Web Flow, a framework for writing conversational use cases on the web. This project, originally developed by Erwin Vervaet and brought into the Spring Framework fold by Keith Donald, allows you to declaratively build use cases that span multiple requests. Colin Yates provided these chapters.

- Appendix A introduces an excellent tool for documenting your Spring applications. The BeanDoc tool, written and maintained by Darren Davison, is like Javadoc for your bean definition XML files. This handy and easy tool integrates with your build to produce HTML documentation complete with images of the dependencies between beans. This appendix was contributed by Darren Davison, author of BeanDoc.

- Appendix B provides a bit of a sidebar; it introduces one way to integrate AJAX technologies into your Spring-powered web application. Darren Davison explains how to integrate DWR, or Direct Web Remoting (`http://getahead.ltd.uk/dwr`), with your Spring MVC applications.

Target Audience

Even though this book's title contains the word *expert*, you don't need to be an expert in Java or Spring to take advantage of it. However, to get the most out of this book, you should be familiar with Java and have created at least one web application with it.

You won't find discussions on basic Servlet API constructs or how to set up and configure your favorite servlet container. Many great books and resources—including countless web resources—already exist for this. We assume that you have at least a passing knowledge of what the Servlet API provides and how to deploy a Java web application. We also assume you are a competent Java developer, familiar with the language and its APIs.

Although you need not be a Spring Framework expert, it helps if you have investigated it to get a feel for what it is and what it brings to the table. We merely provide an introduction to the framework in this book. We recommend that you have a reference resource handy to turn to when we mention a Spring concept that you might not be familiar with.

If you are familiar with Java web programming and curious how Spring MVC stacks up against other request/response web frameworks, then this book will certainly help you determine that.

If you have built a few web applications with Spring MVC, we believe this book can still offer you great value. We provide many little tips and tricks, including some best practices for making the most from the web architecture in general. This book also covers some of the motivations for the designs of the components of Spring MVC, providing valuable insight into why the elements were built that way and how they connect.

For More Information

When you run into a situation that this book can't cover, you'll find that the Spring Framework has a vibrant and supportive community ready to help you out. The Spring community is made up of Java developers who take OOP, testability, and good design seriously, so you'll be in good company.

- The Spring Framework's home page, `http://www.springframework.org`, is the place to get news about the framework and links to many resources found on the web. Use this as a jumping-off point to downloads, forums, CVS, and issue tracker services.

- The Spring Framework Support Forums, `http://forum.springframework.org`, are your first choice when you want to ask a question or have a problem. Here you can choose from many forums, including those dedicated to Spring MVC and Spring Web Flow, and even one on architectural issues. These forums are active and helpful.

- The user mailing list is largely deprecated in favor of the support forums. However, you can access the archives via Spring's SourceForge page, `http://sourceforge.net/projects/springframework`. There you will also find the developers' mailing list, useful if you want to track development issues.

- You will find that the excellent Reference Manual, available from `http://www.springframework.org/documentation`, is up-to-date and quite full of content. Spring is one open-source project that does not skimp on its bundled documentation.

- Spring uses JIRA for its issue and bug tracking, found at `http://opensource2.atlassian.com/projects/spring/secure/Dashboard.jspa`. You can use this site to register new bugs you have found or to check whether someone else has discovered the issue first. This site also has the roadmap for future versions of the framework.

- For more on Spring Web Flow, that project has a very active Wiki page found at `http://opensource2.atlassian.com/confluence/spring/display/WEBFLOW/Home`. There you will find more tutorials, documentation, and links to articles on this up-and-coming project.

With the Spring Framework, there is no shortage of support options available, including many other books and professional consulting organizations and individuals.

Sample Applications

Sometimes looking at raw code is the only way to make the light bulb go off. If you're stuck and want to see how others might do it, Spring comes with many sample applications with full source code. These are excellent opportunities to investigate real working apps to see examples of Spring MVC and its integration with the rest of the application.

The sample applications can be found in the `samples` directory of the Spring Framework distribution or CVS repository.

Table 1-1. *Sample Web Applications*

Name	Description
countries	Demonstrates paged list navigation, locale and theme switching, localized view definitions, page composition through view definitions, and generation of PDF and Excel views.
imagedb	Demonstrates BLOB/CLOB handling, native JDBC connection handling, multipart file uploads, and Velocity integration.
jasperdemo	Demonstrates using JasperReports as the view technology.
JPetStore	Full application with all layers, using either Spring MVC or Struts for the web layers. Also demonstrates different remoting options.
PetClinic	Demonstrates integration with JDBC, Hibernate, Apache OJB, and Oracle TopLink. Also demonstrates JMX integration.
webapp-minimal	Minimal web application structure, including build scripts.

Spring 2.0

This book was written while Spring 2.0 was under development, so everything mentioned here will work with 2.0 or earlier. Nothing is 2.0 specific, so don't worry if you are using an earlier version of the framework.

The biggest addition to Spring's web capabilities with Spring 2.0 is the formal bundling of Spring Web Flow and Spring Portlet support. Spring MVC stays largely the same as previous versions, but does gain a few helpful simplifications and shortcuts. The changelog for the latest version is currently found at `http://static.springframework.org/spring/docs/current/changelog.txt`.

Summary

With so many options available for web frameworks, many of them perfectly fine solutions, it might come down to which framework is simply more enjoyable to work with. We believe that using Spring MVC will not only lead you to better designs and code, but also inspire *fun* developing with it. It really is a joy to apply good OOP design techniques and to write applications that are easily tested.

We have found that using Spring MVC has enhanced our ability to develop and deliver quality applications, and we want you to have the same level of success that we have enjoyed. So go forth, use Spring MVC, and bring OOP back to web programming!

CHAPTER 2

■■■

Spring Fundamentals

The Spring Framework has pumped new life into Java development. In the period immediately following the dot com bubble burst, Java applications were facing an uncertain future. The initial promises of J2EE had been thoroughly debunked, .NET was poised to offer a strong alternative, and the industry was generally sobering. Companies began to expect more application for less money and effort, and it wasn't certain that the J2EE platform would be able to deliver.

After the release of Rod Johnson's *Expert One-on-One J2EE Design and Development (Programmer to Programmer)* (Wrox, 2002) and its eventual evolution into the Spring Framework, the Java landscape had a new beacon of hope. The Spring Framework encapsulates a refreshing new beginning to Java development. First and foremost, it has enabled the return of the plain old Java object (POJO) to enterprise development. The framework combines best practices learned from actual deployments, with best-of-breed third-party utilities, to deliver a complete package.

Before we dive into Spring MVC and Web Flow, we feel it important to touch on a few very important concepts from the Spring Framework that we will rely on for the rest of the book. The Spring Framework has a unique, lightweight/full-featured duality, and we won't attempt to glance over the framework in this chapter. That job has been performed quite successfully by other works such as *Pro Spring*, or the Spring documentation. We wish to reintroduce only the core principles we believe to be important. If you are new to Spring, or need a refresher, there are many great resources available. Refer to *Pro Spring*, by Harrop and Machacek (Apress, 2005), or the online Spring Framework documentation (http://www.springframework.org).

Inversion of Control

You might hear the terms *Inversion of Control* and *Dependency Injection* used interchangeably, but in fact they are not the same thing. Inversion of Control is a much more general concept, and it can be expressed in many different ways. Dependency Injection is merely one concrete example of Inversion of Control.

Inversion of Control (or IoC) covers a broad range of techniques that allow an object to become a passive participant in the system. When the IoC technique is applied, an object will relinquish control over some feature or aspect to the framework or environment. Some examples of control include the creation of objects or the delegation to dependent objects. IoC can remove these concerns from objects with Dependency Injection and aspect-oriented programming, respectively.

IoC Example

Many systems of medium to large scale require some sort of a security system. Performing authorization, authentication, and accounting is a concern of the application that typically cuts across the entire object model.

A first attempt at implementing security might place the authorization calls directly inside the domain object, effectively forcing the object to control security itself. This can lead to a bloated object model implementation, because now the security code has become interlaced across the system, obscuring the business logic (Listing 2-1).

Listing 2-1. *Simple POJO with Control of Security*

```
public class BankAccount {
    public void transfer(BigDecimal amount, BankAccount recipient) {
        SecurityManager.hasPermission(this, Permission.TRANSFER,
            SecurityContext.getCurrentUser());
        recipient.deposit(this.withdraw(amount));
    }

    public void closeOut() {
        SecurityManager.hasPermission(this, Permission.CLOSE_OUT,
            SecurityContext.getCurrentUser());
        this.open = false;
    }

    public void changeRates(BigDecimal newRate) {
        SecurityManager.hasPermission(this, Permission.CHANGE_RATES,
            SecurityContext.getCurrentUser());
        this.rate = newRate;
    }
}
```

Listing 2-1 shows a simple BankAccount class with typical business logic methods (transfer, closeout, changeRates). These method implementations are cluttered with nearly duplicate security-related checks, obscuring the original intent of the business logic. In addition, the SecurityManager calls add a dependency that will be difficult to work with when we unit test this class.

To remove the clutter and simplify the implementation, the BankAccount should let go of this security responsibility altogether (Listing 2-2). In effect, the control over security should be turned inside out from the object to the surrounding framework.

Listing 2-2. *Simple POJO with Security Concerns Relinquished*

```
public class BankAccount {
    public void transfer(BigDecimal amount, BankAccount recipient) {
        recipient.deposit(this.withdraw(amount));
    }

    public void closeOut() {
        this.open = false;
    }

    public void changeRates(BigDecimal newRate) {
        this.rate = newRate;
    }
}
```

This *Inversion of Control* has freed the object from the cross-cutting constraint of security authorization. The end result is a removal of duplicate code and a simplified class that is focused on its core business logic.

So how do we get the security checks back into the system? You can add the authorization mechanism into the execution path with a type of IoC implementation called *aspect-oriented programming (AOP)*. Aspects are concerns of the application that apply themselves across the entire system. The SecurityManager is one example of a system-wide aspect, as its hasPermission methods are used by many methods. Other typical aspects include logging, auditing, and transaction management. These types of concerns are best left to the framework hosting the application, allowing developers to focus more on business logic.

An AOP framework, such as Spring AOP, will interject (also called *weaving*) aspect code transparently into your domain model at runtime or compile time. This means that while we may have removed calls to the SecurityManager from the BankAccount, the deleted code will still be executed in the AOP framework. The beauty of this technique is that both the domain model (the BankAccount) and any client of the code are unaware of this enhancement to the code.

To explain a little more, it helps to talk about a concrete implementation of AOP as applied by Spring. The Spring Framework uses what is called *proxy-based AOP*. These proxies essentially wrap a target object (the BankAccount instance) in order to apply aspects (SecurityManager calls) before and after delegation to the target object. The proxies appear as the class of the target object to any client, making the proxies simple drop-in replacements anywhere the original target is used.

■**Note** Spring also supports AspectJ, which is implemented not with proxies but with compile-time weaving. Weaving is a more capable AOP implementation and a nice alternative to the more simple proxy solution.

Figure 2-1 illustrates the sequence of calls when a BankAccount is closed out, using proxy-based AOP to perform the security checks.

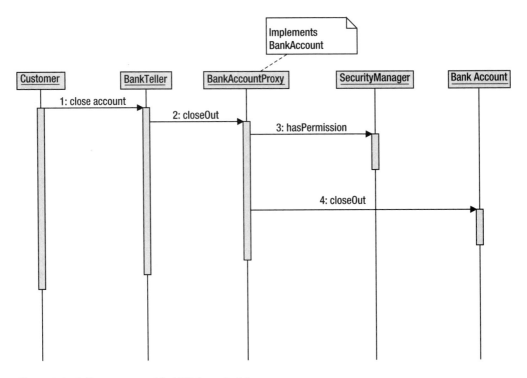

Figure 2-1. *Call sequence with AOP SecurityManager*

As you can see from the preceding diagram, the SecurityManager calls are handled by the proxy before it delegates to the real BankAccount class.

For more information on aspect-oriented programming, we recommend Ramnivas Laddad's *AspectJ in Action* (Manning Publications, 2003) or Adrian Colyer's *Eclipse AspectJ: Aspect-Oriented Programming with AspectJ and the Eclipse AspectJ Development Tools* (Eclipse/Addison-Wesley, 2004). For more information on how Spring supports and implements AOP, consult *Pro Spring*.

Summary

When you apply an AOP solution to your system, you are actually applying a form of IoC. For instance, introducing security aspects to your object model is merely inverting the responsibility from the object layer to the framework layer.

The Spring Framework provides a robust implementation of AOP. Every time you use the declarative transaction management, you are using AOP. Thus, you are using another form of IoC. In this form, the object model becomes a passive participant in transaction management, relinquishing control over when to commit or roll back to the framework.

To summarize, Inversion of Control is the broad concept of giving control back to the framework. This control can be control over creating new objects, control over transactions, or control over the security implementation. Aspect-oriented programming is one technique to implement IoC. Dependency Injection is another technique to implement, which we will discuss in the following section.

Dependency Injection

The concept of Dependency Injection is core to the Spring Framework. A specialization of Inversion of Control, Dependency Injection is a technique that frameworks use to wire together an application. The framework performs the work of connecting an application's dependencies together, removing the wiring logic and object creation from the application code completely.

We will contrast Dependency Injection with an older technique named the Service Locator pattern. We will show how the Service Locator pattern harms the testability and flexibility of an application. We then show how Dependency Injection, and Spring's implementation, fix this issue.

In nearly all applications there are at least two participants, and these two participants are required to somehow collaborate. The trick is to connect these two objects without locking in the connection or requiring a certain environment to even exist for the connection to be made.

For our example, we will consider the following use case. A cash register must obtain up-to-date prices for items being purchased. The prices are stored and calculated inside a large legacy system, but the cash register is physically located at the point of sale. The CashRegister object must have a reference to the price database to perform its work.

We begin by defining the interface to represent the cash register. It has one method, calculateTotalPrice, which takes a shopping cart and returns the total price for all items in the cart.

```
public interface CashRegister {
    public BigDecimal calculateTotalPrice(ShoppingCart cart);
}
```

Next, we define the interface for the service that will provide the real time price lookup. This interface has one method, lookupPrice, to return the price for an item.

```
public interface PriceMatrix {
    public BigDecimal lookupPrice(Item item);
}
```

Finally, we will create the implementation of the CashRegister interface. It simply creates its own dependency, an instance of PriceMatrix.

```
public class CashRegisterImpl implements CashRegister {
    private PriceMatrix priceMatrix = new PriceMatrixImpl();

    public BigDecimal calculateTotalPrice(ShoppingCart cart) {
        BigDecimal total = new BigDecimal("0.0");
        for (Item item : cart.getItems()) {
            total.add(priceMatrix.lookupPrice(item));
        }
        return total;
    }
}
```

There are three major issues with the preceding implementation. The first is that every instance of CashRegisterImpl has a separate instance of PriceMatrixImpl. If it is costly to create or maintain that object, then this is a waste of system resources. With heavy services (those that are remote or those that require connections to external resources such as databases) it is preferable to share a single instance across multiple clients.

The second and most important issue is that the CashRegisterImpl now has concrete knowledge of the implementation of PriceMatrix. The CashRegisterImpl class should not know the details of the implementation of its dependency interfaces. By explicitly creating the instance of PriceMatrixImpl, the CashRegisterImpl has tightly coupled itself to the concrete implementation class.

The third issue with the preceding implementation is a direct result of the tight coupling to the implementation class. By explicitly creating its own dependent objects, the CashRegisterImpl creates a difficult test situation. One of the most important tenets of writing unit tests is to divorce them from any environment requirements. The unit test itself should run without connecting to outside resources. If we were to test the calculateTotalPrice method as is, we would have no choice but to require a fully functioning PriceMatrixImpl. Not only would this slow down our unit test runs, it would now couple our tests to resources we can't control. What if the price returned by lookupPrice changes over time? Our unit tests would have to stay in sync with the physical resource, increasing the burden of maintaining the tests.

If we can't interact with a real PriceMatrix, how do we test our calculateTotalPrice method? We will create a stub instance of PriceMatrix, one where we can control the conditions and outcomes of the method calls. This technique is called a *mock*, and it is very useful in unit tests. For a full explanation of mock objects and their uses, refer to *JUnit in Action* by Husted and Massol (Manning Publications, 2003). In the meantime, it is sufficient to think about a mock object as a fake object that looks like a particular class, but whose behavior is controlled by the test author.

As you can see, we have noticed three deficiencies of the above implementation. The responsibility of creating the object is left to the method, prohibiting the use of a shared PriceMatrixImpl. The method is also difficult to test, as we need to somehow insert a mock object in place of the real thing. Most importantly, the client code is now aware of implementation details of its dependency, creating two tightly coupled classes.

To address the first issue, we will remove the explicit instantiation of the PriceMatrix dependency. This frees the CashRegisterImpl from the burden of object creation and from the knowledge of any physical implementation details. More importantly, the PriceMatrixImpl is no longer located inside the CashRegisterImpl instance. By moving the dependency out of the client object, it is no longer solely owned by CashRegisterImpl, and can now easily be shared among all classes. The question then becomes, how do we now locate the dependency?

Service Locator

Enter the *Service Locator pattern*, our first attempt at fixing the method. The Service Locator pattern encapsulates the actions taken to obtain a reference to the object required. This shields the client from knowing how, or even where, to obtain a reference to the object.

This pattern emerged as a workaround from using Java Naming and Directory Interface (JNDI) to obtain references to other Enterprise JavaBeans (EJBs) in a J2EE application. Using JNDI to obtain a simple object reference can be cumbersome and can require a lot of defensive programming. To protect the client, and to reduce code duplication, the Service Locator pattern was born. It usually manifests itself as a static method, returning a single instance of the requested object.

We can now change our initial code to the following:

```
public class CashRegisterImpl implements CashRegister {

    private PriceMatrix priceMatrix;

    public CashRegisterImpl() {
        priceMatrix = ServiceLocator.getPriceMatrix();
    }

    public BigDecimal calculateTotalPrice(ShoppingCart cart) {
        BigDecimal total = new BigDecimal("0.0");
        for (Item item : cart.getItems()) {
            total.add(priceMatrix.lookupPrice(item));
        }
        return total;
    }

}
```

Using this Service Locator, the class no longer has to manage object creation. The location of the actual instance of PriceMatrix is now independent of the client class. In a managed environment, such as J2EE servers, this point is critical. The act of obtaining the resource is now hidden from the client so that it may get on with the work at hand. The first problem we had with the original implementation has been solved.

The other benefit of using this Service Locator is that our client has no knowledge of the concrete implementation of PriceMatrix. This shields the client, allowing the implementation of PriceMatrix to evolve independently of CashRegisterImpl.

The third problem, the lack of testability, is unfortunately still with us, even after the change to the Service Locator. Creating a unit test for the preceding method is extremely difficult, because the implementation relies on a functioning PriceMatrix object. The test should be written with a mock PriceMatrix, but there is no way to insert the mock object during testing.

The Service Locator pattern, implemented here as a static method, falls down in a test scenario. The static ServiceLocator.getPriceMatrix is difficult to change during a test run. The locator method has to be told to return a mock PriceMatrix during the test, and a real PriceMatrix during deployment.

This situation has illustrated the need to swap different implementations of PriceMatrix without affecting the client. To effectively do this, the client (in this case, the calculateTotalPrice method) must not actively participate in the construction or retrieval of the resource. The resource must be *given* to the client.

Dependency Injection

Instead of the lookup call to the Service Locator, the framework can provide a reference of type PriceMatrix to the CashRegisterImpl class. This reduces the active work the client has to do to obtain a reference to zero, making it a passive client of the framework.

The responsibility for object creation and object location has been inverted, from the class to the framework. This wiring of dependencies is Dependency Injection in action.

Spring supports Dependency Injection in two main ways, and both are extremely simple. In fact, both use plain old Java idioms.

■**Tip** There is a third way, called *method-based injection*, which takes advantage of Spring's AOP support. It's more complicated, however no less useful, so it is not mentioned here. Consult the documentation or *Pro Spring* for more information on method-based injection.

The first type of Dependency Injection we will cover is *constructor-based injection*. This concept merely means the dependency is provided via the constructor at object creation time. For instance, to use constructor-based injection on our CashRegisterImpl object, the class would look as shown in Listing 2-3.

Listing 2-3. *Constructor-Based Dependency Injection*

```
public class CashRegisterImpl implements CashRegister {
    private PriceMatrix priceMatrix;

    public CashRegisterImpl(PriceMatrix priceMatrix) {
        this.priceMatrix = priceMatrix;
    }

    public BigDecimal calculateTotalPrice(ShoppingCart cart) {
        BigDecimal total = new BigDecimal("0.0");
        for (Item item : cart.getItems()) {
            total.add(priceMatrix.lookupPrice(item));
        }
        return total;
    }
}
```

That's it! The framework is responsible for obtaining the reference to a PriceMatrix object and then calling the constructor of the CashRegisterImpl and providing the PriceMatrix object.

The class is obeying what is commonly called the Hollywood Principle. In other words, the framework's contract is "Don't call me; I'll call you." Even more technically, the contract is "Don't ask for the resource; I'll give it to you."

Another type of Dependency Injection that's more popular with Spring is setter-based injection; just what it sounds like, it uses setter methods to inject the dependency. To use setter-based injection, the constructor will be removed and replaced with a simple JavaBean-compliant setter, as shown in Listing 2-4.

Listing 2-4. *Setter-Based Dependency Injection*

```
public class CashRegisterImpl implements CashRegister {
    private PriceMatrix priceMatrix;

    public setPriceMatrix(PriceMatrix priceMatrix) {
        this.priceMatrix = priceMatrix;
    }

    public BigDecimal calculateTotalPrice(ShoppingCart cart) {
        BigDecimal total = new BigDecimal("0.0");
        for (Item item : cart.getItems()) {
            total.add(priceMatrix.lookupPrice(item));
        }
        return total;
    }
}
```

The framework simply calls the setter with the PriceMatrix instance, and now CashRegister has everything it needs. By not using the constructor, the CashRegister object can now be created without the immediate availability of a PriceMatrix, making its life cycle a bit more flexible.

Which type should you use, constructor-based injection or setter-based injection? This is purely a matter of taste. The Spring Framework does not mandate one method or the other. In fact, you may even use both methods on the same bean. Those who prefer constructor-based injection claim that it enforces a correctly initialized object due to the intrinsically self-validating nature of constructors. A potential downside to constructor-based injection is the risk of a proliferation of constructors to accommodate different use cases. As use cases grow, each requiring different sets of dependencies, so shall grow the number of constructors.

Those who prefer setter-based injection argue that it is more flexible (able to mix and match for different situations) or that it is self-documenting. For instance, compare the following two bean definition examples in Listings 2-5 and 2-6, and consider which tells you more about the relationship between the object and its dependencies.

Listing 2-5. *Example A*

```
<bean id="addressService" class="org.example.addr.AddressServiceImpl">
  <constructor-arg ref="zipCodeService" />
  <constructor-arg ref="uspsValidator" />
  <constructor-arg ref="googleMapService" />
</bean>
```

Listing 2-6. *Example B*

```
<bean id="addressService" class="org.example.addr.AddressServiceImpl">
  <property name="zipCodeService" ref="zipCodeService" />
  <property name="postalServiceValidator" ref="uspsValidator" />
  <property name="mappingService" ref="googleMapService" />
</bean>
```

You don't have to know how to read Spring's bean definition XML format to tell which configuration exposes more information. Example B uses setter-based injection, clearly indicating which properties have which value.

The choice of Dependency Injection methods is yours; feel free to mix and match the two approaches in your application.

The main point is that the framework is responsible for wiring the application together, before the application starts. Dependencies are injected into objects without those objects actively requesting anything. Another benefit of Dependency Injection is the client doesn't know the details of the physical implementation of the dependency. In other words, the client code is not coupled to any concrete implementation. As long as the dependency implements the interface requested, the contract is fulfilled.

Unit Testing Benefits

Dependency Injection easily solves our concern of testability. By using a setter method and removing the Service Locator (potentially removing tremendous amounts of JNDI code), we've divorced our CashRegisterImpl object from any sort of environment prerequisite. This means we can easily run CashRegisterImpl outside of any container and even independently of the framework itself.

The following JUnit test example illustrates how easy it is to test a method that doesn't use a Service Locator. The code creates a mock to stand in for a real PriceMatrix. The mock then is set into the CashRegisterImpl class we are testing. This isolates our class so that the only code that is being tested is the CashRegisterImpl. All dependencies are under our control, through their mock replacements.

```
public void testCalculateTotalPrice() {
  Mock mockPriceMatrix = mock(PriceMatrix.class);
  PriceMatrix priceMatrix = (PriceMatrix) mockPriceMatrix.proxy();
  cashRegister.setPriceMatrix(PriceMatrix);
  // mock object expectations set…
  assertEquals(42.00, cashRegister.calculateTotalPrice(cart));
}
```

In the context of a unit test, the framework itself is absent. There's no mention of Spring. That's what we call *lightweight*.

Summary

Dependency Injection is a technique to wire an application together without any participation by the code that requires the dependency. The client usually exposes setter methods so that the framework may inject any needed dependencies. The client now allows others to manage the life cycle of the dependencies. The client also becomes much more testable. The client has no environment-specific code to tie it to a particular framework.

Dependency Injection is a core concept of the Spring Framework, and we will take advantage of it throughout all the code that appears in this book. This has been a high-level overview of the capabilities of IoC. You may find more helpful information in *Pro Spring* or via Martin Fowler's Dependency Injection article (http://www.martinfowler.com/articles/injection.html).

Spring ApplicationContexts

Looking specifically to the Spring Framework, we now turn our attention to the ApplicationContext. It is this object that actually forms the heart and soul of a Spring application. It is inside the ApplicationContext that the actual Dependency Injection is performed. If Dependency Injection is the core concept of Spring, then the ApplicationContext is its core object.

The ApplicationContext is a specialization of a BeanFactory, which is the registry of all the objects managed by Spring. Under normal circumstances, the BeanFactory is responsible for creating the beans, wiring them with any dependencies, and providing a convenient lookup facility for the beans. The BeanFactory is also aware of some Spring-specific interfaces, such as BeanNameAware and InitializingBean. These interfaces, along with others, help to define the life cycle of beans managed by the BeanFactory.

The ApplicationContext can be thought of as a full-service BeanFactory. Applications typically interact with an ApplicationContext instead of a BeanFactory. Web applications, for instance, have their own specialized WebApplicationContext.

ApplicationContexts add additional features to a BeanFactory. They can automatically process the BeanFactory after initialization by running BeanFactoryPostProcessors. They provide internationalization (i18n) facilities for resolving messages, an event-routing mechanism for loosely coupled producers and consumers, and support life cycle interfaces such as ApplicationContextAware.

The ApplicationContext is normally configured via an XML file. This file uses a simple DTD that sacrifices brevity for readability. A simple Spring applicationContext.xml looks like this:

```
<?xml version="1.0"?>
<!DOCTYPE beans PUBLIC "-//SPRING//DTD BEAN//EN"
"http://www.springframework.org/dtd/spring-beans.dtd">
<beans>
  <bean id="cashRegister" class="org.example.CashRegisterImpl">
    <property name="priceMatrix" ref="priceMatrixBean" />
  </bean>
  <bean id="priceMatrixBean" class="org.example.PriceMatrixImpl" />
</beans>
```

The previous configuration specified two beans for the ApplicationContext to create and manage. The first is the CashRegister instance, the second being an instance of PriceMatrix. The <property> tag defines a property for Dependency Injection. In this case, we want the ApplicationContext to find a bean inside its context with the name of priceMatrixBean, and use it when calling the setPriceMatrix method on the cashRegister instance.

The preceding example can be roughly translated into the following Java code:

```
CashRegister cashRegister = new CashRegisterImpl();
PriceMatrix priceMatrixBean = new PriceMatrixImpl();
cashRegister.setPriceMatrix(priceMatrixBean);
```

Following the tenets of zero impact of the framework on your code, you usually won't interact with the ApplicationContext directly. To keep your system lightweight, avoid interacting directly with the ApplicationContext. We'll cover suggested application design later, showing how to use the ApplicationContext without embedding it into your object model.

The ApplicationContext has a lot of features and is very powerful. If you are not already comfortable with this object, we recommend you review the capabilities of the BeanFactory and the ApplicationContext using *Pro Spring*. It covers the capabilities, features, and configuration of these core Spring objects in great detail. We will also use the XML file format tremendously, so we encourage you to become familiar with it.

The Return of the POJO

We've covered Dependency Injection and the Spring ApplicationContext, the two most central concepts in the Spring Framework. They are but tools, created only to enable applications (yes, even web applications) to be written entirely with plain old Java objects (POJOs). You can now develop web applications that are object oriented and without a trace of the framework in your core business logic. The Spring Framework and, by extension, Spring MVC go out of their way to get out of your way. This applies to the whole range of applications you might write, from simple web applications to large enterprise web applications.

One of the most important topics this book covers is that your web applications can be built using strong OO principles. You will find yourself focusing on the business logic embedded in your object model, instead of inside framework-specific code. This opens up the door to all of the design patterns, principles, and practices for effective object-oriented development. We will show you how to build out the domain object model first, and then the framework will enhance it and expose it as a web application.

The POJO has come full circle and regained its place at the top of the food chain. You can now take advantage of all those concepts you learned about when studying OOP, such as inheritance, encapsulation, and polymorphism. The Spring Framework is all about transparently serving and enhancing your business domain objects. You no longer have to sacrifice a design principle just to fit into the framework.

For example, instead of subclassing a framework abstract class (and destroying your one chance at inheritance) you are free to subclass whatever class makes sense. The Spring Framework is considered lightweight because it doesn't weigh down your application code by imposing intrusive restrictions. Your POJOs remain POJOs and your domain object model remains independent of any framework or environment.

We will take advantage of Spring's acceptance of POJOs throughout our coverage of Spring MVC. Developing systems with POJOs allows us to concentrate on business logic and solid OO design principles.

Impact on Web Applications

What does all this mean for developing web applications, specifically Spring MVC? Simply put, you will find that your web applications will become simpler as your business logic is unencumbered by the framework. The web framework's role in your application will be minimized to providing translation layer between the HTTP world and your business domain world.

You will write more POJOs, and you will build more successful object hierarchies and domain models. You will write more tests because it will be easier to isolate pieces of code. This will increase the quality of your code, and thus the application. Having a strong test suite will increase the confidence you have in the application functioning correctly. This confidence will allow you to refactor more, take risks, and react to evolving business requirements faster.

Summary

We reintroduced the Spring Framework and pointed out the three concepts we consider most important to understand.

Dependency Injection, a type of Inversion of Control, is a mechanism to insert dependencies into application code. The application code is a passive participant, allowing it to remain free of framework-specific code. By relying on Dependency Injection, the application does not manage dependency creation or have to actively locate it. The application code becomes very testable.

The `ApplicationContext` is Spring's main object registry and integration point. It is usually configured via an XML file in which beans and their dependencies are declared. The `ApplicationContext` has many features, but its central role is object creation and Dependency Injection. In most cases, the `ApplicationContext` will be a transparent piece of our applications, freeing our application logic from Spring-specific integration.

Finally, all of this has been leading up to an emphasis on developing systems with plain old Java objects. The POJO is a simple concept with powerful repercussions. Using strong object-oriented development techniques, systems developed with POJOs are testable and flexible. Most importantly, they allow the developer to concentrate on business logic and the problem domain instead of how to deal with the framework.

In the next chapter, we will cover principles for web application design, including typical layers and where the Spring Framework fits in.

CHAPTER 3

■ ■ ■

Spring MVC Application Architecture

Before we begin our exploration of the internals of Spring MVC, it is important to discuss how a typical Spring MVC is built. In this chapter, we will answer such questions as, "Where should the business logic live?" and "What are the correct levels of abstractions?" We will present the entire picture of a Spring MVC web application to better explain the individual roles that Spring MVC plays and where it fits in the overall architecture.

Mastering a new framework requires more than studying its APIs. Examining and understanding the architecture of a complete Spring MVC web application provides you with clues and motivations for the design of the framework itself. This allows for a higher level of understanding, allowing you to make more contextually sound choices when building your application.

Layers of Abstractions

Spring MVC applications are broken down into a series of layers. We consider a *layer* to be a discrete, orthogonal area of concern within an application. For instance, all of the persistence code is considered a separate layer from the view rendering code. Layers are abstractions within an application, and interfaces provide the contract by which layers interact. Some layers might be well hidden, used only by the layer immediately above it. In contrast, the most important layer (the domain model itself) spans nearly all the other layers in the system.

Layers are conceptual boundaries and are not necessarily physically isolated. More often than not, all of the layers will be located within the same virtual machine for a web application. For a good discussion on application distribution, consult Rod Johnson's *Expert One-on-One J2EE Design and Development* (Wrox, 2002).

Note Are layers the same thing as tiers? Many people use the two terms interchangeably, but separating the two helps when discussing the application and its deployment. A *layer* is a logical abstraction within an application. A *tier* is best thought of as a physical deployment of the layers. Thinking in layers can help the software developer, while thinking in tiers can assist the system administrator. Layers are mapped onto tiers.

Thinking in layers can help conceptualize the flow through an application. Visualizing the application's layers as a cake (layers of cake stacked one on another) is a common and convenient way to illustrate how the application is organized. Typical metaphors such as "down into persistence" and "back up to the user interface" refer to a cake, and denote a sense of vertical direction, reinforcing the metaphor. Figure 3-1 illustrates the common, highly generalized layers for web applications.

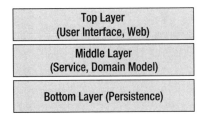

Figure 3-1. *General, high-level layers in a web application*

Typically, any persistence functionality is at the bottom of the cake, while the user interface is at the top. What is found in the middle, and how it is organized, is the subject of this chapter. We will use this metaphor when explaining our architecture.

Breaking it down further, typical Spring MVC applications have at least five layers of abstraction that you as a developer will code to. The layers are

- user interface

- web

- service

- domain object model

- persistence

You might notice that common applications elements, such as transaction management or security, are not in the preceding list. If you are familiar with the Spring Framework and its extensive use of aspect-oriented programming (AOP), this won't come as a surprise. Transaction management, for instance, is considered a transparent aspect of a system, not a full layer.

Figure 3-2 more specifically illustrates the relative placement of the different layers.

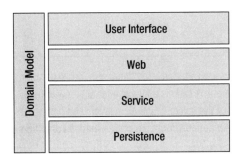

Figure 3-2. *Spring MVC application layers*

You will notice that the domain model vertically spans all the other layers. This is because all the other layers have a dependency on the domain model. It is the only layer that crosscuts all the rest.

Layer Isolation

Isolating problem domains, such as persistence, web navigation, and user interface, into separate layers creates a flexible and testable application. Implementations of each layer will vary independently, increasing the flexibility of the application. Decreasing the coupling between areas of the application will increase the testability, making it easier to test each part of the application in isolation.

This isolation is accomplished by minimizing the amounts of dependencies between the layers. The fewer dependencies a layer has upon itself, the less costly it is to change that layer. It is a best practice to ensure that a layer is required only by one or two other layers. Avoid having one single layer required by many different parts of the application.[1]

You can avoid dependency explosion in at least two ways. If a layer begins to employ too many layers, consider creating a new layer of abstraction wrapping all the previous interactions. On the other hand, if you find that a layer has permeated throughout many layers, consider if that layer is itself an aspect of the system. If the functionality can be applied across great swaths of the system transparently, use Spring's AOP functionality to remove the explicit dependency from your code.

The important point to remember is that one of the great benefits of layering an application is it creates a decoupled design. When you discover a layer or facet of the application that is too intrusive, refactor it to another abstraction or through AOP. This will keep your application flexible and testable.

Java Interface As Layer Contract

The Java interface is the key enabler to building an application with layers. The interface is a contract for a layer, making it easy to keep implementations and their details hidden while enforcing correct layer usage.

The benefits of low coupling provided by interfaces have been well known for some time. Their full benefits have been hindered because the instantiation of concrete types was still required. The promise of implementation abstraction wasn't quite realized—this is, before Spring and other Dependency Injection frameworks. Spring helps interfaces truly shine, because it handles the creation of the objects instead of your application code.

Treating an interface as a contract between layers is very helpful in large team settings. Coordinating the many resources often required by large projects is difficult, and it is rare that integration between layers happens precisely. Interfaces help to speed development between teams because of their lightweight nature. Developers program against the interface, while its implementation continues to be built and tested.

On a practical level, the Spring Framework works especially well with interfaces. Its AOP facilities are built around JDK proxies,[2] making it easy to extend an implementation of an interface with additional services.

---

1. Exception to this rule is the domain model, which typically spans many layers.
2. Spring can weave aspects into classes without interfaces, but a few caveats are involved. For one, the use of cglib (`http://cglib.sourceforge.net`) is required.

Using interfaces to define interactions between components makes unit testing much simpler. By using frameworks such as EasyMock (http://www.easymock.org) or jMock (http://www.jmock.org) you can easily create mock implementations of your interfaces with just a few lines of code and use these mocks when testing an object and its interactions with its collaborators. Although both EasyMock and jMock can create mocks of classes rather than interfaces, they require runtime bytecode generation and have some caveats that are not present with interface-based mocks.

■**Note** We will provide extensive coverage of testing a Spring MVC application later in the book. You will learn how to use a mock objects library to help test individual layers of your application.

Connecting layers with interfaces also has an added benefit of reducing compile times and creating more modular builds. Concrete implementation classes can now change without requiring a recompile of any clients dependent on it (because the clients don't have a physical dependency on any concrete classes). For large systems, this can be very helpful at build and deploy time.

Using interfaces also enables systems to be so flexible that their implementations can be chosen at startup, or even while the application is runtime. Because the client is compiled against the interface, the implementation class can be swapped in and out at runtime. This creates a highly dynamic system, further increasing flexibility and decreasing coupling. Many systems take advantage of this ability, such as Spring itself.

In summary, each layer is exposed as an interface. The interface provides a layer of abstraction, making it easy to change the implementation of the layer without affecting the rest of the application.

Layers in a Spring MVC Application

This section contains discussions of each major layer in a typical Spring MVC application. We will also cover some potential deviations from this design. A few discussions will touch on Spring MVC interfaces or classes. Do not fear; we explain each subject in detail in following chapters.

User Interface Layer

The user interface layer is responsible for presenting the application to the end user. This layer renders the response generated by the web layer into the form requested by the client. For instance, cell phones usually require WML or at least specializations of XHTML. Other clients may want PDFs for their user interface. And, of course, browsers want the response rendered as XHTML. We keep the user interface rendering layer separate from the web layer (discussed next) so that we can reuse the web layer as much as possible.

■**Note** From the perspective of a web developer, the user interface layer is a very important level of abstraction. It's easy to consider the user interface as a sublayer below the full web layer, and this view is not incorrect. For the purposes of this book, specializing in web applications, we've elevated the user interface to a formal layer because it has its own set of concerns and implementation details.

The user interface layer is typically the top layer. Conceptually, this means it is the last layer in the processing chain before the bytes are sent to the client. By this point, all the business logic has been performed, all transactions are committed, and all resources have been released.

Being last, in this case, is a good thing. The user interface layer is responsible for rendering the bytes that are sent to the client. The client, in a web application, is remote and connected via an unreliable network.[3] The transfer of bytes can slow down, be repeated, or even stop. The UI layer is kept separate from the other layers because we want the system to continue to process other requests, with valuable resources such as database connections, without having to wait on network connections. In other words, the act of rendering a response for a client is separate from the act of gathering the response.

Another reason for isolating the user interface into its own layer is the practical reality that there are many toolkits for rendering the user interface. Some examples include JSP, Velocity, FreeMarker, and XSLT (all of which are well supported by Spring). Putting the UI concerns behind its own layer allows the rendering technology to change without affecting the other layers. The other layers of the system should be hidden from the choice of the rendering toolkit. There are simply too many options, each with its own pros and cons, to tie a particular toolkit directly into the system.

Teams with a dedicated UI specialist benefit greatly by separating this layer. UI designers typically work with a different toolset and are focused on a different set of concerns than the developers. Providing them with a layer dedicated to their needs shields them from the internal details of much of the system. This is especially important during the prototyping and interface design stages of development.

Spring MVC's User Interface Layer

Spring MVC does a nice job of isolating the UI concerns into a few key interfaces. The org.springframework.web.servlet.View interface represents a view, or page, of the web application. It is responsible for converting the result of the client requested operation (the response model) into a form viewable by the client.

■**Note** The model is a collection of named objects. Any object that is to be rendered by the View is placed into the model. The model is purposely generic so that it may work with any view rendering technology. The view rendering toolkit is responsible for rendering each object in the model.

---

3. See fallacy number one, "The network is reliable," in *The Eight Fallacies of Distributed Computing* by Peter Deutsch (http://today.java.net/jag/Fallacies.html).

The `View` interface is completely generic and has no specific view rendering dependencies. Each view technology will provide an implementation of this interface. Spring MVC natively supports JSP, FreeMarker, Velocity, XSLT, JasperReports, Excel, and PDF.

The `org.springframework.web.servlet.ViewResolver` provides a helpful layer of indirection. The `ViewResolver` provides a map between view instances and their logical names. For instance, a JSP page with a filename of `/WEB-INF/jsp/onSuccess.jsp` can be referred to via the name "success". This decouples the actual `View` instance from the code referencing it. It's even possible to chain multiple `ViewResolvers` together to further create a flexible configuration.

Dependencies

The view layer typically has a dependency on the domain model (see the following discussion). This is not always the case, but often it is very convenient to directly expose and render the domain model. Much of the convenience of using Spring MVC for form processing comes from the fact that the view is working directly with a domain object.

For example, the model is typically filled with instances from the domain model. The view technology will then render the pages by directly querying the domain model instances.

Some may argue this creates an unnecessary coupling in the system. We believe that the alternatives create such an inconvenience that it outweighs any benefits of divorcing the two layers. For example, Struts promotes a class hierarchy for its model beans that is completely separate from the domain model. This creates an odd parallel class hierarchy, with much duplicated effort. Often the system isn't that decoupled because the view-specific classes are nearly one-to-one reflections on the domain classes.

To keep things simple, Spring MVC promotes integrating the domain classes to the view. We consider this acceptable, but in no way is it enforced or required.

Summary

The user interface layer (also known as the *view*) is responsible for rendering output for the client. Typically, this means XHTML for a web application, but Spring MVC supports many different view rendering technologies for both text and binary output. The key interfaces are `org.springframework.web.servlet.View` (representing a single page) and `org.springframework.web.servlet.ViewResolver` (providing a mapping between views and logical names). We cover Spring MVC's view technology in Chapter 7 and 8.

Web Layer

Navigation logic is one of two important functions handled by the web layer. It is responsible for driving the user through the correct page views in the correct order. This can be as simple as mapping a single URL to a single page or as complex as a full work flow engine.

Managing the user experience and travels through the site is a unique responsibility of the web layer. Many of the layers throughout this chapter assume much more of a stateless role. The web layer, however, typically does contain some state to help guide the user through the correct path.

There typically isn't any navigation logic in the domain model or service layer; it is the sole domain of the web layer. This creates a more flexible design, because the individual functions of the domain model can be combined in many different ways to create many different user experiences.

The web layer's second main function is to provide the glue between the service layer and the world of HTTP. It becomes a thin layer, delegating to the service layer for all coordination of the business logic. The web layer is concerned with request parameters, HTTP session handling, HTTP response codes, and generally interacting with the Servlet API.

The HTTP world is populated with request parameters, HTTP headers, and cookies. These aspects are not business logic–specific, and thus are kept isolated from the service layer. The web layer hides the details of the web world from the business logic.

Moving the web concerns out of the business logic makes the core logic very easy to test. You won't be worrying about setting request variables, session variables, HTTP response codes, or the like when testing the business layer. Likewise, when testing the web layer, you can easily mock the business layer and worry only about issues such as request parameters. Chapter 10 offers a more detailed discussion on testing the web layer.

Divorcing the web concerns from the service layer also means the system can export the same business logic via multiple methods. This reduces code duplication and allows the system to easily add connection mechanisms, such as HTTP, SOAP, or XML-RPC, quickly and easily. The web layer becomes just another client connection mechanism, providing access to core business functionality, but never implementing the functionality directly.

The web layer can be implemented as simply as servlets, for instance. These servlets will perform the work of turning request parameters into meaningful objects for the service layer, and then calling a method on a service interface. The web layer is also responsible, among other things, for turning any business exceptions into appropriate error messages for end users.

Higher-level frameworks, such as Spring MVC and Tapestry, offer sophisticated mechanisms for this translation between the raw request parameters and the business logic layer. For instance, Spring MVC will map request parameters onto plain old Java objects (POJOs) that the business logic can operate on directly. Spring MVC also implements sophisticated work flows for processing requests, structuring the way the request is handled and making extension easy.

There are two main types of web layer implementations: request/response frameworks and component frameworks. A request/response framework is built to interact directly with the Servlet API and the `HttpServletRequest` and the `HttpServletResponse`. These types of frameworks are considered to have a push model, because the user code will compile a result and then push it out to be rendered. Spring MVC is considered a request/response framework.

Other frameworks have adopted different approaches to processing a web request. Some frameworks, such as Tapestry and JavaServer Faces (JSF), are considered component-based. Those frameworks attempt to not only hide the Servlet API from you, but also make programming for the web feel like programming a Swing application. Those frameworks are essentially event-driven, as the components respond to events originally coming from the web layer.

Both types of programming models have their advantages and disadvantages. We believe Spring MVC is a good balance. It provides a rich hierarchy of implementations for handling requests, from the very basic to the very complex. You can choose how tightly you wish to couple yourself to the Servlet API. Using the base Spring MVC classes does expose you to the Servlet API. On the other hand, you will see that with Spring Web Flow or the `ThrowawayController`, the Servlet API can be hidden completely. As with many things in the Spring Framework, the developer is left to choose what is best for that particular situation.

Dependencies

The web layer is dependent on the service layer and the domain model. The web layer will delegate its processing to the service layer, and it is responsible for converting information sent in from the web to domain objects sufficient for calls into the service layer.

Spring MVC Web Layer

Spring MVC provides an org.springframework.web.servlet.mvc.Controller interface and a very rich class hierarchy below it for its web layer contract. Put very simply, the Controller is responsible for accepting the HttpServletRequest and the HttpServletResponse, performing some unit of work, and passing off control to a View. At first glance, the Controller looks a lot like a standard servlet. On closer inspection, the Controller interface has many rich implementations and a more complete life cycle.

Out of the box, Spring MVC provides many Controller implementations, each varying in its complexity. For instance, the Controller interface simply provides a method analogous to the servlet's doService method, assisting very little in the way of navigation logic. On the other hand, the SimpleFormController implements a full single-form work flow, from initial view of the form, to validation, to form submission. For very complex work flows and user experiences, Spring Web Flow provides a declarative means to navigate a user through a set of actions. Spring Web Flow contains a full-featured state machine so that all of the logic for a user's path through the system is moved out of the Controllers. This simplifies the wiring and configuration of complex work flows.

When a Controller wants to return information to the client, it populates a ModelAndView. The ModelAndView encapsulates two pieces of information. It contains the model for the response, which is merely a Map of all the data that makes up the response. It also contains a View reference, or the reference name for a View (to be looked up by a ViewResolver).

Summary

The web layer manages the user's navigation through the site. It also acts as the glue between the service layer and the details of the Servlet API.

Spring MVC provides a rich library of implementations of the Controller interface. For very complex user work flows, Spring Web Flow builds a powerful state machine to manage a user's navigation.

Service Layer

The service layer plays very important roles for the both the client and the system. For the client, it exposes and encapsulates coarse-grained system functionality (use cases) for easy client usage. A method is *coarse grained* when it is very high level, encapsulating a broad work flow and shielding the client from many small interactions with the system. The service layer should be the only way a client can interact with the system, keeping coupling low because the client is shielded from all the POJO interactions that implement the use case.

For the system, the service layer's methods represent transactional units of work. This means with one method call, many POJOs and their interactions will be performed under a single transaction. Performing all the work inside the service layer keeps communication between the client and the system to a minimum (in fact, down to one single call). In a highly transactional system, this is important to keep transaction life span to a minimum. As an added benefit, moving the transactions to a single layer makes it easy to centralize the transaction configurations.

Each method in the service layer should be stateless. That is, each call to a service method creates no state on the object implementing the service interface. No single method call on a service object should assume any previous method calls to itself. Any state across method calls is kept in the domain model.

In a typical Spring MVC application, a single service layer object will handle many concurrent threads of execution, so remaining stateless is the only way to avoid one thread clobbering another. This actually leads to a much more simple design, because it eliminates the need to pool the service objects. This design performs much better than a pool of instances, because there is no management of checking the object in and out of the pool. Using a singleton for each service object keeps memory usage to a minimum as well.

This layer attempts to provide encapsulations of all the use cases of the system. A single use case is often one transactional unit of work, and so it makes sense these two aspects are found in the service layer. It also makes it easy to refer to one layer for all the high-level system functionality.

Consolidating the units of work behind a service layer creates a single point of entry into the system for end users and clients. It now becomes trivial to attach multiple client communication mechanisms to a single service interface. For instance, with Spring's remoting capabilities, you can expose the same service via SOAP, RMI, Java serialization over HTTP, and, of course, standard XHTML. This promotes code reuse and the all-important DRY (Don't Repeat Yourself) principle by decoupling the transactional unit of work from the transport or user interface. For more information on Spring's remoting capabilities, refer to *Pro Spring* by Rob Harrop (Apress, 2005) or to the online documentation (http://www.springframework.org/documentation).

Example

As just mentioned, the service layer provides an interface for clients. A typical interface has very coarse-grained methods and usually looks something like Listing 3-1.

Listing 3-1. *Coarse-Grained Service Layer Interface*

```
public interface AccountManager {
  void activateAccount(String accountId);

  void deactivateAccount(String accountId);

  Account findAccountByUsername(String username);
}
```

You can see why these methods are considered coarse grained. It takes one simple call for the client to achieve completion of a single use case. Contrast this to a fine-grained interface (see Listing 3-2), where it would take many calls, to potentially many different objects, to accomplish a use case.

Listing 3-2. *Fine-Grained Service Layer Interface*

```
public interface FineGrainedAccountManager {
  Account findAccountByUsername(String username);

  void setAccountToActive(Account account);

  boolean accountAbleToBeActivated(Account account);

  void sendActivationEmail(Account account, Mailer mailer);
}
```

With the preceding example, too much responsibility is given to the client. What is the correct order of the method calls? What happens if there is a failure? There's no way to guarantee that the same account instance is used for every call. This fine-grained interface couples the client too closely to *how* the use case is implemented.

In environments where the client is remote, a coarse-grained interface is an important design element. Serialization is not a cheap operation, so it is important to serialize at most once per call into the service layer. Even in systems where the client is in the same virtual machine, this layer plays a crucial role when separating the concerns of the system and making it easier to decouple and test.

Dependencies

The service layer is dependent upon the domain model and the persistence layer, which we discuss in the following sections. It combines and coordinates calls to both the data access objects and the domain model objects. The service layer should never have a dependency on the view or web layers.

It is important to note that it is usually unnecessary for this layer to have any dependencies on framework-specific code, or infrastructure code such as transaction management. The Spring Framework does a good job of transparently introducing system aspects so that your code remains highly decoupled.

Spring's Support for the Service Layer

The Spring Framework does provide any interfaces or classes for implementing the business aspects of the service layer. This should not be surprising, because the service layer is specific to the application.

Instead of defining your business interfaces, Spring will help with the programming model. Typically, the Spring Framework's `ApplicationContext` will inject instances of the service into the web `Controllers`. Spring will also enhance your service layer with services such as transaction management, performance monitoring, and even pooling if you decide you need it.

Summary

The service layer provides a stateless, coarse-grained interface for clients to use for system interaction. Each method in the service layer typically represents one use case. Each method is also one transactional unit of work.

Using a service layer also keeps coupling low between the system and the client. It reduces the amount of calls required for a use case, making the system simpler to use. In a remote environment, this dramatically improves performance.

Domain Model Layer

The domain object model is the most important layer in the system. This layer contains the business logic of the system, and thus, the true implementation of the use cases. The domain model is the collection of nouns in the system, implemented as POJOs. These nouns, such as `User`, `Address`, and `ShoppingCart`, contain both state (user's first name, user's last name) and behavior (`shoppingCart.purchase()`). Centralizing the business logic inside POJOs makes it possible to take advantage of core object-oriented principles and practices, such as polymorphism and inheritance.

Note We've talked a lot about interfaces and how they provide good contracts for layer interaction. Interfaces are used tremendously with the service layer but aren't as common inside the domain model. The use of interfaces inside the domain model should be driven by pure object-oriented design considerations. Add them into the domain model when it makes sense, but don't feel obligated to add interfaces merely to put interfaces in front of everything.

When we say *business logic*, what do we mean? Any logic the system performs to satisfy some rule or constraint dictated by the customer is considered business logic. This can include anything from complex state verification to simple validation rules. Even a seemingly simple CRUD (create, read, update, and delete) application will have some level of business logic in the form of database constraints.

You might have noticed a contradiction just now. Can you spot it? Earlier, we advocated that the domain model should encapsulate the business logic of the system. Yet we have acknowledged that there are some business rules that live in the database, in the form of constraints such as UNIQUE or NOT NULL. While you should strive to put all your business logic inside your domain model, there are cases where the logic will live in other places. We consider this split to be acceptable, because the database does a good job at enforcing these constraints. You can, however, continue to express the business rule found in the database in your domain model. This way, the rule won't be hidden.

For example, let's say that all emails must be unique in the system. We could code this logic into the domain model by loading up all the users and the searching through each one. The performance on this type of operation, however, would be horrible. The database can handle this sort of data integrity requirement with ease. The moral of the story is that the domain model should contain most of the business logic, but place the logic outside the model when there is a good reason.

It's important to note that business logic does not mean just a strong set of relationships between objects. A domain model that contains only state and relationships to other models is what Martin Fowler would call an Anemic Domain Model (http://www.martinfowler.com/bliki/AnemicDomainModel.html). This anti-pattern is found when there is a rich domain model that doesn't seem to perform any work. It might be tempting to place all your business logic into the service layer or even the web layer, but this will negate any benefits of an object-oriented system. Remember, objects have state and behavior.

Dependencies

The domain model, or business object model, is a good example of a layer that largely permeates the other layers. It may be helpful to think of the domain model as a vertical layer. In other words, many other layers have dependencies on the domain model. It is important to note, however, that the object has no dependencies on any other layer.

The domain model should never have any dependencies on the framework, so that it can decouple itself from the environment it will be hosted in. First and foremost, this means the business logic can be tested outside of the container and independently of the framework. This speeds up development tremendously, as no deployments are required for testing. Unit tests become very simple to create, as they are testing simple Java code, without any reliance on database connections, web frameworks, or the other layers in the system.

All of the other layers have a dependency on the domain model. For instance, the service layer typically combines multiple methods from the domain model together to run under one transaction. The user interface layer might serialize the domain model for a client into XML or XHTML. The data access layer is responsible for persisting and retrieving instances of the objects from the model.

As you can see, each layer is responsible for their problem domains, but they all live to service the domain model. The domain model is the first-class citizen of the system, and frameworks like Spring and Spring MVC support this notion. Developing web applications with Spring MVC is refreshing, because there is so much true object-oriented development.

Spring's Support for the Domain Layer

Just like the service layer, Spring does not provide any base interfaces for your object model. Doing so would be completely against the ideologies of a lightweight container such as Spring. However, Spring does provide certain convenience interfaces one might choose to use when needing to integrate tightly with the framework. The need to do so is rare, and we caution against introducing any framework-specific interfaces into your base object model.

Spring can also enhance your domain model via AOP, just like it will with the service layer. To Spring, both the service layer and domain model are simply a set of POJOs.

If you decide to, Spring will perform Dependency Injection on your domain model as well. This is an advanced technique, but it is recommended for advanced object-oriented domain models.

■**Tip** Two ways of Dependency Injecting your domain model objects include an AspectJ approach (`http://www.aspectprogrammer.org/blogs/adrian/2005/03/hacking_with_ha.html`) and a Hibernate Interceptor approach (`org.springframework.orm.hibernate.support.DependencyInjectionInterceptorFactoryBean`, currently in the sandbox).

Dependency Injection for the Domain Model

As you probably know, Spring does an excellent job of creating POJOs and wiring them together. This works well when the object is actually created and initialized by Spring, but this isn't always the case with objects in the domain model. These instances can come from outside the `ApplicationContext`, for instance loaded directly by the database. How do we inject these objects with their dependencies before they enter the application?

If you have an object instance already constructed, but you would like Spring to wire that object with any dependencies, you will need an instance of a `AutowireCapableBeanFactory`. Luckily, `XmlBeanFactory` happens to implement that interface. Listing 3-3 illustrates how to wire an existing POJO with dependencies.

Listing 3-3. *Bean Definition for Wiring an Existing POJO*

```
<?xml version="1.0"?>
<!DOCTYPE beans PUBLIC "-//SPRING//DTD BEAN//EN"
    "http://www.springframework.org/dtd/spring-beans.dtd">

<beans>

  <bean id="account" abstract="true"
    class="com.apress.expertspringmvc.chap3.Account">
      <property name="mailSender" ref="mailSender" />
  </bean>

  <bean id="mailSender"
    class="org.springframework.mail.javamail.JavaMailSenderImpl">
      <property name="host" value="mail.example.com" />
  </bean>

</beans>
```

The preceding bean definition specifies one abstract bean definition for an `Account` object. An `Account` has a `MailSender` as a property. We then define the `MailSender` as the second bean in this bean definition. Note we use `abstract="true"` to ensure it will never be created inside the container.

Listing 3-4. *Simple POJO Requiring an External Resource*

```
package com.apress.expertspringmvc.chap3;

import org.springframework.mail.MailSender;
import org.springframework.mail.SimpleMailMessage;

public class Account {

    private String email;

    private MailSender mailSender;
```

```
    private boolean active = false;

    public String getEmail() {
        return email;
    }

    public void setEmail(String email) {
        this.email = email;
    }

    public void setMailSender(MailSender mailSender) {
        this.mailSender = mailSender;
    }

    public void activate() {
        if (active) {
            throw new IllegalStateException("Already active");
        }
        active = true;
        sendActivationEmail();
    }

    private void sendActivationEmail() {
        SimpleMailMessage msg = new SimpleMailMessage();
        msg.setTo(email);
        msg.setSubject("Congrats!");
        msg.setText("You're the best.");
        mailSender.send(msg);
    }
}
```

The Account POJO in Listing 3-4 has a method called activate() that sets the account instance as active and then sends an activation email. Clearly it needs an instance of MailSender, as it doesn't create one itself. We will use the code in Listing 3-5 to ask Spring to inject this dependency, based on the previous abstract account definition.

Listing 3-5. *Example Dependency Injection of Existing POJO*

```
package com.apress.expertspringmvc.chap3;

import org.springframework.beans.factory.BeanFactory;
import org.springframework.beans.factory.config.AutowireCapableBeanFactory;
import org.springframework.beans.factory.xml.XmlBeanFactory;
import org.springframework.core.io.ClassPathResource;

public class DependencyInjectionExistingPojo {

    public static void main(String[] args) throws Exception {
```

```
    BeanFactory beanFactory = new XmlBeanFactory(
            new ClassPathResource("chapter3.xml"));

    Account account = new Account();
    account.setEmail("email@example.com");

    ((AutowireCapableBeanFactory)beanFactory).applyBeanPropertyValues(
            account, "accountPrototype");

    account.activate();
    }

}
```

The code in Listing 3-5 uses the `applyBeanPropertyValues()` method on `AutowireCapable-BeanFactory` to apply a bean definition's properties to an existing bean. We are linking the `accountPrototype` bean definition from the XML file to the account instance. The `activate()` method now will work, because the `Account` object has its `MailSender` dependency.

The `AutowireCapableBeanFactory` interface also defines an `autowireBeanProperties()` method if you don't want to specify an abstract bean definition. This method will use an autowire strategy of your choice to satisfy any dependencies of the object.

Although this is a good example, most applications aren't quite this simple. The biggest issue will be the account instance, as it will most likely come from the database. Depending on what persistence mechanism you choose, you will want to see if it's possible to intercept the object after it is loaded from the database, but before it is sent back into the application. You can then apply this technique to inject the object with any extra dependencies.

■**Tip** If you are using Hibernate, there is a `DependencyInjectionInterceptorFactoryBean` in Spring's sandbox that will wire objects loaded from Hibernate automatically. It provides a very nice way to transparently inject dependencies into your Hibernate objects as they come out of persistence. You can find this class in the `org.springframework.orm.hibernate.support` package.

Using this technique, you can build a very strong domain model that can support complex business logic. Be careful what you inject into your domain model; you don't want to increase the amount of dependencies the domain model has. For example, the domain model shouldn't know anything about the persistence layer. Let the service layer handle that coordination. You should only be injecting objects that help to implement business logic and rules.

Data Access Layer

The data access layer is responsible for interfacing with the persistence mechanism to store and retrieve instances of the object model. The typical CRUD methods are implemented by this layer.

The data access functionality gets its own layer for two reasons. Delegating the persistence functionality into its own layer protects the system from change and keeps tests quick to run and easy to write.

One of the primary reasons for abstraction in object-oriented systems is to isolate sections of the applications from change. The data access functionality is no different, and it is designed to isolate the system from changes in the persistence mechanisms.

As an example, a business requirement change might force all user accounts to be stored inside an LDAP-compliant directory instead of a relational database. While this might happen rarely, abstracting the persistence operations behind a single interface makes this a low-impact change for the system.

A more likely scenario is a change in the data access layer's implementation and libraries. Many different types of implementations are available, ranging from straight Java Database Connectivity (JDBC) to full-fledged object relational mapping frameworks such as Hibernate. Each offers its own distinct advantages, but they function in significantly different ways. When all data access is delegated to its own layer, changing from one persistence mechanism to another becomes possible. Again, it's unlikely that the persistence framework will be swapped out in a production system, but it's certainly possible.

Building the system to cope with change is important, for they say that we are building tomorrow's legacy software today. Recognizing a discrete problem domain of the system, such as data access, is important. Isolating those problem domains in their own interfaces and layers helps to keep the system adaptable in the face of change.

Keeping the time to run the system tests low is the other key reason the data access layer is isolated. Any unit test that requires more than the method being tested ceases to be a unit test and becomes an integration test. Unit tests are meant to test very small units of code. If the tests had to rely on an external database, then the code under test would not be isolated. If a problem would arise, both the external database and the actual code would have to be checked for problems.

Database connections are expensive resources to create and maintain. Unit tests should be very quick to run, and they will slow down tremendously if they require connections to the RDBMS. Isolating all persistence operations to one layer makes it easy to mock those operations, keeping test runs fast.

The system is built on a solid object model, and therefore the bulk of the unit tests will be against the object model. The data access features are in their own layer to keep the object model from having to manage a concern that is primarily orthogonal to the concern of implementing business logic.

Dependencies

It is important to note that, typically, only the service layer has a dependency on the data access layer. This means that there is typically only one layer that knows anything about the data access layer. There are two reasons for this.

The service layer implements transactional boundaries. The data access layer is concerned only with interacting with the persistence mechanism, and the persistence mechanism is typically transactional. Performing the data access operations within the scope of the service façade means that the current transaction is easily propagated to the data access layer.

Also, the service layer encapsulates many little operations from the POJOs, thus shielding the client from the inner workings of the system. Those POJOs have to be loaded from persistence. From a practical standpoint, the service layer coordinates the data access layer and the POJO layer such that the appropriate POJOs are loaded and persisted for the use case.

It's important to note that the persistence layer does not have to be accessed behind the service layer. The persistence code is just another set of JavaBeans. For very simple applications, directly accessing the Data Access Objects (DAOs) is not necessarily a bad thing. Be aware of handling transactional boundaries correctly, and be sure your domain model does not have any references to the DAOs.

Spring Framework Data Access Layer

The Spring Framework really shines when providing data access interfaces. The framework doesn't have a single common interface for all data access operations, because each toolkit (Hibernate, JDBC, iBATIS, and so on) is so varied. Your business needs will usually dictate the interface design. However, Spring does provide common patterns for interacting with the data access layer. For example, the template pattern is often used by data access operations to shield the implementer from common initialization and cleanup code. You will find template implementations for Hibernate (`HibernateTemplate`), JDBC (`JdbcTemplate`), iBATIS (`SqlMapTemplate`), and others inside the `org.springframework.jdbc` and `org.springframework.orm` packages.

One of the main benefits of Spring is its very rich and deep data access exception hierarchy. The framework can convert all of your database server's specific exceptions into a semantically rich exception, common across all database implementations. For instance, your database server's cryptic "Error 223—Foreign Key Not Found" will be converted to a strongly typed `DataIntegrityViolationException`. All of the exceptions in the `DataAccessException` hierarchy are of type `RuntimeException` to help keep code clean. These exceptions are commonly mapped across both database servers as well as persistence mechanisms. That is, `HibernateTemplate`, `JdbcTemplate`, and the others will throw the same set of exceptions. This helps tremendously with any potential porting required in the future.

For a full discussion of Spring's support for persistence, refer to Rob Harrop's *Pro Spring* (Apress, 2005), or the online documentation. This is a very valuable and powerful aspect of the framework.

For your application-specific code, typically you will first design a data access layer interface independently of any implementation or even the framework. For example, one such DAO interface might look like this:

```
public interface AccountDao {
    public Account findById(String accountId);
    public void deleteAccount(Account account);
    public void saveAccount(Account account);
}
```

The operations in this interface do not mention any persistence technology. This keeps coupling low, because clients of the data access layer will be interacting through this interface. The clients don't care how the data is persisted or retrieved, and the interface shields them from any underlying technologies.

Once you have defined your DAO interface, it is easy to choose one of Spring's convenience classes, such as `HibernateDaoSupport`, to subclass and implement. This way, your class takes advantage of Spring's data access support, while implementing your system's specific DAO contract.

Options: There's More Than One Way to Do It

Is this the only way to construct a Spring MVC application? Are all those layers needed all the time? It is important to note that the preceding discussions are suggestions and guidelines. Many successful web applications don't follow this same pattern.

When choosing the architecture of the system, it's important to recognize what type of application is being built. Will the application live for a long time? Is the application for internal or external use? How many developers will be maintaining the application? Understanding what the initial investment will be will help to dictate the application architecture. You must correctly balance the needs of today with the inevitable needs of tomorrow's growth and maintenance.

We understand that if the web application starts its life as a single page with a single SQL query, implementing all the layers would be overkill. We also understand that applications have a tendency to grow in scope and size. The important steps during development are refactoring constantly and writing unit tests consistently. Although you may not start out with an *n*-layer application, you should refactor toward that goal.

Spring MVC applications certainly encourage your applications to head a certain direction, but they by no means require it. Letting the developer choose what is best for the application is what the Spring Framework and Spring MVC is all about.

No matter how your web application is implemented, it's important to take a few points to heart. Consider using layers in your application to help isolate separate areas of concern. For instance, do not put JDBC code directly in your servlets. This will increase coupling in your application. Separating into layers will structure your application, making it easier to learn and read.

Use interfaces as a means to hide clients from implementations at layer boundaries. This also reduces coupling and increases testability. You can accomplish this very simply these days, because modern IDEs support refactoring techniques such as Extract Interface. Interfaces are especially helpful when used at integration points.

Most importantly, you should put business logic inside POJOs. This exposes the full power of OOP for your domain model. For instance, encapsulate all the business rules and logic to activate an account inside an `activate()` method on the `Account` class (as we did in the "Domain Model Layer" section of this chapter). Think about how to apply common OO features such as polymorphism and inheritance to help solve the business problems. Focus first on the domain model, and accurately reflect the problem domain by building classes with state and behavior. Also, don't let system-wide, non–business-specific concerns like transaction management or logging creep into the domain model. Let the Spring Framework introduce those aspects via AOP.

These principles are not new, and they have been preached for a long time in the object-oriented world. Until the arrival of Inversion of Control containers, with strong Dependency Injection support, these principles were very difficult to implement in medium to large systems. If you have built systems before and had to throw out many of your hard-learned OOP practices, you will soon breathe a welcome sigh of relief. The Spring Framework makes it possible to integrate and develop loosely coupled web application systems.

Summary

We've shown that a typical Spring MVC application has many layers. You will write code to handle the user interface, the web navigation, the service layer, the domain model, and the persistence layer. Each layer is isolated in such a way to reduce coupling and increase testability. The layers use interfaces as their contracts, shielding other layers from implementation details. This allows the layers to change independent of the rest of the system. The system becomes more testable, as each layer can be tested in isolation. The other layers are mocked in the unit tests, keeping test runs quick and focused on testing only the target code.

We've also shown that the most important layer is the object model. The object model contains the business logic of the system. All the other layers play supporting roles and handle orthogonal system concerns such as persistence or transactions. The web layer is kept thin, implementing no business logic and providing a bridge between the world of the web and the object model.

A main goal has been to keep the framework out of our code as much as possible. By using the Spring Framework, we are able to keep framework-specific code out of our object model completely. The interfaces to our data access layer are unaware of any framework. The service façade layer's interfaces are also devoid of any framework code. The Spring Framework binds our layers together transparently, without dictating application design or implementation.

■ ■ ■

CHAPTER 4

Jump into Spring MVC

There's no better way to fully understand Spring MVC than to dive right in and build an application with it. We'll skip over the typical "Hello, world!" demo and instead build something a bit more substantial. For the rest of the chapter, we will build a simple web application for an airline travel site. This application will allow us to highlight some of the most important aspects about Spring MVC so that you can get a cohesive picture of typical system configuration and execution.

Use Cases

Our airline travel site will begin with two simple use cases. We will use the customer's requirements to help drive the design of both the service layer and the web layer. As we design and build this system, we are keeping a close eye on where we place our business logic. We wish to keep the web layer free of any business logic, instead focusing on web navigation and providing the glue between the service layer and the user experience.

Initially, we will cover the following two use cases for our demo application.

1. A list of current special deals must appear on the home page. Each special deal must display the departure city, the arrival city, and the cost. These special deals are set up by the marketing department and change during the day, so it can't be static. Special deals are only good for a limited amount of time.

2. A user may search for flights, given a departure city and time and an arrival city. The results must display the departure city, the arrival city, the total cost, and how many legs the flight will have.

Certainly these initial use cases do not warrant a complicated work flow or user experience. Use case #1 is a read-only page with dynamic content. The second use case will manifest itself as a typical form submission with the resulting page full of dynamic content. For more complicated work flows, such as multipage flows, you should consider using Spring Web Flow, as it can handle complex page flows more elegantly than straight Spring MVC.

Service Interface

As mentioned before, Spring MVC applications are typically layered with the service layer encapsulating the actual use cases. Therefore, we start by creating the service layer interface, helping us keep the business logic out of the web layer. Because the Spring Framework does such a good job at managing plain old Java objects (POJOs) and beans, we're not afraid of creating many well-defined and orthogonal Java objects that together form the entire system.

Creating the interface first also allows development work to begin on the web layer, before the actual interface implementation is complete.

Use Case #1

The first use case doesn't specify any type of uniqueness to the special deals. That is, every user will see the same special deals when they view the home page. For now, the most simple thing to do is create a getSpecialDeals() method on the service interface (Listing 4-6) returning a list of SpecialDeal objects.

The SpecialDeal class (Listing 4-2) is defined by the use case to include three parameters: the departure airport, the arrival airport, and the total cost. The airports will be instances of the Airport class (see Listing 4-1), so that we can encapsulate both the name and airport code.

Listing 4-1. *Airport Class*

```
public class Airport {

    private String name;
    private String airportCode;

    public Airport(String name, String airportCode) {
        this.name = name;
        this.airportCode = airportCode;
    }

    public String getAirportCode() {
        return airportCode;
    }

    public String getName() {
        return name;
    }

    public String toString() {
        return name + " (" + airportCode + ")";
    }

}
```

Like the Airport class, we have made the SpecialDeal class (Listing 4-2) immutable, to make it easier and safer to use. As it stands now, the only use of this class is to return read-only data, so in this case it is justified.

Tip For more notes on immutability for objects, consult Joshua Bloch's excellent book *Effective Java Programming Language Guide* (Addison-Wesley Professional, 2001). See Item 13, "Favor immutability."

Listing 4-2. *SpecialDeal Class*

```
public class SpecialDeal {

    private Airport departFrom;
    private Airport arriveAt;
    private BigDecimal cost;
    private Date beginOn;
    private Date endOn;

    public SpecialDeal(Airport arriveAt, Airport departFrom, BigDecimal cost,
            Date beginOn, Date endOn) {
        this.arriveAt = arriveAt;
        this.departFrom = departFrom;
        this.cost = cost;
        this.beginOn = new Date(beginOn.getTime());
        this.endOn = new Date(endOn.getTime());
    }

    public BigDecimal getCost() {
        return cost;
    }

    public Airport getDepartFrom() {
        return departFrom;
    }

    public Airport getArriveAt() {
        return arriveAt;
    }

    public boolean isValidNow() {
        return isValidOn(new Date());
    }

    public boolean isValidOn(Date date) {
        Assert.notNull(date, "Date must not be null");
        Date dateCopy = new Date(date.getTime());
        return ((dateCopy.equals(beginOn) || dateCopy.after(beginOn)) &&
                (dateCopy.equals(endOn) || dateCopy.before(endOn)));
    }

}
```

For lack of a proper `Money` type, we use `BigDecimal` for all monetary values. Why not simply use `double` type? The short answer is that `double`'s value isn't exact, and there's no absolute control over rounding. With `BigDecimal` you get precise control over rounding, exact decimal values, and immutability. If you find this class inconvenient to use, consider using `int` or `long` to represent pennies (or your smallest unit of money). For applications where rounding imprecisely can cause problems, such as interest calculations, use `BigDecimal`. For our purposes, using `long` to represent the number of pennies would have sufficed, but then we wouldn't have been able to bring you the next plug for *Effective Java*.

■**Tip** For more information on why you should avoid `float` and `double` when exact answers matter, consult Item 31 from *Effective Java*.

Notice how we have also made defensive copies of all `java.util.Date` objects passed into the object. For objects that are not immutable, like `Date`, it's a best practice to make your own copies of the arguments before storing in the class or using with some business logic. By using this technique, you are protecting your class, as the client could change the internal value of the argument after passing in the object, potentially creating odd or inconsistent states. We did not make copies of the `Airport` instances, because they are immutable, as you'll see shortly.

The use case also mentions that special deals are good only for a limited time, which sounds like business logic to our ears. To encapsulate this logic, we've added `beginOn` and `endOn` properties along with `isValidOn()` and `isValidNow()` methods. Even inside `isValidOn()` we make a defensive copy of the Date argument to ensure its consistency during the validity calculation.

Design Decisions

Although we'd much like to believe the opposite, it's not entirely possible to design layers in total isolation. For example, the choice of persistence framework can govern the design decisions we make when building the domain model. A little foresight can alleviate many frustrations later.

Case in point is Listing 4-2's `SpecialDeal` class. We chose to make the class immutable—for safety reasons, and because it models more correctly an immutable concept (a special deal can't change, but it can be deleted and a new one can take its place). However, will the persistence framework of choice be able to populate the fields on load or use classes without a default constructor?

■**Tip** If using Hibernate, set the access type to "field" in order to use reflection to set the fields instead of property access, which uses setters. Also, you can tell Hibernate that the class is immutable by setting mutable to `false`, in which case Hibernate will perform small optimizations.

Use Case #2

The second use case is more complicated because it returns a list of flights based on the user's search conditions. For this service method, we will encapsulate the search criteria inside a FlightSearchCriteria class. We will call the method findFlights() (Listing 4-6), and it will return a list of Flight objects.

The use case in Listing 4-3 defines the parameters for the FlightSearchCriteria class, mentioning that the user can search by arrival and departure information.

Listing 4-3. *SearchFlights Class*

```
public class FlightSearchCriteria {

    private String departFrom;
    private Date departOn;
    private String arriveAt;
    private Date returnOn;

    public Date getReturnOn() {
        return returnOn;
    }
    public void setReturnOn(Date arriveOn) {
        this.returnOn = arriveOn;
    }
    public Date getDepartOn() {
        return departOn;
    }
    public void setDepartOn(Date departOn) {
        this.departOn = departOn;
    }
    public String getArriveAt() {
        return arriveAt;
    }
    public void setArriveAt(String arriveAt) {
        this.arriveAt = arriveAt;
    }
    public String getDepartFrom() {
        return departFrom;
    }
    public void setDepartFrom(String departFrom) {
        this.departFrom = departFrom;
    }

}
```

We've made a conscious decision not to use the Airport class for the departFrom and arriveAt fields. This class represents search criteria, and searching for arrival cities isn't always an exact science. A user might misspell the city name or forget the airport code, for example.

For this reason, we are flexible with the search criteria with the knowledge that the business logic of the system will do the right thing and return the best matches available.

Additionally, we are big fans of creating types to encapsulate concepts, even simple ones. As you'll see, Spring MVC isn't restricted to working with only String classes and primitive types. The classes that encapsulate form submissions can be full of rich types, so don't hesitate to encapsulate types when appropriate.

With all the talk about building immutable classes, you might wonder why we decided to add all these setters for this class. This class is not immutable (it includes public setters) for two reasons: (1) the search criteria can change over time as the user refines his search to find the best deals; and (2) we will take advantage of Spring MVC's flexible usage of POJOs in order to share this class across both the domain model (modeling the search criteria themselves) and web requests. As you'll see shortly, this class will be shared with the web layer to encapsulate the XHTML form submission data. It will be populated automatically by Spring MVC from a form submission, so it must provide both getters and setters (Spring's data binding can bind only properties that follow JavaBean syntax and semantics).

Did we just allow advanced knowledge of the requirements of the web framework to influence the design of our domain model, but enforcing the existence of setters on any object that will encapsulate forms? In this case we did, but we didn't cross any dependency boundaries. In fact, Spring MVC easily allows for domain objects to be used by the web tier, in order to cut down on the amount of classes needed by the system.

As with issues brought up by the choice of your persistence framework, designing your application by considering all the layers is a smart way to create a more cohesive architecture. The domain model doesn't have any compile-time dependencies on any other layers, so we're still safe.

The Flight class (Listing 4-4) encapsulates an airline trip between two cities with zero or more stops. Each stop along the way is an instance of a FlightLeg (Listing 4-5). A nonstop flight, for instance, has only one FlightLeg. This class can also report the total amount of travel time, via the getTotalTravelTime() method.

Along with getTotalTravelTime(), this class includes another business logic method named isNonStop(). Not all business logic has to be big and complicated, but it is important to keep it all in the object model (as much as you can, but be pragmatic about it). Calculated values (e.g., total travel time) or derived answers (e.g., is this flight nonstop?) should be answered by the object you are talking about. Classes contain state *and* behavior, so don't forget to take advantage of that.

Listing 4-4. *Flight Class*

```
public class Flight {

    private List<FlightLeg> legs;
    private BigDecimal totalCost;

    public Flight(List<FlightLeg> legs, BigDecimal totalCost) {
        Assert.notNull(legs);
        Assert.isTrue(legs.size() >= 1, "Flights must have at least one leg");
```

```
        this.legs = legs;
        this.totalCost = totalCost;
    }

    public BigDecimal getTotalCost() {
        return totalCost;
    }

    public boolean isNonStop() {
        return (legs.size() == 1);
    }

    public Airport getDepartFrom() {
        return getFirstLeg().getDepartFrom();
    }

    private FlightLeg getFirstLeg() {
        return legs.get(0);
    }

    private FlightLeg getLastLeg() {
        return legs.get(legs.size()-1);
    }

    public Airport getArrivalAt() {
        return getLastLeg().getArriveAt();
    }

    public int getNumberOfLegs() {
        return legs.size();
    }

    /**
     * @return number of milliseconds for total travel time
     */
    public long getTotalTravelTime() {
        Date start = getFirstLeg().getDepartOn();
        Date end = getLastLeg().getArriveOn();
        Assert.isTrue(end.compareTo(start) > 0,
                "Start date must be before end date");

        return (end.getTime() - start.getTime());
    }
}
```

Listing 4-5. *FlightLeg Class*

```java
public class FlightLeg {

    private Airport departFrom;
    private Date departOn;
    private Airport arriveAt;
    private Date arriveOn;

    public FlightLeg(Airport departFrom, Date departOn, Airport arriveAt,
            Date arriveOn) {
        this.arriveAt = arriveAt;
        this.arriveOn = arriveOn;
        this.departFrom = departFrom;
        this.departOn = departOn;
    }

    public Airport getArriveAt() {
        return arriveAt;
    }

    public Date getArriveOn() {
        return arriveOn;
    }

    public Date getDepartOn() {
        return departOn;
    }

    public Airport getDepartFrom() {
        return departFrom;
    }

}
```

Service Interface

Once the domain model is flushed out, it is now time to define the service interface (see Listing 4-6). This interface provides easy access to the use cases through the façade pattern. These methods are coarse grained and stateless (i.e., multiple calls into the methods may happen concurrently without side effects). We say they are coarse grained to indicate that a single method call will accomplish the use case, instead of many small calls.

Listing 4-6. *FlightService Interface*

```
public interface FlightService {

    List<SpecialDeal> getSpecialDeals();

    List<Flight> findFlights(SearchFlights search);

}
```

For the purposes of our example, we won't concern ourselves with how this interface is implemented. We want to show off Spring MVC, so in the meantime we will create a DummyFlightService implementation of FlightService that returns simple preset values.

In the real world, you would most likely create a Data Access Object (DAO) layer for dealing with persistence. The service implementation would delegate to the DAOs, perform any extra processing necessary, and return the results. The Spring Framework contains many example projects that illustrate this architecture, and we recommend browsing through the source code. For a more in-depth discussion of the implementation of a Spring Framework application, consult the book *Pro Spring* by Rob Harrop and Jan Machacek (Apress, 2005).

ApplicationContext

The FlightService implementation is defined inside this example's main applicationContext.xml. Normally, Dependency Injection would play a role in configuring your services, but for this simple example it is enough to simply define the bean. Later the web components of the application will be injected with this service, so it is important that the FlightService be accessible as a Spring bean.

We are making a deliberate effort to separate our application beans from any web components by creating separate ApplicationContexts. This ensures an obvious separation between the different areas of the application.

For instance, in Listing 4-7, we are defining the DummyFlightService bean in an ApplicationContext that is separate from any web components.

Listing 4-7. *applicationContext.xml*

```
<?xml version="1.0"?>
<!DOCTYPE beans PUBLIC
    "-//SPRING//DTD BEAN//EN"
    "http://www.springframework.org/dtd/spring-beans.dtd">
<beans>

  <bean id="flightService"
    class="com.apress.expertspringmvc.flight.service.DummyFlightService" />

</beans>
```

Summary

Before any work was done on the web layer, we first analyzed the use cases to develop both a domain object model and a service layer. Focusing first on these layers forces us to design the core of the system without dependencies on the web layer. We also are forced into keeping all of the core business logic in the object model.

The two use cases influenced the FlightService interface, supporting both a read-only method (getSpecialDeals()) and a query-and-response method (findFlights()).

As the last step, the FlightService implementation is defined as a Spring bean inside the applicationContext.xml so that it may be easily injected into our web components.

Web Components

With the service layer built, it is now time to expose the use cases to the web. In this section we will both create the classes and configure the web application to initialize and host the code.

JAR Dependencies

The Spring Framework ships with a main spring.jar containing everything you will need. This book and all of its examples will work with version 1.2 or later. You may obtain this JAR, along with the source code, from http://www.springframework.org.

If for some reason disk space is a real issue, you may prefer to use the smaller JAR files also packaged with the distribution. These JAR files package each section of the framework individually, offering you the ability to pick and choose which features of the Spring Framework you wish to bundle with the application. If you choose to use the smaller individual JARs, refer to Table 4-1 for the minimum required.

Table 4-1. *Minimum Module-Specific Required Spring JARs*

JAR	Contents	Dependencies
spring-core	Core utilities	commons-logging
spring-beans	JavaBeans support, bean container	spring-core
spring-context	ApplicationContext, validation, JNDI, UI context support	spring-beans
spring-web	WebApplicationContext, MultipartResolver, web utilities, third-party framework support	spring-context, servlet
spring-webmvc	Framework servlets, Web mvc framework, web controllers, web views	spring-web

■**Caution** The upcoming release of Spring 2.0 will have a different JAR packaging strategy. To be safe, continue to use the full spring.jar, and monitor the release notes, which is the safest option for future upgrades.

Table 4-1 is represented graphically in Figure 4-1.

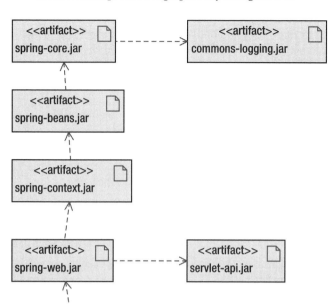

Figure 4-1. *Module-specific JAR dependencies for Spring 1.2.x and earlier*

■**Tip** Because Spring MVC requires so many parts of the Spring Framework and you are likely to use more than the minimum, we recommend sticking with the full `spring.jar` file. Updates to new versions will be faster too.

Third-Party JAR Dependencies

No matter which configuration you choose, you will also need `commons-logging.jar`, the only required external dependency of the Spring Framework.

Installation

As with all Java web applications, these JAR files must be placed into the `/WEB-INF/lib` directory of your web application.

Before we build the home page, we will first quickly introduce the central trinity of a Spring MVC application: the `Controller`, `View,` and `ModelAndView` classes.

Controllers

Spring MVC delegates the responsibility for handling HTTP requests to Controllers. Controllers are much like servlets, mapped to one or more URIs and built to work with HttpServletRequest and HttpServletResponse objects. The Controller API makes no attempt to hide its dependence to the Servlet API, instead fully embracing it and exposing its power.

Controllers are responsible for processing HTTP requests, performing whatever work necessary, composing the response objects, and passing control back to the main request handling work flow. The Controller does not handle view rendering, focusing instead on handling the request and response objects and delegating to the service layer.

The Controller class hierarchy is rich with implementations, spanning a wide range of functionality. Some of the included Controllers are

- simple request handlers with no work flow

- form controllers handling complete the XHTML form life cycle

- wizard controllers, providing multipage work flows

- WebWork-esque one-off controllers

- flexible, multi-action controllers

Controllers are intended to be singletons, just like servlets. As singletons, they will handle concurrent requests,[1] so they should never maintain state during a request.

Views

The response from a Controller is rendered for output by an instance of the View class. The Controller does not perform any view rendering, nor is it aware of the view rendering technology used.

Spring MVC has excellent support for many different view rendering technologies, including template languages such as

- JSP and JSTL

- Velocity (http://jakarta.apache.org/velocity)

- FreeMarker (http://freemarker.sourceforge.net)

Views can render more than just text output. Other bundled view rendering toolkits include

- PDF

- Excel

- JasperReports (an open-source reporting tool, http://jasperreports.sourceforge.net)

---

1.   This is true, unless the Controller is an instance of a ThrowAwayController. See Chapter 6.

Because the `Controllers` are totally unaware of the view technology, it is easy to mix and match the rendering toolkits and even use multiple toolkits concurrently in the same application.

ModelAndView

When processing is complete, the `Controller` is responsible for building up the collection of objects that make up the response (the Model) as well as choosing what page (or `View`) the user sees next. This combination of Model and `View` is encapsulated in a class named (drum roll...) `ModelAndView`.

Spring MVC makes a special effort to keep the `Controller` unaware of any view technologies used, helping to keep coupling low. Therefore, the Model is a `Map` of arbitrary objects, and the `View` is typically specified with a logical name. The view's name is later resolved to an actual `View` instance, later in the processing pipeline. It is the `View`'s responsibility to intelligently display and render the objects in the `Model`.

Building the Home Page Use Case

With the very basics of Spring MVC components introduced, we will now implement the first use case. Because this is the first use case we are building, we will also set up and configure the web application.

Spring MVC Components

For Use case #1, we need to build a home page that displays special deals for the user. These special deals aren't static—presumably they originate from a database—so a regular XHTML page isn't enough. Therefore, we will create a `Controller` that delegates to the service layer to load up the special deals so that the `View` can render them into XHTML.

The most basic `Controller` implementation is an `org.springframework.web.servlet.mvc.` `AbstractController`, perfect for read-only pages and simple requests. It provides a simple callback for handling a request, along with facilities such as controlling caching via HTTP headers and enforcing certain HTTP methods. For *extremely* simple `Controllers`, you may implement the `Controller` interface directly, although we don't recommend it because `AbstractController` provides many useful features applicable to all types of web requests.

■**Tip** The `AbstractController` is well suited for web resources that return dynamic information but don't respond to input.

Controller

Let's begin by taking a look at the code, shown in Listing 4-8. We have created a `Controller` named `HomeController`, to handle the dynamic home page of the application. The method to notice is `handleRequestInternal()`, where the real work is performed.

Listing 4-8. *HomeController*

```
public class HomeController extends AbstractController {

    private static final int FIVE_MINUTES = 5*60;
    private FlightService flights;

    public HomeController() {
        setSupportedMethods(new String[]{METHOD_GET});
        setCacheSeconds(FIVE_MINUTES);
    }

    public void setFlightService(FlightService flightService) {
        this.flights = flightService;
    }

    @Override
    protected ModelAndView handleRequestInternal(HttpServletRequest req,
            HttpServletResponse res) throws Exception {
        ModelAndView mav = new ModelAndView("home");
        mav.addObject("specials", flights.getSpecialDeals());
        return mav;
    }

}
```

The constructor configures this Controller to respond only to HTTP GET requests, because GET has semantics that most closely match that of "read." In the case of a read-only web page, such as the home page, this restriction prohibits potentially malicious clients from exploiting the system in unintended ways.

■**Tip** For a full discussion on all of the available HTTP request methods and their semantics, consult section 9 of the HTTP RFC at http://www.w3.org/Protocols/rfc2616/rfc2616-sec9.html. The choice of request method has a profound impact on application design and web architecture. Respond only to request methods that are semantically appropriate—for example, GET for reads and POST for writes or modifications.

The constructor also instructs the superclass to send the appropriate HTTP headers to enable caching. Thus, any caches or browsers that request the home page will be told it is acceptable to cache the response for five minutes. Depending on the liveliness of your data, this can be a simple way to reduce bandwidth and CPU cycles for your application. In our case, the special deals won't be changing faster than five minutes, so we are telling browsers it's OK to cache the home page for that long.

Note By default, `AbstractController` will send the appropriate headers to disable caching.

It is important to note that these types of configurations can also be set in the bean definition of the `Controller`. It is not uncommon to see the above `setCacheSeconds()` method replaced by a `<property name="cacheSeconds" value="300" />` XML snippet. The choice of configuration methods is up to you. However, we believe that the less XML in a system, the better. For configuration elements that have almost no chance of changing, configuring them in straight Java code feels like a better solution. We like XML for external issues such as wiring the classes together, or for configuration elements that have a reasonable chance of changing. The choice is yours, but whatever you choose it always helps to remain consistent.

The `setFlightService()` method is a clear sign that the `HomeController` will require Dependency Injection to obtain an instance of `FlightService`. `Controllers` are declared, configured, and managed by the Spring Framework just like all other beans in the system. Therefore, it is common and recommended to use Dependency Injection, and the full feature set of the Spring Framework, when building and configuring `Controllers`.

The `handleRequestInternal()` method is analogous to the `service()` method of a servlet, in that it accepts a `HttpServletRequest` and `HttpServletResponse` in order to perform some work. One of the main differences, as you can see here, is that instead of returning `void`, this method returns an instance of `ModelAndView`.

The main implication of this difference is that `Controllers` are not intended to render the response. Instead, this task is delegated to other components of Spring MVC. This is a benefit to `Controller` design, as it can now focus on delegation to the service layer and safely ignore response rendering issues.

The special deals are pulled from the `FlightService` and placed directly into the model with the name `specials`. The view layer will use this name to locate the list of special deals. The `ModelAndView` instance is constructed with the view name `home`, used to identify which view to render for this `Controller`. These logical view names are used to keep the `Controller` decoupled from the view technology.

Controller Configuration

Just like there is an `ApplicationContext` for the `FlightService`, the web components have their own `ApplicationContext`. The `HomeController` will be defined and configured in a `spring-servlet.xml` file, whose name has special meaning as we'll see in a moment.

To make things simple, we will map the URI for the `Controller` at the same time we define the `Controller`. By default, Spring MVC will search for all beans configured with a name parameter that begins with a / (forward slash) and will use those names as URI mappings. We are mapping the `HomeController` to the URI /home (as shown in Listing 4-9), which will be prefixed by the `WebApplicationContext` path and the servlet mapping to form the full path to the `Controller`. We will cover how a `Controller` is fully mapped in more detail when we introduce the `web.xml` configuration (see the section "URI Mapping to Controllers" later in this chapter).

■**Note** The URI-to-Controller mapping strategy is fully pluggable, making it easy to change if the default is not sufficient.

Listing 4-9. *spring-servlet.xml*

```
<?xml version="1.0"?>
<!DOCTYPE beans PUBLIC
    "-//SPRING//DTD BEAN//EN"
    "http://www.springframework.org/dtd/spring-beans.dtd">
<beans>

  <bean name="/home"
    class="com.apress.expertspringmvc.flight.web.HomeController">
    <property name="flightService" ref="flightService" />
  </bean>

</beans>
```

As you can see, we have also configured the FlightService property of the HomeController, thus resolving its dependencies.

The spring-servlet.xml file will be stored in the /WEB-INF directory for now (which is the default location), but the location is completely configurable.

View

With the Controller built and configured, it's time now to build and configure the View. To review, in the handleRequestInternal() (from Listing 4-8) method we retrieved a list of special deals and placed them in the model. We will now render the list of special deals into XHTML.

For our examples, and to keep things simple, we will use JSP to render the views, including the home page. Listing 4-10 contains the full JSP for the home page.

Listing 4-10. *home.jsp*

```
<?xml version="1.0" encoding="ISO-8859-1" ?>
<%@ taglib uri="http://java.sun.com/jsp/jstl/core" prefix="c" %>
<!DOCTYPE html PUBLIC "-//W3C//DTD XHTML 1.0 Strict//EN"
  "http://www.w3.org/TR/xhtml1/DTD/xhtml1-strict.dtd">
<html xmlns="http://www.w3.org/1999/xhtml">
<head>
<meta http-equiv="Content-Type" content="text/html; charset=ISO-8859-1" />
<title>Flight Booking Service</title>
</head>
<body>
<h1>Welcome to the Flight Booking Service</h1>
<p>We have the following specials now:</p>
```

```
<ul>
  <c:forEach items="${specials}" var="special">
  <li>${special.departFrom.name} - ${special.arriveAt.name} from
$${special.cost}</li>
  </c:forEach>
</ul>

<p><a href="search">Search for a flight.</a></p>

</body>
</html>
```

■**Caution** Always place the XML declaration (`<?xml?>`) on the first line of your JSP, as the XML specification requires this. If you place any JSP elements, such as the `<%@ taglib %>` directive on the first line, a
blank line will appear when the content is rendered to the client. This will create non-conforming XHTML.

Notice that we are iterating over a variable named specials, the same variable placed into
the model by the HomeController. There are no Spring MVC–specific elements in this JSP file,
keeping the learning curve low as you can rely on standard JSP elements and tags.

As you can see, the model object named specials were exposed to the JSP page as request
scoped attributes for easy scripting. Each view technology is responsible for exposing and
obtaining the objects from inside the model.

View Configuration

If you recall, the HomeController created a ModelAndView with a view name of home. How does
that logical View name lead to an actual View instance (in this case a JSP page)? An instance of
org.springframework.web.servlet.ViewResolver steps in and provides the mappings between
View names and the View instance.

For our JSP files, the simple org.springframework.web.servlet.view.
InternalResourceViewResolver will provide the perfect view resolution. In this context,
Internal Resource refers to any resource accessible via the Servlet API's RequestDispatcher.

We like using the InternalResourceViewResolver for two reasons. First, unlike other
ViewResolver implementations, the InternalResourceViewResolver does not require explicit
mappings between View names and View instances, which significantly reduces the amount
of configuration required. This works when your logical View names from the ModelAndView
match filename substrings of your JSP pages. The second reason why we like this particular
ViewResolver is that it defaults to supporting JSP pages as Views, further reducing the configuration necessary.

■**Tip** Learn all about the many different Views and ViewResolver options in Chapters 7 and 8.

To turn on an `InternalResourceViewResolver`, simply define it as a bean in the `spring-servlet.xml` file, as we have done in Listing 4-11. You must then configure this resolver with a prefix and suffix to be used when generating the full path to the view resource. For instance, all of the JSP files are in the `/WEB-INF/jsp/` directory, and they all have the file extension `.jsp`. Therefore, with a view name of `home`, a prefix of `/WEB-INF/jsp/`, and a suffix equal to `.jsp`, the full path to the view resource becomes `/WEB-INF/jsp/home.jsp`.

Listing 4-11. *ViewResolver Addition to spring-servlet.xml*

```
<bean id="viewResolver"
  class="org.springframework.web.servlet.view.InternalResourceViewResolver">
  <property name="prefix" value="/WEB-INF/jsp/" />
  <property name="suffix" value=".jsp"/>
</bean>
```

■**Tip** It is good practice to place all view pages, including JSP pages, inside or below the `/WEB-INF` directory. This protects the pages from being retrieved independently of the `Controller`s that configure them.

Summary

Let's recap what we have done so far. Focusing on the home page use case, we have created a `Controller` named `HomeController` and a JSP file for the view.

The `HomeController` delegates to the `FlightService` to find any special deals and then places those deals inside a `ModelAndView`. This `ModelAndView` object is returned from the `Controller`, bringing along with it the name of the view to render.

The view name is resolved to a JSP file by an `InternalResourceViewResolver`, which creates a full resource path by combing a prefix, the view name, and a suffix.

The `InternalResourceViewResolver` and `HomeController` are defined and configured in the `spring-servlet.xml` file, which defines all the beans that make up the web components application context.

With the web layer components complete we will now configure the `web.xml` file to initialize the Spring MVC environment.

Web Application Configuration

The configuration of the `web.xml` file is quite simple for a Spring MVC application. Most of the actual configuration is done via Spring's bean definition XML files, so we will use the `web.xml` to bootstrap our application and to define the central entry point.

Initializing the Root ApplicationContext

Spring MVC applications usually have two `ApplicationContexts` configured in a parent-child relationship. The parent context, or root `ApplicationContext`, contains all of the non–web-specific beans such as the services, DAOs, and supporting POJOs. For our example, the root

ApplicationContext contains the FlightService implementation, and is named applicationContext.xml. This ApplicationContext must be initialized before the web-specific resources are started because it provides services required by the web application.

To create the root ApplicationContext, there are two choices. The first is to use the ContextLoaderListener, responding to the contextInitialized() callback of a ServletContextListener. This class is the recommended method for root ApplicationContext creation, but is only viable for Servlet 2.3 or higher containers.

■**Caution** Some Servlet 2.3 containers do not initialize listeners before servlets, which is incorrect behavior. If this is the case for your container, you must use the ContextLoaderServlet.

If you are using a Servlet 2.2 container, or if your Servlet 2.3 container does not follow the correct order for loading components, you will need to use the ContextLoaderServlet. However, for the rest of the example, we will use and illustrate the ContextLoaderListener.

Configure the ContextLoaderListener by defining a <listener> element in the web.xml file (refer to Listing 4-12), with a <listener-class> of org.springframework.web.context. ContextLoaderListener. Upon initialization, it will attempt to use the default location of /WEB-INF/applicationContext.xml to find the configuration file for the root ApplicationContext (of course, the file location is configurable). Once the ApplicationContext is built it will be placed into the application scope of the web application so that the entire application may access it. However, because of Dependency Injection, it is rare to ever need to access an ApplicationContext directly.

Listing 4-12. *web.xml*

```xml
<?xml version="1.0" encoding="UTF-8"?>
<web-app version="2.4"
  xmlns="http://java.sun.com/xml/ns/j2ee"
  xmlns:xsi="http://www.w3.org/2001/XMLSchema-instance"
  xsi:schemaLocation="http://java.sun.com/xml/ns/j2ee
  http://java.sun.com/xml/ns/j2ee/web-app_2_4.xsd">

  <display-name>JumpIntoSpringMVC</display-name>

  <listener>
    <listener-class>
      org.springframework.web.context.ContextLoaderListener
    </listener-class>
  </listener>

</web-app>
```

With the root application configured, the last piece of this puzzle is now required. The main servlet for the application, which provides the central entry point for the application, needs to be specified. The `org.springframework.web.servlet.DispatcherServlet` plays this role, coordinating the processing pipeline for each incoming web request.

DispatcherServlet

The `DispatcherServlet` is the Front Controller of the system, handling all incoming requests and coordinating the different subsystems of Spring MVC. For instance, the `DispatcherServlet` shuttles the `ModelAndView` returned by `Controllers` to the appropriate `ViewResolvers`. These, and many other, subsystems are combined to create a sophisticated and flexible processing pipeline, with each step abstracted for easy customization.

The `DispatcherServlet` also creates the `WebApplicationContext`, which contains the web-specific components such as the `Controllers` and `ViewResolver`. The `WebApplicationContext` is then nested inside the root `ApplicationContext` so that the web components can easily find their dependencies.

■**Tip** For more on `ApplicationContext` nesting, please consult the book *Pro Spring*.

To locate the XML for the `WebApplicationContext`, the `DispatcherServlet` will by default take the name of its servlet definition from `web.xml`, append `-servlet.xml`, and look for that file in `/WEB-INF`. For instance, if the servlet is named `spring`, it will look for a file named `/WEB-INF/spring-servlet.xml`. Of course, as with nearly everything in Spring MVC, the location of the `WebApplicationContext` configuration file is itself configurable.

Let's add the `DispatcherServlet` to `web.xml` now (see Listing 4-13).

Listing 4-13. *Adding the DispatcherServlet to web.xml*

```
<servlet>
  <servlet-name>spring</servlet-name>
  <servlet-class>
    org.springframework.web.servlet.DispatcherServlet
  </servlet-class>
</servlet>

<servlet-mapping>
  <servlet-name>spring</servlet-name>
  <url-pattern>/app/*</url-pattern>
</servlet-mapping>
```

As you can see, we also took this opportunity to define the URL mapping for the servlet.

URI Mapping to Controllers

This is a good time to review how a full URI is mapped to a Controller. There are three components to a mapped URI path, the WebApplicationContext path, the servlet mapping, and the Controller mapping.

If you recall, we defined the HomeController with /home as its URL, which gets appended to the mapping of the servlet, which has just been mapped to /app/*. The third piece of the puzzle is the WebApplicationContext path. In this case, if the context path is JumpIntoSpringMVC, the full URL to the HomeController would be http://www.example.com/JumpIntoSpringMVC/app/home.

Full web.xml

Putting it all together, we now present the full web.xml, shown in Listing 4-14.

Listing 4-14. *Full web.xml*

```xml
<?xml version="1.0" encoding="UTF-8"?>
<web-app version="2.4"
  xmlns="http://java.sun.com/xml/ns/j2ee"
  xmlns:xsi="http://www.w3.org/2001/XMLSchema-instance"
  xsi:schemaLocation="http://java.sun.com/xml/ns/j2ee
  http://java.sun.com/xml/ns/j2ee/web-app_2_4.xsd">

  <display-name>JumpIntoSpringMVC</display-name>

  <listener>
    <listener-class>
      org.springframework.web.context.ContextLoaderListener
    </listener-class>
  </listener>

  <servlet>
    <servlet-name>spring</servlet-name>
    <servlet-class>
      org.springframework.web.servlet.DispatcherServlet
    </servlet-class>
  </servlet>

  <servlet-mapping>
    <servlet-name>spring</servlet-name>
    <url-pattern>/app/*</url-pattern>
  </servlet-mapping>

  <welcome-file-list>
    <welcome-file>index.html</welcome-file>
    <welcome-file>index.jsp</welcome-file>
  </welcome-file-list>

</web-app>
```

File Layout and Distribution

The file layout for the web application should now look like the one in Figure 4-2.

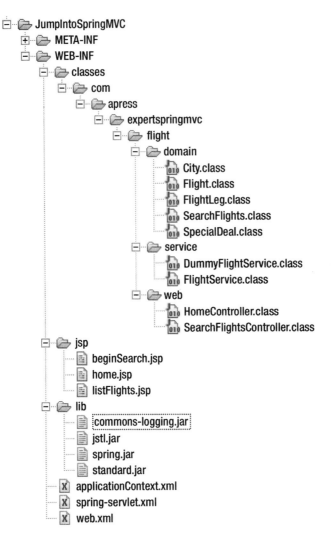

Figure 4-2. *Web application file layout*

Start the Application

You are now ready to deploy the application. The deployment process is specific to each servlet container. If you are using Tomcat, simply create a directory named JumpIntoSpringMVC in the $TOMCAT_HOME/webapps directory and place all of the files inside. Be sure to match the file layout as shown in Figure 4-2.

Once deployed, start your browser and load the URL http://localhost:8080/ JumpIntoSpringMVC/app/home. You should see a page that looks like the one in Figure 4-3.

Figure 4-3. *Home page*

If you see the home page, then congratulations! If you are experiencing errors, check that all the files are in the right location and that the web application has been deployed correctly to your servlet container. You may need to create a WAR file before you can deploy the application. Check your servlet container's documentation for specific deployment instructions.

Request Handling Sequence

Figure 4-4 details the work flow performed when an HTTP request enters the system. Notice how the DispatcherServlet drives the work flow, taking the ModelAndView returned by the Controller and then delegating to the ViewResolver to locate the View. As you will see in following chapters, the DispatcherServlet coordinates the full life cycle for the request, called the *processing pipeline*. What you are seeing in this diagram is but a small piece of the overall work performed by the DispatcherServlet. However, it does accurately reflect the important life cycle events related to the HomeController and FlightService objects.

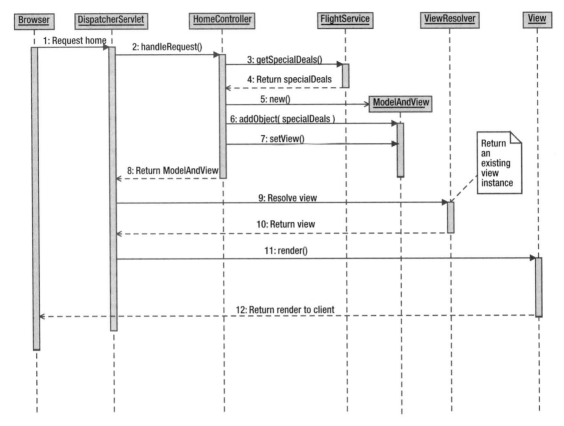

Figure 4-4. *Sequence for HomeController*

Summary

We have built, from the ground up, a Spring MVC application complete with a service layer and an object model. Nearly all of the configuration work is complete as well, making it quite easy to add functionality as the application grows.

You have been introduced to many of the core elements of a Spring MVC application, including the Controller, ModelAndView, ViewResolver, View, and DispatcherServlet. The Controllers and Views you will build and configure, while the ViewResolver and DispatcherServlet typically require only configuration.

A Spring MVC application is initialized via the web.xml file, the standard configuration file for a Java web application, but the configuration is performed via the bean definition XML files such as applicationContext.xml and spring-servlet.xml. Both the DispatcherServlet and the ContextLoaderListener are defined in the web.xml file, providing the initialization and bootstrap process for the entire Spring MVC application. Controllers and the ViewResolver appear in spring-servlet.xml. The service layer and non–web-specific supporting services appear in applicationContext.xml.

Having built a fully functional application, we will now implement the second use case. The Search for Flights use case will be much simpler because we've completed the initial configuration of the application. Its implementation will illustrate how Spring MVC handles XHTML form processing.

Building the Search for Flights Use Case

To review, the second use case allows the user to search for a flight by departure location and time, arrival location, and return time. We have already built the business logic and service layer for this use case, using the class `SearchFlights` and the service method `findFlights()`. To implement this feature, we will now implement the XHTML form and the form handling `SimpleFormController`.

Form handling in Spring MVC works similar to Struts, in that it will create a bean on form submission and populate it with the fields from the form. This bean is then provided to a `Controller` for processing.

Unlike Struts, Spring MVC is able to populate any JavaBean, no matter what class or interface the bean implements. In other words, Spring MVC does not mandate a particular superclass like Struts does with its `FormBean` class. For this reason, form handling in Spring MVC is very flexible, able to populate both simple JavaBeans as well as complex, deeply nested beans. It is even common to use the domain object model for the form beans, in order to minimize the number of classes required in the system.

SimpleFormController

When handling forms in Spring MVC, the `SimpleFormController` is the class you will most often extend. This `Controller` implements a well-defined form handling life cycle, and it provides many points for extension, making it extremely customizable.

Figure 4-5 illustrates a simplified default version of the form submission work flow for `SimpleFormController`. Keep in mind that much of this work flow is configurable based on your needs. A much more detailed version of this work flow diagram can be found in Chapter 6.

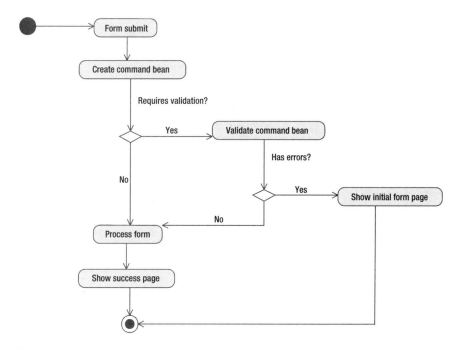

Figure 4-5. *Basic form submission work flow for SimpleFormController*

The first thing to note about `SimpleFormController` is that it is intended to handle both the viewing of the form and the submission of the form. That is, this `Controller` will respond to both an initial HTTP GET request for the form itself, as well as the HTTP POST request when the form is submitted.

Command Bean

The `SimpleFormController` creates and populates a *command bean*, which contains all the parameters from the form as JavaBean properties accessible via getters and setters. The command bean will be validated if validation is enabled, and if no errors are found, the command bean will be processed. Otherwise, the original form page will be shown again, this time with the errors from validation.

■**Tip** For more on validation, consult Chapter 9.

Command beans can be any POJO that implements JavaBean-style getters and setters, and they are not required to subclass any framework-specific class or interface. Also of benefit is that Spring MVC allows for the properties of the command class to be of any type or class. Properties of command beans can be simple types (such as `int` or `boolean`), simple classes (such as `String` or `Long`), or even complex classes (such as `Date`).

Spring will use `PropertyEditors`, which come from the JavaBean specification, to provide the conversion between request parameters (which are only `Strings`) and the specific type required by the command class. For instance, we will use a `CustomDateEditor`, which can convert strings such as "2005-06-30" to `java.util.Date` instances, when we are populating `SearchFlights`' `Date` properties.

The framework ships with many useful `PropertyEditors`, and it is easy to create your own for your own custom types and classes. We will cover the full range of `PropertyEditors` when we cover `Controllers` in Chapter 6.

Binding to a Form

On a form submission, the properties of the command bean are populated via JavaBean-compatible getters and setters. When the `SimpleFormController` encounters a request parameter, it will use the parameter name to identify which command bean property to set with the value.

For instance, we will use the `SearchFlights` class for the command bean for this use case, and it has a property named `departFrom`. When creating an XHTML text input element, the name of the corresponding form field must also be `departFrom`. Refer to Listing 4-15.

Listing 4-15. *departFrom Text Input*
```
<input type="text" name="departFrom" />
```

■**Note** Convenience tags are available to help with rendering form elements for some view technologies. Consult Chapters 7 and 8 for details.

Summary

Command beans are POJOs that encapsulate the data from a form submission. Command bean classes must have getters and setters whose property names match the names of the form fields. Spring MVC uses PropertyEditors to help convert String values from the request into the expected types of the properties of the command bean class.

SearchFlightsController

With the service layer and the SearchFlights class already created, we can quickly build the SearchFlightsController, shown in Listing 4-16.

Listing 4-16. *SearchFlightsController Class*

```
public class SearchFlightsController extends SimpleFormController {

    private FlightService flights;

    public SearchFlightsController() {
        setCommandName("searchFlights");
        setCommandClass(SearchFlights.class);
        setFormView("beginSearch");
        setSuccessView("listFlights");
    }

    public void setFlightService(FlightService flights) {
        this.flights = flights;
    }

    @Override
    protected void initBinder(HttpServletRequest req,
            ServletRequestDataBinder binder) throws Exception {
        binder.registerCustomEditor(Date.class, new CustomDateEditor(
                new SimpleDateFormat("yyyy-MM-dd HH"), true));
    }

    @Override
    protected ModelAndView onSubmit(Object command) throws Exception {
        SearchFlights search = (SearchFlights) command;
        ModelAndView mav = new ModelAndView(getSuccessView());
        mav.addObject("flights", flights.findFlights(search));
        mav.addObject("searchFlights", search);
        return mav;
    }

}
```

The constructor is used to declaratively configure the class, defining the command bean, the command name, and the view names for the form work flow.

- `setCommandName()` defines the name of the command bean, when referenced by the view page. You will see this name referenced with the `<spring:nestedPath>` tag in the JSP in Listing 4-8, defining the bean to be used for the entire XHTML form.

- `setCommandClass()` defines the class to be used for the command bean. This can be any POJO with getters and setters, and it can include both simple and complex types for properties.

- `setFormView()` defines the logical name for the view used when initially viewing the form. This view will also be displayed if validation fails, so that the user can correct any mistakes. Remember that this view name is resolved to an actual `View` instance via the `ViewResolver`.

- `setSuccessView()` defines the logical name for the view to display when form submission finished correctly. This view will receive the objects from the model when form processing is complete.

■**Note** You may choose to define these properties in the bean definition XML file when you declare the `Controller`. However, because these configurations are fairly static, we recommend the constructor as a better place to set the properties. Anything to keep the amount of XML to a minimum is usually helpful.

Notice that what you don't see in the code is any special handling to display the form itself. The `SimpleFormController` handles the initial HTTP GET request and displays the initial form view. Most of the time, you will concern yourself only with handling the form submission.

Just like with the `HomeController`, this `Controller` delegates the real work of the form submission to the service layer. We see that this `Controller` includes the `setFlightService()` method so that the `ApplicationContext` can inject this dependency.

The `initBinder()` method is a life cycle callback method provided so that you may register any custom `PropertyEditors` required for your command bean. Because the `SearchFlights` bean has properties of type `java.util.Date`, we need to create an instance of `CustomDateEditor` with the allowed date format. The `registerCustomEditor()` method essentially says, "Whenever you see a property of type `Date.class`, use this `CustomDateEditor` to convert the `String` from the request parameter into an instance of `Date.class`."

■**Note** Spring, out of the box, is configured with many different `PropertyEditors` to support many of the basic types, such as `ints`, `booleans`, and arrays of `Strings`. These `PropertyEditors` you do not need to register. You are required to register an editor only if it requires specific information in order to function, as is the case here with a custom date format.

The real action happens inside onSubmit(), the life cycle callback for handling the command bean when the form is submitted. If this method is called, it is assumed that the bean was successfully created, populated with values from the form, and validated correctly. By now you can assume that the command bean is ready to be processed.

The onSubmit() method should delegate to the service layer, as we are doing here with the call to findFlights(). It also is responsible for generating the ModelAndView object, to be used when rendering the success view. As you can see, we are including the search results and the original command bean into the model, so that we can display the matching flights and the original search criteria.

With the matching flights located and included in the model, the success view will be rendered.

SearchFlightsController Configuration

Like we did for HomeController, the SearchFlightsController will be defined inside the spring-servlet.xml and thus the WebApplicationContext. We will also map this controller to the URI /search, which will be used for both viewing the search form and handling the form submission. Refer to Listing 4-17.

Listing 4-17. *spring-servlet.xml Additions for SearchFlightsController*

```
<bean name="/search"
  class="com.apress.expertspringmvc.flight.web.SearchFlightsController">
  <property name="flightService" ref="flightService" />
</bean>
```

No other configuration is required, for the environment was previously configured for the first use case.

Summary

The SearchFlightsController is a basic implementation of the SimpleFormController. It leaves nearly all of the work flow up to the superclass, implementing only the onSubmit() method to process the command bean. The processing is simply delegated to the service layer, creating a clean separation of concerns.

As seen in the constructor, a SimpleFormController requires two Views, one for the initial form view, containing the XHTML form, and one for the success view, rendered after a successful form submission. Let's look at both of these JSP pages now.

Form View

The first XHTML page we will create contains the search form, shown in Listing 4-18. Again, for simplicity's sake, we will use JSP as the template language, but you can use any of Spring's supported template systems that best suits your needs.

Note that, for the time being, we are ignoring validation issues such as displaying validation errors. All of the work we do here is completely compatible with validation, but for the sake of showing you the most functionality in this chapter without spilling over to hundreds of pages, we are glossing over validation. We're big fans of validated data, but there's a whole chapter that covers it nicely.

As you review Listing 4-18, don't worry about those `<spring:nestedPath>` and `<spring:bind>` tags; we will explain them momentarily.

Listing 4-18. *Search for Flights XHTML Form*

```
<?xml version="1.0" encoding="ISO-8859-1" ?>
<%@ taglib uri="http://www.springframework.org/tags" prefix="spring" %>
<!DOCTYPE html PUBLIC "-//W3C//DTD XHTML 1.0 Strict//EN"
  "http://www.w3.org/TR/xhtml1/DTD/xhtml1-strict.dtd">
<html xmlns="http://www.w3.org/1999/xhtml">
<head>
<meta http-equiv="Content-Type" content="text/html; charset=ISO-8859-1" />
<title>Search For Flights</title>
</head>
<body>

<h1>Search for Flights</h1>

<spring:nestedPath path="searchFlights">
<form action="" method="post">
<table>

<tr>
  <td>Depart From:</td>
  <td>
    <spring:bind path="departFrom">
      <input type="text" name="${status.expression}" value="${status.value}" />
    </spring:bind>
  </td>
  <td>Depart On:</td>
  <td>
    <spring:bind path="departOn">
      <input type="text" name="${status.expression}" value="${status.value}" />
    </spring:bind>
    <span style="font-size:smaller">(yyyy-MM-dd HH)</span>
  </td>
</tr>

<tr>
  <td>Arrive At:</td>
  <td>
    <spring:bind path="arriveAt">
      <input type="text" name="${status.expression}" value="${status.value}" />
    </spring:bind>
  </td>
  <td>Return On:</td>
  <td>
```

```
    <spring:bind path="returnOn">
      <input type="text" name="${status.expression}" value="${status.value}" />
    </spring:bind>
    <span style="font-size:smaller">(yyyy-MM-dd HH)</span>
  </td>
</tr>

<tr>
  <td />
  <td><input type="submit" value="Search" /></td>
  <td />
  <td />
</tr>

</table>
</form>
</spring:nestedPath>

</body>
</html>
```

This XHTML will generate a page like the example in Figure 4-6.

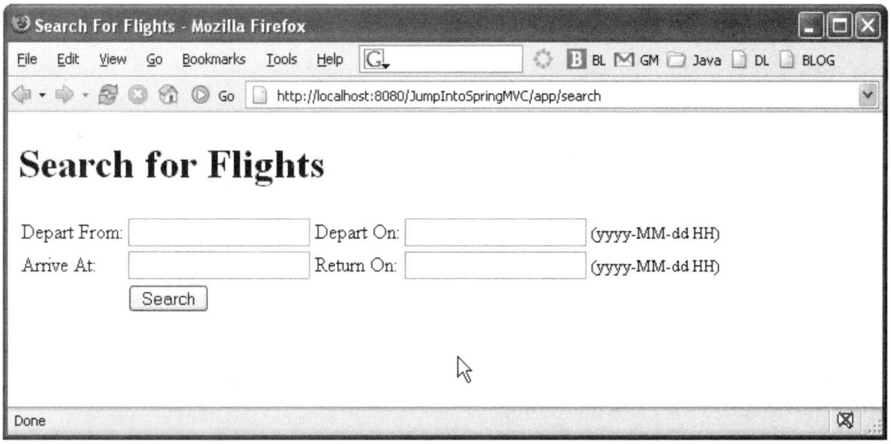

Figure 4-6. *Search for Flights form*

Spring JSP Tags

For the first time, we have used Spring-specific tags in our XHTML, namely the `<spring:nestedPath>` and `<spring:bind>` tags. These tags work together to create full paths to properties on the command bean, in order to pull values from the bean and return any validation errors on the field. These tags aren't required, but are recommended as they provide a standard way to retrieve metadata about a form field and its relationship to a property of the command bean.

Listing 4-19 includes a snippet of the rendered XHTML that is sent to the browser to illustrate what the Spring tags are actually doing. Notice how the names of the form input elements match the names of the properties from the `SearchFlights` class, as well as the paths from the `<spring:bind>` tags.

Listing 4-19. *Rendered XHTML for Search Flights Page*

```
<tr>
  <td>Depart From:</td>
  <td>

      <input type="text" name="departFrom" value="" />

  </td>
  <td>Depart On:</td>
  <td>

      <input type="text" name="departOn" value="" />

    <span style="font-size:smaller">(yyyy-MM-dd HH)</span>
  </td>
</tr>
```

If you recall that we declared the `SearchFlights` class as the command bean, then the paths from the `<spring:bind>` tags will look familiar. The path names used in the tags are the same as the bean's property names.

The `<spring:nestedPath>` tag sets a path name that all enclosed `<spring:bind>` tags will use as a prefix. We are using this tag to effectively set the name of the command bean once, to avoid repeating it with each `<spring:bind>` tag.

The `<spring:bind>` tag will bring a `status` variable into scope, which is an object that contains the metadata for a bean property from the command bean. The `status.value` variable is the current value of the property defined by the path, retrieved from executing the getter method. On initial page views, this won't render anything, as the command bean has not been populated yet. The `status.expression` variable is the name of the property itself (minus the name of the command bean).

While it might look like overkill at this point to use the Spring tags, their true benefit appears when validation is enabled and errors are generated. By using the `<spring:bind>` tag, you can easily retrieve any errors associated with a property or retrieve the current value of the property. When validation fails, and the page is re-rendered, these abilities make it easy to display what the user already entered into the form with the appropriate error messages.

■Tip Using the convenience tags for form elements (available for JSP, Velocity, and FreeMarker) can hide much of the usage of the Spring tags. Chapters 7 and 8 have more details.

Summary

We will cover these tags in much more detail in Chapter 7, so don't worry if you don't see the payoff right away. For now, the take away from this section is this: the `<spring:bind>` tag provides a way to expose the property of a command bean to the form, as well as metadata about the property such as errors, full path name, and the current value. When working with validators, this tag provides an easy way to integrate with any potential errors. Because most forms use validation in one form or another, we recommend the use of these tags, even if validation isn't currently enabled.

Success View

When a `SimpleFormController` successfully completes its processing of a form submission, the success view will render the results. The success view for this use case will iterate through the search results to display them to the user, as shown in Listing 4-20.

Listing 4-20. *Success View XHTML JSP*

```
<?xml version="1.0" encoding="ISO-8859-1" ?>
<%@ taglib uri="http://java.sun.com/jsp/jstl/core" prefix="c" %>
<!DOCTYPE html PUBLIC "-//W3C//DTD XHTML 1.0 Strict//EN"
   "http://www.w3.org/TR/xhtml1/DTD/xhtml1-strict.dtd">
<html xmlns="http://www.w3.org/1999/xhtml">
<head>
<meta http-equiv="Content-Type" content="text/html; charset=ISO-8859-1" />
<title>List Flights</title>
</head>
<body>

<h1>List Flights</h1>

<p>
You searched for flights leaving ${searchFlights.departFrom} on or about
${searchFlights.departOn}, heading to ${searchFlights.arriveAt}, returning on
or about ${searchFlights.returnOn}.
</p>

<table>
  <thead>
    <tr>
      <th>Number of Legs</th>
      <th>Total Travel Time</th>
      <th>Total Cost</th>
```

```
    </tr>
  </thead>
  <tbody>
  <c:forEach items="${flights}" var="flight">
  <tr>
    <td>${flight.numberOfLegs}</td>
    <td>${flight.totalTravelTime}</td>
    <td>$${flight.totalCost}</td>
  </tr>
  </c:forEach>
  </tbody>
</table>

</body>
</html>
```

At this point, this page shouldn't look too exciting. After rendering, the browser should display a page that looks like the one in Figure 4-7.

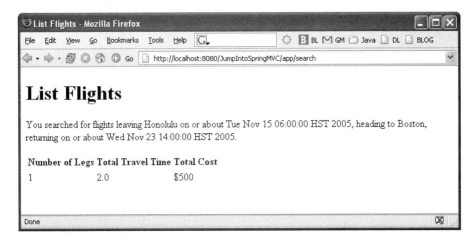

Figure 4-7. *The success view for Find Flights*

Summary

The second use case, searching for available flights, introduced Spring MVC's support for XHTML forms. Many new classes and techniques were introduced for the first time, none as important as the SimpleFormController.

The go-to class for handling form submissions is definitely the SimpleFormController, for it manages the entire life cycle of an XHTML form from viewing the form, to validation, to processing, and finally to directing to the success page. This Controller is as powerful as it is configurable, but its defaults are more than enough to quickly handle forms.

XHTML forms are encapsulated by POJOs named command beans, containing getters and setters matching the fields found in the form. Command beans can contain properties of all different types, from simple types to simple and complex classes. PropertyEditors are used when conversion is required from the simple `Strings` returned by the `HttpServletRequest` to more complex types found in the command bean. Spring ships with many `PropertyEditors` handling common conversions, and it is easy to add your own.

Properties from the command bean are bound into XHTML form elements using the JSP tag `<spring:bind>`. This tag exposes a `status` variable with metadata about the property, including its value, any errors, and the path name to the variable.

Now Let's Learn How to Swim

At this point, you've seen the most important elements of the Spring MVC system, but you've only begun to explore how configurable, flexible, and powerful they can be. Let's review what we've see so far.

- `Controllers` perform an action when a web resource is requested by a client. They can be simple, as is the case with `AbstractController`, or complex like `SimpleFormController`. Spring MVC provides a rich assortment of `Controllers` that provide a solid foundation to build your application.

- `Views` are single pages, usually created with a template language such as JSP, Velocity, or FreeMarker. Spring MVC also supports such technologies as PDF, Excel, and JasperReports. View systems can be mixed and matched in an application.

- `ViewResolvers` translate a logical view name into a physical `View` instance. This class is used to keep the `Controllers` blissfully unaware of the actual view technology in use. `ViewResolvers` can be chained together if multiple strategies are required.

- The `DispatcherServlet` manages the entire processing pipeline of a HTTP request, delegating to a wide array of components to complete the request and generate the response. You've seen some of these components, such as `Controllers` and `ViewResolvers`, but there are many more such as file upload handlers and `Locale` managers. The `DispatcherServlet` is the Front Controller for the application, handling all incoming requests and choosing the right `Controller` for the job.

- Spring MVC provides JSP tags for binding properties from the command bean to form elements. These tags provide metadata about the bean property, such as any errors from validation or its current value. These tags are also available as macros for the template languages Velocity and FreeMarker.

This introduction has shown you only the tip of the iceberg in terms of functionality and configuration options. There is a wide array of `Controller` implementations to review, as well as whole chapters devoted to validation and testing. But first thing's first. In Chapter 5 we will closely examine the processing pipeline provided by the `DispatcherServlet`, where you'll see what it takes to handle an incoming HTTP request.

■■■

CHAPTER 5

The Processing Pipeline

Spring MVC applications are highly configurable and extensible, and most of that power comes from its software architecture. Inside Spring MVC, as is the case with the Spring Framework as a whole, interfaces and abstractions are provided so that you can easily customize the behavior and work flow of your web application. In this chapter we will examine the `DispatcherServlet` and the processing pipeline that it controls in order to understand how a request is handled, as well as how best to tap into the many extension points and life cycle events.

Processing Requests

A new HTTP request entering the system is passed to many different handlers, each playing its own small part in the overall processing of the request. We will now look at the timeline of a new request and the order in which the handlers are activated.

Request Work Flow

1. Discover the request's `Locale`; expose for later usage.

2. If the request is a multipart request (for file uploads), the file upload data is exposed for later processing.

3. Locate which request handler is responsible for this request (e.g., a `Controller`).

4. Locate any request interceptors for this request. Interceptors are like filters, but customized for Spring MVC.

5. Call `preHandle()` methods on any interceptors, which may circumvent the normal processing order (see "HandlerInterceptors" in Chapter 6).

6. Invoke the `Controller`.

7. Call `postHandle()` methods on any interceptors.

8. If there is any exception, handle it with a `HandlerExceptionResolver`.

9. If no exceptions were thrown, and the `Controller` returned a `ModelAndView`, then render the view. When rendering the view, first resolve the view name to a `View` instance.

10. Call `afterCompletion()` methods on any interceptors.

Functionality Overview

As you can see, the `DispatcherServlet` provides Spring MVC much more functionality than `Controllers` and `Views`. The main theme here is pluggability, as each piece of functionality is abstracted behind a convenient interface. We will visit each of these areas with more depth later in this chapter, but for now let's look at what Spring MVC is really capable of.

Locale Aware

Especially important with applications sensitive to internationalization (i18n) issues, Spring MVC binds a `Locale` to all requests. Typically, the servlet container will set the `Locale` by looking at HTTP headers sent by the client, but Spring MVC abstracts this process and allows for the `Locale` to be retrieved and stored in arbitrary ways. By extending the `LocaleResolver` interface, you can discover and set the `Locale` for each request based on your application's requirements. The `Locale` is then available during the entire request processing, including view rendering.

■Tip See section 14.4 of the HTTP RFC for more on the Accept-Language header: `http://www.w3.org/Protocols/rfc2616/rfc2616-sec14.html#sec14.4`.

Multipart File Uploads

A standard functionality requirement for all web application frameworks, file uploads (also known as multipart requests) are handled in a pluggable manner. Spring MVC integrates with the two well-known Java file upload libraries, Jason Hunter's COS library (`http://www.servlets.com/cos`, from his book *Java Servlet Programming* (O'Reilly, 2001)) and Jakarta Commons' FileUpload library (`http://jakarta.apache.org/commons/fileupload`). If neither of these libraries covers your application's needs, you may extend the `MultipartResolver` interface to implement your custom file upload logic.

Request HandlerAdapters

While all the examples in this book will cover `Controllers` as the primary way to handle incoming requests, Spring MVC provides an extension point to integrate any request handling device. The `HandlerAdapter` interface, an implementation of the adapter pattern, is provided for third-party HTTP request handling framework integration.

■Tip Learn more about the adapter pattern, which adapts one system's API to be compatible with another's, inside the book *Design Patterns: Elements of Reusable Object-Oriented Design* (Gamma, Helm, Johnson, and Vlissides; Addison Wesley, 1995).

Mapping Requests to Controllers

The `HandlerMapping` interface provides the abstraction for mapping requests to their handlers. Spring MVC includes many implementations and can chain them together to create very flexible and partitioned mapping configurations. Typically a request is mapped to a handler (Controller) via a URL, but other implementations could use cookies, request parameters, or external factors such as time of day.

Intercepting Requests

Like servlet filters wrapping one or more servlets, HandlerInterceptors wrap request handlers and provide explicit ways to execute common code across many handlers. HandlerInterceptors provide useful life cycle methods, much more fine grained than a filter's simple doFilter() method. An interceptor can run before a request handler runs, after a request handler finishes, and after the view is rendered. Like servlet filters, you may wrap a single request handler with multiple interceptors.

Custom Exception Handling

Spring MVC allows for more exact exception handling than the standard web.xml file through its HandlerExceptionResolver interface. It's still possible to simply map exceptions to error pages, but with a HandlerExceptionResolver your exception mappings can be specific to the request handler plus the exception thrown. It's possible to chain these resolvers to create very specific exception handling mappings.

View Mapping

The extremely flexible view mapping mechanism, through the ViewResolver interface, is one of Spring MVC's most useful features. ViewResolvers are Locale aware, converting a logical view name into a physical View instance. Complex web applications are not limited to a single view technology; therefore Spring MVC allows for multiple, concurrent view rendering toolkits.

Pieces of the Puzzle

As you can see, the request is passed between quite a few different processing elements. While this might look confusing, Spring MVC does a good job hiding this work flow from your code. The work flow (see "Request Work Flow" earlier in this chapter) is encapsulated inside the DispatcherServlet, which delegates to many different components providing for easy extension and customization.

DispatcherServlet

As mentioned in Chapter 4, the DispatcherServlet is the front controller of the web application. It gets its name from the fact that it dispatches the request to many different components, each an abstraction of the processing pipeline.

Declaration

Typically, you will only declare and configure this class. All the customization is done through configuring different delegates instead of extending or modifying this class directly.

■**Caution** The DispatcherServlet will be marked final in the near future, so avoid subclassing this class.

You saw the declaration and configuration of this servlet in Chapter 4. To quickly review, this servlet is configured in your application's web.xml file, as shown in Listing 5-1.

Listing 5-1. *DispatcherServlet in the web.xml*

```
<servlet>
  <servlet-name>spring</servlet-name>
  <servlet-class>
    org.springframework.web.servlet.DispatcherServlet
  </servlet-class>
</servlet>

<servlet-mapping>
  <servlet-name>spring</servlet-name>
  <url-pattern>/app/*</url-pattern>
</servlet-mapping>
```

Of course, the URL pattern you choose for the servlet-mapping element is up to you.

■**Tip** Many servlet containers will validate the web.xml against its DTD or schema file, so be sure to place the elements in the right order and in the right place.

Initialization

When the DispatcherServlet initializes, it will search the WebApplicationContext for one or more instances of the elements that make up the processing pipeline (such as ViewResolvers or HandlerMappings).

■**Tip** Remember that the WebApplicationContext is a special ApplicationContext implementation that is aware of the servlet environment and the ServletConfig object.

For some of the component types such as ViewResolvers (see Table 5-1), the DispatcherServlet can be configured to locate all instances of the same type. The servlet will then chain the components together and order them, giving each the chance to handle the request.

■**Note** The DispatcherServlet uses the Ordered interface to sort many of its collections of delegates. To order anything that implements the Ordered interface, simply give it a property named order. The lower the number, the higher it will rank.

Usually, the first element to respond with a non-null value wins. This is very useful if your application requires different ways to resolve view names, for instance. This technique also allows you to create modular configurations of request handlers and then chain them together at runtime.

The DispatcherServlet searches for its components using the algorithm pictured in Figure 5-1. The path through the algorithm is dependent on many factors, including if multiple components of the same type can be detected and if there is a default strategy available if none are found in the ApplicationContext. For many types of components, if you disable the automatic detection by type, then the DispatcherServlet will fall back to searching for a single component with a well-known bean name.

Table 5-1 lists the discovery rules and interfaces of the components managed by the DispatcherServlet.

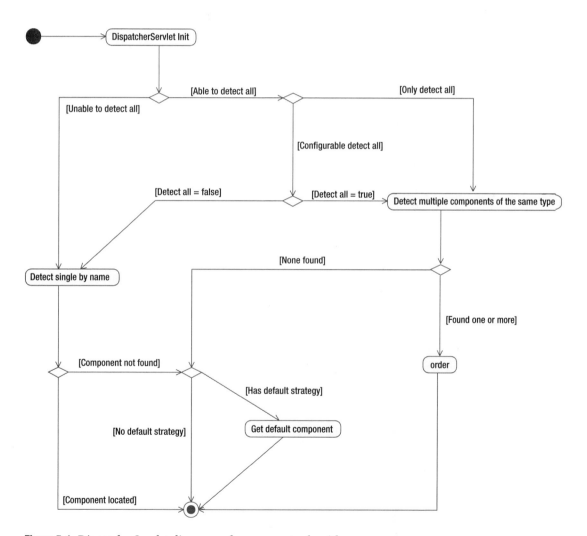

Figure 5-1. *DispatcherServlet discovery of components algorithm*

Table 5-1. *Interfaces of the Processing Pipeline*

Interface Name	Default Bean Name	Purpose	Chain Multiple?	Can Detect All?
org.springframework.web.servlet. HandlerMapping	handlerMapping	Maps requests to handlers (e.g., Controllers)	Yes	Yes
org.springframework.web.servlet. HandlerAdapter	none	Instance of adapter pattern, decouples handlers from the DispatcherServlet	Yes	No
org.springframework.web.servlet. ViewResolver	viewResolver	Maps view names to view instances	Yes	Yes
org.springframework.web.servlet. HandlerExceptionResolver	handlerExceptionResolver	Map exceptions to handlers and views	Yes	Yes
org.springframework.web.multipart. MultipartResolver	multipartResolver	Strategy interface to handle file uploads	No	No
org.springframework.web.servlet. LocaleResolver	localeResolver	Strategy interface for resolving the Locale of a request	No	No
org.springframework.web.servlet. ThemeResolver	themeResolver	Strategy interface for resolving a theme for this request (not used directly in the DispatcherServlet)	No	No

During initialization, the DispatcherServlet will look for all implementations by type of HandlerAdapters, HandlerMappings, HandlerExceptionResolvers, and ViewResolvers. However, you may turn off this behavior for all types but HandlerAdapter by setting to false the detectAllHandlerMappings, detectAllHandlerExceptionResolvers, or detectAllViewResolvers properties. To set one or more of these properties, you must use the web.xml where you initially declared the DispatcherServlet. Listing 5-2 shows an example of disabling the detection of all ViewResolvers.

■Note At the time this was written, there is no way to turn off automatic detection of all HandlerAdapters.

Listing 5-2. *Disable Detection of all View Resolvers*

```
<servlet>
  <servlet-name>spring</servlet-name>
  <servlet-class>
    org.springframework.web.servlet.DispatcherServlet
  </servlet-class>
  <init-param>
    <param-name>detectAllViewResolvers</param-name>
    <param-value>false</param-value>
  </init-param>
</servlet>
```

If you do disable the automatic discovery, you will then need to name at least one bean of each type with the default bean name. Consult Table 5-1 for each type's default bean name.

The DispatcherServlet is configured with default implementations for most of these interfaces. This means that if no implementations are found in the ApplicationContext (either by name or by type), the DispatcherServlet will create and use the following implementations:

■Caution There is no default implementation for MultipartResolver, HandlerExceptionResolver, or ViewResolver.

- org.springframework.web.servlet.handler.BeanNameUrlHandlerMapping

- org.springframework.web.servlet.mvc.SimpleControllerHandlerAdapter

- org.springframework.web.servlet.view.InternalResourceViewResolver

- org.springframework.web.servlet.i18n.AcceptHeaderLocaleResolver

- org.springframework.web.servlet.theme.FixedThemeResolver

Let's now take a closer look at each element in the processing pipeline, starting with the HandlerAdapter interface.

HandlerAdapter

The org.springframework.web.servlet.HandlerAdapter is a system level interface, allowing for low coupling between different request handlers and the DispatcherServlet. Using this interface, the DispatcherServlet can interact with any type of request handler, as long as a HandlerAdapter is configured.

■**Tip** If your application consists of only Controllers, then you may safely ignore this section. Controllers are supported by default, and no explicit configurations for HandlerAdapters are required. However, read on if you are interested in integrating a third-party framework into Spring MVC.

Why not just require all request handlers to implement some well-known interface? The DispatcherServlet is intended to work with any type of request handler, including third-party frameworks. Integrating disparate software packages is often difficult because the source code isn't available or is very difficult to change. The Adapter design pattern attempts to solve this problem by adapting the third party's interface to the client's expected interface. The seminal book *Design Patterns* (Gamma, Helm, Johnson, and Vlissides; Addison Wesley, 1995) defines this pattern's goal as follows: "Convert the interface of a class into another interface clients expect. Adapter lets classes work together that couldn't otherwise because of incompatible interfaces."

Spring's HandlerAdapter achieves this adaptation by delegation. Listing 5-3 shows the HandlerAdapter interface.

Listing 5-3. *HandlerAdapter Interface*

```
package org.springframework.web.servlet;

public interface HandlerAdapter {

  boolean supports(Object handler);

  ModelAndView handle(HttpServletRequest request, HttpServletResponse response,
      Object handler) throws Exception;

  long getLastModified(HttpServletRequest request, Object handler);

}
```

The DispatcherServlet will check whether the HandlerAdapter supports a handler type with a call to supports(). If so, the DispatcherServlet will then ask the adapter to delegate the request to the handler via the handle() method. Notice how this interface is provided the handler instead of looking one up via the ApplicationContext.

If your application uses only Controllers, which nearly all Spring MVC applications do, then you will never see this interface. It is intended, along with its default subclass SimpleControllerHandlerAdapter, to be used by the framework internally. However, if you are intending to integrate an exotic web framework, you may use this class to integrate it into the DispatcherServlet.

Listing 5-4 provides a simple example of an implementation of a HandlerAdapter for some exotic web framework.

Listing 5-4. *Example HandlerAdapter*

```
public class ExoticFrameworkHandlerAdapter implements HandlerAdapter {

    public boolean supports(Object handler) {
        return (handler != null) && (handler instanceof ExoticFramework);
    }

    public ModelAndView handle(HttpServletRequest req, HttpServletResponse res,
        Object handler) throws Exception {
        ExoticResult result = ((ExoticFramework)handler).executeRequest(req, res);
        return adaptResult(result);
    }

    private ModelAndView adaptResult(ExoticResult result) {
        ModelAndView mav = new ModelAndView();
        mav.getModel().putAll(result.getObjectsToRender());
        return mav;
    }

    public long getLastModified(HttpServletRequest req, Object handler) {
        return -1;  // exotic framework doesn't support this
    }

}
```

Configuring the DispatcherServlet to use this HandlerAdapter is quite easy, as the DispatcherServlet by default looks into the ApplicationContext for all HandlerAdapters. It will find all adapters by their type, and it will order them, paying special attention to any adapters that implement the org.springframework.core.Ordered interface.

Listing 5-5 contains the bean definition for the ExoticFrameworkHandlerAdapter.

Listing 5-5. *ApplicationContext with ExoticFrameworkHandlerAdapter*

```
<?xml version="1.0"?>
<!DOCTYPE beans PUBLIC
  "-//SPRING//DTD BEAN//EN"
  "http://www.springframework.org/dtd/spring-beans.dtd">
<beans>
    <bean id="exoticHandlerAdapter"
        class="com.apress.expertspringmvc.chap4.ExoticFrameworkHandlerAdapter"
    />
</beans>
```

It does not matter what the name of the HandlerAdapter is, because the DispatcherServlet will look for beans of type HandlerAdapter.

Note that by specifying any HandlerAdapter, the default SimpleControllerHandlerAdapter will not be used. If your application requires two or more HandlerAdapters, you will need to explicitly specify all HandlerAdapters, including the default.

Summary

The HandlerAdapter, an example of the Adapter design pattern, is a system-level interface to promote easy integration between the DispatcherServlet and third-party frameworks. Unless using third-party frameworks, this interface and its implementations are normally hidden from the developer. The DispatcherServlet will also chain multiple adapters if found in the ApplicationContext and will order them based on the Ordered interface.

HandlerMapping

No web application is complete without mapping its request handlers to URLs. As with all things in Spring MVC, there is no one way to map a URL to a Controller. In fact, it's very possible to create a mapping scheme and implementation that doesn't even rely on URLs at all. However, because the provided implementations are all based on URL paths, we will now review the default path matching rules.

Path Matching

Path matching in Spring MVC is much more flexible than a standard web.xml's servlet mappings. The default strategy for path matching is implemented by org.springframework.util. AntPathMatcher. As its name hints, path patterns are written using Apache Ant (http://ant. apache.org) style paths. Ant style paths have three types of wildcards (listed in Table 5-2), which can be combined to create many varied and flexible path patterns. See Table 5-3 for pattern examples.

Table 5-2. *Ant Wildcard Characters*

Wildcard	Description
?	Matches a single character
*	Matches zero or more characters
**	Matches zero or more directories

Table 5-3. *Example Ant-Style Path Patterns*

Path	Description
/app/*.x	Matches all .x files in the app directory
/app/p?ttern	Matches /app/pattern and /app/pXttern, but not /app/pttern
/**/example	Matches /app/example, /app/foo/example, and /example
/app/**/dir/file.*	Matches /app/dir/file.jsp, /app/foo/dir/file.html, /app/foo/bar/dir/file.pdf, and /app/dir/file.java
/**/*.jsp	Matches any .jsp file

Path Precedence

The ordering and precedence of the path patterns is not specified by any interface. However, the default implementation, found in `org.springframework.web.servlet.handler.AbstractUrlHandlerMapping`, will match a path based on the longest (most specific) matching pattern.

For example, given a request URL of `/app/dir/file.jsp` and two path patterns of `/**/*.jsp` and `/app/dir/*.jsp`, which path pattern will match? The later pattern, `/app/dir/*.jsp`, will match because it is longer (has more characters) than `/**/*.jsp`. Note that this rule is not specified in any high-level interface for matching paths to request handlers, but it is an implementation detail.

Mapping Strategies

The `HandlerMapping` interface (shown in Listing 5-6) doesn't specify exactly how the mapping of request to handler is to take place, leaving the possible strategies wide open.

Listing 5-6. *HandlerMapping Interface*

```
package org.springframework.web.servlet;

public interface HandlerMapping {
  HandlerExecutionChain getHandler(HttpServletRequest request) throws Exception;
}
```

As you can see in Listing 5-6, a `HandlerMapping` returns not a `HandlerAdapter`, but a `HandlerExecutionChain`. This object encapsulates the handler object along with all handler interceptors for this request. The `HandlerExecutionChain` is a simple object and is used only between the `DispatcherServlet` and implementations of `HandlerMapping`. If you are not implementing your own custom `HandlerMapping`, then this object will be hidden from you.

Out of the box, Spring MVC provides three different mappers, all based on URLs. However, mapping is not tied to URLs, so feel free to use other mechanisms such as session state to decide on which request handler shall handle an incoming request.

BeanNameUrlHandlerMapping

The default strategy for mapping requests to handlers is the `org.springframework.web.servlet.handler.BeanNameUrlHandlerMapping` class. This class treats any bean with a name or alias that starts with the / character as a potential request handler. The bean name, or alias, is then matched against incoming request URLs using Ant-style path matching. Listing 5-7 provides an example bean definition with a bean name containing a URL path.

Listing 5-7. *A Controller Mapped by a Bean Name*

```
<bean name="/home"
  class="com.apress.expertspringmvc.flight.web.HomeController">
  <property name="flightService" ref="flightService" />
</bean>
```

Caution You may not use a bean definition's `id` attribute to specify URL paths, because the XML specification forbids the `/` character in XML `id`s. You can, however, have both an `id` attribute and a name attribute on a single bean definition.

Path Components

Now how does that mapping translate to a full URI used by a client? Many paths are at work here, including the web application's context path, the servlet's mapped path, and then this `Controller`'s mapped path. How are they all combined and parsed when mapping a request to a handler?

By default, the path provided in the bean definition is inside the servlet's URL path. The servlet, in this case, is the `DispatcherServlet` that is declared and configured in the `web.xml`. For example, in Listing 5-8 we have mapped the `DispatcherServlet` to handle all requests for `/app/*`.

Listing 5-8. *Example DispatcherServlet Configuration*

```
<servlet>
  <servlet-name>spring</servlet-name>
  <servlet-class>
    org.springframework.web.servlet.DispatcherServlet
  </servlet-class>
</servlet>

<servlet-mapping>
  <servlet-name>spring</servlet-name>
  <url-pattern>/app/*</url-pattern>
</servlet-mapping>
```

Therefore, to access the `HomeController` with a bean name of `/home`, a client must use the following full URI: `http://example.org/servletcontext/app/home`. In this case, `servletcontext` is the name of the servlet context this application is currently deployed to.

The default behavior, to be relative to the servlet mapping, is useful and preferable because it is decoupled from the URL pattern used to map the `DispatcherServlet` (in this case, `/app/*`). If the pattern changes, the bean name mappings do not need to change.

If you wish to write bean name mappings that include the servlet path mapping, you may do so by setting `alwaysUseFullPath` to `true` on an instance of `BeanNameUrlHandlerMapping`. To do this, simply declare an instance of `BeanNameUrlHandlerMapping` in your `ApplicationContext`. See Listing 5-9.

Listing 5-9. *Setting alwaysUseFullPath to True*

```
<bean
  class="org.springframework.web.servlet.handler.BeanNameUrlHandlerMapping">
  <property name="alwaysUseFullPath" value="true" />
</bean>

<bean name="/app/home"
  class="com.apress.expertspringmvc.flight.web.HomeController">
  <property name="flightService" ref="flightService" />
</bean>
```

Multiple Mappings per Handler
You may also assign multiple mappings to a single handler. Simply separate each mapping
with one or more spaces inside the bean name attribute, as shown in Listing 5-10.

Listing 5-10. *Multiple Mappings for a Single Handler*

```
<bean name="/home /homepage /index"
  class="com.apress.expertspringmvc.flight.web.HomeController">
  <property name="flightService" ref="flightService" />
</bean>
```

Because wildcards are supported, the example shown in Listing 5-10 could be shortened
to Listing 5-11.

Listing 5-11. *Multiple Mappings with Wildcards*

```
<bean name="/home* /index"
  class="com.apress.expertspringmvc.flight.web.HomeController">
  <property name="flightService" ref="flightService" />
</bean>
```

Tip This convenient mapping technique is useful with `MultiActionControllers`, which are controllers
that handle multiple URIs with separate methods. For more information, see the section "MultiActionControllers" in Chapter 6.

Default Mapping
It is also possible to set a default handler, in the case that no other mapping can satisfy the
request. If you wish to designate a default handler, simply map that handler with /*, as shown
in Listing 5-12.

Listing 5-12. *Setting a Controller As the Default Handler*

```
<bean name="/*"
  class="com.apress.expertspringmvc.flight.web.HomeController">
  <property name="flightService" ref="flightService" />
</bean>
```

The order in which you define your beans and mappings does not matter to the
BeanNameUrlHandlerMapping. It attempts to find the best match at request time.

Match Algorithm

As you can see, there are many different strategies for mapping a request handler with a URL
path. The AbstractUrlHandlerMapping class uses the following algorithm when performing a
match.

1. Attempt an exact match. If found, exit from search.

2. Search all registered paths for a match. The most specific (longest) path pattern will win.

3. If no matches are found, use the default mapping (/*) if present.

BeanNameUrlHandlerMapping Shortcomings

While it is very convenient, there are shortcomings with BeanNameUrlHandlerMapping. This
implementation of HandlerMapping is not able to map to prototype beans. In other words,
all request handlers must be singletons when using BeanNameUrlHandlerMapping. Normally,
Controllers are built as singletons, so this doesn't become an issue. However, as we'll see
in the chapter covering Controllers, there are a few types of controllers that are indeed
prototypes.

■**Note** Prototype beans are non-singleton beans. A new bean instance is created for every call to getBean()
on the ApplicationContext. For more information, consult *Pro Spring*.

The BeanNameUrlHandlerMapping has another problem when your application begins to
integrate interceptors. Because there is no explicit binding between this handler mapping and
the beans it is mapping, it is impossible to create complex relationships between controllers
and interceptors. We will cover interceptors in detail in Chapter 6.

If more complex handler mapping requirements arise, you may use the
SimpleUrlHandlerMapping along with BeanNameUrlHandlerMapping.

SimpleUrlHandlerMapping

Created as an alternative to the simple BeanNameUrlHandlerMapping, the
SimpleUrlHandlerMapping addresses the former's two shortcomings. It is able to map to
prototype request handlers, and it allows you to create complex mappings between handlers
and interceptors.

The path matching algorithms default to the same mechanism as BeanNameUrlHandlerMapping, so the patterns used to map URLs to request handlers remains the same.

To use a SimpleUrlHandlerMapping, simply declare it inside your ApplicationContext. The DispatcherServlet will recognize it by type, and it will not create an instance of BeanNameUrlHandlerMapping. This means that if you wish to use both mapping strategies, you must declare both in your ApplicationContext.

■Tip The DispatcherServlet will chain handler mapping strategies, allowing you to mix and match as you see fit. Handler mappings also implement the Ordered interface.

To begin, we will port the previous mapping to use a SimpleUrlHandlerMapping, as shown in Listing 5-13.

Listing 5-13. *SimpleUrlHandlerMapping Example*

```
<bean
  class="org.springframework.web.servlet.handler.SimpleUrlHandlerMapping">
  <property name="urlMap">
    <map>
      <entry key="/home" value-ref="homeController" />
    </map>
  </property>
</bean>

<bean id="homeController"
  class="com.apress.expertspringmvc.flight.web.HomeController">
  <property name="flightService" ref="flightService" />
</bean>
```

Unfortunately, it is a bit more verbose when mapping two different URL patterns to the same request handler. You must create two different mappings, as shown in Listing 5-14.

Listing 5-14. *Two Mappings for One Controller with SimpleUrlHandlerMapping*

```
<bean
  class="org.springframework.web.servlet.handler.SimpleUrlHandlerMapping">
  <property name="urlMap">
    <map>
      <entry key="/home*" value-ref="homeController" />
      <entry key="/index" value-ref="homeController" />
    </map>
  </property>
</bean>
```

As you can see, we are mapping a URL directly to a request handler instance (in this case, the singleton `homeController`). If your request handlers are prototypes, you may instead use the `mappings` property of `SimpleUrlHandlerMapping`. Using this property, the mapping is between a URL and a bean name (as a `String`), thus decoupling the mapping from the actual bean instance. Using the `mappings` property, you are able to map to prototype request handlers, as they are looked up every time a request enters the system. See Listing 5-15.

Listing 5-15. *Mapping URLs to Bean Names for Use with Prototype Handlers*

```
<bean
  class="org.springframework.web.servlet.handler.SimpleUrlHandlerMapping">
  <property name="mappings">
    <props>
      <prop key="/home">homeController</prop>
    </props>
  </property>
</bean>
```

The `SimpleUrlHandlerMapping` maps default handlers in the same way as the `BeanNameUrlHandlerMapping`. To set a request handler as the default handler, simply map it to the path `/*`.

One of the main reasons to use `SimpleUrlHandlerMapping` is to take advantage of interceptors. While you can configure interceptors with `BeanNameUrlHandlerMapping`, it is very difficult to create different combinations of handlers and interceptors. Using `SimpleUrlHandlerMapping` makes it easy to create custom handler chains per request handler. We will visit interceptors in Chapter 6.

Custom Mapping Strategy

The power and flexibility of Spring MVC's request mapping really shines when a non–URL-based mapping strategy is required. Because the `HandlerMapping` interface doesn't require a URL to be involved in the mapping, the possibilities are quite open.

To illustrate a mapping strategy not based on URLs, let's consider mapping requests to handlers based solely on request parameters.

To begin with, we will subclass `AbstractHandlerMapping` to take advantage of ordering, the ability to set a default handler, and other life cycle callbacks. The new `RequestParameterHandlerMapping` class (Listing 5-16) will map request parameter values from a specified parameter name to handler instances.

Listing 5-16. *RequestParameterHandlerMapping*

```
public class RequestParameterHandlerMapping extends AbstractHandlerMapping
        implements InitializingBean {

    public final static String DEFAULT_PARAM_NAME = "handler";
    private String parameterName = DEFAULT_PARAM_NAME;

    private final Map<String, Object> paramMappings =
        new HashMap<String, Object>();
```

```
    public final void setParamMappings(Map<String, Object> paramMappings) {
        this.paramMappings.putAll(paramMappings);
    }

    public final void setParameterName(String parameterName) {
        this.parameterName = parameterName;
    }

    @Override
    protected Object getHandlerInternal(HttpServletRequest request)
            throws Exception {
        String parameterValue = request.getParameter(parameterName);
        return paramMappings.get(parameterValue);
    }

    public void afterPropertiesSet() throws Exception {
        Assert.hasText(parameterName,
          "parameterName must not be null or blank");
    }

}
```

Because this class extends `AbstractHandlerMapping`, if no handler exists for the request parameter, then the `AbstractHandlerMapping` will attempt to load the default handler, which can be set via the XML bean definition. See Listing 5-17.

Listing 5-17. *RequestParameterHandlerMapping XML Definition*

```
<bean
  class="com.apress.expertspringmvc.chap5.RequestParameterHandlerMapping">
  <property name="defaultHandler" ref="defaultController" />
  <property name="parameterName" value="action" />
  <property name="paramMappings">
    <map>
      <entry key="load" value-ref="loadController" />
      <entry key="save" value-ref="saveController" />
    </map>
  </property>
</bean>
```

With this configuration, the URL `http://example.org/springapp/app?action=load` would be routed to the `loadController`. Remember that `/app` is just the `DispatcherServlet` mapping and not specific to any controller or request handler.

Summary

Mapping incoming requests to request handlers is very flexible in Spring MVC. Out of the box, URL mapping methods are provided, but it's very easy to create mapping strategies that use any information available in the HttpServletRequest.

The BeanNameUrlHandlerMapping is the default mapping strategy and is used if no other mapping strategies are defined in the ApplicationContext. This strategy, while simple and easy, does have a few limitations. If you require complex interceptor mapping or the use of prototype beans for handlers, you will need to use the SimpleUrlHandlerMapping.

Handler mapping strategies can be ordered using the Ordered interface, allowing you to utilize multiple methods to resolve incoming requests to handlers.

HandlerExceptionResolver

When an exception occurs from handling a request, Spring MVC can catch the exception for you and route the request to a particular error page or other exception handling code. The HandlerExceptionResolver will handle any exception thrown inside the HandlerInterceptors, the Controllers, or the View rendering. Typically, an exception is mapped to a particular error page, but it is easy to extend this functionality for your particular error handling needs.

By using a HandlerExceptionResolver, shown in Listing 5-18, it is easy to centralize error handling and configuration. Otherwise, each controller and interceptor would have to contain duplicate code and logic for each exception that could be thrown.

Listing 5-18. *HandlerExceptionResolver Interface*

```
package org.springframework.web.servlet;

public interface HandlerExceptionResolver {

    ModelAndView resolveException(
        HttpServletRequest request, HttpServletResponse response,
        Object handler, Exception ex);

}
```

The DispatcherServlet is configured by default to look for all beans in its ApplicationContext of type HandlerExceptionResolver. If it finds one or more, it will order them using the org.springframework.core.Ordered interface if the bean implements it. If no HandlerExceptionResolver is found, no exception resolving will take place. Of course, any mapped exceptions you have specified in the web.xml will still apply if the exception isn't handled by a HandlerExceptionResolver.

You may also tell the DispatcherServlet to use only a single exception resolver, ignoring all others that may be present in the ApplicationContext. Simply set the detectAllHandlerExceptionResolvers property of the DispatcherServlet to false, and then define a single bean with the name handlerExceptionResolver.

The default implementation of this interface is the `org.springframework.web.servlet.` `handler.SimpleMappingExceptionResolver`. This class maps exceptions to view names by the exception class name or a substring of the class name. This implementation can be configured for individual `Controllers` or for globally for all handlers. The example configuration in Listing 5-19 illustrates these options.

Listing 5-19. *Example SimpleMappingExceptionResolver ApplicationContext*

```
<?xml version="1.0"?>
<!DOCTYPE beans PUBLIC
    "-//SPRING//DTD BEAN//EN"
    "http://www.springframework.org/dtd/spring-beans.dtd">
<beans>
  <bean id="exceptionMapping"
    class="org.springframework.web.servlet.handler.SimpleMappingExceptionResolver">
    <property name="exceptionMappings">
      <props>
        <prop key="ApplicationException">appErrorView</prop>
        <prop key="SomeOtherException">someErrorView</prop>
        <prop key="java.lang.Exception">genericErrorView</prop>
      </props>
    </property>
  </bean>
</beans>
```

The `exceptionMappings` property is a `java.util.Properties` with substrings (explained later in this section) of exception class names as keys and `View` names as values. Notice how you can specify a fully qualified class name or only part of a class name for the key. The error `View` name will be ultimately resolved by a `ViewResolver`.

Listing 5-19 does not specify a particular request handler, so it will be applied to any mapped exception by any handler. However, you can bind an exception resolver to specific handlers to create very specific mappings. Use this technique when you require displaying different error pages for the same exception thrown by two different controllers.

Caution Mapping exceptions to individual handlers only works if the handler is a singleton. Unless you are using `ThrowawayControllers`, this should not be an issue because normally `Controllers` are singletons. However, it is always possible to run any controller as a prototype.

Listing 5-20 provides two examples, one for mapping an exception resolver to a single request handler, and the other for mapping to multiple request handlers.

Listing 5-20. *Two Exception Resolvers for Specific Handlers*

```
<?xml version="1.0"?>
<!DOCTYPE beans PUBLIC
```

```xml
                    "-//SPRING//DTD BEAN//EN"
                    "http://www.springframework.org/dtd/spring-beans.dtd">
  <beans>
    <bean id="exceptionMappingForSingleController"
        class="org.springframework.web.servlet.handler.SimpleMappingExceptionResolver">
        <property name="mappedHandlers">
            <set>
                <ref bean="someController" />
            </set>
        </property>
        <property name="exceptionMappings">
            <props>
                <prop key="ApplicationException">appErrorView</prop>
                <prop key="SomeOtherException">someErrorView</prop>
                <prop key="java.lang.Exception">genericErrorView</prop>
            </props>
        </property>
    </bean>

    <bean id="exceptionMappingForMultipleControllers"
        class="org.springframework.web.servlet.handler.SimpleMappingExceptionResolver">
        <property name="mappedHandlers">
            <set>
                <ref bean="anotherController" />
                <ref bean="mainController" />
            </set>
        </property>
        <property name="exceptionMappings">
            <props>
                <prop key="java.lang.Exception">differentErrorView</prop>
            </props>
        </property>
    </bean>
  </beans>
```

Two exception resolvers are defined in the ApplicationContext in Listing 5-20. Each defines a set of mapped handlers that will define when the exception resolver is applied. If an exception resolver encounters an exception from a handler it is not mapped to, it will simply ignore the exception. Note that this behavior is only for exception resolvers that are mapped to at least one handler.

You can control the order in which the DispatcherServlet will call each exception resolver. To do this, simply add a property named order and set it to a positive integer. Any exception resolvers not specified with an order will be randomly placed at the end of the ordered list.

Listing 5-21 provides an example of setting an order priority.

Listing 5-21. *Example of Ordered Exception Resolver*

```
<bean id="anotherExceptionMapping"
  class="org.springframework.web.servlet.handler.SimpleMappingExceptionResolver">
  <property name="order" value="1" />
  <property name="mappedHandlers">
    <set>
```

Pattern Matching Rules

The rules for pattern matching of the exception names might not be obvious, so we cover them here. There are two rules to be aware of.

Rule Number One

The first rule to be aware of is that the shorter the pattern string, the higher priority it will receive. For example, the mapping Excep will match any exception whose class name contains that substring (in other words, nearly every exception). Even if you have another mapping with the exact class name, the shorter Excep mapping will resolve first. Listings 5-22 through 5-24 illustrate this.

Listing 5-22 contains the two exception classes we'll use for this example. It is a simple class hierarchy, with ExceptionChild subclassing ExceptionParent.

Listing 5-22. *Example Exception Classes*

```
public class ExceptionParent extends Exception { }
public class ExceptionChild extends ExceptionParent { }
```

Listing 5-23 illustrates an exception resolver with two mappings. The first is a very general mapping, handling any exception whose name includes the substring Excep. The second mapping is an explicit mapping for an exception whose names includes the fuller ExceptionChild.

Listing 5-23. *Exception Mapping Example*

```
<?xml version="1.0"?>
<!DOCTYPE beans PUBLIC
    "-//SPRING//DTD BEAN//EN"
    "http://www.springframework.org/dtd/spring-beans.dtd">
<beans>
 <bean id="exceptionMapping"
  class="org.springframework.web.servlet.handler.SimpleMappingExceptionResolver">
  <property name="exceptionMappings">
    <props>
      <prop key="Excep">exceptionPage</prop>
      <prop key="ExceptionChild">moreSpecificPage</prop>
    </props>
  </property>
 </bean>
</beans>
```

Listing 5-24 contains sample code that programmatically illustrates what view name is resolved when an `ExceptionChild` exception is thrown.

Listing 5-24. *Test Case*

```
ModelAndView mav = resolver.resolveException(req, res, handler,
    new ExceptionChild());
assertEquals("exceptionPage", mav.getViewName());   // true!
```

Notice how, in Listing 5-24, the `SimpleMappingExceptionResolver` returned the view name exceptionPage, even though there was a rule to map an `ExceptionChild` exception.

Rule Number Two

The second rule comes in two parts. Exception mappings are aware of their superclasses, so a mapping for a class will resolve to that class and all of its subclasses. Given the exception classes from the previous example, the code in Listing 5-25 illustrates this rule.

Listing 5-25. *Exception Resolver Configuration for ExceptionParent*

```
<?xml version="1.0"?>
<!DOCTYPE beans PUBLIC
    "-//SPRING//DTD BEAN//EN"
    "http://www.springframework.org/dtd/spring-beans.dtd">
<beans>
 <bean id="exceptionMapping"
  class="org.springframework.web.servlet.handler.SimpleMappingExceptionResolver">
  <property name="exceptionMappings">
    <props>
      <prop key="ExceptionParent">parentPage</prop>
    </props>
  </property>
 </bean>
</beans>
```

Listing 5-26 simply shows that even those an `ExceptionChild` was thrown, the mapping for `ExceptionParent` resolves.

Listing 5-26. *Test Case*

```
ModelAndView mav = resolver.resolveException(req, res, handler,
    new ExceptionChild());  // throwing child subclass
assertEquals("parentPage", mav.getViewName());   // true!
```

Now, here is the second part of the rule. If you specify both the parent exception and the child exception, then the child exception will resolve. So, even though the resolving logic will scan the exception class hierarchy for a match, it will prefer a match lower in the tree.

Listing 5-27 contains a simple mapping with both `ExceptionParent` and `ExceptionChild`. Which one will resolve is based on which exception is thrown. Listing 5-28 shows that when throwing `ExceptionChild`, the view name `childPage` resolves because `ExceptionChild` is more specific than `ExceptionParent`.

Listing 5-27. *Exception Resolver Mapping Both ExceptionParent and ExceptionChild*

```xml
<?xml version="1.0"?>
<!DOCTYPE beans PUBLIC
    "-//SPRING//DTD BEAN//EN"
    "http://www.springframework.org/dtd/spring-beans.dtd">
<beans>
 <bean id="exceptionMapping"
  class="org.springframework.web.servlet.handler.SimpleMappingExceptionResolver">
  <property name="exceptionMappings">
    <props>
      <prop key="ExceptionParent">parentPage</prop>
      <prop key="ExceptionChild">childPage</prop>
    </props>
  </property>
 </bean>
</beans>
```

Listing 5-28. *Test Case*

```java
ModelAndView mav = resolver.resolveException(req, res, handler,
    new ExceptionChild());  // throwing child subclass
assertEquals("childPage", mav.getViewName());    // true!
```

Of course, if you configured that last exception resolver with a mapping of `Exce`, then that would take precedence over either previous mapping.

Summary

To summarize, the `HandlerExceptionResolver` interface provides a mechanism to centralize exception handling and remove it from the primary work flow logic. You can configure multiple exception resolvers in an `ApplicationContext`, and they can be ordered by priority.

Spring provides a single implementation of this interface called `SimpleMappingExceptionResolver` that maps exception names to error pages. This implementation can match full class names or substrings, will prefer a shorter name, and is aware of the class hierarchy when attempting to match the exception.

The `DispatcherServlet` is aware of all exception resolvers in the `ApplicationContext` and can order them based on priority. You can change this behavior by setting the `DispatcherServlet`'s `detectAllHandlerExceptionResolvers` property to `false`, in which case you will need to define a single exception resolver with the name `handlerExceptionResolver`.

LocaleResolver

The `org.springframework.web.servlet.LocaleResolver` is a Strategy interface for retrieving and setting a `java.util.Locale` during a web request. The Gang of Four, authors of *Design Patterns* (Addison Wesley, 1995), write this of the Strategy pattern: "Define a family of algorithms, encapsulate each one, and make them interchangeable. Strategy lets the algorithm vary independently from clients that use it."

■**Tip** The Strategy pattern is heavily implemented within the Spring Framework. One of the reasons this pattern is preferred is because class inheritance is generally avoided as a means to share behavior. The Strategy pattern allows you to share behavior much more easily.

The `LocaleResolver` defines the contract of `Locale` resolution and modification. It leaves the details of these methods up to implementations. Most importantly, the implementations can be exchanged freely without affecting the system.

The `Locale` is mostly used when the application needs to display translated text for the user interface, although it is also useful for formatting numbers and currencies. It assists the general internationalization (i18n) features of the Java platform (http://java.sun.com/docs/books/tutorial/i18n) and Spring MVC for providing language and culture independent applications. You will see many examples of this in Chapter 7, which covers user interface options. For now, it's important to know that the `Locale` is set per user and intended to be accessible to both the work flow and the user interface.

By default, generic Java web applications will respect the Accept-Language (http://www.w3.org/Protocols/rfc2616/rfc2616-sec14.html#sec14.4) header of a HTTP request. The servlet container will map the languages specified in the header into `Locale` objects and set the primary choice as the chosen `Locale`.

■**Tip** For more information on how Java web applications handle this header, see section 4.8 of the Servlet 2.4 Specification (http://jcp.org/aboutJava/communityprocess/final/jsr154/index.html) or HttpServletRequest's `getLocale()` and `getLocales()` methods.

Many applications, however, require more control when selecting the user's `Locale` or modifying it. This strategy interface allows you to customize where the `Locale` information comes from and how to change it. First, let's look at the `LocaleResolver` interface, shown in Listing 5-29 and Figure 5-2.

Listing 5-29. *LocaleResolver Interface*

```
package org.springframework.web.servlet;

public interface LocaleResolver {
    Locale resolveLocale(HttpServletRequest request);

    void setLocale(HttpServletRequest request, HttpServletResponse response,
        Locale locale);
}
```

■Tip To clear out the locale using this strategy interface, simply set the `locale` property of the `LocaleResolver` implementation to `null`.

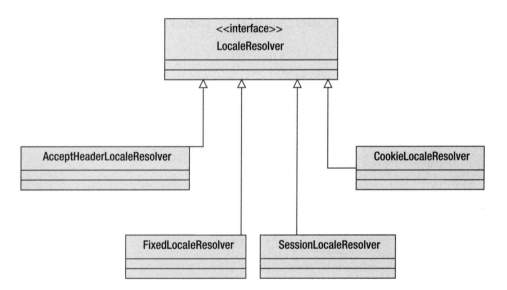

Figure 5-2. *LocaleResolver class hierarchy*

Once you have chosen an appropriate `LocaleResolver`, you need to register it with the `DispatcherServlet` by creating a bean definition with the name `localeResolver` in your `ApplicationContext`. The `DispatcherServlet` will look for that name before falling back to its default implementation, the `AcceptHeaderLocaleResolver`.

The `LocaleResolver` interface defines how to query and set a `Locale`, but it does not define when or how you should use it. Spring MVC's i18n infrastructure (discussed in Chapters 7 and 9) will read out the `Locale` when performing translations and culture-specific formatting. This work is typically done under the hood, so your job as a developer is to set the locale via the `LocaleResolver`.

This action is often a manual operation, helped tremendously by the chosen strategy, because many users and clients cannot be trusted to set their browser's language preferences correctly. In other words, you probably can't trust that the Accept-Language HTTP header is correctly configured all the time.

■**Note** The DispatcherServlet does not support chaining LocaleResolvers, so you are allowed to choose only one implementation.

Setting a Locale

Your application's design will dictate when you should call setLocale, normally in response to some user action. For example, the application might provide a page with language choices, and the user will be able to choose one and submit it back to the server.

In one possible implementation, you would create a Controller that delegates to a LocaleResolver in order to store the user's chosen Locale. Listings 5-30 and 5-31 show you how to do this.

Listing 5-30. *HTML Form, Choosing Language*

```
<form action="setLocale" method="post">
  <p>
  Language: <select name="language">
            <option value="en">English</option>
            <option value="de">German</option>
            </select>
  </p>
  <p>
  <input type="submit" />
  </p>
</form>
```

Listing 5-31. *SetLocaleController*

```
public class SetLocaleController extends AbstractController {

  @Override
  protected ModelAndView handleRequestInternal(HttpServletRequest req,
          HttpServletResponse res) throws Exception {
    String language = req.getParameter("language");
    Locale locale = StringUtils.parseLocaleString(language);

    // How did we get a reference to the localeResolver?
    // See Listings 5-32 and 5-34 for the two strategies
    // for obtaining a reference
    // to this localeResolver instance
```

```
    localeResolver.setLocale(req, res, locale);

    return new ModelAndView("setLocaleSuccess");
  }

}
```

■**Tip** Spring MVC provides a `LocaleChangeInterceptor` that performs the exact same operation as the above example `Controller`. This interceptor is recommended, especially if many forms all have the same locale request parameters.

Retrieving a LocaleResolver

Clearly you may use the `LocaleResolver` to set the locale, but what is the best way to obtain a reference to the `localeResolver` from inside the `Controller`? There are at least two ways to get the `LocaleResolver` object, each with different advantages. Which way you choose will be up to you.

The most obvious way to get the `LocaleResolver` is to rely on Dependency Injection. The `LocaleResolver` instance is a bean in the `ApplicationContext` like all other objects in the system, so Spring will be happy to set this object into your `Controller` via DI for you. The `DispatcherServlet` will recognize only one `LocaleResolver` in the `ApplicationContext` (it won't chain multiple resolvers of this type), so typically there will be only one instance in the application. If you have defined a `LocaleResolver` in the context, consider altering your `Controller` to allow for injection of the resource, as shown in Listings 5-32 and 5-33.

Listing 5-32. *Adding a Setter Method for Dependency Injection*

```
private LocaleResolver localeResolver;

public void setLocaleResolver(LocaleResolver localeResolver) {
  this.localeResolver = localeResolver;
}
```

Listing 5-33. *SetLocaleController ApplicationContext*

```xml
<?xml version="1.0"?>
<!DOCTYPE beans PUBLIC
    "-//SPRING//DTD BEAN//EN"
    "http://www.springframework.org/dtd/spring-beans.dtd">

<beans>

  <bean id="localeResolver"
    class="org.springframework.web.servlet.i18n.SessionLocaleResolver" />
```

```
<bean id="setLocaleController"
  class="com.apress.expertspringmvc.chap4.SetLocaleController">
  <property name="localeResolver" ref="localeResolver" />
</bean>
```

```
</beans>
```

There are situations where simple Dependency Injection won't work, such as when Spring doesn't manage the life cycle of the handler object. For instance, the HandlerAdapter interface was created to allow any request handler to be easily integrated into the DispatcherServlet. In cases such as these, the DispatcherServlet places some of the framework objects, such as the LocaleResolver, into the servlet request as request scoped attributes. This allows for any object handling the HttpServlerRequest to be able to access the LocaleResolver.

To conveniently access the resolver without Dependency Injection, use the org. springframework.web.servlet.support.RequestContextUtils class and its helpful getLocaleResolver() method. This utility method encapsulates the knowledge of where the LocaleResolver is placed in the request scope, making retrieval safer for the client. The Controller can be modified as shown in Listing 5-34.

Listing 5-34. *RequestContextUtils.getLocaleResolver Example*

```
@Override
protected ModelAndView handleRequestInternal(HttpServletRequest req,
          HttpServletResponse res) throws Exception {
  String language = req.getParameter("language");
  Locale locale = StringUtils.parseLocaleString(language);
  LocaleResolver localeResolver = RequestContextUtils.getLocaleResolver(req);
  localeResolver.setLocale(req, res, locale);
  return new ModelAndView("setLocaleSuccess");
}
```

This class no longer needs the setLocaleResolver() method, as Dependency Injection is no longer used.

Which method should you use? Using Dependency Injection is always easier to test than using RequestContextUtils, so the DI solution is preferable.

You have now seen the LocaleResolver interface and the different options of interacting with it. How the Locale, once it is set, affects the i18n features will be covered in Chapters 7 and 9. It's time now to look in detail at the different implementations of LocaleResolver.

AcceptHeaderLocaleResolver

The DispatcherServlet will default to the org.springframework.web.servlet.i18n. AcceptHeaderLocaleResolver class if no other LocaleResolvers are specified in the ApplicationContext. This implementation simply delegates to the HttpServletRequest's getLocale() method, thus obeying the Accept-Language HTTP header. Because the header originates from the client, there is no way to change the Locale, so the AcceptHeaderLocaleResolver will throw an exception if setLocale() is called.

There is no need to specify this class in your ApplicationContext, as the DispatcherServlet will create it if no implementations can be found.

FixedLocaleResolver

The simplest implementation is the FixedLocaleResolver. This class allows you to define the Locale in the ApplicationContext, and because the Locale choice is fixed, it's one size fits all with this Strategy. This is a useful and easy way to override and ignore any client's language choice, for example. Simply define an instance of this class in your ApplicationContext with the bean name localeResolver, and the DispatcherServlet will recognize it automatically.

Listing 5-35 contains an example configuration of a FixedLocaleResolver.

Listing 5-35. *Sample FixedLocaleResolver*

```xml
<?xml version="1.0"?>
<!DOCTYPE beans PUBLIC
    "-//SPRING//DTD BEAN//EN"
    "http://www.springframework.org/dtd/spring-beans.dtd">

<beans>

  <bean id="fixedLocaleResolver"
    class="org.springframework.web.servlet.i18n.FixedLocaleResolver">
    <property name="defaultLocale" value="en" />
  </bean>

</beans>
```

Using the configuration from Listing 5-35, no matter what the client advertises via its headers, the framework will force the locale to be en.

You might notice that the defaultLocale property is of type java.util.Locale, yet all we specified in the above configuration is the string en. Spring will use its LocaleEditor property editor to convert from the string to a full Locale instance. LocaleEditor is one of the many property editors that Spring will create and register by default.

■**Tip** Spring's use of PropertyEditors from the Java Bean specification is quite extensive. Take the time to learn what editors Spring provides out of the box (a subset is covered in Chapter 6).

If your applications require providing each user their own unique experience, the FixedLocaleResolver falls quite short. With the default class AcceptHeaderLocaleResolver (while it does provide a personalized experience) it's impossible for the application to change its value. There are two other implementations of LocaleResolver that allow the application to change the Locale for the user, the CookieLocaleResolver and the SessionLocaleResolver. Both of these implementations support changing and storing the Locale across requests.

CookieLocaleResolver

The CookieLocaleResolver sets and retrieves the Locale object via a browser cookie. This strategy is useful when the application does not support sessions and the state must be kept client side.

Simply declare this class in your ApplicationContext to use it. Note that you can configure the name of the cookie if you choose, but the class provides a sensible default. If you wish to clear the Locale cookie, simply call setLocale() and pass in a null locale.

Listing 5-36 contains a sample bean definition for a CookieLocaleResolver.

Listing 5-36. *CookieLocaleResolver Bean Definition*

```xml
<?xml version="1.0"?>
<!DOCTYPE beans PUBLIC
    "-//SPRING//DTD BEAN//EN"
    "http://www.springframework.org/dtd/spring-beans.dtd">

<beans>

  <bean id="cookieLocaleResolver"
    class="org.springframework.web.servlet.i18n.CookieLocaleResolver" />

</beans>
```

> **Note** If there is no Locale cookie present, this class will fall back to ServletRequest's getLocale() method. The getLocale() method returns the client's preferred Locale, as dictated by the Accept-Language HTTP header. If the client did not specify an Accept-Language header, the method returns the default Locale of the server.

SessionLocaleResolver

The SessionLocaleResolver stores the user's Locale inside the HttpSession object, and it supports both retrieval and modification. It offers a nice alternative to storing the locale state in a cookie. As with the CookieLocaleResolver, if no Locale is found in the session, this class will fall back to the getLocale() method of HttpServletRequest.

This implementation (see Listing 5-37) is as easy to declare as the CookieLocaleResolver.

Listing 5-37. *SessionLocaleResolver Bean*

```xml
<?xml version="1.0"?>
<!DOCTYPE beans PUBLIC
    "-//SPRING//DTD BEAN//EN"
    "http://www.springframework.org/dtd/spring-beans.dtd">

<beans>
```

```
<bean id="sessionLocaleResolver"
  class="org.springframework.web.servlet.i18n.SessionLocaleResolver" />

</beans>
```

Summary

So how do you choose which locale management strategy to use? It all depends on what your application requirements are, and as usual, Spring doesn't force one decision for you. In fact, if your needs aren't covered by the included strategy implementations, the LocaleResolver interface is simple enough to create a customization if required.

■**Tip** Never feel constrained by the provided solutions and implementations. More often than not, there's an interface or abstract class for easy customization.

If your application doesn't allow your users to change their Locale, but you do want to acknowledge their browser's defaults, then stick with the default AcceptHeaderLocaleResolver. This strategy emulates the Servlet specification's default behavior and requires no configuration. It's also the option of least surprise, as it performs as most people would expect.

If you need to force a particular Locale and it can never be changed, then FixedLocaleResolver is the one for you. This class is very simple to set up, but is quite limiting.

When your application requires Locales to be changed by the user from inside the web application, then the CookieLocaleResolver and the SessionLocaleResolver are your two choices. If your application is already using sessions, then the SessionLocaleResolver is a logical choice. However, if you require the Locale choice to persist longer than the session, then the CookieLocaleResolver is your only choice. There is no clear winner here, so choose the option that best fits your situation.

MultipartResolver

Handling file uploads is a standard feature of web frameworks, and Spring MVC's org.springframework.web.multipart.MultipartResolver provides the strategy interface for this functionality. Like many other features, Spring doesn't reinvent the wheel when it comes to file upload handling. Out of the box, Spring provides two implementations of MultipartResolver, one for Jakarta Commons' FileUpload (http://jakarta.apache.org/commons/fileupload) and one for Jason Hunter's COS (http://www.servlets.com/cos).

■**Tip** COS stands for com.oreilly.servlet, as the library was originally written for Jason Hunter's *Java Serlvet Programming* (O'Reilly, 2001).

HTTP file uploading, or "Form-based File Upload in HTML," is defined in RFC 1867 (http://www.ietf.org/rfc/rfc1867.txt). By creating an HTML input field of type="file" and setting the form's enctype="multipart/form-data", the browser can send a text or binary file to the server as part of a HTTP POST request.

The DispatcherServlet will look for a single bean in the ApplicationContext with the name multipartResolver. If one is found, it will pass each incoming request to the resolver in order to wrap the HttpServletRequest with a subclass that can expose the file upload. If a multipart resolver is not located, then no multipart file handling will be available. Note that the DispatcherServlet does not chain MultipartResolvers.

Unlike previous resolvers such as LocaleResolver, client code is never intended to interact with this interface directly. The DispatcherServlet manages the work flow of the MultipartResolver, and the client code will simply cast the request object to an org.springframework.web.multipart.MultipartHttpServletRequest wrapper object in order to get the uploaded file(s).

Listing 5-38 contains the MultipartResolver interface.

Listing 5-38. *MultipartResolver Interface*

```
package org.springframework.web.multipart;

public interface MultipartResolver {

  boolean isMultipart(HttpServletRequest request);

  MultipartHttpServletRequest resolveMultipart(HttpServletRequest request)
    throws MultipartException;

  void cleanupMultipart(MultipartHttpServletRequest request);

}
```

The isMultipart() method is called by the DispatcherServlet in order to determine if the incoming request is a multipart request. The implementation will most likely check the Content-Type of the request for a value of multipart/form-data, but this can be only part of the heuristics.

If the request does indeed contain uploaded files, the resolveMultipart() method is called, returning the MultipartHttpServletRequest (see Listing 5-39). This wrapping object adds methods to retrieve the uploaded files.

■**Caution** The MultipartResolver will only wrap requests with a MultipartHttpServletRequest if the request actually contains file uploads.

Listing 5-39. *MultipartHttpServletRequest Interface*

```
package org.springframework.web.multipart;

public interface MultipartHttpServletRequest extends HttpServletRequest {

  Iterator getFileNames();

  MultipartFile getFile(String name);

  Map getFileMap();

}
```

Before the end of the request life cycle and after the handling code has had a chance to work with the uploaded files, the DispatcherServlet will then call cleanupMultipart(). This removes any state left behind by the file upload implementation code, such as temporary files on the file system. Therefore, it is important that any request handling code should work with the uploaded files before request processing finishes.

So which library should you use, Commons' FileUpload or COS? The choice is up to you, as both have been around for years and are considered stable. However, keep in mind that Commons' FileUpload will probably receive more maintenance in the future. Of course, if neither provides the features you require, you may implement a new MultipartResolver.

Example

Working with file uploads is actually quite simple, as most of the mechanisms are handled by the DispatcherServlet and thus hidden from request handling code. For an example, we will register a Jakarta Commons FileUpload MultipartResolver and create a Controller that saves uploaded files to a temporary directory.

Listing 5-40 contains the configuration required for the CommonsMultipartResolver.

Listing 5-40. *MultipartResolver ApplicationContext*

```xml
<?xml version="1.0"?>
<!DOCTYPE beans PUBLIC
    "-//SPRING//DTD BEAN//EN"
    "http://www.springframework.org/dtd/spring-beans.dtd">

<beans>

  <bean id="multipartResolver"
    class="org.springframework.web.multipart.commons.CommonsMultipartResolver">
    <property name="maxUploadSize" value="2000000" />
  </bean>

  <bean name="/handleUpload"
    class="com.apress.expertspringmvc.chap4.HandleUploadController">
    <property name="tempDirectory" value="/tmp" />
```

```
  </bean>

</beans>
```

Note that we declared the multipart resolver in the same ApplicationContext as our Controller. We recommend grouping all web-related beans in the same context.

Next, we create the form for the file upload, as shown in Listing 5-41.

▪Tip It's very important to set the enctype attribute of the <form> element to multipart/form-data.

Listing 5-41. *HTML File Upload Form*

```
<?xml version="1.0" encoding="ISO-8859-1" ?>
<!DOCTYPE html PUBLIC "-//W3C//DTD XHTML 1.0 Transitional//EN"
  "http://www.w3.org/TR/xhtml1/DTD/xhtml1-transitional.dtd">
<html xmlns="http://www.w3.org/1999/xhtml">
<head>
  <meta http-equiv="Content-Type" content="text/html; charset=ISO-8859-1" />
<title>File Upload Form</title>
</head>
<body>

<form action="spring/handleUpload" method="post" enctype="multipart/form-data">

  File: <input type="file" name="uploaded" />

  <input type="submit" />

</form>
</body>
</html>
```

The Controller that handles the request is shown in Listing 5-42. Notice how it must cast the request object to a MultipartHttpServletRequest before extracting the file. The utility class FileCopyUtils, provided by Spring, contains convenience methods such as copying an input stream to an output stream.

Listing 5-42. *File Upload Controller*

```
public class HandleUploadController extends AbstractController
    implements InitializingBean {

  private File destinationDir;

  public void setDestinationDir(File destinationDir) {
    this.destinationDir = destinationDir;
  }
```

```
public void afterPropertiesSet() throws Exception {
  if (destinationDir == null) {
    throw new IllegalArgumentException("Must specify destinationDir");
  } else if (!destinationDir.isDirectory() && !destinationDir.mkdir()) {
    throw new IllegalArgumentException(destinationDir + " is not a " +
      "directory, or it couldn't be created");
  }
}

protected ModelAndView handleRequestInternal(HttpServletRequest req,
        HttpServletResponse res) throws Exception {
    res.setContentType("text/plain");

    if (! (req instanceof MultipartHttpServletRequest)) {
        res.sendError(HttpServletResponse.SC_BAD_REQUEST,
            "Expected multipart request");
        return null;
    }

    MultipartHttpServletRequest multipartRequest =
        (MultipartHttpServletRequest) req;
    MultipartFile file = multipartRequest.getFile("uploaded");
    File destination = File.createTempFile("file", "uploaded",
            destinationDir);
    FileCopyUtils.copy(file.getInputStream(),
            new FileOutputStream(destination));

    res.getWriter().write("Success, wrote to " + destination);
    res.flushBuffer();
    return null;
}

}
```

If you are creating command beans (see BaseCommandController and SimpleFormController in Chapter 6) to encapsulate the request parameters from forms, you can even populate a property of your command object from the contents of the uploaded file. In other words, instead of performing the manual operation of extracting the file from the MultipartFile instance (as we did in the preceding example in Listing 5-42), Spring MVC can inject the contents of the uploaded file (as a MultipartFile, byte[], or String) directly into a property on your command bean. With this technique there is no need to cast the ServletRequest object or manually retrieve the file contents.

We'll cover binding request parameters from forms in the next chapter, so we won't jump ahead here and confuse the topic at hand. But we will provide the hint required to make the file contents transparently show up in your command bean: you must register either `ByteArrayMultipartFileEditor` or `StringMultipartFileEditor` with your data binder (for instance, inside the `initBinder()` method of your form controller). What does that mean? Hang tight, or skip to Chapter 7.

As long as the contents of the uploaded file aren't too large, we recommend the direct property binding because it is less work for you and certainly more transparent.

ThemeResolver

Spring MVC supports a concept of *themes*, which are interchangeable looks and feels for your web application. Often called *skins*, themes are a way to abstract a look and feel (color scheme, logo, size of buttons, and so on) from the user interface. This is helpful to the user interface implementer, because the skin information can be rendered at runtime, instead of simply duplicating each page once for each look and feel. We will cover themes in greater detail in the Chapter 7. For now, we will focus on how to choose and manipulate themes for each user's requests. You will find that the concepts here are very similar to the `LocaleResolver`.

Listing 5-43 contains the `ThemeResolver` interface.

Listing 5-43. *ThemeResolver Interface*

```
package org.springframework.web.servlet;

public interface ThemeResolver {
  String resolveThemeName(HttpServletRequest request);

  void setThemeName(HttpServletRequest request, HttpServletResponse response,
    String themeName);
}
```

As you can see, the `ThemeResolver` interface resembles the `LocaleResolver` interface very closely. One major difference between the two is `ThemeResolver` returns strings instead of a strongly typed objects. The resolution of the theme name to a `org.springframework.ui.context.Theme` object is done via an `org.springframework.ui.context.ThemeSource` implementation.

The `ThemeResolver` interface has the same types of implementations as the `LocaleResolver` interface. Out of the box, Spring MVC provides a `FixedThemeResolver`, a `CookieThemeResolver`, and a `SessionThemeResolver`. Just like their `LocaleResolver` counterparts, both `CookieThemeResolver` and `SessionThemeResolver` support retrieving and changing the theme, while `FixedThemeResolver` only supports a read-only theme.

Figure 5-3 illustrates the class hierarchy for the ThemeResolver and its subclasses.

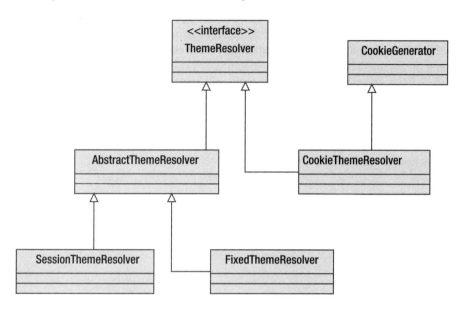

Figure 5-3. *ThemeResolver class hierarchy*

The DispatcherServlet does not support chaining of ThemeResolvers. It will simply attempt to find a bean in the ApplicationContext with the name themeResolver. If no ThemeResolvers are located, then the DispatcherServlet will create its own FixedThemeResolver configured only with the defaults.

Working with the configured ThemeResolver is no different than working with the LocaleResolver. The DispatcherServlet places the ThemeResolver into each request as an HttpServletRequest attribute. You then access this object through the RequestContextUtils utility class and its getThemeResolver() method.

Summary

A theme is a skin, or look and feel, for your web application that is easily changed by the user or application. The ThemeResolver interface encapsulates the strategy for reading and setting the theme for a user's request. Similar to the LocaleResolver, the ThemeResolver supports a fixed theme, or storing the theme in a cookie or in the HttpSession object.

The DispatcherServlet will look for a bean with the name themeResolver in the ApplicationContext upon startup. If it does not find one, it will use the default FixedThemeResolver.

We'll discuss themes in detail in Chapter 7. For now, it's important to know that there is one for each DispatcherServlet and the default, if none are specified, is the FixedThemeResolver.

Summary

Spring MVC has a full-featured processing pipeline, but through the use of sensible abstractions and extensions, it can be easily extended and customized to create powerful applications. The key is the many interfaces and abstract base classes provided for nearly every step along the request's life cycle.

As a developer, you are encouraged to implement and extend the provided interfaces and implementations to customize your users' experiences. Don't be constrained by the provided implementations. If you don't see something you need, chances are it's very easy to create.

For more information on themes and views, including the `ViewResolver`, continue on to Chapter 7. For more information on `Controllers` (Spring MVC's default request handlers) and interceptors, let's now continue on to Chapter 6.

CHAPTER 6

■■■

The Controller Menagerie

A Controller is the workhorse of Spring MVC, providing the glue between the core application and the web. We've mentioned Controllers several times up to this point, and we will now provide an in-depth review of the different available Controller implementations.

This chapter will also cover many of the details surrounding form submission, including details on binding form data to POJOs. Related to data binding are simple validation and how PropertyEditors help convert Strings to complex types. We'll cover both in this chapter.

Introduction

It is important to note that a Controller in Spring MVC is not the same thing as a *Front Controller*. Martin Fowler in *Patterns of Enterprise Application Architecture* (Addison Wesley, 2002) defines a Front Controller as "a controller that handles all requests for a Web site." By that definition, the DispatcherServlet serves the role of a Front Controller. A Spring MVC Controller is really a Page Controller, which Fowler defines as "an object that handles a request for a specific page or action on a Web site."

In Spring MVC there are two high-level types of Controllers: Controllers and ThrowawayControllers. Controllers are (typically) singleton, multithreaded page controllers fully aware of the Servlet API (e.g., HttpServletRequest, HttpServletResponse, and so on). A ThrowawayController is an executable command object (providing an execute() method) that is populated directly with request parameters and has no awareness of the Servlet API. A ThrowawayController is not intended for multithreaded use, but instead for one-off execution (hence its name).

■**Tip** Admittedly the naming convention leads you to believe a ThrowawayController is a subclass of Controller, but in fact a ThrowawayController works very differently than a Controller, and it is not a subclass of Controller. We will discuss both types in this section, but be aware that a Controller is treated differently than a ThrowawayController.

How do you choose which controller type to implement? We believe this decision has a lot to do with you and how you think about how requests are processed. If you are comfortable with how the standard servlet model works, then you will feel right at home with the Controller interface. Controllers are typically implemented and deployed as singletons, therefore all requests for the same resource (or page) are routed through the same instance. This design forces you to keep all of the state for the request outside the Controller, instead in places such as the HttpSession or stateful session beans. The advantage of this design is that it is very familiar (Struts Actions follow this design, as well as standard servlets, for example) and very scalable due to the stateless nature of the request processing and its minimal impact on garbage collection.

If you prefer to think about the incoming request as a thing to be executed, then you might find the ThrowawayController easier to work with (fans of WebWork (http://www.opensymphony. com/webwork), I'm talking to you). With this controller type you are not restricted to writing state-less controllers, as this controller encapsulates both state (parameters from the request) and behavior (the execute() method). Although we still recommend that you delegate business logic to the domain model, if you like programming to a model where the command is encapsulated as first-class citizen, this controller is for you.

As with all things in Spring MVC, the choice is yours, and there is no intrinsic bias toward one method or the other. Feel free to mix and match controller types in the same application to give yourself ultimate flexibility. If you are unsure, fear not! We will cover both in detail in this chapter. One thing to note, however, is that Spring MVC appears to favor Controllers over ThrowawayControllers, simply by the number of implementations available for Controller.

The Controller Interface and Implementations

To review, the Controller interface (presented again in Listing 6-1) contains a simple, stateless method that accepts an HttpServletRequest and an HttpServletResponse and optionally returns a ModelAndView. In true Spring MVC style, there are many Controller implementations to choose from, each building upon its superclass to extend its life cycle and work flow.

Listing 6-1. *Controller Interface*

```
public interface Controller {
  ModelAndView handleRequest(HttpServletRequest request,
    HttpServletResponse response) throws Exception;
}
```

A Look at Design

Before we begin our tour of the different Controllers, we will first discuss one of the important design principles behind the class hierarchy. When studying the different Controllers, new users encounter plenty of methods marked final. These are often encountered when a user wishes to add functionality to a subclass of a Controller implementation but is prohibited from doing so. These final methods can be frustrating, but they are there for an important reason.

To understand the developers' intentions, we must look at an important principle of object-oriented design entitled the Open-Closed Principle. Quoting Bob Martin,[1] as he paraphrases Bertrand Meyer,[2] this principle is defined as follows:

> *Software entities (classes, modules, functions, etc.) should be open for extension, but closed for modification.*

In other words, this principle states that a class should protect itself from alteration while at the same time providing well-defined extension points. At first glance, these two objectives seem contradictory, for isn't implementing an extension point just another way to alter a class?

Good object-oriented design places a high premium on *encapsulation*, which is the hiding of both data and implementation details. This principle states that a class should protect itself from not only outside influence (something we are very familiar with, as we mark any method as `private`), but also internal influence. Internal influence can be anything that might have intimate knowledge of the class structure, such as subclasses (which are in a much more powerful position to modify the behavior of a class). A well-designed class conforming to the Open-Closed Principle considers even subclasses as potentially harmful, which is why you will see so many methods marked as `final`.

So what type of harm is the class protecting itself from? Without the `final` modifier, a subclass is able to re-implement any non-private method of its superclass. This method overriding is potentially very dangerous, as it might ignore or change the original implementation's intents. Any redefinition of a method would effectively break the contract the superclass has with the rest of the system, leading to potentially unintended consequences.

But I hear you saying that your overriding method can simply call `super.doMethod()`, ensuring that the original method's logic is run (thus preserving the original method definition). This is the crux of the problem, as there is no way to force an overriding method to call `super.doMethod()`. Also, does the subclass call the method before or after the overriding method's code? For libraries intended to be used across many different systems, this type of uncertainly is not acceptable.

However, libraries intended for wide use must allow for customization, and this is where "open for extension" comes in. Instead of allowing a class's behavior to change, you should allow a class to be extended. Extension happens via well-defined life cycle callback methods (typically with method names such as `onXxx()` in the Spring Framework). These callback methods are intended to be overridden, because they don't define the core business logic of the class. While the core business logic method is marked as `final`, it might call one or more extension methods allowing a subclass to *add* in extra behavior.

To illustrate this principle in action, we will look at the high-level implementation of the `Controller` interface, which is the `org.springframework.web.servlet.mvc.AbstractController`. This first class in the `Controller` hierarchy remains fairly simple. However, it provides the first good example of the Open-Closed Principle in action, plus it gives us a good starting point to examine the `Controller` options.

---

1. Bob Martin, The Open-Closed Principle, `http://www.objectmentor.com/resources/articles/ocp.pdf`, 1996.
2. Bertrand Meyer, *Object Oriented Software Construction* (Upper Saddle River, NJ: Prentice Hall, 1988) p 23.

AbstractController

This class provides the basic building blocks for all other Controllers. You shouldn't have to implement your own Controller class, as this class is built for subclassing.

The first thing to notice about this class is that it marks the handleRequest() method (from the Controller interface) as final. At first glance, this seems to make the class useless for subclasses. Looking closer, we see a protected method named handleRequestInternal(), clearly intended for subclasses. Why not just allow overriding of the handleRequest() method? The answer, in short, is because this class obeys the Open-Closed Principle.

Each Controller in the hierarchy defines a clear work flow and life cycle. For instance, the AbstractController will

1. check whether the HTTP request method (GET, POST, etc) is supported by this Controller;

2. check whether a session exists, if this Controller requires a session;

3. send cache control headers, if required;

4. synchronize around the session, if required;

5. run custom logic, via handleRequestInternal().

The first four steps are well defined, and each subclass relies on them to run in a well-known manner. In other words, they should never change, because if they did, the very definition of AbstractController changes. For this reason, the class marks the handleRequest() method as final, to be *closed for modification*. This class's work flow is now set in stone, so to speak.

Of course, if the class only performed the first four items, it wouldn't be of much use. To be *open for extension*, it defines a handleRequestInternal() method specifically for subclasses to have a well-known extension point to place custom logic. This way, subclasses are free to customize this class without the possibility of changing its well-defined work flow. This is a perfect manifestation of the Open-Closed Principle, and you will see many examples of it throughout the Controller hierarchy.

This example also illustrates the Template pattern, a popular design pattern also found throughout the Spring Framework. The Template pattern is used to separate the variant sections of an algorithm from the invariant sections to allow for easy customization and substitution. In other words, a template of the algorithm is created, with the specifics intended to be filled in later.

The AbstractController's implementation of handleRequest() applies the Template pattern, as it defines a well-known work flow (the algorithm) but provides an extension point for specifics via the handleRequestInternal() method. This pattern is another perfect example of the Open-Closed Principle, and you can find it across the Spring Framework from Spring MVC to Spring JDBC.

AbstractController Functionality

By examining the work flow of AbstractController, we will see the common functionality that is applied to all Controllers.

Enforcing HTTP Methods

By default, an AbstractController supports HEAD, GET, and POST methods. If an HTTP
method is used for the request that is not in that list, a RequestMethodNotSupportedException
will be thrown. Note that the AbstractController doesn't define what should happen for each
type of request, but that other subclasses do make the distinction between different methods.
Setting the list of supported methods is often a good idea, enforcing the contract for a particular Controller. For example, some Controllers may display only read-only data, so setting its
supported methods to only GET enforces this usage.

■**Note** The HTTP RFC, http://www.w3.org/Protocols/rfc2616/rfc2616-sec9.html, defines each
method, its semantics, and its intended usage.

For example, you can set the supported methods via the bean definition (Listing 6-3) or
simply inside the Controller's constructor (Listing 6-2).

■**Tip** Set the supported methods to only those that the Controller specifically supports. When a client
attempts a non-supported HTTP method, the correct error message and status will be generated, creating
helpful error messages. Plus, your Controller will be protected against incorrect (and potentially damag-
ing) usage.

Listing 6-2. *Setting Supported Methods via the Constructor*

```
public SimpleController() {
  setSupportedMethods(new String[]{"GET","POST"});
}
```

Listing 6-3. *Setting Supported Methods via the Bean Definition*

```
<bean>
  <bean name="/sample"
class="com.apress.expertspringmvc.chap4.SimpleAbstractController">
    <property name="supportedMethods" value="GET,POST" />
  </bean>
</bean>
```

These two examples are identical, so choose the method that best works for you.

■Tip We recommend that for configuration elements that will not change, such as the supported methods for a `Controller`, the constructor is the best place to set them. The XML bean definitions are excellent places for configuration elements that will change or are external to the definition of the bean itself.

How did Spring convert the string `"GET,POST"` into an array of `Strings`? Spring used the `org.springframework.beans.propertyeditors.StringArrayPropertyEditor`, automatically registered for `ApplicationContexts`. Learn more about `PropertyEditors` later in this chapter.

Require Sessions

The `AbstractController` will also, if configured to do so, check for an existing HTTP session in the request. If a session is not found, then the `Controller` will fail fast with a `SessionRequiredException`. This may be useful when a `Controller` is part of a work flow that requires a session to already exist, as it should fail in a consistent manner and with a semantically rich exception if no session exists.

To configure this behavior, simply set the `requiresSession` property to `true`. The default behavior is to not require a session. Again, this can be done inside the constructor or in the bean definition.

Cache Header Management

With a few simple configuration properties, the `AbstractController` will also manage the sending of cache control headers in the response. These headers will instruct the client, and any caches between the client and server, on how to cache the document returned by the `Controller`. By default, the `Controller` will not send any cache headers with the response.

To send cache control headers, simply set the `cacheSeconds` property to a value greater or equal to zero. With zero as the value, the `Controller` will tell the client that no caching is allowed. If the value is greater than zero, the `Controller` will send the appropriate headers to indicate the content shall be cached for that many seconds. Of course, the client is free to ignore any or all of these headers, so treat them as hints.

■Tip HTTP caching is a large concept with many nuances. Begin your research with the HTTP RFC's section on caching (`http://www.w3.org/Protocols/rfc2616/rfc2616-sec13.html#sec13`). Used correctly, caching can save both bandwidth and system resources. At a minimum, enable caching for read-only pages with static (or infrequently changing) content.

By default, both HTTP/1.0 and HTTP/1.1 cache manipulation headers will be sent by `AbstractController`. Note that there are few clients out in the wild that speak only HTTP/1.0, but sending both 1.0 and 1.1 headers is normally done to accommodate broken client implementations. For safety, and unless there is some other explicit reason, send both versions of headers. To control sending of HTTP/1.0 headers, use the `useExpiresHeader` property. To control sending of HTTP/1.1 headers, use the `useCacheControlHeader` property.

If you have set the property cacheSeconds to zero, the following headers will be sent:

- Pragma: No-cache (universal)

- Expires: n (where n = current system date + one second, as HTTP-formatted date) (HTTP/1.0)

- Cache-Control: no-cache (HTTP/1.1)

- Cache-Control: no-store (HTTP/1.1, for Firefox)

If you wish to inform the client to cache the document, the following headers will be sent:

- Expires: n (where n = current system date + seconds, as HTTP-formatted date) (HTTP/1.0)

- Cache-Control: max-age=s (where s = seconds documents should be cached for) (HTTP/1.1)

There is one more element of caching your Controller can configure, but not through setting properties. Your Controller implementation may also implement the interface org.springframework.web.servlet.mvc.LastModified (shown in Listing 6-4) to indicate that it provides a last modified time for the document. This interface contains one method.

Listing 6-4. *LastModified Interface*

```
package org.springframework.web.servlet.mvc;
public interface LastModified {
  long getLastModified(HttpServletRequest request);
}
```

If your Controller implements this (which AbstractController does *not* by default), then the cache control code can send an extra hint to the client via cache headers. By providing a last modified date, the Cache-Control header will contain the value max-age=s, must-revalidate, which instructs the client that it must revalidate the document once it has become stale in the cache.

The most common way a client will revalidate the document is to issue a conditional request using the Last-Modified header inside the HTTP request. When the client requests the document again, it will send a Last-Modified header set to the date when it last received the document. The document is considered valid if it has not been modified since this date.

■**Tip** For more on how a client may revalidate a resource, consult section 13.3 of the HTTP RFC, http://www.w3.org/Protocols/rfc2616/rfc2616-sec13.html#sec13.3.

As you can see, by implementing LastModified, your Controller will be able to accurately tell the server when its contents last changed. Thus, AbstractController is able to incorporate the must-revalidate instruction in its Cache-Control headers.

To be clear, the `AbstractController` does not implement the `LastModified` interface. It is up to you to provide this functionality, if your data supports it.

Cache control is a broad topic but, if implemented correctly, it can help to manage bandwidth and CPU consumption considerably. For example, if the `Controller`'s main responsibility is to pull static information from a database to be rendered in HTML, instructing clients to cache the document will save repeated trips to the database, bandwidth, and processing load (always a good thing).

Synchronized Session

The last bit of functionality the `AbstractController` will perform on behalf of subclasses is optionally synchronizing the handling of the request around the session object. By setting `synchronizeOnSession` to `true`, the `Controller` will synchronize every call to `handleRequestInternal()` around the user's `HttpSession` object. If there is no session, then no synchronizing will take place no matter the value of `synchronizeOnSession`.

This is useful if the `Controller` must ensure multiple requests from the same client are to be handled in a serialized and nonconcurrent manner. When would you have to do this? If it is possible to directly modify state that is stored in the session, it's useful to serialize access to the session in order to ensure that multiple processes don't interfere with each other.

As browsers become more sophisticated and pre-fetch more pages (the Google Web Accelerator does this, for example), the chances of web requests being performed in the background increase. Be aware that the client may be creating multiple concurrent requests without the user's involvement. You may want to investigate the `synchronizeOnSession` property to protect your `Controllers` from such activity.

Summary

The `AbstractController` provides the basis for all `Controller` implementations in Spring MVC. It adheres to the Open-Closed Principle to protect its work flow and life cycle methods, while providing a well-known extension hook in the form of `handleRequestInternal()`. The `AbstractController` handles session checking, HTTP method checking, cache control, and synchronization, all configured by either the bean definition in the XML or through simple setters called in the constructor.

For simple `Controller` implementations, subclass this class instead of merely implementing `Controller`. For more robust work flows, we will now begin examining subclasses of `AbstractController`.

BaseCommandController

While `AbstractController` is a good class for read-only web resources, an interactive web application will require HTML forms support. Native servlet applications would require working directly with the `HttpServletRequest` and its `getParameter()` method to read submitted form values. This method is error prone and cumbersome, as the developer needs to handle missing values and potential type conversion. Modern web frameworks usually provide a mechanism to automatically convert the raw request parameters into classes and properties, so that the request handling code can interact with a strongly typed object instead of a collection of `Strings`.

The `org.springframework.web.servlet.mvc.BaseCommandController` class provides the basic feature set for supporting form submits, including creating JavaBeans from the request, and registering `Validators`. It does not support the notion of a page view work flow, nor does it do anything with the JavaBean once created. This class is the parent for classes such as `SimpleFormController` that build upon its functionality to bring coordinated page views to the user.

Tip If you are looking to handle form submits, look past the `BaseCommandController` to `SimpleFormController`. `BaseCommandController` does not provide any work flows that you can extend easily, but it does provide much of the base functionality.

`BaseCommandController` subclasses `AbstractController` and provides the concept of a command object. A command, in this scenario, is a JavaBean whose properties are set from HTTP request parameters.

Note Do not confuse a command bean with the Gang of Four's Command design pattern. The formal Command pattern implies the object has a well-known execution interface (some sort of `execute()` method, for instance), encapsulating a callback. In contrast, the `BaseCommandController` does not call any methods on its command object once it is created. Of course, you could extend `BaseCommandController` and implement the Command pattern (or simply use `ThrowawayController`), but know that there is no such built-in callback work flow in this class.

One important note about `BaseCommandController` is that it does not, itself, define any work flow. That is, while it provides functionality such as binding request parameters to beans and life cycle methods for validation, it does *not* put them together to create anything meaningful. Its subclasses, such as `AbstractFormController` and `SimpleFormController`, will add the value.

Our interest in this class is to explain how Spring MVC converts, or binds, request parameters to JavaBean properties. This feature is not unique, as many web frameworks have been doing this for years. Spring MVC's benefit is that it does not force a particular type, or superclass, for the command class. You are free to use any class that conforms to the JavaBeans model, and this freedom can lead to significantly fewer classes in your system. This means that you will be able to populate domain classes directly from requests, removing the need for otherwise duplicate form classes.

Before we show you how to work with a freshly bound command object, we will first cover the capabilities and limitations of populating beans from HTML form submits, also known as *data binding*. Because the `BaseCommandController` doesn't have any work flow, when we talk about form processing, we will introduce the `SimpleFormController`. For now, we present data binding for beans. Note that while Spring MVC takes advantage of data binding, the binding framework is not web-specific and can be used with ease outside of the web framework.

Binding a Form to a Bean

Spring MVC encourages the use of command beans with a wide variety of property types. However, the Servlet API returns form parameters only as Strings. To fully take advantage of richly typed command beans, Spring provides the ability to convert string form parameters into nearly any other Java class. This technique, called *data binding*, is the act of taking a name-value pair, such as name.firstName=joe, and converting it to getName().setFirstName("joe"). Spring MVC uses data binding to set form bean properties from request parameters. This technique is similar to what is often called an *expression language*, such as the JSTL's Expression Language (EL) or the Object Graph Navigation Language (OGNL). It is very useful as a shorthand way to refer to bean properties, even deeply nested properties.

The binding functionality is achieved through the use of Spring's org.springframework. validation.DataBinder class and its subclass, org.springframework.web.bind. ServletRequestDataBinder. As you can see from its package, the DataBinder class is not specific to the web framework. This means the capabilities and facilities of data binding are available to any type of application. The ServletRequestDataBinder merely makes it easy to bind from Servlet request parameters.

The DataBinder will happily bind string values to properties of type String. Given the previous example, the firstName property is a String, so setting the value joe to a String is trivial. Of course, not every property on every object is a String, so the DataBinder supports converting a String to some arbitrary type via PropertyEditors. We will see more of PropertyEditors soon, but they are a standard JavaBean mechanism to covert Strings to other types, such as integers, collections, or nearly any other class. Spring uses PropertyEditors heavily, and we can take advantage of them as we populate command classes from HTTP requests.

To be exact, the DataBinder merely coordinates these activities, delegating the actual binding and PropertyEditor support to a BeanWrapper (which we will visit shortly). From the point of view of a BaseCommandController and its subclasses, you will interact with the DataBinder instead of BeanWrappers.

It's best to simply jump in and discover what kind of functionality the DataBinder can support. To begin with, we will create a simple bean that we will use for the command class. We will want to take servlet request parameters and bind their values into an instance of a Name class, shown in Listing 6-5.

Listing 6-5. *Example Command Class*

```
package com.apress.expertspringmvc.chap4.binding;

public class Name {

    private String firstName;
    private String lastName;

    public String getFirstName() {
        return firstName;
    }
    public void setFirstName(String firstName) {
        this.firstName = firstName;
```

```
    }
    public String getLastName() {
        return lastName;
    }
    public void setLastName(String lastName) {
        this.lastName = lastName;
    }

}
```

The Name class comes straight from a domain object model, as it is a simple plain old Java object (POJO). We wish to create an instance of this class when a form is submitted and populate it from form fields. Listing 6-6 contains the example HTML form with fields that correspond to our Name POJO.

Listing 6-6. *CommandBean HTML Form*

```
<form>
<p>
First Name: <input type="text" name="firstName" />
</p>
<p>
Last Name: <input type="text" name="lastName" />
</p>
<p><input type="submit" /></p>
</form>
```

We see the first requirement when using the DataBinder framework here in the form. The form field names match the property names of the Name class. More specifically, the form field names match the JavaBean translation of the Name getters and setters. For example, the method setFirstName() is converted via JavaBean semantics to "the setter for the firstName property." The DataBinder performs this conversion from getter and setter methods to property names so that it can match the form fields from the HTTP request.

■**Caution** When using the DataBinder, the bean that you are binding to must have a public setter for the property. If the bean is missing the setter or if it is spelled differently, no error is generated, and the property will not be set. It is also important to have a public getter for the property, so that the field may be retrieved by the view. The DataBinder cannot perform direct field access; it must go through setters or getters.

To demonstrate how simple the binding process is, we have created a JUnit TestCase (contained in Listing 6-7) that binds the parameters of a HttpServletRequest to a JavaBean of type Name. We are isolating the actual binding here, so that you may get a clear picture of how a bean's properties are populated. Know that this is all hidden from you when working with BaseCommandController and its subclasses.

We are using an org.springframework.mock.web.MockHttpServletRequest to simulate an
HttpServletRequest object. Spring provides a complete set of mock objects for the servlet
environment, making it easy to write tests for your Spring MVC components that will run outside of a container. We will cover testing of Spring MVC applications in a future chapter, but
for now it's sufficient to know that these mock classes allow us to control and simulate the
external elements of a web request, such as an HttpServletRequest or HttpServletResponse.

Listing 6-7. *Simple DataBinder TestCase*

```
public class CommandBeanBindingTest extends TestCase {

    private Name name;
    private ServletRequestDataBinder binder;
    private MockHttpServletRequest request;

    public void setUp() throws Exception {
        name = new Name();
        binder = new ServletRequestDataBinder(name, "nameBean");
        request = new MockHttpServletRequest();
    }

    public void testSimpleBind() {
        // just like /servlet?firstName=Anya&lastName=Lala
        request.addParameter("firstName", "Anya");
        request.addParameter("lastName", "Lala");

        binder.bind(request);     // performed by BaseCommandController
                                  // on submit so you don't have to

        assertEquals("Anya", name.getFirstName());   // true!
        assertEquals("Lala", name.getLastName());    // true!
    }
}
```

Note that when using the BaseCommandController or its subclasses, the actual bind() call
is performed automatically. By the time your code obtains the command bean, it will be created and populated by request parameter values. We explicitly show it here so that you may
understand what is going on under the hood.

The ServletRequestDataBinder is initialized with the bean to be populated and the name
nameBean. This name is used when generating an Errors instance and error messages, in the case
of errors during binding. The name can be any String, though it is best to use names that are
easily compatible with properties files (which is where you typically define error messages). If
not provided the name will default to target. However, when this DataBinder is used in the MVC
framework, the default name of the JavaBean is command.

The unit test in Listing 6-7 creates a MockHttpServletRequest so we can illustrate how the
request is actually bound to the bean. We simulate a request submission by adding parameters, being careful to match the parameter name to the name of the property on the bean. The
bind() method then delegates to a BeanWrapperImpl class to translate the string expressions,

such as firstName, into JavaBean setters, such as setFirstName(). After bind returns, the bean is populated and ready to be used by the Controller.

If all domain object classes simply had strings for properties and never any child objects, our discussion could be finished! However, Spring MVC supports and encourages a rich domain model, and this means the DataBinder can support binding to deeply nested classes, primitives, and even different types of collections and arrays.

Nested Properties

The real power of the DataBinder shows up when binding string values to nested object graphs. The example in Listing 6-7 used two simple independent properties, a firstName and lastName. A reasonable refactoring would move the name properties into a new Name class, as shown in Listing 6-8.

Listing 6-8. *NestedCommandBean Class*

```
package com.apress.expertspringmvc.chap4.binding;

public class NestedCommandBean {

    private Name name = new Name();

    public Name getName() {
        return name;
    }

    public void setName(Name name) {
        this.name = name;
    }

}
```

It's important to see that we initialized the name reference to a non-null object. The DataBinder is not able to set properties on nested objects that are null. Remember that a string of name.firstName will convert to getName().setFirstName("value"). If getName() returns null, we have a nasty NullPointerException on our hands. This is especially tricky when it comes to collections, as we will see later. You do not need to initialize the nested object in exactly the way we have shown (i.e., the same place as the declaration), but be certain that the object is not null before any binding is to take place.

The firstName and lastName properties are now moved to a Name class, shown in Listing 6-9.

Listing 6-9. *Name Class*

```
package com.apress.expertspringmvc.chap4.binding;

public class Name {

    private String firstName;
    private String lastName;
```

```
    public String getFirstName() {
        return firstName;
    }
    public void setFirstName(String firstName) {
        this.firstName = firstName;
    }
    public String getLastName() {
        return lastName;
    }
    public void setLastName(String lastName) {
        this.lastName = lastName;
    }

}
```

The `DataBinder` supports nested objects and properties with a simple dot notation, similar to the JSTL's EL. An example, contained in Listing 6-10, best illustrates this nesting.

Listing 6-10. *NestedCommandBeanTest*

```
    public void setUp() throws Exception {
        bean = new NestedCommandBean();
        binder = new ServletRequestDataBinder(bean, "beanName");
        request = new MockHttpServletRequest();
    }

    public void testSimpleBind() {
        // just like /servlet?name.firstName=Anya&name.lastName=Lala
        // or name.firstName=Anya&name.lastName=Lala as the payload
        // of a POST request
        request.addParameter("name.firstName", "Anya");
        request.addParameter("name.lastName", "Lala");

        binder.bind(request);
        assertEquals("Anya", bean.getName().getFirstName());  // true!
        assertEquals("Lala", bean.getName().getLastName());   // true!
    }
```

The property name `name.firstName` is converted to `getName().setFirstName()`. The root bean, in this case a `NestedCommandBean`, is implicit, and thus it is not mentioned in the binding string name.

There is no limit to the nesting of objects and properties. Just remember that any object whose property you are trying to set cannot be `null` (including collections and objects inside of collections). The property itself (in this case, `firstName`) can be `null`, however.

Binding to Collections

Along with nested classes, the DataBinder supports binding properties of objects inside collections. Your command bean class and its nested classes can contain Lists, Maps, and arrays.

Just like nested classes, the object in the collection that you are attempting to set a property value on must not be null. This means that, before binding, you must not only initialize
the collection, but populate it with objects.

Binding to Lists

To begin, we will create a new command bean that contains a List of Name objects, as shown in
Listing 6-11.

Listing 6-11. *NestedCollectionsCommandBean Class*

```
public class NestedCollectionsCommandBean {
    private List<Name> names = new ArrayList<Name>();

    public NestedCollectionsCommandBean() {
        names.add(new Name());
        names.add(new Name());
    }

    public List<Name> getNames() {
        return names;
    }
    public void setNames(List<Name> names) {
        this.names = names;
    }
}
```

Notice how we not only had to initialize the List, but also populate it. We added two Name
objects into the list in the constructor for convenience, but normally the objects will be added
as the result of some web request or business logic.

The DataBinder uses a familiar [index] notation to reference items in a List or array. For
instance, the string names[0].firstName is the same as getNames().get(0).setFirstName("value").
Listing 6-12 shows an example of binding to object properties inside collections.

Listing 6-12. *NestedCollectionsCommandBeanTest*

```
public void setUp() throws Exception {
  bean = new NestedCollectionsCommandBean();
  binder = new ServletRequestDataBinder(bean, "beanName");
  request = new MockHttpServletRequest();
}
```

```
public void testSimpleBind() {
  // just like /servlet?names[0].firstName=Anya&names[0].lastName=Lala
  request.addParameter("names[0].firstName", "Anya");
  request.addParameter("names[0].lastName", "Lala");

  binder.bind(request);

  assertEquals("Anya", bean.getNames().get(0).getFirstName());   // true!
  assertEquals("Lala", bean.getNames().get(0).getLastName());    // true!
}
```

Of course, you aren't limited to binding to properties of objects inside Lists. You may also reference a particular String inside a List just as easily as a String property of an object in the List. To illustrate this, take the example command bean shown in Listing 6-13.

Listing 6-13. *StringListCommandBean Class*

```
public class StringListCommandBean {

    private List<String> strings = new ArrayList<String>();

    public List<String> getStrings() {
        return strings;
    }

    public void setStrings(List<String> strings) {
        this.strings = strings;
    }

}
```

In this case, to reference the first String in the List, the property name would be strings[0]. When you are setting the values, it's perfectly legal to refer to Strings in the List in random order, such as strings[4] and then strings[2]. Of course, if you are trying to read the value of strings[0] before setting it, you will receive a null value.

Listing 6-14 illustrates how binding directly to Strings inside a List is performed.

Listing 6-14. *StringListCommandBean Unit Test*

```
public void setUp() throws Exception {
  bean = new StringListCommandBean();
  binder = new ServletRequestDataBinder(bean, "beanName");
  request = new MockHttpServletRequest();
}

public void testSimpleBind() {
 // just like /servlet?strings[0]=Anya&strings[1]=Lala
 request.addParameter("strings[0]", "Anya");
 request.addParameter("strings[1]", "Lala");
```

```
binder.bind(request);

assertEquals("Anya", bean.getStrings().get(0));  // true!
assertEquals("Lala", bean.getStrings().get(1));   // true!
}
```

Binding to Arrays

Arrays work in an identical manner to Lists. The DataBinder expression for an array is the same as for the List. Listing 6-15 changes a List of Name objects into an array.

Listing 6-15. *NestedArrayCommandBean Class*

```
public class NestedArrayCommandBean {

    private Name[] names = new Name[]{new Name(), new Name()};

    public Name[] getNames() {
        return names;
    }
    public void setNames(Name[] names) {
        this.names = names;
    }

}
```

The unit test, contained in Listing 6-16, looks nearly identical, and the binding expressions remain the same. As with Lists, when binding properties to objects in arrays, make sure the object exists in the array first. The DataBinder won't create a new instance of the object if it is null; instead it will generate a NullPointerException.

Listing 6-16. *NestedArrayCommandBeanTest*

```
public void setUp() throws Exception {
  bean = new NestedArrayCommandBean();
  binder = new ServletRequestDataBinder(bean, "beanName");
  request = new MockHttpServletRequest();
}

public void testSimpleBind() {
  // just like /servlet?names[0].firstName=Anya&names[0].lastName=Lala
  request.addParameter("names[0].firstName", "Anya");
  request.addParameter("names[0].lastName", "Lala");

  binder.bind(request);

  assertEquals("Anya", bean.getNames()[0].getFirstName());  // true!
  assertEquals("Lala", bean.getNames()[0].getLastName());   // true!
}
```

Binding to Maps

Binding to properties inside objects inside Maps is similar to Lists. The brackets remain, but instead of a numerical index, you will use the string value of the key inside the map. For instance, we will modify the command bean to support a Map of Name objects, one for a nickname and one for a formal name. Thus, the string expression names['nickname'].firstName translates to getNames().get("nickname").setFirstName("value") in Java code.

Just like Lists and arrays, you can also bind request parameters directly to objects inside the Map, instead of properties of objects inside the Map. For instance, if you have a Map<String, String> stringMap, then you can refer to elements inside the Map using the expression stringMap['key'].

Listing 6-17 is an example of a Map and nested objects.

Listing 6-17. *NestedMapCommandBean Class*

```java
public class NestedMapCommandBean {

    private Map<String,Name> names = new HashMap<String,Name>();

    public NestedMapCommandBean() {
        names.put("nickname", new Name());
        names.put("formal", new Name());
    }

    public Map<String, Name> getNames() {
        return names;
    }
    public void setNames(Map<String, Name> names) {
        this.names = names;
    }

}
```

Listing 6-18 contains a unit test that illustrates how to use the expression language to refer to elements in the Map.

Listing 6-18. *NestedMapCommandBean Unit Test*

```java
public void setUp() throws Exception {
  bean = new NestedMapCommandBean();
  binder = new ServletRequestDataBinder(bean, "beanName");
  request = new MockHttpServletRequest();
}
```

```
public void testSimpleBind() {
  // just like /servlet?names['nickname'].firstName=Anya \
  // &names['nickname'].lastName=Lala
  request.addParameter("names['nickname'].firstName", "Anya");
  request.addParameter("names['nickname'].lastName", "Lala");

  binder.bind(request);

  // true!
  assertEquals("Anya", bean.getNames().get("nickname").getFirstName());

  // true!
  assertEquals("Lala", bean.getNames().get("nickname").getLastName());
}
```

The DataBinder can only refer to objects in a Map with keys of type String. This shouldn't be a concern, as the keys are HTTP request properties, which themselves are Strings.

Binding to Sets

Binding to properties of objects in Sets is possible, but is not as exact as working with Lists or arrays. Sets in Java are unordered collections of unique objects, so referring to a single object within the Set is not possible directly through the Set interface. Spring's DataBinder works around this limitation by iterating through the Set to find the object indicated by the index specified. Obviously, which object resolves to the index is dependent on the Set implementation. If you will be using Sets with the DataBinder, you should use a LinkedHashSet or some other implementation that has a predictable iteration order.

■**Caution** We strongly recommend against using Sets inside JavaBeans that will be used as command objects. There is simply no way to replace or set a value into a Set, which severely limits its usefulness in this context.

In contrast, the DataBinder is not able to set the value of objects in a Set. While the DataBinder is able to iterate through the Set to locate an object whose properties need to be set, there is no way to set a particular object directly into a Set at some location. The following two examples, illustrated in Listings 6-20 and 6-21, shows what is and isn't possible when working with Sets and the DataBinder. Listing 6-19 first sets[3] up a command bean with Sets as properties.

---

3. No pun intended.

Listing 6-19. *NestedSetCommandBean Class*

```java
public class NestedSetCommandBean {

    Set<Name> names = new LinkedHashSet<Name>();
    Set<String> strings = new LinkedHashSet<String>();

    public NestedSetCommandBean() {
        names.add(new Name());
        strings.add("first string");
    }

    public Set<Name> getNames() {
        return names;
    }

    public void setNames(Set<Name> names) {
        this.names = names;
    }

    public Set<String> getStrings() {
        return strings;
    }

    public void setStrings(Set<String> strings) {
        this.strings = strings;
    }

}
```

The following unit test, Listing 6-20, illustrates the limits of using the DataBinder with a Set by showing what *is* possible.

Listing 6-20. *NestedSetCommandBean Unit Test*

```java
public void setUp() throws Exception {
  bean = new NestedSetCommandBean();
  binder = new ServletRequestDataBinder(bean, "beanName");
  request = new MockHttpServletRequest();
}

public void testSimpleBind() {
  // just like /servlet?names[0].firstName=Anya&names[0].lastName=Lala
  request.addParameter("names[0].firstName", "Anya");
  request.addParameter("names[0].lastName", "Lala");

  binder.bind(request);
```

```
    // true!
    assertEquals("Anya", bean.getNames().iterator().next().getFirstName());
    // true!
    assertEquals("Lala", bean.getNames().iterator().next().getLastName());
}
```

The preceding unit test passes, as we have chosen a LinkedHashSet as the Set implementation and we're setting properties of objects inside of the Set. However, the following unit test, Listing 6-21, fails. Notice how we're attempting to set the value of a String directly in the Set.

Listing 6-21. *NestedSetCommandBean Unit Test (Fails)*

```
public void testBindToStrings() {
    // just like /servlet?strings[0]=Anya
    request.addParameter("strings[0]", "Anya");

    binder.bind(request);    // errors at this point
}
```

■**Note** The DataBinder supports setting properties directly on individual objects, or objects in arrays, Lists, Sets, or Maps only. It only supports setting objects directly, or objects in Lists, arrays, or Maps.

Up to this point, we have covered using the DataBinder to set properties of objects directly, or within collections. However, all of the examples have used properties of type String. The DataBinder supports more than simple String properties through its use of PropertyEditors. It's possible to set properties of nearly any type, including primitives.

Non-String Properties

We've shown you a few examples of PropertyEditors before, normally connected with bean definitions and the ApplicationContext. The same facilities apply here with the DataBinder. For a quick review, a PropertyEditor's job is to convert between a String value and a strongly typed object, and back again. For instance, a UrlPropertyEditor would convert the String http://www.example.com to a java.net.URL class with the value of http://www.example.com, and from a java.net.URL object back to a String.

Out of the box, the DataBinder, and its BeanWrapper, supports many different PropertyEditors. This means your command beans can use a wide variety of property types, and the DataBinder and its facilities will handle all of the conversion for you.

Table 6-1 lists the default PropertyEditors that come registered to the DataBinder by default. If you require a type not covered in Table 6-1, it is very easy to create and register your own PropertyEditors.

Table 6-1. *BeanWrapper Default PropertyEditors*

PropertyEditor	Result	Description
ByteArrayPropertyEditor	byte[]	String to a byte[] with getBytes().
ClassEditor	Class	Similar to Class.forName().
FileEditor	java.io.File	Via new File(pathname).
InputStreamEditor	java.io.InputStream	See also ResourceEditor.
LocaleEditor	java.util.Locale	See also Locale's toString() method for format.
PropertiesEditor	java.util.Properties	See format in java.util.Properties.
ResourceArrayPropertyEditor	Resource[]	Wildcard resource locations, e.g. file:c:\my*.txt.
StringArrayPropertyEditor	String[]	Comma-separated String to String array.
URLEditor	java.net.URL	Fully qualified standard URL or Spring's classpath: prefix URL.
CustomCollectionEditor	java.util.Collection subclass	Converts one collection type to another. It will convert a String to a single element collection. It does not convert the collection to a String.
CharacterEditor	char or Character	Single character String to Character.
CustomBooleanEditor	boolean or Boolean	true/on/yes/1 for true, and false/off/no/0 for false.
CustomNumberEditor	Primitive number or Number wrapper, BigDecimal or BigInteger	Can use a NumberFormat for Locale-specific formatting or default to valueOf() and toString().

Spring provides a few more PropertyEditors, such as the CustomDateEditor, which require manual registration and configuration, and it is simple to create others specific to your needs.

PropertyEditors are applied intelligently to the data binding process. You begin by declaring any PropertyEditors not already in the default set, and the DataBinder's process will automatically apply them when it encounters a property not of type String.

For example, to begin, let us create a simple command bean with properties other than String. We will first create a bean (Listing 6-22) with properties that the DataBinder already knows about. Then we will declare a CustomDateEditor (a custom PropertyEditor provided by Spring) to handle java.util.Date objects. Last, we will create our own PropertyEditor to handle a specific internal domain class.

Listing 6-22. *MultiTypeCommandBean Class*

```
public class MultiTypeCommandBean {

    private int intProperty;
    private Integer integerProperty;
    private Class classProperty;
    private URL urlProperty;

    public Class getClassProperty() {
        return classProperty;
    }
    public void setClassProperty(Class classProperty) {
        this.classProperty = classProperty;
    }
    public Integer getIntegerProperty() {
        return integerProperty;
    }
    public void setIntegerProperty(Integer integerProperty) {
        this.integerProperty = integerProperty;
    }
    public int getIntProperty() {
        return intProperty;
    }
    public void setIntProperty(int intProperty) {
        this.intProperty = intProperty;
    }
    public URL getUrlProperty() {
        return urlProperty;
    }
    public void setUrlProperty(URL urlProperty) {
        this.urlProperty = urlProperty;
    }
}
```

Using the command bean in Listing 6-22, we have four different properties, each of different types, including intProperty, which is a primitive.

We are simulating the following form, shown in Listing 6-23, with the unit test. Note that input fields for the HTML form are handled like regular text inputs. The actual conversion happens inside the DataBinder.

Listing 6-23. *MultiTypeCommandBean HTML Form*

```
<form>
<p>
Int Property: <input type="text" name="intProperty" />
</p>
<p>
```

```
Integer Property: <input type="text" name="integerProperty" />
</p>
<p>
Class Property: <input type="text" name="classProperty" />
</p>
<p>
URL Property: <input type="text" name="urlProperty" />
</p>
<p><input type="submit" /></p>
</form>
```

In Listing 6-24 we simulate a HTTP request that will use the DataBinder to populate these varied type properties.

Listing 6-24. *MultiTypeCommandBean Unit Test*

```
public void setUp() {
  bean = new MultiTypeCommandBean();
  request = new MockHttpServletRequest();
  binder = new ServletRequestDataBinder(bean, "bean");
}

public void testBind() throws Exception {
  request.addParameter("intProperty", "34");
  request.addParameter("integerProperty", "200");
  request.addParameter("classProperty", "java.lang.String");
  request.addParameter("urlProperty", "http://www.example.com/");

  binder.bind(request);

  // all true!
  assertEquals(34, bean.getIntProperty());
  assertEquals(new Integer(200), bean.getIntegerProperty());
  assertEquals(String.class, bean.getClassProperty());
  assertEquals(new URL("http://www.example.com/"), bean.getUrlProperty());
}
```

As you can see, all the property values begin as Strings inside the HTTP request. When the binder encounters a property type other than String, it will consult its list of PropertyEditors. When it finds a match based on the property's class, it will delegate the conversion to the PropertyEditor. Because Spring provides so many default PropertyEditors, for most cases, you won't have to perform extra configuration, and the editors will gracefully perform the conversions.

Non-default PropertyEditors

Some types of classes can't be created from Strings without context specific configurations. For instance, there are many different valid text representations of a java.util.Date, so it is impractical to provide a default Date PropertyEditor to handle all the different cases. To allow you to control the format used for conversion, Spring's Date PropertyEditor, the CustomDateEditor, allows you to define the format you expect the date to be entered as. Once configured, you simply register the PropertyEditor with the DataBinder.

For example, we will create a simple command bean (shown in Listing 6-25) with a single property of type java.util.Date. We then create an HTML form (Listing 6-26) that requests the user enter a date with the format YYYY-MM-DD, as a single String (e.g., 2005-03-21). We will register a CustomDateEditor to handle the conversion, delegating to a java.text.SimpleDateFormat class.

Listing 6-25. *DateCommandBean Class*

```
public class DateCommandBean {

    private Date date;

    public Date getDate () {
        return dateProperty;
    }

    public void setDate (Date date) {
        this.date = date;
    }

}
```

Listing 6-26. *DateCommandBean HTML Form*

```
<form>
<p>
Date: <input type="text" name="date" /> (YYYY-MM-DD)
</p>
<p><input type="submit" /></p>
</form>
```

For this example, we will configure the CustomDateEditor to use the text format yyyy-MM-dd, as defined by the java.text.SimpleDateFormat class. Listing 6-27 illustrates these concepts together.

Listing 6-27. *DateCommandBean Unit Test*

```
protected void setUp() throws Exception {
  bean = new DateCommandBean();
  request = new MockHttpServletRequest();
  binder = new ServletRequestDataBinder(bean, "bean");
}


public void testBind() throws Exception {
  SimpleDateFormat dateFormat = new SimpleDateFormat("yyyy-MM-dd");
  Date expected = dateFormat.parse("2001-01-01");

  CustomDateEditor dateEditor = new CustomDateEditor(dateFormat, true);
  binder.registerCustomEditor(Date.class, dateEditor);

  request.addParameter("date", "2001-01-01");

  binder.bind(request);

  assertEquals(expected, bean.getDate()); // true!
}
```

The registerCustomEditor(Class, PropertyEditor) (shown in Listing 6-27) configures the DataBinder to use the PropertyEditor any time it encounters a property with the given Class.

A second form, registerCustomEditor(Class, String, PropertyEditor), (not shown in Listing 6-27) takes a third parameter, which is the full path name to a property. If you specify the property name, the Class parameter can be null, but should be specified to ensure correctness. If the property name points to a collection, then PropertyEditor is applied to the collection itself if the Class parameter is a collection, or to each element of the collection if the Class parameter is not a collection.

Working with PropertyEditors not supported in the default set requires a bit more work, but still results in a fairly simple setup. You will first create an instance of the CustomDateEditor and provide it with your chosen DateFormat object. The PropertyEditor is then registered with the DataBinder, assigning it to a class it will be responsible for converting (in this case, the Date class). After you register it, proceed as normal, and the CustomDateEditor will handle any property of type Date.

As you may guess, when you register a PropertyEditor with the DataBinder, that PropertyEditor is then used any time the Date class is encountered. While most times this may be what you want, there are some situations where you may want two different date formats for two different properties of the same object.

To handle this situation, you may register a PropertyEditor to be used for a specific property, instead of for every instance of that class. Using this type of registration provides very specific data binding on a per-property basis instead of the default per-class basis.

For example, we will create a command bean with two Date properties. One property we will require the user to use the format YYYY-MM-DD, while the other property will require the format DD-MM-YYYY. We will create two CustomDateEditors, each with its own date parsing format. Then, we will register each CustomDateEditor to their specific properties. Listing 6-28 contains the new command bean with two Dates.

Listing 6-28. *TwoDatesCommand Class*

```
public class TwoDatesCommand {

    private Date firstDate;
    private Date secondDate;

    public Date getFirstDate() {
        return firstDate;
    }
    public void setFirstDate(Date firstDate) {
        this.firstDate = firstDate;
    }
    public Date getSecondDate() {
        return secondDate;
    }
    public void setSecondDate(Date secondDate) {
        this.secondDate = secondDate;
    }
}
```

Listing 6-29 simply shows the XHTML form for both dates.

Listing 6-29. *TwoDates HTML Form*

```
<form>
<p>
First Date: <input type="text" name="firstDate" /> (YYYY-MM-DD)
</p>
<p>
Second Date: <input type="text" name="secondDate" /> (DD-MM-YYYY)
</p>
<p><input type="submit" /></p>
</form>
```

Listing 6-30. *TwoDatesCommand Unit Test*

```
protected void setUp() throws Exception {
  bean = new TwoDatesCommand();
  request = new MockHttpServletRequest();
  binder = new ServletRequestDataBinder(bean, "bean");
}

public void testBind() throws Exception {
  SimpleDateFormat firstDateFormat = new SimpleDateFormat("yyyy-MM-dd");
  Date firstExpected = firstDateFormat.parse("2001-01-01");

  SimpleDateFormat secondDateFormat = new SimpleDateFormat("dd-MM-yyyy");
  Date secondExpected = secondDateFormat.parse("01-01-2001");
```

```
    CustomDateEditor firstDateEditor = new CustomDateEditor(firstDateFormat, true);
    CustomDateEditor secondDateEditor = new CustomDateEditor(secondDateFormat, true);

    binder.registerCustomEditor(Date.class, "firstDate", firstDateEditor);
    binder.registerCustomEditor(Date.class, "secondDate", secondDateEditor);

    request.addParameter("firstDate", "2001-01-01");
    request.addParameter("secondDate", "01-01-2001");

    binder.bind(request);

    assertEquals(firstExpected, bean.getFirstDate()); // true!
    assertEquals(secondExpected, bean.getSecondDate()); // true!
}
```

As you can see in Listing 6-30, when we register the PropertyEditor to the DataBinder, we can also specify which property, or field, the PropertyEditor should apply to. This overrides any PropertyEditor already bound to a class.

Custom PropertyEditors

Although Spring provides many useful PropertyEditors, often times you will wish to convert some String value to a specific domain class from your object model. Creating and registering your own PropertyEditors is as simple as registering any PropertyEditor to the DataBinder.

For example, consider a typical PhoneNumber class. This class might encapsulate a typical phone number, consisting of an area code and the number. The HTML form might allow a phone number to be entered with a single text input field, as long as it conforms to the standard (xxx) xxx-xxxx format.

To begin, let us define a simple PhoneNumber class in Listing 6-31.

Listing 6-31. *PhoneNumber Class*

```java
public class PhoneNumber {

    private String areaCode;
    private String prefix;
    private String suffix;

    public String getAreaCode() {
        return areaCode;
    }
    public void setAreaCode(String areaCode) {
        this.areaCode = areaCode;
    }
    public String getPrefix() {
        return prefix;
    }
    public void setPrefix(String prefix) {
```

```
        this.prefix = prefix;
    }
    public String getSuffix() {
        return suffix;
    }
    public void setSuffix(String suffix) {
        this.suffix = suffix;
    }

    public String toString() {
        return "(" + areaCode + ") " + prefix + "-" + suffix;
    }
}
```

We will need a command class to contain a PhoneNumber property so that it may be set by the DataBinder. Of course, Spring MVC doesn't require nesting your domain class inside some command bean. If you wish to create a form with input fields directly mapping to properties of the PhoneNumber, then there is no need for a custom PropertyEditor (because all properties of a PhoneNumber are String in this case). Listing 6-32 illustrates how to convert a single text field into a (relatively) complex domain object, so we will treat the PhoneNumber as a property itself.

Listing 6-32. *PhoneNumberCommand Bean*

```
public class PhoneNumberCommand {

    private PhoneNumber phoneNumber;

    public PhoneNumber getPhoneNumber() {
        return phoneNumber;
    }

    public void setPhoneNumber(PhoneNumber phoneNumber) {
        this.phoneNumber = phoneNumber;
    }


}
```

For the real fun of this example, we now create the PhoneNumberPropertyEditor (shown in Listing 6-33) that knows how to convert a string with the format ^(\d{3}) \d{3}-\d{4}$ (as a regular expression) into a PhoneNumber instance.

Listing 6-33. *PhoneNumberEditor Class*

```
public class PhoneNumberEditor extends PropertyEditorSupport {

    private Pattern pattern = Pattern.compile("^\\((\\d{3})\\) (\\d{3})-(\\d{4})$");

    @Override
```

```java
    public void setAsText(String text) throws IllegalArgumentException {
        if (! StringUtils.hasText(text)) {
            throw new IllegalArgumentException("text must not be empty or null");
        }

        Matcher matcher = pattern.matcher(text);
        if (matcher.matches()) {
            PhoneNumber phoneNumber = new PhoneNumber();
            phoneNumber.setAreaCode(matcher.group(1));
            phoneNumber.setPrefix(matcher.group(2));
            phoneNumber.setSuffix(matcher.group(3));

            setValue(phoneNumber);
        } else {
            throw new IllegalArgumentException(text +
                    " does not match pattern " + pattern);
        }
    }

    @Override
    public String getAsText() {
        return getValue().toString();
    }

}
```

The HTML form with a phone number input field would look something like that in Listing 6-34.

Listing 6-34. *PhoneNumber HTML Form*

```html
<form>
<p>
Phone Number: <input type="text" name="phoneNumber" /> (XXX) XXX-XXXX
</p>
<p><input type="submit" /></p>
</form>
```

The following unit test, Listing 6-35, simulates the HTTP request with a value of (222) 333-4444 as the user's phone number.

Listing 6-35. *PhoneNumberEditor Binding Unit Test*

```java
protected void setUp() throws Exception {
 bean = new PhoneNumberCommand();
 request = new MockHttpServletRequest();
 binder = new ServletRequestDataBinder(bean, "bean");
```

```
  expected = new PhoneNumber();
  expected.setAreaCode("222");
  expected.setPrefix("333");
  expected.setSuffix("4444");
}

public void testBind() {
  PhoneNumberEditor editor = new PhoneNumberEditor();
  binder.registerCustomEditor(PhoneNumber.class, editor);

  request.addParameter("phoneNumber", "(222) 333-4444");

  binder.bind(request);
  assertEquals(expected.getAreaCode(), bean.getPhoneNumber().getAreaCode());
  assertEquals(expected.getPrefix(), bean.getPhoneNumber().getPrefix());
  assertEquals(expected.getSuffix(), bean.getPhoneNumber().getSuffix());
}
```

This all works because the property on the command bean is of type PhoneNumber, so the PhoneNumberPropertyEditor can easily be called upon to do the String to PhoneNumber conversion. There is no limit to the number of PropertyEditors you can declare and register to a DataBinder. You can also replace a registered PropertyEditor in the DataBinder if you wish to redefine which editor is called upon for each class.

As mentioned, you may also choose to map each property of the PhoneNumber class to an HTML text field. In this case, you will not need a custom PropertyEditor. However, if you find that you need to use a single text field to contain the entire value of a bean, even if that bean has multiple properties, then a custom PropertyEditor will allow you to handle this scenario. In other words, when you need to convert a single String value into a single complex object (potentially with many properties of its own), use a custom PropertyEditor.

Controlling Which Fields Are Bound

By default, the DataBinder will bind to any property on a bean that it can. That is, if the HTTP request contains a parameter name that matches a property of the bean, the bean's setter for that property will be called. Depending on the situation, this may or may not be what you will want. It is possible to control when fields can become bound, in order to provide an extra layer of protection from outside manipulation.

For instance, in Spring MVC, it's very common to bind request parameters directly to domain object models. Although this streamlines development and reduces the amount of classes in the system, it does present a potential security risk for the system. The binding process exposes the domain object directly to outside information. An attacker can, if enough knowledge of the system is gained, manipulate the domain object by sending an unintended request property and value with the form submit. This action would potentially bypass validation, and otherwise incur a risky situation.

To provide extra security for handling incoming data, the DataBinder can be configured to allow only accepted and approved properties. Properties not in the approved list will be dropped, and binding will continue.

To allow certain properties, simply call the setAllowedFields() method with a full list of all properties to be considered for binding. You will need to set this list before binding will take place.

The example in Listing 6-36 illustrates how to secure the binding process to only bind allowed fields. We're using the simple Name class (Listing 6-5) for this example, and we prohibit the lastName from being bound.

Listing 6-36. *Allowed Fields Test*

```
public void setUp() {
  name = new Name();
  binder = new ServletRequestDataBinder(name, "name");
  request = new MockHttpServletRequest();
}

public void testAllowedFields() {
  // only allow firstName field, ignore all others
  binder.setAllowedFields(new String[]{"firstName"});

  request.addParameter("firstName", "First");
  request.addParameter("lastName", "Last");

  binder.bind(request);   // only print log message on non-allowed fields
                          // allow binding to continue

  assertEquals("First", name.getFirstName());
  assertNull(name.getLastName());
}
```

By specifying which fields should be allowed for a particular binding, you can ensure that only intended fields from the HTML form will eventually make their way into the domain objects. Otherwise, there is no protection from misconfigured or malicious request parameters.

Rudimentary Validation

While Spring MVC support's Spring's flexible validation framework (covered in great detail in Chapter 9), the DataBinder provides a sort of "first line of defense" through its basic validation support. The DataBinder can be configured to check for required fields, or type mismatches, and any errors from these rules flow right into the main Validation system.

Although we will dedicate an entire chapter to Spring MVC's validation framework, to fully understand the DataBinder's basic validation support we will very briefly cover some of the fundamental constructs here. For every instance of data binding, there is a corresponding instance of a org.springframework.validation.BindException. This object is created automatically when binding begins, and encapsulates all the errors—either general object errors or field level errors—resulting from the binding and validation process.

Errors that apply to the entire object being bound to are instances of org.springframework.validation.ObjectError and are created when a validation rule that is not specific to any field is violated. Errors that are field-specific are instances of org.springframework.validation.FieldError. These error types are more common, as they encapsulate the specific error (e.g., a required field is missing) and the field that caused the error.

Configuring the DataBinder to check for required fields is similar to enforcing allowed fields (see the previous section, "Controlling Which Fields Are Bound"). By calling the setRequiredFields() method with a list of properties, the DataBinder will register an error if that property is missing from the request parameters. The error is an instance of org.springframework.validation.FieldError and is added to the DataBinder's instance of org.springframework.validation.BindException.

For the example, we will use the trusty Name class, and we will require the presence of the firstName field. Listing 6-37 contains the unit test illustrating required fields.

Listing 6-37. *Required Field Validation Test*

```
protected void setUp() throws Exception {
  name = new Name();
  binder = new ServletRequestDataBinder(name, "name");
  request = new MockHttpServletRequest();
}

public void testRequired() {
  binder.setRequiredFields(new String[]{"firstName"});

  // missing firstName parameter
  request.addParameter("lastName", "Smith");

  binder.bind(request);

  BindException errors = binder.getErrors();
  FieldError error = errors.getFieldError("firstName");

  assertNotNull(error);    //true!
  assertEquals("required", error.getCode());   //true!
}
```

The DataBinder will also generate an error if the request parameter value cannot be coerced into the field's type. For instance, if the parameter value is Smith but the field type is a java.lang.Integer, the DataBinder will intelligently create an error for this situation. This behavior, in fact, is automatic, and requires no explicit configuration on the DataBinder.

For the example, we will use a MultiTypeCommandBean (Listing 6-24) and attempt to set a String value into intProperty field, which is an int. Listing 6-38 contains the unit test illustrating error generation.

Listing 6-38. *Type Conversion Error Test*

```
protected void setUp() throws Exception {
  bean = new MultiTypeCommandBean();
  binder = new ServletRequestDataBinder(bean, "bean");
  request = new MockHttpServletRequest();
}

public void testRequired() {
  request.addParameter("intProperty", "NOT_A_NUMBER");

  binder.bind(request);

  BindException errors = binder.getErrors();
  FieldError error = errors.getFieldError("intProperty");

  assertNotNull(error);    //true!
  assertEquals("typeMismatch", error.getCode());  //true!
}
```

These two techniques should not be viewed as a replacement for the full validation framework. The DataBinder's validation functionality is limited to either declarative required field checking or automatic type conversion error generation, so for more complicated validation logic, you will have to use the org.springframework.validation framework. However, it does generate errors that are fully compatible to the full validation framework. The two types of validation mechanisms certainly complement each other.

Another thing to note is that typically, you will not have to deal with pulling the BindException object out of the DataBinder, or otherwise do any manual checking for errors. Controllers that implement a full form viewing and submitting work flow (such as SimpleFormController; see the section after next) will automatically detect the presence of errors and route the user to the correct view. We presented Listing 6-39 to give you an understanding of what is happening under the covers.

Summary

To summarize, the DataBinder is responsible for setting object properties from expression strings and their values. These expressions, in the form of property.property[2].property, are the names of HTML fields inside HTML forms. The values come from the submitted HTTP request parameters. The expression is converted into a series of JavaBean getters and setters to retrieve or manipulate the data.

The DataBinder supports setting properties of type String, primitives, and nearly any type, through its use of PropertyEditors. The DataBinder, through its BeanWrapper, supplies many different PropertyEditors by default, and it is trivial to create and register your own PropertyEditor to meet your specific needs.

You can also bind to properties of objects that live inside collections, such as Sets, Insert arrays, after Lists, and Maps. You can bind directly to objects that live in Lists, arrays or Maps (but not Sets, as there is no way to set a member of a Set directly).

We recommend that you control which properties can be bound to, to guard against malicious binding attempts. Using the DataBinder's setAllowedFields() method, you can declare the names of properties to be bound to request parameters. If the request parameter is not in that list, it will be silently dropped and will not be set into the bean.

An error will be generated when a request parameter cannot be converted into the field's type. For instance, if a String value is given to a field expecting an integer, a FieldError will be created and stored inside the BindException object. This functionality happens without any explicit configuration on the DataBinder.

Data binding is provided for you via the BaseCommandController class, which knows only how to bind request parameters to command classes. Subclasses of this class build upon this base functionality to create cohesive work flows.

The command classes, encapsulating form submissions, do not require a special class type; the DataBinder will happily bind to any class that obeys JavaBean conventions with standard getters and setters. We encourage you to use your domain model objects as the command classes and populate them directly from form submissions.

Now that we have thoroughly covered data binding, it's time now to look at the SimpleFormController class. This class builds upon the BaseCommandController to provide a very full-featured work flow for HTML forms. You will see how to apply your new data binding skills and how to process a command class once it has been populated by form fields.

SimpleFormController and Handling Forms

The org.springframework.web.servlet.mvc.SimpleFormController is a very powerful Controller responsible for handling the entire life cycle of HTML form interaction. This Controller manages and coordinates viewing the form, through validation, and finally to handling the submission. If your page or resource does not have to handle any form submits, you can move up the class hierarchy to use a simpler controller such as AbstractController. If you need to display a form and handle its submission, then this is the Controller for you.

■**Tip** This controller extends AbstractController, so it inherits all of the work flow from AbstractController. It does not attempt to change or replace the logic of AbstractController.

One very nice aspect of this class is that it models the entire life cycle of form interaction. It handles all the details and provides very explicit extension points allowing you to append functionality during the process of form viewing or submission.

SimpleFormController is configured through many different properties (listed in Table 6-2). Because this class attempts to obey the Open-Closed Principle, the properties are provided to declaratively configure the work flow and behavior of the controller.

Table 6-2. *SimpleFormController Properties*

Property Name	Default	Description	Found In
formView	null	The name of the view that contains the form.	SimpleFormController
successView	null	The name of the view to display on successful completion of form submission.	SimpleFormController
bindOnNewForm	false	Should parameters be bound to the form bean on initial views of the form? (Parameters will still be bound on form submission.)	AbstractFormController
sessionForm	false	Should the form bean be stored in the session between form view and form submission?	AbstractFormController
commandName	"command"	Logical name for the form bean.	BaseCommandController
commandClass	null	The class of the form bean.	BaseCommandController
validator(s)	null	One or more Validators that can handle objects of type configured by commandClass property.	BaseCommandController
validateOnBinding	true	Should the Controller validate the form bean after binding during a form submission?	BaseCommandController

This class's work flow can be split into two parts: viewing the form and handling the submission of the form. This controller provides both actions from a single URL, or HTTP resource. In other words, you will use the URL /app/editPerson.html to view the form and to submit the form. Semantically, using the same resource (URL) for both viewing (via HTTP GET) and submitting (via HTTP POST) maps very well to HTTP's modeling of a resource and how best to interact with the resource.

■**Tip** The HTTP specification specifies eight verbs, or commands, for accessing resources on the web. The two most popular verbs are GET and POST. GET is used when fetching, or reading, the resource, and the results are intended to be cacheable and repeatable without repercussions on the resource (i.e., GET is an idempotent action). In contrast, POST is meant for altering or modifying the resource, which is why it is used most often for form submissions. A POST action is not meant to be repeated without explicit approval from the user.

This controller has a complex work flow, and we will break it down into its core components. Then, we will show you the best extension points for altering the work flow in the controller. We begin by illustrating all possible paths through the controller.

Figure 6-1 illustrates the many paths through the work flow of handling forms with `SimpleFormController`.

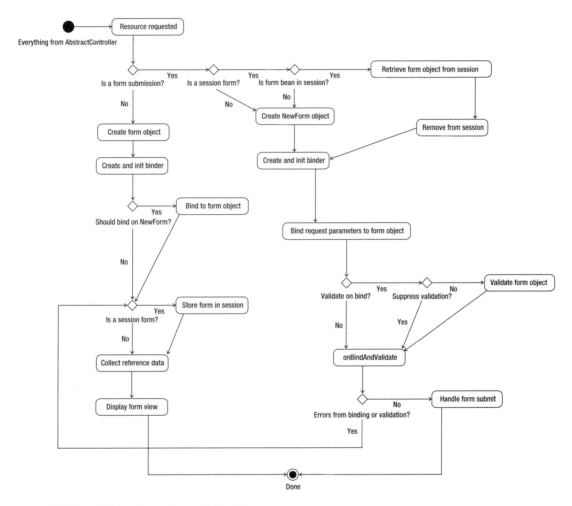

Figure 6-1. *SimpleFormController activity diagram*

We will focus on the initial retrieval of the HTML form first. The controller uses the method `isFormSubmission()` to determine if the HTTP request is either a form viewing or form submission. The default implementation of this method merely checks the HTTP method, and if it is a POST then `isFormSubmission()` returns `true`. The controller does not consider a HTTP GET request a form submission. However, this method is not final, so your implementation is free to define whatever criteria is appropriate to indicate the request should be treated as a submission. If indeed the request is not a form submission, the controller will then consider this request as the first of two requests (the second being the actual form submission). It will create an instance of the form object (a.k.a. command bean) using the `formBackingObject()` method. By default, this method will return an instance of the class specified with `setCommandClass()`. The `formBackingObject()` method is not final, so you will use this method to configure, if necessary, the form object class, possibly setting any dependencies or properties. This is the time to manipulate the form object before it enters the work flow.

Once the instance of the form object is ready, the controller then creates the `DataBinder` and calls the `initBinder()` life cycle method. Override this method to register any custom `PropertyEditors` required when binding to the form object. By default, this method does nothing.

Now that the `DataBinder` instance is ready, you have the choice of performing a binding using any parameters sent with this initial HTTP GET request. This action is determined by the `bindOnNewForm` property, enabled by (you guessed it) calling the `setBindOnNewForm()` method. Typically, on the first view of a form, no parameters have been sent with the request, so it is safe to leave `bindOnNewForm` equal to `false` (the default). However, if you set the property to `true`, and any errors occurred from the binding process, those errors will be available to the initial form view.

The `SimpleFormController` has the ability to store the form object in the session for the duration of the controller's work flow. That is, the form will live in the session between the initial form view and the form submission. To enable this feature, simply call `setSessionForm()` with a value of `true`. Once the form object has been created, and after it is possibly bound by the `DataBinder`, it will be stored in the session if this property is `true`.

If you load the form bean from persistence using an object-relational mapping (ORM) tool, you may find the session form functionality useful. Many ORM tools support the concept of reattaching, or merging, a detached bean back into persistence. If you require this type of behavior, using the session form functionality is a nice way to load the form bean only once during initial form view. That same instance will then be used during the form submission stage, avoiding the need to pull the instance from persistence again. Most persistence strategies can handle pulling the instance twice (once on form view and once on form submission), so weigh the pros with the cons of increased memory usage for the session, among other issues.

■**Caution** Storing the form in the session should not be chosen lightly if the application is to be clustered. Typically, in a clustered environment, session data is serialized and often replicated among different nodes in the cluster. Serialization is a costly procedure, and it can place a heavy burden on cluster bandwidth. Check with your application server's clustering strategies, and be sure to understand the impact of session storage.

At this point, the form view is about to be returned to the user. Before the view is rendered, the `referenceData()` callback is called. This life cycle method allows you to assemble and return any auxiliary objects required to render the view. The form object will automatically be sent to the form view, so use this method to put anything else into the model the form page might need. By default, this method does not manipulate the model in any way.

If you've made it this far, the Controller will assemble the full model with the form object, any possible errors from potential binding, and the model from referenceData(). It will then send this combined model to the View named by the formView property. This is the name of the View that contains the actual HTML form.

Form Submission with SimpleFormController

The SimpleFormController has completed half of its job by displaying the HTML form to the user. Once the user hits the submit button of the form, the SimpleFormController roars back to life to handle the submission. It will bind the request parameters to the form bean, validate the bean, and choose to show either the original form again if there were errors or the form success view if everything worked as expected. We will walk you through this process now, pointing out the useful life cycle callback methods along the way.

The first method in this controller that determines the form bean's fate is again the isFormSubmission() method. Your HTML forms *should* use the POST method for form submissions for both technical (it can handle much more data) and architectural (POST actions are intrinsically non-idempotent) reasons. Also, the default implementation of isFormSubmission() returns true if the action is a POST. You are free to override this method to further define what a form submission looks like, but the default should work fine for most situations.

In this case, because we are tracking the form submission work flow, this method will return true. The SimpleFormController will now check whether or not the form bean is stored in the session, via the isSessionForm() method. If the form bean is stored in the session, then the Controller will retrieve the form bean, put there originally when the user viewed the form. The Controller then removes the form bean from the session, as it is likely the form bean will be successfully submitted during this work flow (thus no longer needed in the session). If, in fact, there are errors during the submission process, the form bean will be placed back into the session later.

If the form bean was not stored in the session, then the controller will simply create another instance of the form bean using the formBackingObject() method. This is the same method used to create the form bean during the initial form view.

■**Tip** If your form bean requires dependencies to be injected by Spring's ApplicationContext, overriding formBackingObject() provides the opportunity to request the bean from the BeanFactory. Of course, to avoid having to manually pull the bean using the getBean() method on the BeanFactory you can use Spring's support for method injection (refer to *Pro Spring* by Rob Harrop and Jan Machacek (Apress, 2005) for more information). In any case, don't restrict your form beans to simple POJOs as you may use Spring's dependency injection for your form beans quite easily.

At this point, the form bean instance has been obtained. The Controller now creates the DataBinder and calls the initBinder() callback method. As with the work flow for viewing the form, use this method to register any custom PropertyEditors you need during binding.

With the form bean created, and the DataBinder created with custom PropertyEditors registered, the request parameters are now bound to the form bean. The binding process will also capture any binding errors, such as type conversion errors or any configured required fields.

Of course, most forms require more complicated validation than what is provided by the DataBinder. At this point in the work flow, the Controller consults the method isValidateOnBinding() to determine if it should now run the form bean through the Validators. This method defaults to true, and it is marked final so the only way to change its behavior is through setValidateOnBinding().

If your situation requires a more exact control over when validation is performed after a binding, you may override the suppressValidation() method. While this method defaults to false, this method allows you to choose on a request-by-request basis whether or not to run through the validators.

By default, the controller will allow each configured validator to validate the form bean. After all the validators have run, the controller will then call the onBindAndValidate() life cycle method. This callback method is your chance to perform any custom validation logic or general logic after binding and validation.

Note The onBindAndValidate() method will run even if suppressValidation() returns true or if isValidateOnBinding() returns false. In other words, onBindAndValidate() will always run, even if validation did not.

After onBindAndValidate() runs, the Controller makes a decision based on whether any errors exist. These errors would have resulted from the binding process or through automatic validation or custom validation in onBindAndValidate(). If there are any errors, the Controller then begins the process of displaying the original form. If no errors exist, then the form bean can finally be processed.

If errors are present and the isSessionForm() method returns true, then the form bean is placed back into the session. Remember that the form bean is removed from the session at the beginning of the form submission handling work flow. However, when there are errors, the original form is displayed again, and so the form bean is stored in the session again to be bound again once the errors are addressed by the user. The referenceData() method is called once more to populate the model with objects for the form. Finally, the form view is displayed again, with the errors and the form bean.

If there are no errors, the controller then calls the onSubmit() life cycle method. This signals that the form bean is ready to be processed. There are several overloaded onSubmit() methods, each method simply calling the other with one fewer method argument. This flow, illustrated in Figure 6-2, is arranged this way to allow you to pick the method with the exact number of parameters you will need to process the form. There is no need to implement all onSubmit() methods; just choose the one that will work for you.

There is also a very simple doSubmitAction(), which is the most simple callback method to override and implement. If you do not implement any of the onSubmit() methods, you will need to implement this method. This method simply provides the form bean to be processed. You may use this method when there is no model to construct and when the default success view is appropriate. If you need to construct a model, or if you need to choose the view to show dynamically, implement one of the onSubmit() methods.

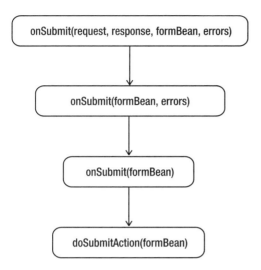

Figure 6-2. *Order in which callback methods are called*

■Tip Choose the best form submit callback to implement based on which objects you need and whether the default success view is always appropriate. Implement only one callback method.

SimpleFormController Examples

It is time to see the SimpleFormController in action. To begin, we will create a form for a simple person. This example brings together what we have covered from the DataBinder and the work flow of the SimpleFormController.

The Person class used in this example (shown in Listing 6-39) has three properties: a Name, when he was born, and his favorite programming language. To make things more interesting, the name property is an example of a nested Name object (shown in Listing 6-40), and the bornOn property will require a custom PropertyEditor.

Listing 6-39. *Person Bean*

```
public class Person {

    private Name name = new Name();
    private Date bornOn;
    private String favoriteProgrammingLanguage;

    public Date getBornOn() {
        return bornOn;
    }
    public void setBornOn(Date bornOn) {
        this.bornOn = bornOn;
    }
```

```java
    public String getFavoriteProgrammingLanguage() {
        return favoriteProgrammingLanguage;
    }
    public void setFavoriteProgrammingLanguage(String favoriteProgrammingLanguage) {
        this.favoriteProgrammingLanguage = favoriteProgrammingLanguage;
    }
    public Name getName() {
        return name;
    }
    public void setName(Name name) {
        this.name = name;
    }
    @Override
    public String toString() {
        StringBuffer sb = new StringBuffer();
        sb.append("Name: [");
        sb.append(name.toString());
        sb.append("], ");
        sb.append("Born On: [");
        sb.append(bornOn);
        sb.append("], ");
        sb.append("Favorite Programming Language: [");
        sb.append(favoriteProgrammingLanguage);
        sb.append("]");
        return sb.toString();
    }
}
```

Listing 6-40. *Name Bean*

```java
public class Name {

    private String first;
    private String last;

    public String getFirst() {
        return first;
    }
    public void setFirst(String first) {
        this.first = first;
    }
    public String getLast() {
        return last;
    }
    public void setLast(String last) {
        this.last = last;
    }
    @Override
    public String toString() {
```

```
        return first + " " + last;
    }
}
```

Listing 6-41 contains the XHTML that matches the Person object, while Figure 6-3 shows how the form is rendered. Note that Listing 6-41 deliberately omits the use of the <spring:bind> tags, in order to illustrate the raw XHTML required. This is the XHTML as the browser would see it. Obviously, this also illustrates that the use of <spring:bind> and related tags are not required, though they are recommended for any real projects.

Listing 6-41. *XHTML Form for Person*

```
<?xml version="1.0" encoding="ISO-8859-1" ?>
<!DOCTYPE html PUBLIC "-//W3C//DTD XHTML 1.0 Strict//EN"
    "http://www.w3.org/TR/xhtml1/DTD/xhtml1-strict.dtd">
<html xmlns="http://www.w3.org/1999/xhtml">
<head>
<title>Person Form</title>
</head>
<body>

<form method="post" action="">
<table>
<tr>
    <td>First Name:</td>
    <td><input type="text" name="name.first" /></td>
</tr>
<tr>
    <td>Last Name:</td>
    <td><input type="text" name="name.last" /></td>
</tr>
<tr>
    <td>Born On:</td>
    <td><input type="text" name="bornOn" /></td>
</tr>
<tr>
    <td>Favorite Programming Language:</td>
    <td><input type="text" name="favoriteProgrammingLanguage" /></td>
</tr>
<tr>
    <td />
    <td><input type="submit" /></td>
</tr>
</table>
</form>

</body>
</html>
```

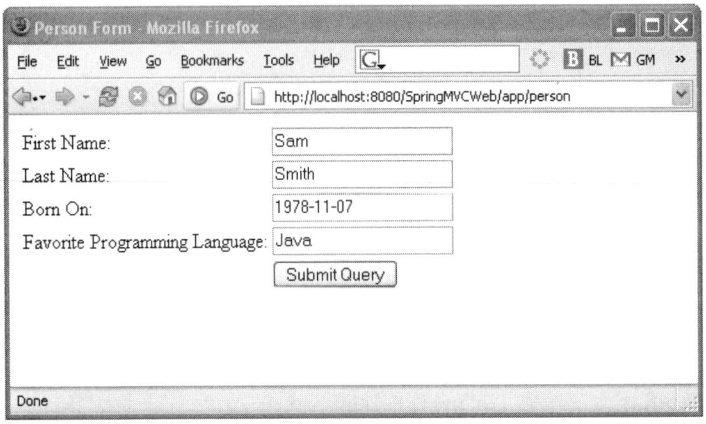

Figure 6-3. *Initial form view*

The XHTML shown in Listing 6-41 has some interesting aspects. First, notice that we are using the POST method for the form. This should be the preferred method for form submissions, as discussed earlier. Second, notice how we used action="" instead of specifying a particular URI. This is a convenience trick to avoid specifying the page's URI, which would tightly couple the page to the URI that indicates it. By not specifying an action, the browser will submit the form back to the originating URI (which, in the case of SimpleFormController, is just what we want). Lastly, notice how the form input element names correspond to the property names from the Person object. This should be familiar from the discussion about the DataBinder.

Next, we show the SimpleFormController implementation (Listing 6-42) for the form in Listing 6-41. For our example, it will simply print out the Person via toString(), but it's easy to imagine using a data access object to persist the person.

Listing 6-42. *PersonFormController*

```java
public class PersonFormController extends SimpleFormController {

    public PersonFormController() {
        setCommandName("person");
        setCommandClass(Person.class);
        setFormView("newPerson");
        setSuccessView("newPersonSuccess");
    }

    @Override
    protected void initBinder(HttpServletRequest request,
            ServletRequestDataBinder binder) throws Exception {
        binder.registerCustomEditor(Date.class,
                new CustomDateEditor(new SimpleDateFormat("yyyy-MM-dd"), false));
    }

    @Override
```

```
protected void doSubmitAction(Object command) throws Exception {
    Person person = (Person) command;
    // persist the object, or some other business logic
}

}
```

The bornOn parameter of the Person object is of type java.util.Date, so we are required to use a custom PropertyEditor to convert the string parameter into a true Date object. This Controller relies on the default behavior of forwarding to the successView once the form is submitted, so we chose to implement doSubmitAction() because it requires the least amount of code.

By default, the form bean will placed into the model on successful form submission. Therefore, the form success view can access the form bean with the identifier set via setCommandName(). The following XHTML page (Listing 6-43) shows this in action.

Listing 6-43. *newPersonSuccess XHTML Page*

```
<?xml version="1.0" encoding="ISO-8859-1" ?>
<!DOCTYPE html PUBLIC "-//W3C//DTD XHTML 1.0 Strict//EN"
    "http://www.w3.org/TR/xhtml1/DTD/xhtml1-strict.dtd">
<html xmlns="http://www.w3.org/1999/xhtml">
<head>
<title>New Person Success</title>
</head>
<body>

<p>${person}</p>

</body>
</html>
```

Listing 6-43's JSP page will render the following result to the browser (Figure 6-4).

Figure 6-4. *Form success view*

The Controller in this example is using logical View names to identify which views should be rendered. This provides a nice decoupling between the controller and how the Views are actually implemented. The DispatcherServlet will delegate these View names to a ViewResolver to resolve the actual View instances. For our example, we will use an InternalResourceViewResolver. This ViewResolver works well with JSP files and lets us hide the actual JSP files behind the /WEB-INF directory to prohibit unauthorized client access.

■**Tip** You should place any restricted or otherwise hidden files inside the /WEB-INF directory of your web application. That directory, and all of its subdirectories, is protected by the servlet container.

The ViewResolver is declared and configured with a prefix and suffix, used to create a fully qualified filename for the view. This bean definition (Listing 6-44) will typically reside in the spring-servlet.xml file with the rest of the controller definitions and other web-specific beans.

Listing 6-44. *ViewResolver Configuration*

```
<bean id="jspViewResolver"
  class="org.springframework.web.servlet.view.InternalResourceViewResolver">
  <property name="viewClass" value="org.springframework.web.servlet.view.JstlView"/>
  <property name="prefix" value="/WEB-INF/jsp/"/>
  <property name="suffix" value=".jsp"/>
</bean>
```

With our example controller using a view name of newPerson, the ViewResolver in Listing 6-45 will attempt to locate the file /WEB-INF/jsp/newPerson.jsp.

We obviously haven't mentioned Validators or what happens if there is a validation error. Validation is a large topic, so we are postponing a full discussion about validation to Chapter 9.

To continue with this example, we now want to modify the code to restrict the choices of favorite programming language. The predetermined choices must be loaded before the initial page view; thus we will override the referenceData() method.

First, we will create the list of approved languages to pick a favorite from. For the example, the List's contents are static, so we will create a simple array to be shared among requests.

It is common to require objects from persistence to be returned by referenceData(). If that information is static, for performance reasons, load the objects only once at startup. This will save on pulling them from the database for every request. In this case, your controller may implement InitializingBean, which is a Spring-specific interface indicating that the bean requires initializing before servicing requests.

■**Tip** For more information about the InitializingBean interface, consult the book *Pro Spring* or the online documentation. An alternative to InitializingBean is the init-method attribute in the XML bean definition, which avoids the need to implement a framework interface.

Listing 6-45 contains the entire PersonFormController code, highlighting the referenceData() method.

Listing 6-45. *PersonFormController with Reference Data*

```java
public class PersonFormController extends SimpleFormController {

    private String[] languages = new String[]{"Java", "Ruby", "Python"};

    public PersonFormController() {
        setCommandName("person");
        setCommandClass(Person.class);
        setFormView("newPerson");
        setSuccessView("newPersonSuccess");
    }

    @Override
    protected Map referenceData(HttpServletRequest req) throws Exception {
        Map data = new HashMap();
        data.put("languages", languages);
        return data;
    }

    @Override
    protected void initBinder(HttpServletRequest request,
            ServletRequestDataBinder binder) throws Exception {
        binder.registerCustomEditor(Date.class,
                new CustomDateEditor(new SimpleDateFormat("yyyy-MM-dd"), false));
    }

    @Override
    protected void doSubmitAction(Object command) throws Exception {
        Person person = (Person) command;
    }

}
```

Now that we are providing a list of favorite languages, we can modify our form XHTML to loop through them to build the <select> and <option> tags, as shown in Listing 6-46.

Listing 6-46. *XHTML Snippet of Favorite Programming Languages*

```
<tr>
    <td>Favorite Programming Language:</td>
    <td>
    <select name="favoriteProgrammingLanguage">
      <c:forEach items="${languages}" var="language">
```

```
        <option>${language}</option>
      </c:forEach>
    </select>
    </td>
</tr>
```

Of course, it's common to return extra information to the View after a form submission. You may, for example, want to provide a confirmation message after the submission completes. In our example so far, we have implemented the doSubmitAction() method, which does not allow for any model to be returned. Again, the doSubmitAction() method is useful when the default success view is sufficient. When you need to return objects required by the success view, you will need to implement an onSubmit() method.

For example, we will extend our PersonFormController to persist the person instance into the database, and we will recommend a book to read based on their favorite programming language. We will remove our doSubmitAction() method and override onSubmit() so that we may return a model with the book recommendation, as shown in Listing 6-47.

Listing 6-47. *PersonFormController with onSubmit()*

```
public class PersonFormController extends SimpleFormController {

    private String[] languages = new String[]{"Java", "Ruby", "Python"};

    private PersonDao personDao;

    public PersonFormController() {
        setCommandName("person");
        setCommandClass(Person.class);
        setFormView("newPerson");
        setSuccessView("newPersonSuccess");
    }

    public void setPersonDao(PersonDao personDao) {
        this.personDao = personDao;
    }

    @Override
    protected Map<String, String[]> referenceData(HttpServletRequest req)
            throws Exception {
        Map<String, String[]> data = new HashMap<String, String[]>();
        data.put("languages", languages);
        return data;
    }
}
```

```
@Override
protected void initBinder(HttpServletRequest request,
        ServletRequestDataBinder binder) throws Exception {
    binder.registerCustomEditor(Date.class,
            new CustomDateEditor(new SimpleDateFormat("yyyy-MM-dd"), false));
}

@Override
protected ModelAndView onSubmit(Object command) throws Exception {
    Person person = (Person) command;
    personDao.persist(person);

    Map<String, String> model = new HashMap<String, String>();
    model.put("suggestedBook",
            suggestBook(person.getFavoriteProgrammingLanguage()));
    model.put(getCommandName(), person);

    return new ModelAndView(getSuccessView(), model);
}

private String suggestBook(String favoriteProgrammingLanguage) {
    Language language = Language.create(favoriteProgrammingLanguage);
    return language.recommendBookTitle();
}

}
```

As you may have noticed, the controller now delegates persistence to a PersonDao class. Thus, a setter method is provided, setPersonDao(), so that the ApplicationContext can easily inject an instance.

The old doSubmitAction() is now replaced with the more flexible onSubmit() method, allowing us to return a ModelAndView object. Notice how we simply call getSuccessView() to return the configured success view. We are also now required to manually add the person object into the model, which was previously automatically added.

Tip If you return null from onSubmit(), a default ModelAndView will be created with getSuccessView() and errors.getModel().

The business logic of choosing a recommended book title is delegated to a Language object. This follows the recommendations of delegating any business logic to the service layer or other POJOs in the system.

All objects in the model are exposed to the View instance, so the success view XHTML page can now easily display the recommended book, as shown in Listing 6-48.

Listing 6-48. *XHTML for Recommended Book Title*

```
<body>

Welcome, ${person.name}! You chose ${person.favoriteProgrammingLanguage}
as your favorite programming language. Therefore, we can recommend you
check out ${suggestedBook}.

</body>
```

Redirect After Submit Pattern

There is a common problem with the way we are handling the display of the confirmation page, which needs to be fixed. The success view is rendered in the same request as the initial POST, leaving the browser in a state with the ability to replay the form submit. In other words, after the success view is shown, the user can simply reload the page, resubmitting the form. This can lead to inconsistencies, with the best-case scenario of a confused user and a worst-case scenario of multiple identical Person instances being saved into the database.

Any form that alters data in persistence, or performs any type of potentially destructive operation, is at risk of being resubmitted. Multiple solutions exist that can ensure that the user must view the form before submitting, thus preventing double submissions. We will cover one of the most common solutions, the Redirect After Submit pattern, in the next example. This pattern simply redirects the user to the success view instead of internally forwarding the request. The redirect forces the browser to obtain a new page, and any reloads will now safely reload the new page instead of the form page.

■**Caution** A client redirect is not the same as a RequestDispatcher.forward() or RequestDispatcher. include(). These two methods internally redirect a request to another handler inside the servlet container. A client redirect instructs the client to issue another GET request.

This pattern is implemented via browser redirects, which are initiated from the server and are built into the HTTP protocol. This means this technique can be used independent of the view technologies used. To initiate a client redirect, the server will send a 302 response code (or 303 if HTTP/1.1 only) plus a Location: header to the client. The HTTP response code 302 indicates that a resource[4] has temporarily moved or that the browser should look elsewhere for the resource. When the browser encounters a 302, it will look for a Location: header to indicate where the resource can now be found.

---

4. More accurately, that the representation of the resource has moved.

Tip For the exact differences between 302 and 303 response codes, please consult the HTTP RFC at `http://www.w3.org/Protocols/rfc2616/rfc2616-sec10.html`. The 303 response code was added to HTTP/1.1 specifically for the redirect after post pattern, but is only understood by HTTP/1.1 clients. Luckily, most HTTP/1.1 clients will treat a 302 response identically to a 303.

There are at least three different ways to accomplish a client redirect with Spring MVC and the Servlet API. The first method, `HttpServletResponse.sendRedirect()`, uses the Servlet API to correctly send the redirect response. You may use this method only if the response has not been committed, however.

Spring MVC treats redirects as just another type of view with its `org.springframework.web.servlet.view.RedirectView` class. This class encapsulates the redirect, the conversion of model objects to query parameters, and the logic to handle a HTTP/1.0 or HTTP/1.1 redirect. This view is then resolved like all other `Views` in the system, hiding the exact view details from the controller.

While the `RedirectView` is very simple to use, if your application is already using an `InternalResourceViewResolver`, you will need to create another view resolver that is able to resolve non-file system views. Because we already have an `InternalResourceViewResolver` configured, we will need to chain the `ViewrResolvers` allowing each the chance to resolve the view name. Once a resolver is able to handle the `View` name, resolving stops and the view instance is returned.

To handle a `RedirectView`, we will define an `XmlViewResolver` (Listing 6-49), which reads its list of view names from a Spring XML file. This `ViewResolver` will be defined inside `spring-servlet.xml` alongside the `InternalResourceViewResolver`. The `XmlViewResolver`, however, will be configured to appear before the `InternalResourceViewResolver` in the chain, so that it has a chance to resolve the view names first. We also specify where the resolver will find its configuration (in this case, in `/WEB-INF/views.xml`).

Listing 6-49. *Two View Resolvers, Chained*

```
<bean id="jspViewResolver"
class="org.springframework.web.servlet.view.InternalResourceViewResolver">
  <property name="viewClass" value="org.springframework.web.servlet.JstlView"/>
  <property name="prefix" value="/WEB-INF/jsp/"/>
  <property name="suffix" value=".jsp"/>
</bean>

<bean id="auxViewResolver"
class="org.springframework.web.servlet.view.XmlViewResolver">
  <property name="order" value="1"/>
  <property name="location" value="/WEB-INF/views.xml"/>
</bean>
```

Now it is simply a matter of defining the RedirectView instance in views.xml (as shown in Listing 6-50). The bean's name will match the view name the controller is using (i.e., newPersonSuccess). We are setting contextRelative to true so that the RedirectView will prepend the context path name for the web application to the URL value.

Listing 6-50. *views.xml*

```
<?xml version="1.0"?>
<!DOCTYPE beans PUBLIC
    "-//SPRING//DTD BEAN//EN"
    "http://www.springframework.org/dtd/spring-beans.dtd">
<beans>

  <bean id="newPersonSuccess"
    class="org.springframework.web.servlet.view.RedirectView">
    <property name="contextRelative" value="true" />
    <property name="url" value="/personSuccess" />
  </bean>

</beans>
```

One of the benefits of the RedirectView is that it will convert each object from the model and place them in the query string of the full URL. However, for this to work correctly, those objects are converted to Strings. Therefore, if you will be using the RedirectView with objects in the model, ensure that the next page expects only Strings from the model. We will now slightly modify our Controller (as shown in Listing 6-51), explicitly adding each property we will need for the success page.

Listing 6-51. *Modified onSubmit Using Only Strings in the Model*

```
Map<String, Object> model = new HashMap<String, Object>();
model.put("suggestedBook",
          suggestBook(person.getFavoriteProgrammingLanguage()));
model.put("personName", person.getName());
model.put("personFavoriteProgrammingLanguage",
          person.getFavoriteProgrammingLanguage());
```

Our success page's message (shown in Listing 6-52) will now be changed to reference the new model properties. Notice how we are accessing the model objects from the request parameters (as indicated by the param prefix). This is because the objects in the model are sent to the next page via the query string, such as /personSuccess?personName=joe&suggestedBook= title automatically by the RedirectView.

Listing 6-52. *New Success Page Text*

```
Welcome, ${param.personName}! You chose ${param.personFavoriteProgrammingLanguage}
as your favorite programming language. Therefore, we can recommend you
check out ${param.suggestedBook}.
```

And finally, we will add a `Controller` to handle the new success page. Why do we need a `Controller` for a simple JSP page? A `Controller` can hide the implementation of the `View` from the client, and it provides a uniform URL address space. For consistency's sake, it's a good idea to front even simple `Views` with a `Controller`. As you'll see, Spring MVC make this a straight-forward process.

The view name `newPersonSuccess` is now being used for the redirect view, which redirects to the controller identified by `/personSuccess`. In this case, we simply wish to display the success message so we aren't interested in coding up a `Controller` just to forward to a JSP page. Luckily, Spring MVC provides an `org.springframework.web.servlet.mvc.UrlFilenameViewController` that can convert the last part of the request URL to a view name. This avoids the need to write a custom `Controller` for resources that are only implemented as `Views`.

For instance, given the URL `/app/address.x`, the `UrlFilenameViewController` will convert the URL into the view name `address`. This is a very easy way to expose `View` resources such as JSP pages while continuing to hide their implementation technology.

Tip For resources that are only views, hide them behind simple controllers such as `UrlFilenameViewController` or `ParameterizableViewController`. This hides implementation revealing clues, such as the .jsp extension, and can provide a uniform URL address space. This also allows you to place your view files in the protected `/WEB-INF` directory.

For the example, we now add the bean definition for the `/personSuccess` resource (shown in Listing 6-53), which the client will be redirected to upon successful form submission. This definition should go in `spring-servlet.xml` with the other web-specific beans.

Listing 6-53. */personSuccess Bean Definition*

```
<bean name="/personSuccess"
  class="org.springframework.web.servlet.mvc.UrlFilenameViewController" />
```

With this last change, the `Controller` now correctly redirects the client after the form submission. We accomplished this by using a `RedirectView` and an `XmlViewResolver`, which is a good strategy when you wish to keep the `Controller` unaware of the implementations of any views.

However, quite a bit of infrastructure was required for this configuration. Spring MVC provides shorthand for redirect views, allowing you to forgo the definition of any `RedirectViews` or the configuration of an explicit `XmlViewResolver`. The `UrlBasedViewResolver` (the superclass for `InternalResourceViewResolver`) recognizes the special prefix `redirect:`, which simply triggers a client redirect instead of being resolved through the standard process.

Converting the `PersonFormController` to use this shorthand is quite easy, and involves mostly deleting code we just created. The `Controller`'s success view name will now be changed to use the `redirect:` prefix (as shown in Listing 6-54), alleviating the need for a `RedirectView` definition or an `XmlViewResolver` definition.

Listing 6-54. *Person Controller Constructor with Redirect:Pprefix*

```
public PersonFormController() {
  setCommandName("person");
  setCommandClass(Person.class);
  setFormView("newPerson");
  setSuccessView("redirect:/app/personSuccess");
}
```

Redirect After Submit Summary

The *redirect after submit* pattern, sometimes known as *redirect after POST*, is a method to protect the client from resubmitting a form. By sending a HTTP redirect, the client is sent to a different page after the form is submitted, effectively leaving the original form's page. Any attempts to reload the page will simple reload the success page instead of the original form.

MultiActionController

SimpleFormController is great when you need to model a form work flow with one page view and one form submission. There are, however, some situations where you might want one Controller to handle more than one work flow. For instance, you may have a logical group of read-only operations, and subclassing an AbstractController for each operation might be a bit verbose for your application. The MultiActionController provides a way to group multiple actions, or request handlers, together in one controller.

The benefits of the MultiActionController include

- fewer physical controllers, thus fewer classes in the system

- logical grouping of actions in one class

- flexible mapping for action methods.

The disadvantages of MultiActionController include

- form handling work flow isn't explicit, unlike SimpleFormController

- possibility for large, confusing controllers handling many tasks

- no compile-time checks can be performed due to the use of reflection.

So when does using MultiActionController make sense? We believe it is a perfect way to consolidate actions that have a similar theme into one controller, when those actions do not require a full form handling work flow. It's also useful when the actual processing is performed by a shared delegate. However, be wary of putting too many request handling methods inside one MultiActionController, for it can quickly become too large and unwieldy.

■**Note** The MultiActionController is similar in nature to Struts' DispatchAction, only much more flexible.

The MultiActionController has the following capabilities:

- flexible action method mapping, defaulting to URL to method name mapping

- command bean binding

- support for one or more Validators

- per-action "last modified" timestamp control

- exception handling

■**Caution** Even though this Controller supports Validators and command bean binding, it does not define a form handling work flow.

On initialization, this class searches all of its methods for any that conform to the request handler signature. Any method that will handle a request must conform to the following features:

- returns ModelAndView

- accepts an HttpServletRequest as a first parameter

- accepts an HttpServletResponse as a second parameter

- optionally, accept either an HttpSession or an Object (to be treated as the command bean) as a third parameter

---

■**Note** The name of the method does not matter when locating potential request handling methods.

Listing 6-55 contains a simple MultiActionController with three different but valid request handling methods.

Listing 6-55. *Example Request Handling Method Signature*

```
public class MyMultiController extends MultiActionController {
    public ModelAndView doStuff(HttpServletRequest req,
        HttpServletResponse res) { … }

    public ModelAndView doOtherStuff(HttpServletRequest req,
        HttpServletResponse res, HttpSession session) { … }

    public ModelAndView doStuff(HttpServletRequest req,
        HttpServletResponse res, CommandBean command) { … }
}
```

Now the question becomes, how does `MultiActionController` know which method to call when it handles a request? This decision process is encapsulated into the strategy `MethodNameResolver`, whose job it is to take an `HttpServletRequest` and return a method name as a `String`.

InternalPathMethodNameResolver

The default strategy, if none is specified, is the `org.springframework.web.servlet.mvc.multiaction.InternalPathMethodNameResolver`. To quote the Javadocs, this strategy is a "Simple implementation of `MethodNameResolver` that maps URL to method name." This class will convert the last path section of the URL, ignoring any file extensions, into a method name. For instance, it will turn `/app/account/delete.x` into the method name `delete`.

If the method names in your controller vary in a uniform way from the URL path section, then a prefix or suffix can be configured. For instance, if your method name is `dodelete`, but you want to continue to use `/app/account/delete.x`, then you can configure the prefix property of `InternalPathMethodNameResolver` to equal "do."

Because this strategy is the default, no configuration is required if you choose to use it. However, if you want to configure a prefix or suffix, then you will have to specify its bean definition. Listing 6-56 contains a sample configuration.

Listing 6-56. *Example Configuration of an InternalPathMethodNameResolver*

```
<bean id="methodNameResolver"
  class="o.s.web.servlet.mvc.multiaction.InternalPathMethodNameResolver">
  <property name="prefix" value="do" />
</bean>
<bean name="/account/*"
  class="com.apress.expertspringmvc.flight.web.ViewAccountController">
  <property name="methodNameResolver" ref="methodNameResolver" />
  <property name="accountService" ref="accountService" />
</bean>
```

ParameterMethodNameResolver

If you are looking for behavior that matches Struts' `DispatchAction`, then you can use the `org.springframework.web.servlet.mvc.multiaction.ParameterMethodNameResolver`. This strategy actually is a combination of two separate strategies, both looking at request parameters for method name resolution.

The first strategy will look for a parameter by name, and its value will be treated as the method name. By default, the name of the parameter is `action`, but you can change it by calling `setParamName()`. Unlike `InternalPathMethodNameResolver`, there are no prefix and suffix capabilities, so the value of the action parameter must match exactly the method name.

The second strategy is to look for the mere presence of a request parameter, whose name will point to the method name. The `ParameterMethodNameResolver` will look for any parameter whose name is found in the `methodParamNames` array, and the first match wins.

> **■Tip** The second strategy will take precedence over the first, even if the first successfully resolves a match.

Over time, code gets refactored and URL links change, so the ParameterMethodNameResolver supports a mapping between request parameter and the true method name found in the controller. The strategy includes a logicalMappings java.util.Properties, containing a map between the request parameter name or value and the actual method name. This can come in very handy if you do not wish to expose real method names to the view layer.

Finally, this ParameterMethodNameResolver can be configured with a default method name, if no other method name can be resolved. To configure a default method name, configure the defaultMethodName property.

An example usage of this MethodNameResolver is contained in Listing 6-57, configuring a list of parameters to look for and their mappings to real method names.

Listing 6-57. *Example of ParameterMethodNameResolver*

```
<bean id="methodNameResolver"
  class=
  "org.springframework.web.servlet.mvc.multiaction.ParameterMethodNameResolver">
  <property name="methodParamNames">
    <list>
      <value>hello</value>
    </list>
  </property>
  <property name="logicalMappings">
    <props>
      <prop key="hello">index</prop>
    </props>
  </property>
</bean>
```

With the example in Listing 6-57, if a URL like /app/controller?hello=true is used, the index() method will be called on the controller. Note that the value of the hello parameter does not matter when using the methodParamNames matching strategy, as only the presence of the parameter is what matters.

PropertiesMethodNameResolver

A third option for method name resolution is the org.springframework.web.servlet.mvc.multiaction.PropertiesMethodNameResolver, which happens to be the most flexible of the strategies. As its name implies, the mapping is done via java.util.Properties, with URL paths acting as keys and the values as method names. The URL path can use the same Ant-style pattern matching you've seen with other URL path matching strategies.

This strategy will first attempt an exact match on the URL path, excluding the web app contact name and the servlet mapping, but including the mapping for the Controller. If this exact match does not work, all the mappings will be attempted in iteration order through the Properties instance until a match is found.

Listing 6-58 contains an example bean definition and configuration of a
PropertiesMethodNameResolver.

Listing 6-58. *Example of PropertiesMethodNameResolver*

```
<bean id="methodNameResolver"
  class=
  "org.springframework.web.servlet.mvc.multiaction.PropertiesMethodNameResolver">
  <property name="mappings">
    <props>
      <prop key="/account/findByUsername">findByUsername</prop>
      <prop key="/account/*">index</prop> <!-- treated as default -->
    </</props>
  </property>
</bean>

<bean name="/account/*"
  class="com.apress.expertspringmvc.flight.web.ViewAccountController">
  <property name="methodNameResolver" ref="methodNameResolver" />
  <property name="accountService" ref="accountService" />
</bean>
```

The default case, in the preceding listing as /account/*, should be the last property
specified, so it will attempted last. Also, notice how the mapping path begins with the
mapping specified for the controller. If you wish to change this behavior, consult the
AbstractUrlMethodNameResolver superclass for options on how to configure the treatment
of the URL path.

MethodNameResolver Summary

You've seen three distinct strategies for mapping a request to a method on a
MultiActionController. The InternalPathMethodNameResolver will parse the URL path for the
last element and use it as a method name. The ParameterMethodNameResolver looks for request
parameters, either by value or by name, to resolve a method name. This strategy also supports
a default method name if no name was resolved. Finally, the PropertiesMethodNameResolver is
the least restrictive of the bunch, as it allows for a mapping of arbitrary URL paths to method
names.

Which one should you use? As with everything Spring Framework, the choice is ultimately
yours, and the framework doesn't lean toward any preference. You should weigh how much
configuration each strategy will take under your circumstances, as generally less configuration
is better. We favor not relying on request parameters for method names, as we feel URL paths
are cleaner and generally friendlier to work with.

MultiActionController Example

For an example of the MultiActionController, we will create a ViewAccountController that
exposes many different ways to find an Account. For instance, a user may want to find an
Account by username or first name or last name. These are simple read-only methods without

complex form handling, so it's a perfect chance to consolidate these three actions into one controller. We'll also take advantage of the built-in exception handling and rudimentary validation provided by the `DataBinder`, later in this example.

Listing 6-59 contains a full example of a `MultiActionController`.

Listing 6-59. *ViewAccountController Example*

```
public class ViewAccountController extends MultiActionController {

    private AccountService accountService;

    public ViewAccountController() throws ApplicationContextException {
        setSupportedMethods(new String[]{METHOD_GET});
    }

    public void setAccountService(AccountService accountService) {
        this.accountService = accountService;
    }

    public ModelAndView findByUsername(HttpServletRequest request,
            HttpServletResponse response, SearchCriteria criteria) {
        Account account = accountService.findAccountByUsername(
            criteria.getSearchBy());
        return new ModelAndView("viewAccount", "account", account);
    }

    public ModelAndView findByFirstName(HttpServletRequest request,
            HttpServletResponse response, SearchCriteria criteria) {
        List<Account> accounts = accountService.findAccountsByFirstName(
            criteria.getSearchBy());
        return new ModelAndView("viewAccounts", "accounts", accounts);
    }

    public ModelAndView findByLastName(HttpServletRequest request,
            HttpServletResponse response, SearchCriteria criteria) {
        List<Account> accounts = accountService.findAccountsByLastName(
            criteria.getSearchBy());
        return new ModelAndView("viewAccounts", "accounts", accounts);
    }

    public static class SearchCriteria {
        private String searchBy;

        public String getSearchBy() {
            return searchBy;
        }
```

```
        public void setSearchBy(String searchBy) {
            this.searchBy = searchBy;
        }
    }
}
```

Let's chat a bit about this example, which highlights the strengths and weaknesses of this
Controller type. A strength of this Controller is that its superclass AbstractController provides helpful facilities such as enforcing allowed HTTP methods (as done in the constructor
in Listing 6-59). A shortcoming of this ability is that the allowed HTTP methods are common
across all request handlers inside the class, as there is no way to declaratively configure the
list of allowed request methods on a per–request handling basis. In this example, where all
requests are read-only, globally restricting to GET makes sense. If your MultiActionController
can handle different request methods at different times, you will have to declare those allowed
HTTP methods inside each handler method. For instance, the code from Listing 6-60 can be
used.

Listing 6-60. *Ensure HTTP Methods*

```
private void ensureMethod(HttpServletRequest request, String ... methods)
        throws RequestMethodNotSupportedException {
    for (String method : methods) {
        if (request.getMethod().equals(method)) {
            return;
        }
    }
    throw new RequestMethodNotSupportedException("The request method " +
            request.getMethod() + " is not allowed");
}
```

You can use such a method at the beginning of each request handling method (as shown
in Listing 6-61), but be sure to propagate the RequestMethodNotSupportedException as the
superclass knows how to deal with it.

Listing 6-61. *Example of Ensuring HTTP Method for a Request Handling Method*

```
public ModelAndView findByUsername(HttpServletRequest request,
        HttpServletResponse response, SearchCriteria criteria)
        throws RequestMethodNotSupportedException {
    ensureMethod(request, METHOD_GET);
    Account account = accountService.findAccountByUsername(
                criteria.getSearchBy());
    return new ModelAndView("viewAccount", "account", account);
}
```

■**Tip** This technique is nice because it fails fast and can protect the semantics of your request handling method. Plus, it generates the appropriate HTTP error code (405) so that clients know exactly what the error was.

A second strength you can see is that `MultiActionController` supports binding the request to a command bean. For this example each request is using the same bean class, `SearchCriteria`, but in fact each request handling method can use a different command bean class. We are using a static inner class for convenience, but any type of JavaBean can be used.

The `MultiActionController` will, by default, create an instance of the specified command bean by simply calling `Class.newInstance()`. A new instance of the command object is created for every request. If you wish to change this behavior, override `newCommandObject()` in your subclass. Options for alternate object creation include pulling an instance from a `BeanFactory` or using method injection to transparently return a new instance.

A downside of using command beans is that, as we've mentioned before, the `MultiActionController` doesn't provide a form handling work flow. This means that if there is a data binding error, there is no way to trap that exception inside the controller itself. The exception handling facilities alluded to earlier only apply to exceptions thrown from inside the request handling methods. Any data binding exceptions, or errors generated from validation, are thrown outside the class. From there you can use the `DispatcherServlet`'s exception mapping and handling facilities, but this can become complicated. Our advice is to simply not attempt to emulate a form handling, or intelligent command data binding, work flow with `MultiActionController`. It is because of this that you do not see the use of `Validators` in this example.

However, this controller does provide exception handling capabilities, useful for business logic exceptions. We will now append our example (shown in Listing 6-62) to include the handling of a `AccountNotFoundException`, which can be thrown by `AccountService.findAccountByUsername()` in the event that the provided username did not locate an account.

Listing 6-62. *Handling the AccountNotFoundException*

```
public ModelAndView accountNotFound(HttpServletRequest request,
        HttpServletResponse response, AccountNotFoundException e) {
    List<String> errorMessages = new ArrayList<String>();
    errorMessages.add("No account found for " +
            request.getParameter("searchBy"));
    return new ModelAndView("accountFindError", "errorMessages",
            errorMessages);
}
```

The name of the method, in this case `accountNotFound`, has no bearing on the work flow involved. The exception handling method must, however, return `ModelAndView` and have three parameters: `HttpServletRequest`, `HttpServletResponse`, and an instance of `Throwable`.

If no exception handling method is found for a type of exception, a method for its superclass will be searched for, until the class `Throwable` is encountered. This allows you to write one exception handling method to encompass an entire exception class hierarchy.

Summary

In classic Spring Framework style, the `MultiActionController` looks simple and straightforward, but can be very configurable and flexible. It allows for one `Controller` instance to handle many different requests by resolving the HTTP request into a method name. The method, itself a request handler, is invoked via reflection, and its arguments are determined at runtime. The arguments must include an `HttpServletRequest` and an `HttpServletResponse`, and the method must return a `ModelAndView` instance. The method may also take either an `HttpSession` object or a command bean of any type.

If you specify a command bean, it will be instantiated and populated with the request parameters. You may specify one or more `Validators`, but if there are any errors there is no easy way to get a reference to them. For this reason, if you wish to perform any data binding and validation, we recommend you do this inside your request handling method. From there you will be able to direct the request appropriately in the event of validation errors.

The strategy for method name resolution is provided by the interface `MethodNameResolver`, and three different implementations are provided, each with their own pros and cons. The default strategy is the `InternalPathMethodNameResolver`, simply converting the last path element of the URI into a method name.

Finally, we can recommend the `MultiActionController` for situations when you have a logical grouping of read only requests, or for very simple POST requests. In either case, it helps if all the requests have some common element, such as acting on the same type class or using the same service object.

AbstractWizardFormController

The `Controllers` we've mentioned up to this point provide stateless request handling, with no explicit features for a multipage work flow. However, there are many situations that call for an ordered and consistent user experience that spans multiple pages.

For instance, the work flow for creating a new account might take two pages, with the first page checking for username and email uniqueness and the second page accepting billing details. Only after the user completes both pages, and no validation errors exist, will the system create the account.

These multistep use cases, commonly called *wizards*, require complex state management for the user experience. To help with this problem, we will use the `org.springframework.web.servlet.mvc.AbstractWizardFormController`, a specialized `Controller` providing the basic infrastructure for multiple form work flows. You should think of this `Controller` as a `SimpleFormController` that has spread its form across multiple pages.

■**Tip** Explore the `SimpleFormController` before attempting to use `AbstractWizardFormController`, as the two controllers treat forms in a similar manner.

Limitations

The AbstractWizardFormController has some limitations that are important to understand before you begin to use it. The Controller really only supports simple multipage work flows that are essentially a single form spread across multiple pages. This Controller was not designed to support arbitrary decision branching, and in no way can it handle a generic state machine. For that, you should turn to Spring Web Flow, covered later in this book. With Spring Web Flow, you can declaratively create arbitrarily complex work flows, allowing the user to travel back and forth through the state machine.

To summarize, use AbstractWizardFormController when you want to split what otherwise would have been a long form into multiple pages. Also, use the AbstractWizardFormController only when you are populating a single command bean across multiple pages. For anything more complex Spring Web Flow is your solution.

■**Caution** The AbstractWizardFormController is for work flows with strict page progression. Use this controller only for splitting a single form across multiple pages.

State Changes

This controller supports three different types of state changes:

- *Page change*: moving from one page to another, either backward (in the event of valida-tion errors, for instance) or forward on success.

- *Cancel*: exiting the wizard in mid–work flow, typically clearing the state of the wizard. This state change is optional.

- *Finish*: formally completing the work flow. This is the end state for the wizard.

By default, the Controller knows which state to enter by examining different well-known request parameters. You may change the heuristics for detecting a state change by overriding the appropriate method (see Table 6-3).

Table 6-3. *Wizard State Change*

State	Default Parameter	Override Method
Page	_targetXXX, where XXX equals the number of the next page view	getTargetPage()
Cancel	_cancel	isCancelRequest()
Finish	_finish	isFinishRequest()

These parameters are normally included as hidden XHTML elements in the form. Each form submission should contain only one of the above parameters. Their values don't matter; only the existence of the parameter is enough to trigger the state change.

Each form can also specify which page it is in the work flow by including a _pageXXX request parameter. By default, the wizard tracks the current page in the HTTP session, but to correctly support the back button, your form should include the _pageXXX parameter. Just like with _targetXXX, replace XXX with the number of the current page.

Listing 6-63 says that the current form represents the first page, and the user should be directed to the second page on a successful form submission.

Listing 6-63. *Declaring Current Page and Next Page Numbers*

```
<input type="hidden" name="_page0" value="true" />
<input type="hidden" name="_target1" value="true" />
```

It is easy to argue that giving the client the responsibility for specifying the target page is a security concern. For instance, it is easy to specify any target on a form submission. When precise control over page progression is required, implement the getTargetPage() method to perform the correct heuristics for target page determination. If you do this, be sure to take into account support for the Back button of the client's browser. In other words, don't base your decision for the target page solely on information in the session, which isn't necessarily updated when the user clicks the Back button.

We keep talking about page numbers, but what do they represent? The wizard is configured with a set of view names, or page names, generally in the order that they should be presented to the user. The page number is the index into the array of view names.

■**Note** The wizard does not enforce the order of the page views, so each page is free to specify any target page to go to next. In other words, just because the user is on page 2 does not mean she must view page 3 next.

For instance, consider the account example mentioned at the beginning of this section. We require two pages, one for username and email, and the other for billing information. When we configure the Controller, we specify these page names in order.

The configuration can be performed inside the Controller's constructor, shown by Listing 6-64.

Listing 6-64. *Constructor Configuration*

```
public CreateAccountWizardController() {
    setPages(new String[]{"usernameAndEmail", "billingDetails"});
}
```

Or inside the bean definition, as is the case with Listing 6-65.

Listing 6-65. *XML Configuration*

```
<bean name="/createAccount"
  class="com.apress.expertspringmvc.flight.web.CreateAccountWizardController">
  <property name="pages">
```

```
      <list>
        <value>usernameAndEmail</value>
        <value>billingDetails</value>
      </list>
    </property>
</bean>
```

Either way is acceptable, but as we have mentioned before, if the list of pages for the wizard is fairly static, we prefer using the constructor method.

URI Mapping

Be aware that there is a single URI for the entire work flow, including all steps and the finish page. This effectively means that a user is prohibited from entering into the middle of a wizard. Luckily, this protects the wizard from ever being in an incorrect state. Any user who attempts to access the wizard via a bookmark will simply be presented with the first page of the wizard.

Validation

Just like SimpleFormController, the wizard controller supports one or more Validators. However, unlike SimpleFormController, the Validators are not automatically invoked during each request. Because each request only fills out some information of the command bean, the standard Validator has no way of knowing which properties of the command bean are missing or simply haven't been filled out yet. Therefore, doing a full validation of the command only makes sense at the end of the wizard.

To validate the command object during the wizard, you must call the appropriate method on your Validator that matches the current page of the wizard. The controller provides a validatePage(Object command, Errors errors, int pageNumber) method for you to implement, where you will call the appropriate validateXxx() method on your Validator given the pageNumber. In other words, you must control how validation is to be performed, because the validate() method will not be called automatically.

Note that at the end of the work flow, and on the _finish event, the controller will again loop through the number of pages and validate each again. This effectively validates the entire command object before the processFinish() method is called.

Page Change Callback

Although life cycle handlers exist for wizard completion and wizard cancellation, you may also optionally implement postProcessPage() to perform some action after a normal page change request.

This method is very useful when the state of the wizard must be persistent, allowing the user to come back and finish the work flow at a later time. If you wish to support something similar to this, persist the command bean inside postProcessPage() to somewhere more permanent than the HTTP session. You will most likely also need to override formBackingObject() to pull the command bean back out of persistence when the user begins the wizard again. Don't forget to also override getInitialPage(), which you can first check to see whether the user had already started the work flow earlier and return the page he left off on.

Work Flow Cancellation

Optionally, you may decide to allow the user to cancel out of the work flow at any time by overriding the processCancel() method. This allows you to perform any cleanup that might have built up during the wizard.

The default state change trigger is the presence of a _cancel request parameter, but you may change the heuristics by overriding isCancelRequest().

You do not need to remove the command object from the session, as that is handled for you by the Controller. At the very least, simply return a ModelAndView instance directing the user to the appropriate page.

Work Flow Completion

This leads us to talk about processFinish(), the only method you must implement with the wizard controller. When the controller encounters either a _finish request parameter, or if you override isFinishRequest() and return true, the command object is validated again, once for each page in the work flow. If there are no errors after a full validation, processFinish() is called, which is where you perform any business logic. As always, you are required to return a ModelAndView, but note that the view name must be set, as the controller does not populate it from the list of page names.

Wizard Example

Let's put together a two-page wizard for the account creation use case mentioned at the beginning of this section. We'll fill out this example with the XHTML files for both pages, the controller itself, and the Validators required. We're including the Validators so you can see how the work flow is altered after errors from validation.

First off, Figures 6-5 and 6-6 shows you what the two screens will look like for the end user.

Figure 6-5. *Wizard page 1*

If the user enters incorrect information, errors will be displayed above the form with a bulleted list. The error messages and the fields that contain the error will be colored red.

Figure 6-6. *Wizard page 1 with errors*

Once the user correctly enters the information for page 1, page 2 is displayed (Figure 6-7), asking for the user's billing address.

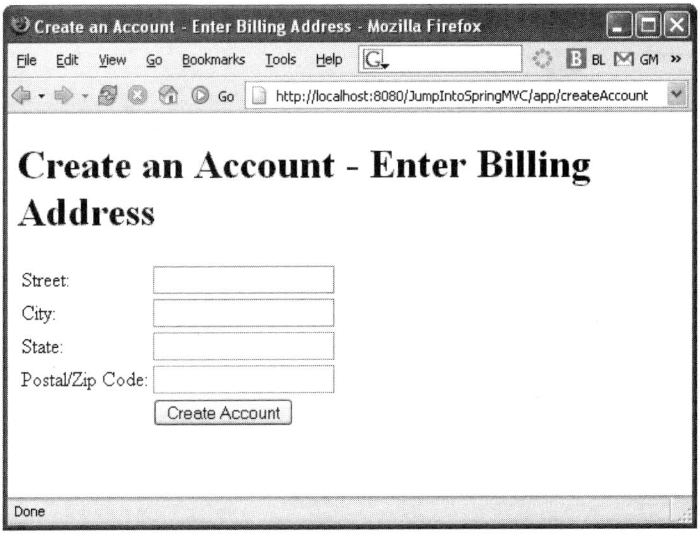

Figure 6-7. *Wizard page 2*

And finally, if there are no errors with page 2, the success screen is displayed (Figure 6-8).

Figure 6-8. *Wizard success page*

Putting it all together, Figure 6-9 illustrates the work flow of the wizard detailing page flow and validation.

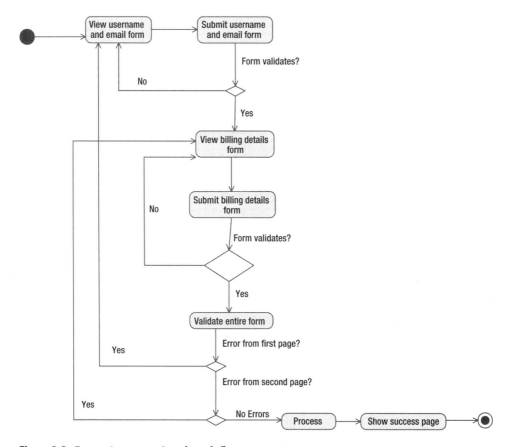

Figure 6-9. *Create Account wizard work flow*

JSP Files

We are taking advantage of many different Spring JSP tags when building these pages. Along with the usual `<spring:bind>` tag, we are also going to use `<spring:hasBindErrors>` and `<spring:message>`. You'll see more about these tags in Chapters 7 and 9, but for now it's important to know that `spring:hasBindErrors` exposes an `errors` attribute to the JSP page if there are validation errors, and `spring:message` performs i18n formatting duties.

We will first build the XHTML page, as shown in Listing 6-66. Pay special attention to the use of the hidden `_page0` and `_target1` form elements.

Listing 6-66. *XHTML for Page 1*

```
<?<?xml version="1.0" encoding="ISO-8859-1" ?>
<%@ taglib uri="http://www.springframework.org/tags" prefix="spring" %>
<%@ taglib uri="http://java.sun.com/jsp/jstl/core" prefix="c" %>
<!DOCTYPE html PUBLIC "-//W3C//DTD XHTML 1.0 Strict//EN"
  "http://www.w3.org/TR/xhtml1/DTD/xhtml1-strict.dtd">
<html xmlns="http://www.w3.org/1999/xhtml">
<head>
<meta http-equiv="Content-Type" content="text/html; charset=ISO-8859-1" />
<title>Create an Account</title>
<link rel="stylesheet" href="<c:url value="/css/main.css" />" type="text/css" />
</head>
<body>

<h1>Create an Account</h1>

<spring:hasBindErrors name="createAccount">
<ul>
<c:forEach items="${errors.allErrors}" var="error">
<li><span class="error"><spring:message message="${error}" /></span></li>
</c:forEach>
</ul>
</spring:hasBindErrors>

<spring:nestedPath path="createAccount">

<form action="" method="post">
<div>
<input type="hidden" name="_page0" value="true" />
<input type="hidden" name="_target1" value="true" />
</div>

<table>

<spring:nestedPath path="account">

<spring:bind path="username">
```

```
<tr>
  <td><label for="${status.expression}"
  <c:if test="${status.error}">class="error"</c:if>>Username:</label></td>
  <td>
      <input type="text" id="${status.expression}" name="${status.expression}"
        value="${status.value}" />

  </</td>
</tr>
</spring:bind>


<spring:bind path="password">
<tr>
  <td><label for="${status.expression}"
  <c:if test="${status.error}">class="error"</c:if>>Password:</label></td>
  <td>
      <input type="password" id="${status.expression}" name="${status.expression}"
        value="${status.value}" />
  </td>
</tr>
</spring:bind>

</spring:nestedPath>

<spring:bind path="confirmPassword">
<tr>
  <td><label for="${status.expression}"
  <c:if test="${status.error}">class="error"</c:if>>Confirm Password:</label></td>
  <td>
      <input type="password" id="${status.expression}" name="${status.expression}"
        value="${status.value}" />
  </td>
</tr>
</spring:bind>

<spring:nestedPath path="account">

<spring:bind path="email">
<tr>
  <td><label for="${status.expression}"
  <c:if test="${status.error}">class="error"</c:if>>Email:</label></td>
  <td>
      <input type="text" id="${status.expression}" name="${status.expression}"
        value="${status.value}" />
  </td>
</tr>
```

```
</spring:bind>
</spring:nestedPath>

<tr>
  <td />
  <td><input type="submit" value="Go to Step 2" /></td>
</tr>

</table>
</form>
</spring:nestedPath>

</body>
</html>
```

The first thing to point out is the two hidden input fields that control the page flow of the wizard. We are specifying both _page and _target to tell the wizard that the user is viewing the first page, and the next page in the wizard is the second page.

As you can see, this page balloons in size when you incorporate all of the Spring JSP tags and appropriate error messaging. We want to take a small diversion from building the wizard to show you a few ways to handle this large JSP file.

Reducing Repetition with JSP Tag Files and Spring JSP Tags

In Listing 6-66, there is a lot of duplicate code that should be eliminated to not only save file size but also to increase readability and reduce typing. There are at least two areas in the file that we can replace with simple tag files, a convenient way in JSP 2.0 to write custom tags as easily as writing JSP pages. Think of a tag file as a JSP include that can take parameters; they are very useful when creating reusable blocks of JSP code.

■**Tip** For more on JSP 2.0 tag files, refer to *JavaServer Pages*, Third Edition, by Hans Bergsten (O'Reilly, 2003).

If you've never heard of JSP 2.0 tag files then don't worry. If you've written any JSP pages they will look very familiar.

Tag files only work in JSP 2.0–compliant environments. This means, among other things, that your servlet container must support JSP 2.0 and that your web.xml file must specify the Servlet 2.4 standard by including version="2.4".

■**Tip** If you are a Tomcat user, make sure you are using Tomcat 5.0 or better to take advantage of the Servlet 2.4, JSP 2.0, and tag files.

The first element we want to pull out of the file is the printing of all the error messages above the form. This code won't change across our wizard pages, and the only unique part is the name of the command bean that errors might be bound to. We will create a tag file for this snippet first.

To create a tag file, create a directory named tags inside WEB-INF. Any file you place in here with an extension of .tag will be available to your JSP pages just like any other JSP tag. The advantage here is that you do not need to write a Tag Library Descriptor (TLD), plus these .tag files are recompiled on the fly just like JSP pages, making development much easier.

Listing 6-67 contains the first tag file, which takes a command bean name and prints any errors.

Listing 6-67. *Errors Tag File*

```
<%@<%@ tag body-content="scriptless" %>
<%@ attribute name="name" required="true" %>
<%@ taglib uri="http://www.springframework.org/tags" prefix="spring" %>
<%@ taglib uri="http://java.sun.com/jsp/jstl/core" prefix="c" %>

<spring:hasBindErrors name="${name}">
<ul>
<c:forEach items="${errors.allErrors}" var="error">
<li><span class="error"><spring:message message="${error}" /></span></li>
</c:forEach>
</ul>
</spring:hasBindErrors>
```

As you can see, the tag file looks a lot like a regular JSP page. The main differences are found at the top of the file, with the tag and attribute elements.

If this looks so much like a JSP file, why not use a simple include instead of this tag file? While includes are perfect for static content, this snippet requires a dynamic name attribute for <spring:hasBindErrors>. By using a tag file instead of an include, we can use this snippet anywhere we want to print out a list of errors from Spring's validation framework.

Can you spot the second grossly repeated snippet from the JSP page? If you suggested that the form input fields and labels look awfully similar, give yourself a hand. Listing 6-68 contains the tagfile for simple <input> form elements. It has two dynamic elements: the path to the field and the name of the field itself.

Listing 6-68. *Form Field Tag File*

```
<%@ tag body-content="scriptless" %>
<%@ attribute name="name" required="true" %>
<%@ attribute name="path" required="true" %>
<%@ attribute name="type" required="false" %>
<%@ taglib uri="http://www.springframework.org/tags" prefix="spring" %>
<%@ taglib uri="http://java.sun.com/jsp/jstl/core" prefix="c" %>

<c:if test="${empty type}">
<c:set var="type" value="text" scope="page" />
</c:if>
```

```
<spring:bind path="${path}">
<tr>
  <td><label for="${status.expression}"
  <c:if test="${status.error}">class="error"</c:if>>${name}:</label></td>
  <td>
      <input type="${type}" id="${status.expression}" name="${status.expression}"
        value="${status.value}" />
  </td>
</tr>
</spring:bind>
```

This tag file encapsulates the printing of the table row, checking whether the field has an error, and filling out the `<input>` tag's attribute values. It can also handle both text and password `<input>` fields by specifying the type attribute, though text is the default.

This tag file can be improved upon, based on your flexibility needs. For instance, the name and path attributes might be considered redundant if you already have a translation of the path attribute in your messages file. You may consider passing the path attribute value into the `<spring:message>` tag to get the current locale's translation for the field name.

Let's put it all together and use these helpful new tag files in our original JSP file, modified in Listing 6-69.

Listing 6-69. *Page 1: JSP File with Tag Files*

```
<?xml version="1.0" encoding="ISO-8859-1" ?>
<%@ taglib uri="http://www.springframework.org/tags" prefix="spring" %>
<%@ taglib uri="http://java.sun.com/jsp/jstl/core" prefix="c" %>
<%@ taglib tagdir="/WEB-INF/tags" prefix="tag" %>
<!DOCTYPE html PUBLIC "-//W3C//DTD XHTML 1.0 Strict//EN"
  "http://www.w3.org/TR/xhtml1/DTD/xhtml1-strict.dtd">
<html xmlns="http://www.w3.org/1999/xhtml">
<head>
<meta http-equiv="Content-Type" content="text/html; charset=ISO-8859-1" />
<title>Create an Account</title>
<link rel="stylesheet" href="<c:url value="/css/main.css" />" type="text/css" />
</head>
<body>

<h1>Create an Account</h1>

<tag:errors name="createAccount" />

<spring:nestedPath path="createAccount">

<form action="" method="post">
<div>
<input type="hidden" name="_page0" value="true" />
<input type="hidden" name="_target1" value="true" />
</div>
```

```
<table>

<spring:nestedPath path="account">

<tag:formField name="Username" path="username" />
<tag:formField name="Password" path="password" type="password"/>

</spring:nestedPath>

<tag:formField name="Confirm Password" path="confirmPassword" type="password"/>

<spring:nestedPath path="account">

<tag:formField name="Email" path="email" />

</spring:nestedPath>

<tr>
  <td />
  <td><input type="submit" value="Go to Step 2" /></td>
</tr>

</table>
</form>
</spring:nestedPath>

</body>
</html>
```

Notice that to the JSP file, the tag files are used just like any other tag element. The only difference is found in the `taglib` declaration: when using tag files, you must specify a `tagdir` attribute instead of a `uri` attribute. As with all JSP tags, the prefix is arbitrary, so feel free to use whatever you like.

At least now the file has more XHTML elements than JSP elements, so I think we did a good job. What should you take away from this? Creating user interface elements should fall under the same scrutiny as your code. If you find yourself repeating yourself with similar snippets in JSP files, take advantage of includes and tag files to minimize repetition and to create more easily understood files.

With the new tag files complete, we are in a good position to create the second page of the wizard, as shown in Listing 6-70.

Listing 6-70. *Page 2: Enter Billing Address*

```
<?xml version="1.0" encoding="ISO-8859-1" ?>
<%@ taglib uri="http://www.springframework.org/tags" prefix="spring" %>
<%@ taglib uri="http://java.sun.com/jsp/jstl/core" prefix="c" %>
<%@ taglib tagdir="/WEB-INF/tags" prefix="tag" %>
```

```
<!DOCTYPE html PUBLIC "-//W3C//DTD XHTML 1.0 Strict//EN"
  "http://www.w3.org/TR/xhtml1/DTD/xhtml1-strict.dtd">
<html xmlns="http://www.w3.org/1999/xhtml">
<head>
<meta http-equiv="Content-Type" content="text/html; charset=ISO-8859-1" />
<title>Create an Account - Enter Billing Address</title>
</head>
<body>

<h1>Create an Account - Enter Billing Address</h1>

<tag:errors name="createAccount" />

<spring:nestedPath path="createAccount">

<form action="" method="post">
<div>
<input type="hidden" name="_page1" value="true" />
<input type="hidden" name="_finish" value="true" />
</div>

<table>

<spring:nestedPath path="account.billingAddress">

<tag:formField name="Street" path="street" />
<tag:formField name="City" path="city" />
<tag:formField name="State" path="state" />
<tag:formField name="Postal/Zip Code" path="postalCode" />

</spring:nestedPath>

<tr>
  <td />
  <td><input type="submit" value="Create Account" /></td>
</tr>

</table>
</form>
</spring:nestedPath>

</</body>
</html>
```

For the second page, we've changed the _page parameter to reflect this page, and we've indicated that this form will trigger the _finish event. The _finish parameter is important to include, as this is the default way the wizard will know if the work flow is complete.

Due to our tag files, this page is fairly succinct and easy to read. Another reason for this is our use of the `<spring:nestedPath>` tag. We take advantage of it to make the tags for the address fields a bit easier to read and write. Without the `<spring:nestedPath path="account.billingAddress">` tag, the `tag:formField` tags would need to include the entire path to the fields: `<tag:formField name="Street" path="account.billingAddress.street" />`. As you can imagine, this would become verbose and tedious. Not only do we save typing by using `<spring:nestedPath>`, but we're now able to create generic address XHTML code without worrying what the full path to the fields are. For instance, we can use the same chunk of XHTML to display an address for both a billing address and a shipping address.

Finally, we present the success page to complete the list of JSP required for the wizard, shown by Listing 6-71.

Listing 6-71. *Wizard Success Page*

```
<?<?xml version="1.0" encoding="ISO-8859-1" ?>
<!DOCTYPE html PUBLIC "-//W3C//DTD XHTML 1.0 Strict//EN"
  "http://www.w3.org/TR/xhtml1/DTD/xhtml1-strict.dtd">
<html xmlns="http://www.w3.org/1999/xhtml">
<head>
<meta http-equiv="Content-Type" content="text/html; charset=ISO-8859-1" />
<title>Account Successfully Created</title>
</head>
<body>

<h1>Account Successfully Created</h1>

<p>
Congratulations, ${account.username}, your account was
created successfully.
</p>

</body>
</html>
```

Command Bean

Every good wizard needs a command bean that contains all the form fields from all those pages. Because we are writing a Spring MVC application, we will use the Account class from our domain model. This class contains the username, password, email address, and billing address of the user.

However, the work flow requires that the user confirm her password, so where does that form field live? We don't want to place confirm password inside the Account class, because after the form is submitted successfully, we don't care about that field anymore. Instead of allowing the UI requirements to influence the design of the domain model, we will create a command bean class (Listing 6-72) that contains both the Account class and the confirm password property. This way we can still use the Account class and directly populate it from the request, as well as incorporate any extra fields required for the work flow.

Listing 6-72. *Wizard Command Class*

```
public class CreateAccount {

    private Account account = new Account();
    private String confirmPassword;

    public Account getAccount() {
        return account;
    }
    public void setAccount(Account account) {
        this.account = account;
    }
    public String getConfirmPassword() {
        return confirmPassword;
    }
    public void setConfirmPassword(String confirmPassword) {
        this.confirmPassword = confirmPassword;
    }

}
```

You might remember all those <spring:nestedPath> tags we used in the JSP files. You can see here why we need to use them, as the Account class is nested inside the command bean (instead of being the command bean itself). And the Address object is inside the Account, requiring another <spring:nestedPath> tag.

■**Tip** The <spring:nestedTag> is not required if you have nested objects in your command bean, but it comes in handy when you begin to modularize your JSP pages.

Controller

It is time to look at the concrete implementation of the wizard itself, which surprisingly isn't that complicated. The AbstractWizardFormController does a good job at performing the work of page flows and validation. All that we have left to do is to fill out the validation logic and save the Account instance at the end of the wizard. Listing 6-73 contains the Controller implementation.

Listing 6-73. *Wizard Controller*

```
public class CreateAccountWizardController extends AbstractWizardFormController {

    private AccountService accountService;

    public CreateAccountWizardController() {
        setCommandName("createAccount");
```

```
        setCommandClass(CreateAccount.class);
        setValidator(new CreateAccountValidator());
        setPages(new String[]{"usernameAndEmail", "billingAddress"});
    }

    public void setAccountService(AccountService accountService) {
        this.accountService = accountService;
    }

    @Override
    protected void validatePage(Object command, Errors errors, int page) {
        CreateAccount createAccount = (CreateAccount) command;
        CreateAccountValidator validator = (CreateAccountValidator) getValidator();
        switch (page) {
        case 0:
            validator.validatePage0(createAccount, errors);
            break;
        case 1:
            validator.validatePage1(createAccount, errors);
            break;
        }
    }

    @Override
    protected ModelAndView processFinish(HttpServletRequest request,
            HttpServletResponse response, Object command, BindException errors)
            throws Exception {
        CreateAccount createAccount = (CreateAccount) command;
        accountService.saveAccount(createAccount.getAccount());
        return new ModelAndView("createAccountSuccess",
                "account", createAccount.getAccount());
    }

}
```

This controller looks a lot like a SimpleFormController, with the exception of the validatePage() method.

Summary

The AbstractWizardFormController provides a multistep wizard work flow, appropriate for splitting large forms across many pages. This wizard works with a single command object, populating it as the user moves through the pages.

The wizard supports three different types of state changes: page change, cancellation, and completion. By default, each state change is triggered by the existence of well-known request parameters, but this behavior is easily overridden with the appropriate methods.

Validation is done in piecemeal style as the user moves through the wizard, validating only parts of the command bean on each step. At the last step in the wizard, all validations are run again in order, effectively validating the complete command bean.

This controller should not be used for arbitrary work flows. Instead you should use Spring Web Flow, which is capable of handling complex state changes and page flows.

ThrowawayController

There are at least two schools of thought on how to model a request/response-type web framework. The first says that the request is something that should be passed around to stateless handlers, which is exactly how servlets and `Controllers` work. The second school of thought says that the request should be modeled with the Command pattern and directly executed. This matches how WebWork (`http://www.opensymphony.com/webwork`) has modeled its request handling, for instance. If this is your cup of tea, Spring MVC provides an `org.springframework.web.servlet.mvc.throwaway.ThrowawayController` that implements the Command pattern for request handling.

Up to now, you've seen `Controllers` as stateless singletons in the system, working directly with the `HttpServletRequest` and `HttpServletResponse` objects in order to process requests. The `ThrowawayController` provides the alternative to this model because it encapsulates both the state of the request as well as the behavior. The `ThrowawayController` is also a prototype bean; a new instance is created for each request. For these reasons, `ThrowawayControllers` are an entirely different breed of request handler, so much so that they don't even implement the `Controller` interface.

■**Tip** Controllers such as `SimpleFormController` do not have to be singletons. You may configure any controller type as a prototype if you wish, but `ThrowawayController` must be a prototype because its design is not thread safe.

`ThrowawayControllers` are meant to act as the command bean and the request handler. This controller literally adds an `execute()` method to a command bean, so that you may directly execute it. Listing 6-74 contains the `ThrowawayController` interface.

Listing 6-74. *ThrowawayController Interface*

```
public interface ThrowawayController {
   ModelAndView execute() throws Exception;
}
```

The request parameters will be bound to your concrete subclass just like a command bean. After binding, and assuming no errors were encountered, the `execute()` method will be called.

Notice how this controller does not have access to any Servlet API classes, such as `ServletRequest` or `HttpSession`. If you require these classes, you will need to use the `Controller` interface.

The lack of the presence of the Servlet API can be considered a benefit, as it makes it easier to test this class. There is no need to create a `MockHttpServletRequest` just to test the controller.

When should you use this controller type instead of the others we've presented? First off, if you find it convenient to treat the request as a true command object then the `ThrowawayController` is exactly what you need. This style of controller makes it easy to route the request around a system, with the ability to call methods on the controller and affect its state. Second, if your controller is really simple and you don't require access to the `HttpServletRequest` and `HttpServletResponse` classes, this class does allow for easier to create tests.

You may not want to use this `Controller` if the request is read-only and does not submit any data. These cases usually do not require any state while performing the request, which negates the need for a Command pattern implementation. Of course, you are free to implement every request handler with `ThrowawayController`, but the downside might be a higher rate of garbage collection (which should only be a problem under very high loads).

Also, the `ThrowawayController` does not implement any form work flow, which makes it more cumbersome to handle forms, validation, errors, and so on.

■**Note** Modern JVMs have sophisticated object creation and lifespan algorithms that can usually cope with the constant creation of objects. The overhead of creating a new instance of `ThrowawayController` is nearly negligible. As always, if under doubt, run your system with a profiler under heavy load and watch for garbage collection performance.

Example

For an example of a `ThrowawayController`, we will add a `CancelAccountController` (Listing 6-75) to the system. A form will request an `Account`'s username, and the `Controller` will attempt to find the account and then cancel it.

Listing 6-75. *CancelAccountController*

```
public class CancelAccountController implements ThrowawayController {

    private AccountService accountService;

    private String username;

    public void setUsername(String username) {
        this.username = username;
    }

    public void setAccountService(AccountService accountService) {
        this.accountService = accountService;
    }
```

```
    public ModelAndView execute() throws Exception {
        if (!StringUtils.hasText(username)) {
            return new ModelAndView("cancelAccount", "errorMessage",
                    "Username must not be blank.");
        }
        try {
            accountService.cancelAccount(username);
            return new ModelAndView("cancelAccountSuccess");
        } catch(AccountNotFoundException e) {
            return new ModelAndView("cancelAccount", "errorMessage",
                    "No account found with username " + username);
        }
    }

}
```

Configuring this `Controller` is similar to all other `Controllers`, except you must specify `singleton="false"` in the bean definition. This will ensure a new instance is created for every request. Otherwise, each request will use the same instance of the `Controller` and risk overwriting the property values. Listing 6-76 contains the bean definition for the `CancelAccountController`.

Listing 6-76. *CancelAccountController Bean Definition*

```
<bean name="/cancelAccount" singleton="false"
  class="com.apress.expertspringmvc.flight.web.CancelAccountController">
  <property name="accountService" ref="accountService" />
</bean>
```

■**Caution** Neither the `DispatcherServlet` nor the `ThrowawayControllerHandlerAdapter` will provide a warning if the controller is a singleton, so double-check your `ThrowawayControllers` are indeed prototypes.

It should be noted that the `ThrowawayController` requires its own `ThrowawayController`➥ `HandlerAdapter` to function. If you have specified and configured one or more handler adapters in your `WebApplicationContext`, you will need to also include `ThrowawayController`➥ `HandlerAdapter` if you choose to use that type of controller. By default, the `DispatcherServlet` will include both `SimpleControllerHandlerAdapter` and `ThrowawayControllerHandlerAdapter`, but it will ignore the defaults if at least one handler adapter is explicitly declared in the `WebApplicationContext`.

As you can tell, there is no way to handle any sort of data binder errors inside the `Controller`. If an error does occur, the `ServletRequestBindingException` will be thrown by the handler adapter, and it will be left up to any exception resolvers found in the `WebApplicationContext` to properly deal with the exception. This is probably not what you want, so if a binding error could occur while populating the `ThrowawayController`, you will need to instead implement a `ValidatableThrowawayController` (covered in the next section).

Summary

The ThrowawayController is an alternate request handling method compared to the Controllers we've seen so far. It is intended to encapsulate both the request parameters as well as the behavior associated with the request. A new ThrowawayController is created for each request, so it must be a prototype bean (by specifying singleton="false" in the bean definition).

Request parameters are bound directly to the controller, and if there are no data binding errors, the controller's execute() method is called to handle the request.

ValidatableThrowawayController

The standard ThrowawayController can't support any fine grained data binding configuration because there is no callback to specify any custom PropertyEditors. If there are any data binding errors, the controller never knows about them, making proper error handling cumbersome.

Enter the ValidatableThrowawayController, as shown in Listing 6-77, which adds a bit more complexity but fills in the gaps of error handling. This controller type is still a stateless Command pattern implementation of a controller, so you should use it wherever you would use a ThrowawayController but require the ability to register custom PropertyEditors or build work flows that take into account any errors.

Listing 6-77. *ValidatableThrowawayController*

```
public interface ValidatableThrowawayController {

    String getName();
    void initBinder(DataBinder binder) throws Exception;
    ModelAndView execute(BindException errors) throws Exception;

}
```

If you wish to use this controller, you must also declare a ValidatableThrowaway➡ControllerHandlerAdapter in your WebApplicationContext. If you do, be sure to also include any other handler adapters, as the defaults are only included if no handler adapter is found in the ApplicationContext.

HandlerInterceptors

The Servlet 2.3 specification introduced the idea of *filters*, common code that can wrap one or more servlets to provide pre- and post-processing of the request and response. Spring MVC supports an analogous concept with its HandlerInterceptors, which wrap request handlers to provide common functionality. Interceptors handle more life cycle events than a standard filter, but filters are more powerful, in that they may directly manipulate or replace the HttpServletRequest and HttpServletResponse objects.

Listing 6-78 contains the HandlerInterceptor interface.

Listing 6-78. *HandlerInterceptor Interface*

```
public interface HandlerInterceptor {

  boolean preHandle(HttpServletRequest request, HttpServletResponse response,
    Object handler) throws Exception;
  void postHandle(HttpServletRequest request, HttpServletResponse response,
    Object handler, ModelAndView modelAndView) throws Exception;

  void afterCompletion(HttpServletRequest request, HttpServletResponse response,
    Object handler, Exception ex) throws Exception;
}
```

Three life cycle points can be intercepted. See Table 6-4.

Table 6-4. *Interceptor Life Cycle Points*

Method Name	Description
preHandle	Called before the request handler is invoked. If it returns false, the request handler is never invoked, and the rest of the interceptor's methods are never called.
postHandle	Called after the handler finishes but before the view is rendered. Useful for placing common objects into the model.
afterCompletion	Called after the view is rendered, even if there was an error in handling the request. Useful for resource cleanup.

HandlerInterceptor Example

Our simple example of a HandlerInterceptor (shown in Listing 6-79) will insert the current time into the model after the controller has finished, but before the view is rendered. The difficult part of using interceptors is not in implementing them but in configuring them.

Listing 6-79. *HandlerInterceptor Example*

```
public class DateInsertionInterceptor implements HandlerInterceptor {

    public boolean preHandle(HttpServletRequest request,
            HttpServletResponse response, Object handler) throws Exception {
        return true;    // always continue
    }

    public void postHandle(HttpServletRequest request,
            HttpServletResponse response, Object handler,
            ModelAndView modelAndView) throws Exception {
        modelAndView.addObject("currentTime", new Date());
    }
```

```
    public void afterCompletion(HttpServletRequest request,
            HttpServletResponse response, Object handler, Exception ex)
            throws Exception {
        // nothing
    }

}
```

HandlerMapping instances create a HandlerChain, combining HandlerInterceptors with the request handler such as a Controller. Therefore, HandlerInterceptors much be bound to HandlerMappings.

If you want the interceptor to apply to all request handlers and you are using only the BeanNameUrlHandlerMapping object, then the configuration is fairly straightforward. Listing 6-80 contains an example configuration and definition for the DateInsertionInterceptor.

Listing 6-80. *HandlerInterceptor Configuration*

```
<bean id="handlerMapping"
  class="org.springframework.web.servlet.handler.BeanNameUrlHandlerMapping">
  <property name="interceptors">
    <list>
      <bean
        class="com.apress.expertspringmvc.flight.web.DateInsertionInterceptor" />
    </list>
  </property>
</bean>
```

The above configuration is more verbose than normal, as now you must declare the BeanNameUrlHandlerMapping, which previously was the implicit default.

■**Note** Here we are taking advantage of Spring's support for inner bean definitions, useful in this context because the interceptor bean is only needed inside this HandlerMapping.

The only way to configure which interceptors will handle each URI is to bind them to the appropriate HandlerMapping instance. This might mean you need to create more HandlerMapping objects just to handle the way you would like the interceptors to be handled.

Summary

HandlerInterceptors are an excellent opportunity to apply common business logic to many Controllers. They act much like filters, in that they intercept the request handling pipeline. They are capable of bypassing the request handling altogether, placing common objects into the model, and cleaning up resources after every request.

Interceptors are bound to HandlerMapping objects, so any request that the handler mapping can handle will be routed through all of its interceptors and a single request handler.

Controllers Summary

One of Spring MVC's major strengths is its rich collection of `Controller` options. From the very simple (`Controller` interface) to the complex (`AbstractWizardFormController`), Spring MVC has a deep controller hierarchy that is extensible and configurable.

The major design theme for these classes is best summed up with the Open-Closed Principle, which states that classes should be open for extension but closed for modification. Many of these controllers lock their behavior down with methods marked as final, but provide useful extension points for subclasses.

Table 6-5 summarizes the different controller options.

Table 6-5. *Controller Options*

Name	Description
`Controller`	Unifying interface, with no work flow defined.
`AbstractController`	Perfect for all read-only request handlers and has many useful features.
`SimpleFormController`	Provides a form handling work flow, including validation.
`AbstractWizardFormController`	Splits a long form across multiple pages; includes validation support.
`MultiActionController`	Handles multiple URIs with different methods inside the controller itself.
`ThrowawayController`	Non-singleton controller; implements the Command pattern; unaware of the Servlet API.
`ValidatableThrowawayController`	Like the `ThrowawayController`, but aware of data binding errors.
`UrlFilenameViewController`	Hides view-only resources behind application URIs; parses the URI itself.
`ParameterizableViewController`	Hides view-only resources behind the application URI by read a configuration parameter.

■**Note** There are often many intermediate subclasses between the `Controller` classes mentioned in the above table, so look for other options when you require specific overridable behavior.

`HandlerInterceptors` provide filter-like abilities to wrap requests and control the processing pipeline. They are able to bypass `Controllers`, interject common objects into the model for views, or even clean up resources after the request is handled. Interceptors are bound to `HandlerMappings`, which in turn create a `HandlerChain` made up of all the interceptors and a single `Controller`.

The `SimpleFormController` and any `Controller` that subclasses `BaseCommandController` will create command objects to encapsulate the form fields from the request. With the help of `PropertyEditors`, the properties of the command objects may be of any type (`Strings`, `ints`, `java.util.Date`, and so on). The `ServletRequestDataBinder` is responsible for performing the actual binding of request parameters to command objects.

This chapter has briefly mentioned validation, which controllers like SimpleFormController and AbstractWizardFormController have explicit support for. Some validation may take place at the DataBinder level, with its support for required fields. For complex validation, however, you must use the Validator interface, covered in Chapter 9.

We briefly mentioned Views in this chapter, as we looked at building the screens for some of the form controllers and the wizard example. Like Controllers, Spring MVC supports a rich selection of view technologies and integrates them nicely into a cohesive package. The next chapter covers the different view options, including JSPs and the Spring JSP tags.

CHAPTER 7

■■■

The View Layer

This chapter discusses the user interface layer, or view layer, of your Web MVC application. We investigate what the goal of a view is, why it should be considered separately in an application, and how Spring's view layer architecture helps you achieve the goal of producing a user interface independent of the Model and the Controllers.

We will take a detailed tour of the mechanisms used by Spring to manage views, and we'll explore the benefits to be gained from this framework design. We'll cover Views, ViewResolvers, and their relationship to Models and Controllers.

What's in a View

Chapter 4 introduced views on the whistle-stop tour of the sample MVC application. It's important to be familiar with those concepts introduced, because in this chapter we're going to find out what really makes them "tick" and how they interact with all the other parts of an MVC application.

A view serves a dual purpose in a Web MVC application. Primarily, a view is responsible for the display of a model that has been generated by a Controller. Additionally, views may also present the user with suitable options for continued interaction with the application. In an MVC application, it's often useful to think of the model as the contract between the Controller and the View: the View can only see what the Controller passes it via the model.

When Controller components generate a model ready for a view to display, that model should be complete. The view concentrates only on displaying the model and on presenting the options your users can choose next. In normal circumstances, the view should never need to call back into any Controller code, access domain logic, or perform data retrieval functions.

■**Note** You may have come across OpenSessionInView, a common counterexample to this maxim. A view may need to retrieve additional pages from a data store after initially rendering, rather than slowing down the application by having all of the data loaded prior to displaying the first page. Here, the data store session remains open while the view is rendered.

If you're developing console applications, your user interface might consist of a menu of options keyed by letter or number. For browser-based views, the more familiar form fields, hyperlinks, buttons, and images are used, while in rich clients, sets of widgets or UI components are available to handle user input. Not all views will implement this function, particularly if the view consists of a nominally read-only data set like an invoice or a report.

Treating Views in Isolation

An application's choice of view technology should be considered independently from the work flow and `Controller` components. This is generally considered good design and is important for several reasons.

- In multiskilled teams, commonly found on all but small projects, there are likely to be people with specific areas of expertise in designing interfaces. These team members need to be able to work unencumbered by programming knowledge, just as the programmers need to do their job without knowledge of how data will be presented.

- Your application may require at the outset, or in the future, that other view types be supported in addition to the primary one. For example, a web application may offer the user the option of viewing the results of some operation as a PDF file rather than as HTML in the browser. Similarly, an application may define a requirement to support different devices such as mobile phones and rich clients

- A separate view layer makes for a more maintainable application, and for most projects, far more money is spent on maintenance than initial development.

Therefore you'll need to consider the functionality of your application distinctly from the code that generates the relevant markup language or windowing objects. In the past, web applications were often developed in a way that meant much of the control and work flow in the application was tied very closely to the view tier. This design is still found today in some Java-based applications, but more commonly in applications developed in languages like PHP and Perl. The JSP architecture is actually partly to blame in J2EE applications, because it makes it too easy to combine complex work flow logic (and in the worst cases, domain and data access logic) with the view. This common "Model 1" design, appropriate for only the most trivial of projects, will often remain in place as applications grow instead of being factored out into a cleaner set of layers as it really should.

Spring's View Interface

The `DispatcherServlet` and Spring `Controllers` treat views in an implementation-agnostic manner. That means you can define one or more views using different technologies and either use them together or switch them around without impacting any of your `Controller` code. In many cases, you need make no more than a single change to a configuration file in order to replace the entire view tier of your application with a new one! Two interfaces— `org.springframework.web.servlet.View` and `org.springframework.web.servlet.ViewResolver`— primarily make this possible. Listing 7-1 shows the definition of the View interface.

Listing 7-1. *View Interface Definition*

```
public interface View {
    void render(Map model, HttpServletRequest request,
HttpServletResponse response) throws Exception;
}
```

■**Note** Many of Spring's high-level interfaces consist only of a single method. This facilitates the maximum amount of reuse from interfaces and makes them good candidates for anonymous inner class implementations.

The interface is simple. It says that, given a model and the servlet's request and response objects, a View will generate, or render, the output. It assumes nothing else, and that means you have the widest possible choice when selecting an implementation. As we'll see later, though, creating your own View implementation is quite rare; more commonly you'll use one of the built-in Spring view types.

Implementing View

The render() method of the View interface returns void. The buck stops here as far as Spring MVC is concerned; it is the responsibility of the view not just to generate the content but to actually return it to the client too, if appropriate.

We could, therefore, successfully implement a view with the example in Listing 7-2.

Listing 7-2. *Example View Implementation*

```
public class ModelIteratorView implements View {
    public void render(Map model, HttpServletRequest request,
        HttpServletResponse response) throws Exception {

        PrintWriter out = new PrintWriter(response.getOutputStream());
        for (Object key : model.keySet()) {
            out.print(key.toString());
            out.print(" = ");
            out.println(model.get(key));
        }
        out.flush();
        out.close();
    }
}
```

OK, so it won't win your website any design awards, but you're fulfilling the very basic requirement of a View. Spring provides many implementations of View that act as hooks for the supported view technologies—for example, InternalResourceView (JSP), VelocityView, AbstractXsltView, and others. We'll cover the specifics of these and others in Chapter 8 as we examine the major view technologies in more detail.

For now, we'll have a quick tour of some of the common supporting functionality that Spring implements and how it applies to the diverse range of subclasses. Figure 7-1 shows the hierarchy of Views that Spring implements for you.

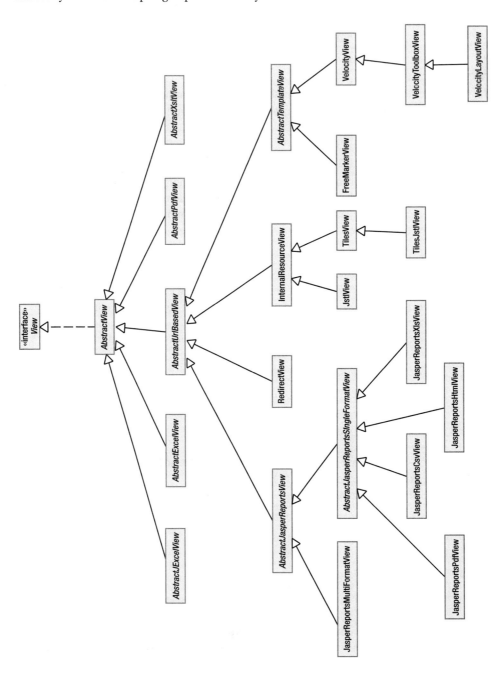

Figure 7-1. *View hierarchy*

The preceding diagram shows that all of the Spring View implementations extend AbstractView and that the majority also descend from AbstractUrlBasedView. Figure 7-2 shows more detail for these classes.

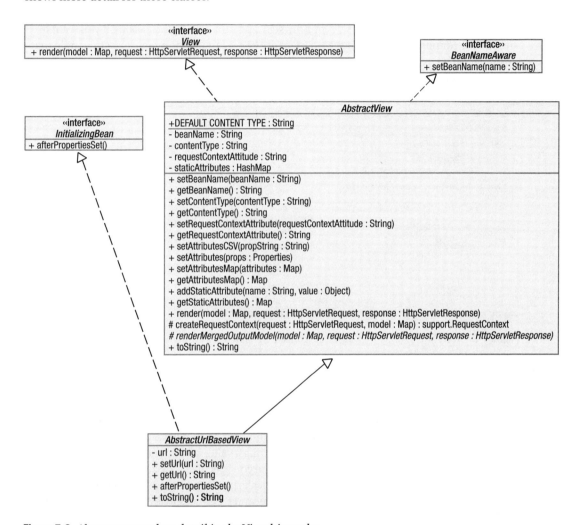

Figure 7-2. *Abstract superclass detail in the View hierarchy*

Spring views don't necessarily need to be HTML-based. In many cases, entirely different content types, including binary, can be rendered to the client. All Spring views support the ability to determine their own content type through AbstractView.setContentType().

By default, this will have the value text/html; charset=ISO-8859-1, and this is appropriate for any view rendering HTML with a Latin character set. The value of the contentType attribute will be used to set the appropriate HTTP headers in the response stream. This indicates to the client device how it should respond. Setting the contentType to a binary MIME type, for example, is likely to cause your browser to pop up a dialog box asking if you want to save the file (or possibly launch it if your machine has an application registered to handle that particular MIME type). Figure 7-3 shows just such an example of a content type that was set in the HTTP response of x-application/pdf.

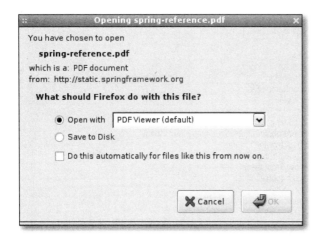

Figure 7-3. *Browser response to a different content type header value*

AbstractView offers the ability to set static attributes on your View instance too. These attributes are independent of the dynamic model generated by the Controllers, and you can set them programmatically or as part of the view configuration. They are useful for including additional data in the view that you don't want to hard-code into, for example, your JSPs or Velocity templates. AbstractView's second contribution to the implementation of your views is the option of declaring a requestContextAttribute name. Setting a value for this will expose the Spring RequestContext object to your view under the name you specified. The RequestContext holds request-specific information such as the theme, locale, binding errors, and localized messages. Support for command and error binding in Velocity and FreeMarker views is based upon exposure of the RequestContext.

Listings 7-3 and 7-4 show how you can use static attributes.

Listing 7-3. *Setting Static Attributes*

```
View view = new InternalResourceView("path");
view.addAttribute("companyName", getThisYearsCompanyName());
view.addAttribute("season", "Summer");
```

Listing 7-4. *Using Attributes in a JSTL View*

```
<p>The name of our company (this year at least) is:
${companyName}</p>
<p>Welcome to our ${season} season of products</p>
```

Once you have added your static attributes to the View instance, they are merged with the dynamic attributes and simply become part of the model as far as the view is concerned.

If any of your dynamic model attributes have the same name as a static attribute, the dynamically generated one will take precedence. This is good because it means that you can define defaults as static attributes and then optionally have your Controller logic override those defaults.

■**Caution** Your attributes must be keyed with Strings. If you use the setAttributesMap() method and the Map contains non-String keys, a runtime exception will be generated.

Obviously your applications aren't going to create views programmatically too often. Much more commonly, you will define the view instances in a configuration file and have Spring create them for you. There are several different ways to do this, and before we dive in and take a look at them, we need to look more closely at the relationship between Controller and View, and to introduce the ViewResolver.

Views and Controllers: Happily Divorced

Spring Controllers specify the following method in their interface shown in Listing 7-5.

Listing 7-5. *Controller Interface Method*

```
ModelAndView handleRequest(HttpServletRequest request,
HttpServletResponse response) throws Exception;
```

The important detail here is the return value from the handleRequest() method. A ModelAndView object is a simple holder enabling your Controller to return two distinct types of object to the caller. The model in question is usually a Map containing keyed object values of the prepared data set that the view will render. The view might either be an implementation itself (of the View interface) or a String holding a name that will later be resolved to an actual View by a ViewResolver, which we'll learn more about in the next section.

Let's look at a sample Controller implementation that takes the first option (Listing 7-6).

Listing 7-6. *Returning a View Instance*

```
public void handleRequestHttpServletRequest request,
HttpServletResponse response) throws Exception {
    Map model = new HashMap();
    model.put("flights", getFlightList());
    View view = new InternalResourceView("/WEB-INF/jsp/flightList.jsp");
    return new ModelAndView(view, model);
}
```

In Listing 7-6, the Controller is responsible for determining the actual view implementation and returns this object along with the model it has generated. Note that this code still makes no assumptions about how that particular view will render the content, and you are still at liberty to change the JSP—or even the implementation of InternalResourceView without reference to any of the Controllers that use it.

The preceding code could be improved by having the Controller look the view up in an ApplicationContext, but it doesn't greatly improve upon the example from a design perspective. The Controller still needs to have too much information about where to find a particular view.

A better alternative, shown in Listing 7-7, is to have the Controller specify a key that names the view. Specifying a name for a view is crucial to how a web framework is able to completely decouple the view from the Controller. A Controller can effectively delegate the choice of view to another object which knows how to find and instantiate a view based on an abstract name. Constructing a ModelAndView with a view name rather than a View instance is much the more common approach in Spring MVC applications and in fact, almost all web frameworks offer a mechanism of addressing views by name.

Listing 7-7. *Returning a Named View*

```
public void handleRequestHttpServletRequest request,
HttpServletResponse response) throws Exception {
    Map model = new HashMap();
    model.put("flights", getFlightList());
    return new ModelAndView("flightList", model);
}
```

In the second example, your Controller knows nothing of the view other than its name. That's good! You are now free to vary the *type* of view that is actually used to render this model, without revisiting even your Controller code.

■**Caution** Be aware that the ModelAndView constructors are slightly counterintuitive, in that you specify the view or view name first, followed by the model.

ViewResolvers

The key to a complete decoupling of the view from the Controller is not to permit the Controller any say in what type of view will be used to render the model. So if the Controller is now divorced from this responsibility, who or what *is* responsible? This job falls to the ViewResolver. ViewResolvers are an important feature in Spring's view layer support.

When your Controller selects a concrete view to return as part of the ModelAndView object, it still knows nothing of *how* that implementation will perform its job. However, it necessarily has knowledge of *which* view will perform the rendering task. In some scenarios this may be acceptable, but in the general case it would be better for your Controllers not to be burdened with this additional responsibility.

This is where a ViewResolver comes into play. Listing 7-8 has the definition for this interface.

Listing 7-8. *The ViewResolver Interface*

```
public interface ViewResolver {
    View resolveViewName(String viewName, Locale locale)
    throws Exception;
}
```

Consistent with many other key Spring interfaces, `ViewResolver` defines a single method for implementation keeping it focused on one particular task.

It should be fairly clear from the interface definition how `ViewResolvers` act as the key link decoupling `Controller` and view.

Putting View Resolution in Context

We've covered much of the detail now of how Spring manages the view tier, decouples views from `Controllers` and operates a sophisticated view resolution strategy. What's missing is an overview of how these objects combine in your Web MVC application—what is responsible for linking them all together?

Let's briefly take a step back up the chain of events and examine a simplified overview of the request/response sequence, noting where the `View` and `ViewResolver` fit in. Figure 7-4 shows a sequence in which the `Controller` returns a `ModelAndView` instance containing the name of a view, rather than a concrete `View` implementation.

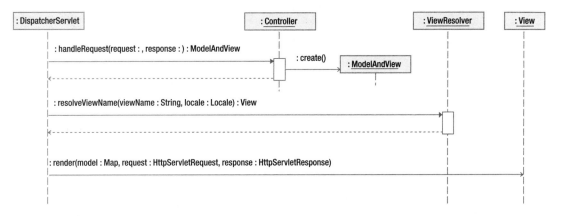

Figure 7-4. *Sequence diagram of named view resolution*

In Figure 7-4 we can see clearly how the view resolution and rendering fits in with the `DispatcherServlet`, which manages the entire operation, and the `Controller` that built our model. The `Controller` plays no part in resolving the view in this sequence and is entirely oblivious of the operation.

Types of ViewResolver

ViewResolver is a strategy interface within the framework. In order to get a better handle on how view resolution is applied through this interface, we'll introduce some of the abstract and concrete implementations. Figure 7-5 details the relationships between various ViewResolver classes.

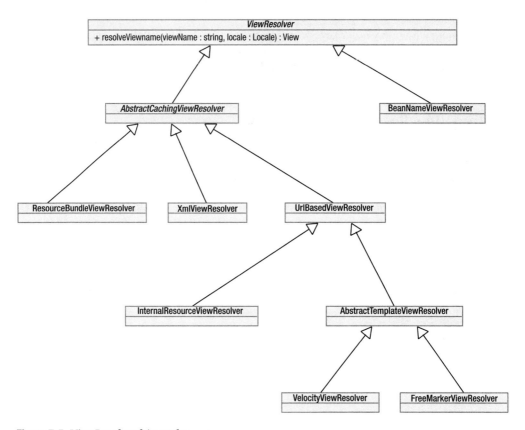

Figure 7-5. *ViewResolver hierarchy*

That's a lot of ViewResolvers, so what do they all do? Let's briefly examine some of the more important ones.

- BeanNameViewResolver is a simple implementation of the interface that is useful in smaller applications. It attempts to resolve views as beans defined in the ApplicationContext, so the name of the view is the id of a bean. This resolver needs no additional configuration, but it has the disadvantage of requiring view beans to be defined in the ApplicationContext file.

- AbstractCachingViewResolver is the superclass to all resolvers that wish to cache their view objects. Creating a View can be an expensive operation, so this is a useful piece of common functionality.

- XmlViewResolver creates views based on an XML definition file. This file (/WEB-INF/ views.xml by default) uses the Spring Beans DTD, which has the advantage of making view definitions both familiar and able to use the full power of Spring's bean factories.

- ResourceBundleViewResolver uses view bean definitions in a ResourceBundle in the class-path. By default the base name for this bundle is views, so it will be located in a file called views.properties in the classpath root. ResourceBundleViewResolver is the only resolver that supports internationalization via the standard ResourceBundle mechanism.

- UrlBasedViewResolver expects the symbolic view name to map directly to a URL with optional prefixes and suffixes. Appropriate where arbitrary mapping definitions are not required. This resolver acts as a superclass for JSP- and template-based views.

The other ViewResolvers are extensions of the ones just described and specialize the ViewResolver functionality for particular view technologies. Most of these we'll encounter later as we discuss the view types themselves that those resolvers are used for. For now we'll take a look at two of the non–view-specific resolvers and how to configure them.

ResourceBundleViewResolver

Listing 7-9 shows an extract from a views.properties file. This file, located in the root of the classpath, can be used to define the views in your application when picked up by a ResourceBundleViewResolver. We'll examine some of the concepts being exposed here.

Listing 7-9. *Sample views.properties*

```
parent-view.class=org.springframework.web.servlet.view.JstlView
parent-view.(abstract)=true
parent-view.attributesCSV=title=FlightDeals.com,season=Summer

homepage.parent=parent-view
homepage.url=/WEB-INF/jsp/home.jsp
listFlights.parent=parent-view
listFlights.url=/WEB-INF/jsp/listFlights.jsp
```

■**Caution** Some of the special properties like abstract (shown in the preceding listing), ref, and singleton are enclosed in parentheses to distinguish them from properties of the same name that your class might have. The parent property does not have this requirement, which is inconsistent. This has been corrected for version 1.3.

Our views.properties file is quite short, but there's a lot going on under the covers. First, this is a generic Spring bean definition file. Although using XML is the more typical approach to defining beans, Spring has always supported property file definitions. From these definitions, three beans would be created in the context with ids:

- parent-view

- homepage

- listFlights

PARENT AND ABSTRACT BEANS

We're declaring a parent view under the name parent-view. This isn't used as an actual view in our application (it doesn't have its own URL), but instead makes use of Spring's native bean hierarchy to impose its values on all other beans that declare it as parent. This is similar to subclassing in your Java applications. For the homepage bean (view), Spring will create an object by instantiating `org.springframework.web.servlet.view.JstlView` based on the `parent-view.class` attribute. It will then call `homepage.setAttributesCSV("title=FlightDeals.com,season=Summer");` and then `homepage.setUrl("/WEB-INF/jsp/index.jsp");`. The same will happen for listFlights and any other views we define in this file. The home page and listFlights views that declare parent-view as their parent will now have the class and attributes that the parent view exposed.

As we've already seen, static attributes are overridden by dynamic model items of the same name, so we have introduced a way to set a default value for a couple of model attributes for all views that can be amended by any `Controller`. Although this concept can be used in any Spring bean definition file, it's a particularly useful and powerful one in the view layer, where you often have many views that will need common values.

XmlViewResolver

Your `ApplicationContext` and `DispatcherServlet` context files are usually written in XML using the Spring Beans DTD file. `XmlViewResolver` allows you to write a view definition file using the same familiar syntax. By default, this file is named `WEB-INF/views.xml`, and that's where the resolver will expect to find it unless you configure it to look elsewhere.

The equivalent XML definition of the preceding `views.properties` file is displayed in Listing 7-10.

Listing 7-10. *WEB-INF/views.xml*

```
<?xml version="1.0" encoding="UTF-8"?>
<!DOCTYPE beans PUBLIC "-//SPRING//DTD BEAN//EN"
"http://www.springframework.org/dtd/spring-beans.dtd">

<beans>
    <bean id="parent-view" abstract="true"
    class="org.springframework.web.servlet.view.JstlView">
        <property name="attributes">
            <props>
                <prop key="title">FlightDeals.com</prop>
                <prop key="season">Summer</prop>
            </props>
        </property>
    </bean>

    <bean id="homepage" parent="parent-view">
        <property name="url"
```

```
                value="/WEB-INF/jsp/home.jsp"/>
    </bean>

    <bean id="listFlights" parent="parent-view">
        <property name="url"
            value="/WEB-INF/jsp/listFlights.jsp"/>
    </bean>
</beans>
```

Making ViewResolvers Known to the Dispatcher

You can define any number of ViewResolvers in your application depending upon your circumstance. A ViewResolver definition resides in the Dispatcher servlet's configuration file (WEB-INF/servletName-servlet.xml by default) and is picked up by the dispatcher based on its class type. Listing 7-11 shows a snippet of the DispatcherServlet context file defining a ViewResolver.

Listing 7-11. *Configuring a ViewResolver in the Context File*

```
<beans>
    <bean id="viewResolver"
        class="org.springframework.web.servlet.view.InternalResourceViewResolver">
        <property name="viewClass"
            value="org.springframework.web.servlet.view.JstlView"/>
        <property name="prefix" value="/WEB-INF/jsp/"/>
        <property name="suffix" value=".jsp"/>
    </bean>

    <!-- other beans -->
</beans>
```

■**Tip** Originally, a ViewResolver definition in the dispatcher context file had to take the name viewResolver. This is still common but no longer required as the servlet will find all ViewResolvers by type. If you *really* want it, you can revert to the old behavior by setting the detectAllViewResolvers property of the DispatcherServlet to false.

Chaining ViewResolvers with the Ordered Interface

If you elect to use more than one ViewResolver it's normally because you want to provide a specific type of resolver for a category of views, perhaps PDFs, falling back to the default resolver for everything else. This is referred to as *chaining* ViewResolvers. Whatever the reason for needing different resolvers, you probably want to be in control of the order in which the DispatcherServlet consults them.

In Spring, many classes of object implement the generic Ordered interface. This is a simple interface that defines a single method, getOrder() : int. Groups or collections of objects can be prioritized if they implement the `Ordered` interface and this is what some of the concrete `ViewResolvers` do. Set the order bean property on the resolver to control chaining order, as demonstrated in Listing 7-12.

Listing 7-12. *Ordering View Resolvers*

```
<bean id="defaultViewResolver"
    class="org.springframework.web.servlet.view.InternalResourceViewResolver">
    <property name="viewClass"
        value="org.springframework.web.servlet.view.JstlView"/>
    <property name="prefix" value="/WEB-INF/jsp/"/>
    <property name="suffix" value=".jsp"/>
</bean>

<!-- this will be consulted first as it has a lower 'order' value -->
<bean id="pdfViewResolver"
    class="org.springframework.web.servlet.view.XmlViewResolver">
    <property name="order" value="1"/>
    <property name="location" value="/WEB-INF/views.xml"/>
</bean>
```

■**Caution** A *lower* value for the order property gives it a *higher* priority in the chain. Values for the order property are usually specified in the range 0 .. `Integer.MAX_VALUE`.

Chaining works in the following manner.

- Each `ViewResolver` in turn, according to its ordered property, gets the option of returning a view.

- If the resolver returns `null`, the next resolver in the chain is consulted.

- If a resolver returns a view instance, the dispatcher uses that view, and no further calls are made to other resolvers that might still be in the chain. View resolution ends at the first successful attempt to resolve a view name.

Bear in mind, however, that not all `ViewResolvers` *can* return `null` even though the contract of the interface permits it. In particular, `InternalResourceViewResolver` never returns `null` because its implementation depends on calling the `RequestDispatcher` internally. There's no other way to discover whether a JSP exists, and the `RequestDispatcher.forward()` method can only be called once. This means that your `ViewResolver` will *always* return a view of some description, and this particular resolver should only ever appear last in the chain. Practically, that means that your application can return 404 errors where you don't want them, so it's always important to configure a generic page to handle this type of error.

A Word on Redirecting

Note This section is naturally about views, but we've left it until after the discussion on `ViewResolvers` because we need a degree of knowledge about resolvers before tackling `RedirectViews` fully.

Sometimes you don't want a view to be rendered as part of a single request-response transaction from the client. This usually applies to form data that is POSTed to a `Controller` where the correct response might be to delegate to another `Controller`. When you do this internally, the delegate `Controller` has access to all of the form POST data, which may not be desirable. In addition, the user can double-post the form data by reloading the current page in the browser after submitting the form.

Both of these problems can be overcome by having the `Controller` that receives the form POST issue a redirect to the client, shown in Figure 7-6. This causes the browser to make a new request the URL in the address bar to change too. Now if the user hits the Reload button, she'll get the page that was the subject of the redirect and won't inadvertently submit a new set of form POST details—something that could involve a credit card purchase. The problem and its "Redirect after POST" solution are commonly understood, so let's take a look at how to deal with this in Spring MVC applications.

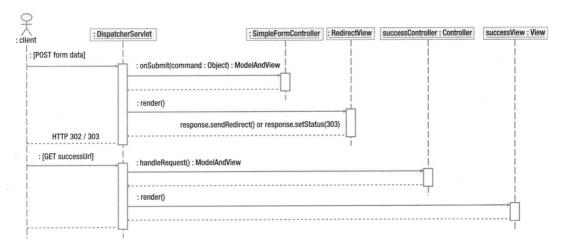

Figure 7-6. *Redirect after POST*

Spring provides a `RedirectView` class—which implements the `View` interface—but under the covers simply sets the response headers to force the client to re-request its configured URL. If you're using `ResourceBundleViewResolver` or `XmlViewResolver`, you can define `RedirectViews` as you would any other view. If, however, you've chosen to use an `UrlBasedViewResolver` or one of its subclasses, then the nature of the resolver makes it impossible to specify a redirect simply by using a logical key as the view name.

You can, of course, simply have your `Controller` create a new `RedirectView` as part of the `ModelAndView` that it returns, but as we've already seen, we don't really want the `Controller` making that decision. The preferred option is to chain two `ViewResolvers` at this point. You should specify an `XmlViewResolver` or `ResourceBundleViewResolver` to resolve views that need to be `RedirectViews`, falling back to the `UrlBasedViewResolvers` for all other views.

If you really can't face chaining `ViewResolvers`, then there is a third alternative—introduced in version 1.1.2 of Spring—specifying a special prefix in the view name. Because a view name can be injected into a `Controller`, this still absolves your controller from knowing that a redirect is going to occur, and hence, you still have completely decoupled components. Listing 7-13 shows the concept.

Listing 7-13. *Using the Redirect Prefix*

```
// viewName should really be injected as a bean property value
String viewName = "redirect:successpage.html";
return new ModelAndView(viewName, model);
```

The actual URL is specified relative to the context root of the web application so that the controller need not be aware of the name that the application was deployed under, although this behavior can be modified in configuration if you really want it.

Themes

You can further enhance your view layer visually through the use of themes. Themes may not be appropriate for all view types—PDF and Excel, for example—but the manner in which you define and use them is consistent across other view types.

Themes are a collection of resources, usually stylesheets (CSS) and images that augment the display of your web pages. Several different themes can coexist in your application together, and a Spring-supplied `ThemeResolver` class does the work of determining which one will be applied in the views.

Let's see an example for better clarity. Listing 7-14 shows the contents of a properties file that specifies some theme keys. We've called this file `winter.properties`.

Listing 7-14. *The Winter Theme Definition Properties File*

```
style=/styles/winter.css
background=/images/snow.png
welcome.message=Brrrr! It's cold.
```

The keys in the theme definition are referred to in your view layer code. In JSP, for example, this can be done with the `<spring:theme>` tag, as shown in Listing 7-15.

Listing 7-15. *Theme Properties Referred to in a JSP*

```
<taglib prefix="spring" uri="http://www.springframework.org/tags"%>
<html>
    <head>
        <link rel="stylesheet"
```

```
            href="<spring:theme code="style"/>"
            type="text/css"/>
  </head>
  <body background="<spring:theme code="background"/>">
    <h1><spring:theme code="welcome.message"/></h1>
    ...
  </body>
</html>
```

The theme tags highlighted in bold will be replaced with the corresponding value from the winter.properties. We might also define a new theme, Summer, that we encapsulate in summer.properties, shown in Listing 7-16.

Listing 7-16. *The "Summer" Theme Definition Properties File*

```
style=/styles/summer.css
background=/images/sun.png
welcome.message=Phew! It's a scorcher.
```

Now, our view can look very different when we switch between winter and summer themes. You can use Spring's theme support to dictate a fixed theme per application that all users see. It can also allow individual users of the application to use a different theme. The missing piece of the puzzle, then, is knowing how the choice of theme is made for any given application or user. Let's see how Spring does that with ThemeSources and ThemeResolvers.

ThemeSources

The properties files that contain the theme's keys are located in the classpath and accessed as resource bundles. By default a ResourceBundleThemeSource is used that will look in the root of the classpath for the properties files.

If you want to place your files elsewhere in the classpath, or if you need to use a custom ThemeSource implementation, you can specify a bean in your context with the reserved name themeSource to do this. A bean with this name will automatically be detected and used by the web ApplicationContext. Listing 7-17 has an example that alters the basename prefix.

Listing 7-17. *ThemeSource Defined in the Web Application Context*

```
<bean id="themeSource"
  class="org.springframework.ui.context.support.ResourceBundleThemeSource">
  <property name="basenamePrefix" value="com.apress.expertspringmvc.themes."/>
</bean>
```

Using the bean definition in the preceding listing, we can place our theme definition files in the specified location of the classpath. Thus, they can be found at com.apress.expertspring-mvc.themes.winter.properties and com.apress.expertspringmvc.themes.summer.properties, respectively.

ThemeResolvers

The ThemeResolver does a very similar job to that of its colleagues, LocaleResolver and ViewResolver. It returns the correct Theme to the dispatcher based upon the application's configuration.

Spring offers three concrete ThemeResolver implementations, shown in Table 7-1.

Table 7-1. *Spring ThemeResolver Implementations*

Implementation	Description
FixedThemeResolver	Always resolves the theme keyed by the name of its defaultThemeName property. All users of the application will see the same theme.
SessionThemeResolver	The name of the theme is stored in the HttpSession for each user. It needs to be set for each user and is not persisted between sessions.
CookieThemeResolver	Similar to the SessionThemeResolver, but the value is stored in a cookie and is persisted between sessions.

The ThemeResolver is listed in the DispatcherServlet's configuration file using the reserved name themeResolver. The dispatcher will automatically use this bean to resolve the correct theme or each application request.

ThemeChangeInterceptor

A final note on theme support: If you need to alter the theme on every request, you can configure a ThemeChangeInterceptor, which is based on Spring's interceptor support that you learned about earlier in the book. A configurable parameter name can alter the theme on a per-request basis.

Internationalization in the View Layer

Internationalization, or *i18n,* is an essential aspect of the view layer. After all, this is the layer that renders your data to the end user and in the global marketplace; your users might be anywhere. The majority of them will expect to see local formatting used for numbers and dates at minimum. Many will expect to be able to read much of your site in their own language.

This section contains a brief tour of the important parts of the view layer that you can leverage in your applications to offer i18n of your site. We independently cover most of the subsections you'll see here elsewhere in this chapter and the next.

Locale Resolution

Recall from earlier in the book that the job of LocaleResolvers was to determine the preferred or default locale of the user making the current request. Much of the support for i18n in other view layer components relies on the job that the LocaleResolver does. We'll recap on the available types of LocaleResolver and how they work in Table 7-2.

Table 7-2. *LocaleResolver Implementations*

Implementation	Description
FixedLocaleResolver	Always returns the same locale for each request that can be set with setDefaultLocale().
AcceptHeaderLocaleResolver	Resolves a locale from the HTTP headers of the client request. Most browsers and other HTTP clients send the current locale in the header accept-language.
SessionLocaleResolver	Resolves the locale from an attribute held in the user's HttpSession. The attribute key can be configured on the resolver. A locale resolved from the session is not persisted between sessions; it must be set once per user per session.
CookieLocaleResolver	Similar to a SessionLocaleResolver, but the choice of locale is persisted between sessions.

■**Note** If you use a SessionLocaleResolver or a CookieLocaleResolver, it will fall back to the accept-language locale in the request headers if a locale cannot be found in the session or cookie, respectively.

Listing 7-18 details the configuration of a LocaleResolver in the ApplicationContext.

Listing 7-18. *Configuring the AcceptHeaderLocaleResolver*

```
<bean id="localeResolver"
  class="org.springframework.web.servlet.i18n.AcceptHeaderLocaleResolver"/>
```

MessageSource Beans

A MessageSource is an object that can resolve messages, given a key to that message. Spring provides two concrete implementations of this interface for use in your applications.

- ResourceBundleMessageSource is based on the familiar standard resource bundle handling in the JVM.

- ReloadableResourceBundleMessageSource works in similar fashion but has the added advantage that changes to the properties files will be picked up without having to restart the web application.

Whichever implementation you choose, the usage of a MessageSource bean is the same. Listing 7-19 shows a MessageSource defined in the ApplicationContext file.

Listing 7-19. *MessageSource Bean Definition*

```
<bean id="messageSource"
  class="org.springframework.context.support.ResourceBundleMessageSource">
  <property name="basename" value="messages"/>
</bean>
```

In the preceding example, a base properties file called `messages.properties` will be located in the classpath and used by the `MessageSource` bean. Various locale-specific files will be used if present such as `messages_es.properties` for values in Spanish. Listings 7-20 and 7-21 show a snippet from a `MessageSource` properties file using two different languages.

Listing 7-20. *Base messages.properties File in the Classpath*

```
homepage.welcome=Hello, welcome.
subpage.title=Books
homepage.footer=&copy; ACME Corp. 2005
```

Listing 7-21. *messages_es.properties File in the Classpath*
```
homepage.welcome=Hola, bienvenidos.
subpage.title=Libros
```

When messages are resolved from the `MessageSource` bean using the preceding resource bundles, the specified key is looked up in the correct bundle depending on the resolved locale. If the key is not found in the locale-specific bundle, the default bundle is searched instead. In the preceding examples, the text for `homepage.footer` will appear exactly the same in both English and Spanish locales, as it is not defined in the `messages_es.properties` file.

View Resolution

`ResourceBundleViewResolver` that we examined earlier fully supports i18n via the standard resource bundle behavior. By default, your views are defined in a file named `views.properties` in the root of the classpath—although this can be configured. If you wish the resolver to return different views per locale, you can define them in specific properties files, such as `views_fr.properties` for French.

If you elect to supply different files for one or more locales, then you can override one or more definitions from the basename file (`views.properties`), and the locale-specific selection will fall back to looking in the default bundle, should a `View` not exist on its own.

The principal advantage of this is being able to specify very different views for different locales—for example, by using a completely different JSP or Velocity template. If all you need to do is modify some or all of the text in a page, you may be better serving the same `View` to users in all locales and relying on the message source features instead.

Theme Resolution

In very similar style to the `ResourceBundleViewResolver` explained in the preceding section, the `ResourceBundleThemeSource` also deals with resource bundles. You can create a `winter_fr.properties` file, for example, that points to theme resources using French text or images and styles.

Bind Support

Binding is the term given to Spring's method of mapping request parameters to domain or command objects. You will most commonly encounter this when dealing with forms in your web pages.

Recap of Binding and Validation Sequence

Unlike Struts, Spring MVC allows you to use any object you like as a command object without constraints on its inheritance or interface implementation. When configuring a command controller, you simply specify the class of the object that will be used to receive the POSTed items from the form.

After form submission from the browser, the work flow can become quite complex and diverse because it depends on many factors. But in the simplest cases, Spring's command "controller hierarchy will take care of the following:

- Instantiating an object from the class you specify as your command class

- Mapping the POST parameters onto fields in your class (*automatically* performing conversions from `Strings` to primitives, or to any other type for which there is `PropertyEditor` support)

- Validating your populated command object with a `Validator` object that you have specified

- Calling an `onSubmit()` or `doSubmitAction()` method, supplying the command object and its validation errors as parameters

- Exposing a "status" object on request that can be accessed from tag libraries and macros containing pertinent information about any given field on your command object such as its name, value, and any validation errors associated with it

Bind Support in View Templates

Bind support in views is currently available via tag libraries for JSP/JSTL views and via macros for Velocity and FreeMarker views. Chapter 8 contains more detail on how to use the <bind> tags or macros for these specific technologies.

Summary

In this chapter we introduced the view part of an MVC application. We looked at what the responsibility of a view is, why a view should be cleanly decoupled from the other layers, and how Spring helps us to achieve these goals. We covered in detail the Spring View implementation hierarchy, how ViewResolvers work and which ViewResolvers can be used for your particular needs.

We've also taken a detailed look at internationalization in the view layer and considered how to further enhance the user experience through the use of themes. Lastly, we recapped bind support prior to detailing it in the following chapter.

This chapter has been quite abstract in nature; the concepts introduced provide the basis for Spring's support of many different view types. In the next chapter, we'll take a good look at those specific view types and how to configure them in your applications.

CHAPTER 8

■ ■ ■

Supported View Types

Spring provides first-class support for the majority of view technologies that you're likely to want to use in your Web MVC application. If you need a view that isn't supported, then you can implement your own View or take advantage of additional functionality by extending AbstractView or another subclass.

As we investigate the various different types of views that Spring supports out of the box, we will concentrate on only the Spring integration of those technologies. A discussion of the working of each of them would be way beyond the scope of this chapter. Please refer to the documentation for any third-party libraries such as FreeMarker, Velocity, JasperReports, and others in order to get the full picture on what that particular view type can do for you.

Let's now dive into some specific technologies and find out what additional benefits you can gain from Spring's integration. We'll cover JSP/JSTL, Velocity and FreeMarker, XSLT, and document-based views (Excel, PDF). In addition, we'll take a brief look at Tiles and JasperReports.

JSP and JSTL

JavaServer Pages (JSP) is the only view technology mandated by Sun's J2EE specification and therefore the only technology that server vendors are compelled to support. This naturally makes them the most popular way to generate web pages in J2EE applications.

JSP has not been without its share of criticism in the community, and the arguments against it are well documented. Essentially, the major issue is the ease with which domain logic and even data access logic can be coded into JSPs since they are compiled into servlets and have the full power of the Java language available to them. We firmly believe that you should treat JSP strictly as a view layer technology in your applications, the goal of which is to display the model generated by your Controller. That means that you should not be able to reference a JSP outside of the application—in other words, you should keep them inside the WEB-INF directory of the WAR file where they are immune from client access.

Spring deals with JSP views via the InternalResourceView class (the name gives you a strong hint about how they should be used!), which subclasses AbstractUrlBasedView. The most popular choice of ViewResolvers for JSP are InternalResourceViewResolver and ResourceBundleViewResolver The example in Listings 8-1 and 8-2 demonstrates best how you can address a JSP to display your carefully crafted model.

Listing 8-1. *Setting Up the InternalResourceViewResolver in the WebApplicationContext*

```
<bean id="viewResolver"
class="org.springframework.web.servlet.view.InternalResourceViewResolver">
  <property name="viewClass"
    value="org.springframework.web.servlet.view.InternalResourceView"/>
  <property name="prefix" value="/WEB-INF/jsp/"/>
  <property name="suffix" value=".jsp"/>
</bean>
```

Listing 8-2. *Specifying Model and View from the Home Controller*

```
@Override
protected ModelAndView handleRequestInternal(
    HttpServletRequest req, HttpServletResponse res)
throws Exception {
    ModelAndView mav = new ModelAndView("home");
    mav.addObject("specials", flights.getSpecialDeals());
    return mav;
}
```

The `Controller` code should be very familiar by now; it simply declares that a `View` with the logical name `home` should be used to handle the model. It doesn't need to know or care that a JSP will actually do that job for you. The model consists of a single object—the list of special deals—keyed under the name `specials`.

The `ViewResolver` definition shown in Listing 8-1 has the interesting information—and is where the magic occurs. First, we specify which `View` implementation class will be used and we specify a prefix and a suffix that will be (surprise) prefixed and suffixed to the logical name. So when the resolver is asked to resolve a `View` name of `home` by the `DispatcherServlet`, it returns an object that wraps the JSP located at `/WEB-INF/jsp/home.jsp`—the physical location of your JSP file in the web application.

Exposing the Model As Request Attributes

Clever stuff—and so far, so good—but what about our model? The `home.jsp` won't be much use if it doesn't have access to the model attributes that our `Controller` obtained from the service layer of the application. This is where the `render()` method of the `View` interface comes into play as it is this method (or more commonly, a delegate method) that is responsible for knowing how to make a generic model available to the specific view technology, in this case JSP.

`InternalResourceView` makes the model available to a JSP in the form of request attributes. An extract from the code in this class shown in Listing 8-3 demonstrates how.

Listing 8-3. *Exposing the Model in InternalResourceView*

```
protected void
exposeModelAsRequestAttributes(Map model, HttpServletRequest request)
throws Exception {
```

```
    Iterator it = model.entrySet().iterator();
    while (it.hasNext()) {
        Map.Entry entry = (Map.Entry) it.next();
        if (!(entry.getKey() instanceof String)) {
            throw new ServletException(
                "Invalid key [" + entry.getKey() +
                "] in model Map - only Strings allowed as model keys");
        }
        String modelName = (String) entry.getKey();
        Object modelValue = entry.getValue();
        if (modelValue != null) {
            request.setAttribute(modelName, modelValue);
        }
        else {
            request.removeAttribute(modelName);
        }
    }
}
```

> **Note** exposeModelAsRequestAttributes is called from the render() method in
> InternalResourceView. We've removed logging statements for clarity.

Displaying the Model

Listing 8-4 shows, for completeness, a fragment of the JSP file that you might use to display
the model.

Listing 8-4. *Displaying the Model in the JSP*

```
<body>
  <h1>Welcome to the Flight Booking Service</h1>

  <p>We have the following specials now:</p>

  <ul>
    <%
    List specials = (List) request.getAttribute("specials");
    for (Iterator i = specials.iterator(); i.hasNext();) {
      SpecialDeal special = (SpecialDeal) i.next();
    %>
    <li>
      <%= special.getDepartFrom().getName() %> -
```

```
      <%= special.getArriveAt().getName() %> from
      $<%= special.getCost() %>
   </li>
   <%
   }
   %>
  </ul>
</body>
```

Naturally, this is a bit "last century"; we don't want to be coding Java in our JSPs but it serves to demonstrate how the Controller, View, ViewResolver, and implementing technology work together in a simple end to end example. Let's see how to use the preferred JSP Standard Tag Library (JSTL) view to give us a nice, clean syntax.

A simple change to our ViewResolver definition from Listing 8-1 denotes that we will use a subclass of InternalResourceView which adds JSTL support: <property name="viewClass" value="org.springframework.web.servlet.view.JstlView"/>. Now we can make the amendments to our JSP shown in Listing 8-5.

Listing 8-5. *JSTL Displays Our Specials List*

```
<%@ taglib uri="http://java.sun.com/jsp/jstl/core" prefix="c" %>
...
<body>
  <h1>Welcome to the Flight Booking Service</h1>

  <p>We have the following specials now:</p>

  <ul>
    <c:forEach items="${specials}" var="special">
    <li>
      ${special.departFrom.name} -
      ${special.arriveAt.name} from
      $${special.cost}
    </li>
    </c:forEach>
  </ul>

  <p><a href="search">Search for a flight.</a></p>
</body>
```

Much better. Figure 8-1 shows the output.

Figure 8-1. *Flight departures output*

JSP Tag Libraries

Spring provides a set of JSP tag libraries for use in your applications. There are tags for simplifying form handling, retrieving internationalized messages from one or more resource bundles (in conjunction with Spring's Locale resolution support), and a few others. Table 8-1 has a summary of what's available.

Table 8-1. *Summary of Spring's JSP Tags*

Tag Name	Description
spring:bind	Used in HTML forms, the <bind> tag exposes a status attribute to the JSP containing information about the command object (or a field on the command object) that it has been bound to. The status attribute holds the name of the field, its present value, if any, and any validation errors associated with that field.
spring:hasBindErrors	Determines whether a field, or command object that has been bound to with the <bind> tag currently has any validation errors.
spring:nestedPath	Exposes a prefix path that can be used to simplify subsequent usage of the <bind> tag.
spring:transform	Allows a non–command object property to be transformed with PropertyEditors in the same way that bound fields can be. This tag can *only* be used inside a <bind> tag.
spring:message	Retrieves localized messages from a MessageSource. Functionally similar to JSTL's <fmt:message> tag, but works with Spring's ApplicationContext and locale support.
spring:htmlEscape	Used to specify a page-level default for HTML escaping. Tags that might emit content containing characters that need to be converted to HTML entities will be affected by this tag.
spring:escapeBody	Custom tag that can be used to escape the content of its own body for HTML, JavaScript, or both.
spring:theme	Look up a value from a theme definition file based on the key supplied to the tag as a parameter. This tag was discussed in the previous chapter in the section on themes.

Forms

Chapter 6 had a recap of the generic work flow used by Spring when you submit a form to one of your command Controllers. Let's see how to link your Views to the command object and the validation errors that Spring makes available for you through the JSP tag libraries.

Listing 8-6 shows a simple form from a JSTL view that takes advantage of the <spring:bind> tag.

Listing 8-6. *Binding to a Command Object Field in a JSTL View*

```
<html>
  <body>
    <h1>Form Submission</h1>
    <p>Please tell us your first name.</p>

    <form action="" method="POST">
      <spring:bind path="command.firstName">
      <input type="text" name="<c:out value="${status.expression}"/>"
        value="<c:out value="${status.value}"/>" /><br>
        <c:forEach var="error" items="${status.errorMessages}">
          <c:out value="${error}"/><br>
        </c:forEach>
      </spring:bind>
      <input type="submit" value="submit"/>
    </form>
  </body>
</html>
```

Calling the <spring:bind> tag will cause an attribute of type BindStatus to be exposed to your JSP. The status is instantiated for the field(s) on your command object denoted by the path attribute you supply to the tag. The BindStatus class is shown in Figure 8-2.

The first time you request the form in your browser with a GET request, the command object will be empty, and the values for command.firstName and status.errorMessages will also be empty. The code will then render the HTML for an empty form in response to this request.

The fun starts when you submit the form. If you submit a valid form—as determined by a suitable Validator class for this particular command object—then the command object's firstName field is set to the value submitted by the user. This is immediately usable in your Controller code and you can pass the command object around in your service layer (or DAO layer) safe in the knowledge that the values already meet the business validation that you specified.

Should binding or validation fail, the default Controller behavior is to show the form again in the browser. This time, the errors part of the status object will not be empty for fields that failed and the code for the form shown above will now display these errors to your user. The actual error messages are normally obtained from a MessageSource object in the ApplicationContext file. All the values that the user submitted originally will still be available on the command object and will be redisplayed, so your user need only correct the fields for which binding or validation failed. When binding failures do occur, the BindStatus values contain exactly what was input by the user, regardless of the binding error, which acts as the principal of least surprise for the user.

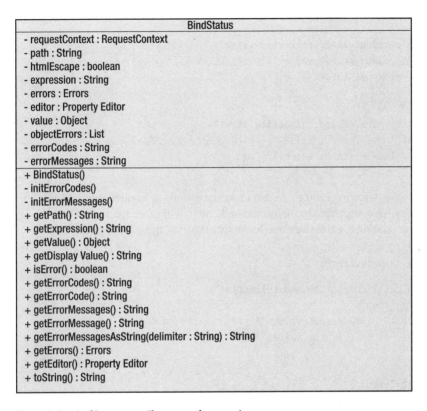

Figure 8-2. *BindStatus attributes and operations*

■**Note** There is a distinction between failure in binding and failure in validation. Binding occurs first, and this can fail if your user submits a value in a field that cannot automatically be converted to the required type, or for which a suitable `PropertyEditor` has not been registered. For example, your command object has a field of type `java.util.Date` and the user enters a value of 3. Validation failure is a failure of bound values to meet business or other validation logic that you supply yourself in the `Validator` class. Neither binding nor validation errors are considered fatal, and they are rounded up together in the errors instance.

Nested Paths

If your forms and command objects are fairly complex, you can take advantage of the `<spring:nestedPath>` tag to make it a little more readable. Setting a nested path affects the bind path for all future binds within the body of the tag, prefixing the bind path with the nested path. Path nesting can be specified multiple times.

We can best explain this by way of example. Listing 8-7 shows a form layout in a JSP that uses several `<bind>` tag uses for various fields and nested fields on the command object.

Listing 8-7. *Binding Without Nesting Paths*

```
<spring:bind path="complexCommand.collection.item">
  <input type="text" name="<c:out value="${status.expression}"/>"
    value="<c:out value="${status.value}"/>"/>
</spring:bind>
<br>
<spring:bind path="complexCommand.collection.item2">
  <input type="text" name="<c:out value="${status.expression}"/>"
    value="<c:out value="${status.value}"/>"/>
</spring:bind>
```

As you can see, we're showing binding to two imaginary items in a collection field of a command object. It's a bit verbose and a maintenance headache if you have a lot of these items to bind fields to. Listing 8-8 has the same form, this time using a nested path.

Listing 8-8. *Binding with Nested Paths*

```
<spring:nestedPath path="complexCommand.collection">
  <spring:bind path="item">
    <input type="text" name="<c:out value="${status.expression}"/>"
      value="<c:out value="${status.value}"/>"/>
  </spring:bind>
  <br>
  <spring:bind path="item2">
    <input type="text" name="<c:out value="${status.expression}"/>"
      value="<c:out value="${status.value}"/>"/>
  </spring:bind>
</spring:nestedPath>
```

Notice now, that when executing inside a nested path, the bind path is significantly shorter, taking its prefix from the path exported by the `<spring:nestedPath>` tag instead.

A Note on Check Box Submissions

Check boxes are handy for displaying Boolean-type data in your forms, but they can be a nuisance too. A deficiency in the way HTML form POSTs work means that if a check box appears on a form but it is not actually checked, then the field will not be submitted by the browser at all in the list of POST parameters.

This can be a problem for your applications. Consider the following scenario:

- A user selects a check box on a form and submits it.

- Other validation errors cause the form to be shown again to the user; the check box is correctly checked as per her original choice.

- She corrects the errors, but also changes her mind about the check box selection and unchecks it.

- When she resubmits the form, the check box field is not transmitted at all, and so Spring doesn't bind a value to it.

- Now, her original selection (check box selected) remains on the command object!

There is fortunately a nice solution to the problem. You can place a hidden field on the form with the same name as the check box field but prefixed with an underscore (_). Listing 8-9 shows a snippet of just such a form.

Listing 8-9. *Hidden Check Box Identifier in the Form*

```
<form ...>
  <spring:bind path="command.acceptTermsAndConditions">
    <input type="checkbox"
      name="${status.expression}"
      value="${status.value}"
      <c:if test="${status.value}">checked="checked"</c:if>
    > I have read the terms and conditions

    <input type="hidden" name="_${status.expression}"/>
  </spring:bind>

  <!-- other form items... -->
</form>
```

When your `Controller` receives the form input the second time, it will see a POST parameter with the name `_command.acceptTermsAndConditions` and know to look for a corresponding parameter of the same name, minus the leading underscore. If it doesn't find it (as it won't in our example), then it knows to reset the value for the field on the command object. Resetting the value depends on the type of field the check box is bound to. If `boolean`, the field is set to `false`. If it's a `String[]`, the field will be set to an empty array, and if it's a `Collection`, it will be set to `null`.

HTML Escaping

Tags might sometimes emit values that are unsafe for HTML and need to be escaped. Characters such as ampersands (&) and apostrophes (') have special meaning and can be replaced with HTML entities such as & and '. There are three ways that you can force conversion of these characters to their entity name counterparts in a Spring MVC application.

The coarsest level of granularity for specifying HTML escaping is application-wide. In your `web.xml` file, you can force a default behavior which will be honored by the Spring tag libraries (and Velocity/FreeMarker macros, which we'll see later). Listing 8-10 shows a snippet of the configuration.

Listing 8-10. *Default HTML Escaping Value Set in web.xml*

```
<web-app>
  <context-param>
    <param-name>defaultHtmlEscape</param-name>
    <param-value>true</param-value>
  </context-param>

  ...
</web-app>
```

Default values for HTML escaping are always false, so you need only specify this context parameter if you want to make escaping the default behavior in your application.

The next level of granularity is at the page scope. Within your JSP you can set a <spring:htmlEscape> tag and the content-producing tags that follow will generate HTML escaped values. Listing 8-11 shows you how.

Listing 8-11. *The <spring:htmlEscape> Tag in Action*

```
<spring:bind path="command.field1">
  ${status.value} <!-- will NOT be html escaped -->
</spring:bind>

<spring:htmlEscape defaultHtmlEscape="true"/>

<spring:bind path="command.field2">
  ${status.value} <!-- WILL be html escaped -->
</spring:bind>
```

Finally, the <bind> tag accepts an optional attribute named htmlEscape that can be used to override the value set in the page by the <spring:htmlEscape> tag, the value set in web.xml, or both. Listing 8-12 explains.

Listing 8-12. *Overriding HTML Escaping in the Bind Tag*

```
<spring:htmlEscape defaultHtmlEscape="true"/>
<spring:bind path="command.field2" htmlEscape="false">
  ${status.value} <!-- will NOT be html escaped -->
</spring:bind>
```

Tagfiles

Version 2.4 of the servlet specification supports the use of tagfiles for JSPs. Tagfiles are similar in nature to macros in FreeMarker and Velocity. They can manipulate the markup language directly (no more need to code them in Java), access standard tag libraries, and be deployed without compilation or tag library descriptor files if you so choose.

Spring currently has no form simplification tagfiles, but they've been on the cards for awhile. It's hoped that they will finally make it into version 1.3, which will probably have been released by the time you read this.

Tiles

Let's take a brief look at Tiles integration before moving to non-JSP view types. Tiles allows you to define separate page components (the *tiles*) that can be configured independently and reused in different page layouts. It was originally a JSP-based technology that grew out of the Struts project and is now considered independent from that framework, although you will still need to include `struts-1.1.jar` or later to use Tiles in your view layer. You'll also need `Commons-BeanUtils`, `Commons-Digester`, and `Commons-Lang` in your classpath.

To get started with Tiles, you must configure it. You can do this with a `TilesConfigurer` bean instance in your `DispatcherServlet`'s configuration file. Listing 8-13 offers just such an example.

Listing 8-13. *Tiles Configuration Bean*

```
<bean id="tilesConfigurer"
  class="org.springframework.web.servlet.view.tiles.TilesConfigurer">
  <property name="definitions">
    <list>
      <value>/WEB-INF/tiles/defs-main.xml</value>
      <value>/WEB-INF/tiles/defs-other.xml</value>
    </list>
  </property>
</bean>
```

In the configuration bean we tell the Tiles subsystem to load definitions (Tiles configurations) from two files located in `WEB-INF/tiles`. Listing 8-14 shows the trivial `defs-main.xml` defining a single home page layout with a single content tile named `content`.

Listing 8-14. *Tiles Definition Configuration for the Home Page*

```
<?xml version="1.0" encoding="ISO-8859-1" ?>

<!DOCTYPE tiles-definitions PUBLIC
  "-//Apache Software Foundation//DTD Tiles Configuration 1.1//EN"
  "http://jakarta.apache.org/struts/dtds/tiles-config_1_1.dtd">

<tiles-definitions>

  <!-- DEFAULT MAIN TEMPLATE -->
  <definition name="home" page="/WEB-INF/jsp/tiles-home.jsp">
    <put name="content" value="/WEB-INF/jsp/home.jsp" type="page"/>
  </definition>

</tiles-definitions>
```

For your Tiles views, Spring provides org.springframework.web.servlet.view.tiles. TilesView, and you can use this as the viewClass property of an InternalResourceViewResolver, or, as always, configure Tiles views individually in a ResourceBundleViewResolver or XmlViewResolver. Listing 8-15 shows an InternalResourceViewResolver that will be used to return TilesViews.

Listing 8-15. *TilesView Resolution*

```
<bean id="viewResolver"
  class="org.springframework.web.servlet.view.InternalResourceViewResolver">
  <property name="requestContextAttribute" value="requestContext"/>
  <property name="viewClass"
    value="org.springframework.web.servlet.view.tiles.TilesView"/>
</bean>
```

To bring it all together, the ViewResolver will resolve the View named home, which our Controller sets as the View's key by looking in the definition file. In WEB-INF/tiles/defs-main.xml shown earlier, the definition has such a key name, so Tiles uses this layout. Listing 8-16 shows the content of the tiles-home.jsp.

Listing 8-16. *Tiles Layout JSP*

```
<%@ taglib prefix="tiles"
    uri="http://jakarta.apache.org/struts/tags-tiles" %>
<%@ taglib prefix="fmt"
    uri="http://java.sun.com/jstl/fmt" %>

<html>
  <head>
    <link rel="stylesheet" type="text/css" href="styles.css"/>
    <title><fmt:message key="title"/></title>
  </head>
  <body>
    <h1>Tiled Home Page</h1>
    <p class="menu">
      <a href="home.html">home</a> |
      <a href="specials.html">specials</a> |
      <a href="search.html">flight search</a>
    </p>

    <tiles:insert name="content"/>

  </body>
</html>
```

Summary

Tiles is a rich technology for creating components in your web pages, and our overview of Spring's Tiles support doesn't scratch the surface of what can be achieved with this view type. If you're new to Tiles, or if you'd like further information on Spring's Tiles support, see *Pro Spring* (Apress, 2004), which has a much more in-depth examination.

Velocity and FreeMarker

Velocity (`http://jakarta.apache.org/velocity`) and FreeMarker (`http://www.freemarker.org`) are both templating technologies. They are purely text-based engines, and both are in widespread use in applications of all kinds that produce text output. Obviously, web applications are one such subset. As our topic is Web MVC applications, though, we're going to consider just that aspect of them both.

CHOOSING A TEMPLATING LANGUAGE

Choosing between Velocity and FreeMarker is a discussion beyond the scope of this book. The only real differences from a technical point of view in applying these engines in a Spring application is in their respective templating languages. If you have no experience of either but would like to try them, we suggest perusing the documentation for both at their respective websites and deciding which suits you and your team best.

Templating Pros and Cons

Unlike JSP, Velocity and FreeMarker templates are not compiled into Java classes; rather, they are interpreted by their respective template engines. This makes them more akin to XSLT than JSP. Despite this, there seems to be no performance penalty in applying either of them in place of JSP. In fact in many benchmarks, Velocity outperforms JSP as the view layer. This is because, although not compiled to byte code, the templates are cached in an efficient binary format by the template engines when they are first read.

An advantage of both over JSP is that you can't easily break out of the templating language and start coding Java, so there's less danger that domain logic will leak into the view layer with either of these solutions.

The disadvantages are that you need a little extra configuration to integrate them smoothly into your application, your preferred IDE may not have good support for them, and, of course, your developers or designers may need to learn an unfamiliar template language. The relevant JAR files will need to be added to your `WEB-INF/lib` (they ship with Spring in case you need them), and for Velocity, you will also need to add `commons-collections.jar` to your application. To be frank, however, the additional configuration is trivial, and the template languages are both significantly simpler than something like Java. In our opinion, the advantages probably just outweigh the disadvantages.

■**Note** The Eclipse IDE (and consequently IBM's WSAD) can be extended with support for both Velocity and FreeMarker template editing through the use of two open-source plugins. See `http://veloedit.sourceforge.net` and `http://freemarker.sourceforge.net/eclipse.html`, respectively. Your mileage may vary with other IDEs.

Basic Configuring for Template Engines

The Velocity (or FreeMarker) engine needs to be configured using one of the Spring-supplied classes. This usually happens in the servlet context file. Listing 8-17 shows you how.

Listing 8-17. *Configuring the Velocity Engine*

```
<bean id="velocityConfigurer"
    class="org.springframework.web.servlet.view.velocity.VelocityConfigurer"
    <property name="resourceLoaderPath" value="WEB-INF/velocity"/>
</bean>
```

■**Note** For `FreeMarkerConfigurer` the property name for the template loading path is `templateLoaderPath`, although from Spring version 1.3 that may be deprecated and you should use `resourceLoaderPath` for either.

`VelocityConfigurer` (and `FreeMarkerConfigurer`) wrap access to the actual template engine (`VelocityEngine` and `Configuration`, respectively). The most important property to set on these objects is the one highlighted in the example. The `resourceLoaderPath` determines where Velocity will look for your template files. As with JSP, it's a good idea to make these inaccessible to web clients by placing them somewhere inside the `WEB-INF` directory.

There are many important properties that can be set on the respective configurer beans, some of which we'll explore later. For now, let's complete the integration by setting up a `ViewResolver`.

Spring's general `ViewResolvers` (`ResourceBundleViewResolver` and `XmlViewResolver`) are perfectly adequate for any kind of `View`, template views included. But often, when your application consists of only one view type it makes sense to take advantage of a specific resolver to keep things a little simpler. For Velocity and FreeMarker, Spring offers `VelocityViewResolver` and `FreeMarkerViewResolver`. Figure 7-5 in the previous chapter showed where these resolvers fit into the general hierarchy. Listing 8-18 shows a simple configuration of them.

Listing 8-18. *ViewResolver Configuration*

```
<bean id="velocityResolver"
  class="org.springframework.web.servlet.view.velocity.VelocityViewResolver">
  <property name="prefix" value="" />
  <property name="suffix" value=".vm"/>
</bean>
```

```
<bean id="freemarkerResolver"
  class="org.springframework.web.servlet.view.freemarker.FreeMarkerViewResolver">
  <property name="prefix" value="" />
  <property name="suffix" value=".ftl"/>
</bean>
```

■**Caution** The prefix property on the `ViewResolver` is relative to the `resourceLoaderPath`. When setting the `resourceLoaderPath` to `WEB-INF/velocity`, as we did earlier, we then needed to ensure that the
`ViewResolver` prefix was empty. This differs a little from the way `InternalResourceViewResolver` is
usually configured for JSPs.

As you'll remember from the discussions on `InternalResourceViewResolver`, your
`Controllers` need only specify the `View` key—in this case home—and the resolver will do
the rest. With Velocity, for example, the resolver looks in the specified template directory
(`WEB-INF/velocity`, which we set on the `VelocityConfigurer` bean) for a file with a prefix of "",
a name of home, and a suffix of `.vm`. In other words, `WEB-INF/velocity/home.vm`.

In the simplest cases you need do no more. Your templates are placed in `WEB-INF/velocity`,
and you've defined the engine configuration and `ViewResolver` beans that form the basis of
Spring's integration for these template languages. For the sample application home page this is
fine. Figure 8-3 shows the file system layout.

Figure 8-3. *WEB-INF directory with several view layers and the libraries required*

Exposing the Model

As always, the specific `View` implementation is responsible for knowing what to do with a model generated by your `Controllers`. For `VelocityView`, each object in the model is added to a `VelocityContext` instance, which is what the Velocity engine uses to merge with the template. FreeMarker works happily with `Map` objects as models, and so no conversion is necessary.

The Template Language

Before moving on, let's take a sneak peek at the actual template files used for the home page. Listing 8-19 shows an example of Velocity Template Language (VTL). In fact, it's the familiar home page of the sample application converted from the JSP example in Listing 8-5.

Listing 8-19. *Sample Home Page in VTL*

```
<body>
  <h1>Welcome to the Flight Booking Service</h1>

  <p>We have the following specials now:</p>

  <ul>
    #foreach ($special in $specials)
    <li>
      ${special.departFrom.name} -
      ${special.arriveAt.name} from
      $${special.cost}
    </li>
    #end
  </ul>

  <p><a href="search">Search for a flight.</a></p>
</body>
```

Listing 8-20 shows the FreeMarker equivalent for completeness. From here on, we'll mostly show just Velocity examples unless there are noteworthy differences in FreeMarker handling.

Listing 8-20. *The Home Page Again—This Time in FTL*

```
<body>
  <h1>Welcome to the Flight Booking Service</h1>

  <p>We have the following specials now:</p>

  <ul>
    <#list specials as special>
    <li>
      ${special.departFrom.name} -
      ${special.arriveAt.name} from
```

```
    $${special.cost}
  </li>
  </#list>
</ul>

<p><a href="search">Search for a flight.</a></p>
</body>
```

As you can see, it's not terribly difficult to get a basic templating solution in place as the view layer. Let's go a little deeper and look at some of the more advanced configurations and also what Spring offers in the way of bind support for Velocity and FreeMarker.

Advanced Configuration Options

Many properties and settings can be used to affect the way your templating engine operates. Certain properties will determine how templates are loaded and cached, how locales are managed, how macros are handled, and more. All of these are beyond the scope of this book, but if you are looking at Velocity or FreeMarker for the first time, we strongly recommend that you familiarize yourself with all these options.

To hook into these advanced options, you can specify the location of an external properties file (you may have one of these if you've previously used Velocity or FreeMarker outside of a Spring application). On the configurer object, set the property named configLocation to wherever the configuration file may be found. The value of configLocation is interpreted as a Spring Resource, which means you can use classpath, file, or URL-based locations. See the Spring reference documentation for information about Spring Resources. You can alternatively set such properties locally on the configurer instance if you have no need to use those properties outside of your MVC application. Listing 8-21 shows an example of both options.

Listing 8-21. *Setting Engine-Specific Properties via the Configurer Bean*

```
<bean id="velocityConfigurer"
  class="org.springframework.web.servlet.view.velocity.VelocityConfigurer">
  <property name="resourceLoaderPath" value="/WEB-INF/velocity"/>
  <!-- inline velocity properties -->
  <property name="velocityProperties">
    <props>
      <prop key="velocimacro.library.autoreload">true</prop>
    </props>
  </property>
</bean>

<bean id="freemarkerConfigurer"
  class="org.springframework.web.servlet.view.freemarker.FreeMarkerConfigurer">
  <property name="templateLoaderPath" value="/WEB-INF/freemarker"/>
  <!-- load freemarker props from the classpath -->
  <property name="configLocation"
    value="classpath:com/apress/expertspringmvc/fm.properties"/>
</bean>
```

Note Check the relevant Velocity and FreeMarker documentation at their respective websites to see the range of properties and settings that can be configured on the two engines.

By default, Spring doesn't expose request or session attributes to your template engines. If you want to access those values in your templates, you need to tell Spring to make them available. This is the same mechanism for both Velocity and FreeMarker, as the relevant properties are part of a common superclass (shown in Figure 8-4).

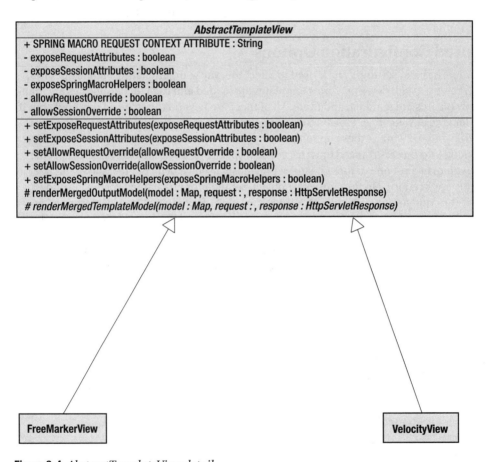

Figure 8-4. *AbstractTemplateView detail*

Listing 8-22 has an example of exposing request and session attributes for a VelocityView instance.

Listing 8-22. *Exposing Session and Request Attributes on a View*

```
attributeView.class=org.springframework.web.servlet.view.velocity.VelocityView
attributeView.exposeRequestAttributes=true
attributeView.exposeSessionAttributes=true
```

■**Tip** You can specify exactly the same values on either `FreeMarkerViewResolver` or `VelocityViewResolver`. All `View`s resolved by the resolver will have those properties set accordingly.

Forms and the SpringBind Macros

Spring's bind support, made available to JSPs via the tag library, has also been extended to Velocity and FreeMarker. This makes either an excellent solution for displaying forms, validation results, and localized messages in your Spring MVC application.

To make the bind support and the Spring macros available to your template, you must configure the relevant `View`. You do this exactly the same way we handled the request and session attribute exposure earlier. On either a `View` or the `ViewResolver`, set the property `exposeSpringMacroHelpers` to `true`.

■**Tip** Spring's Velocity and FreeMarker macros are shipped as part of the `spring.jar` file that you place in your `WEB-INF/lib` folder of your application. They are also copied to the `dist` directory if you build Spring from source. However you *don't* need to copy those files into your application's template directories as Spring configures the template engine to load the macros directly from the `spring.jar` file.

Listing 8-23 shows the `VelocityViewResolver` definition enhanced to make the Spring bind macros available to all of the `View`s that it will resolve.

Listing 8-23. *Making Spring Macros Available to All Velocity Views*

```
<bean id="velocityResolver"
  class="org.springframework.web.servlet.view.velocity.VelocityViewResolver">
  <property name="prefix" value="" />
  <property name="suffix" value=".vm"/>
  <property name="exposeSpringMacroHelpers" value="true"/>
</bean>
```

We covered general bind support in our overview of the JSP tag libraries earlier, so let's get straight to the heart of the templating versions with another Velocity example. Listing 8-24 demonstrates a basic form using the `#springBind` macro, which is the equivalent of the `<spring:bind>` tag in JSP.

Listing 8-24. *Binding to a Command Object Field in a Velocity Template*

```
<html>
  <body>
    <h1>Form Submission</h1>
    <p>Please tell us your first name.</p>

    <form action="" method="POST">
```

```
    #springBind("command.firstName")
    <input type="text" name="$status.expression"
      value="$!status.value" /><br>
    #foreach($error in $status.errorMessages)
    <b>$error</b> <br>
    #end
    <input type="submit" value="submit"/>
  </form>
 </body>
</html>
```

■**Caution** Velocity imports macro definitions into a global namespace, which means all macros are available from all your templates once they have been loaded. FreeMarker, on the other hand, allows macros to be subdivided into separate namespaces. When using the Spring macros in FreeMarker you have to import them into each template that you wish to use them in. Add the following line to the top of your FreeMarker templates: `<#import "spring.ftl" as spring />`.

The binding behavior is exactly the same as we outlined for JSP bind support. It uses the same code under the covers. If you submit a valid form, the command object will have its corresponding field set to the user-submitted value. Conversely, if validation errors occur such as the field being left blank, the form will be redisplayed, and each error in the `status.errorMessages` field can be highlighted to the user. If a value had been submitted in the field, the original incorrect value will be redisplayed in the input field.

So far, so simple. It's no different from JSP's `<spring:bind>` tag behavior, other than the syntactical differences in the template language.

For Velocity and FreeMarker, however, you have (since Spring 1.1) been able to enjoy an additional suite of macros that build upon `#springBind` and generate a lot of the form field content for you based on optional parameters that you supply. Table 8-2 shows the full range of macros available to your templates.

■**Tip** In FreeMarker, the two macros marked (*) in the following table exist but are not actually required, as you can use the normal `formInput` macro, specifying `hidden` or `password` as the value for the `fieldType` parameter.

It's a fairly comprehensive set of form-handling functionality. We'll look at a few common examples and leave you to explore the remainder within your own applications. Listing 8-25 shows a fragment of the `beginSearch.vm` template in the example application. It uses the basic `#springFormInput` macro to generate a couple of input fields.

Table 8-2. *Template Macros Available for Velocity and FreeMarker*

Macro Description	Velocity	FreeMarker
bind	`#springBind($path)`	`<@spring.bind $path>`
message (output a string from a resource bundle based on the code parameter)	`#springMessage($code)`	`<@spring.message code/>`
messageText (output a string from a resource bundle based on the code parameter, falling back to the value of the default parameter)	`#springMessageText($code $default)`	`<@spring.messageText code, default/>`
url (prefix a relative URL with the application's context root)	`#springUrl($relativeUrl)`	`<@spring.url relativeUrl/>`
formInput (standard input field for gathering user input)	`#springFormInput($path $attributes)`	`<@spring.formInput path, attributes, fieldType/>`
formHiddenInput* (hidden input field for submitting non-user input)	`#springFormHiddenInput($path $attributes)`	`<@spring.formHiddenInput path, attributes/>`
formPasswordInput* (standard input field for gathering passwords; note that no value will ever be populated in fields of this type)	`#springFormPasswordInput($path $attributes)`	`<@spring.formPasswordInput path, attributes/>`
formTextarea (large text field for gathering long, freeform text input)	`#springFormTextarea($path $attributes)`	`<@spring.formTextarea path, attributes/>`
formSingleSelect (drop-down box of options allowing a single required value to be selected)	`#springFormSingleSelect( $path $options $attributes)`	`<@spring.formSingleSelect path, options, attributes/>`
formMultiSelect (a list box of options allowing the user to select 0 or more values)	`#springFormMultiSelect($path $options $attributes)`	`<@spring.formMultiSelect path, options, attributes/>`

(Continued)

Table 8-2. *Continued*

Macro Description	Velocity	FreeMarker
formRadioButtons (a set of radio buttons allowing a single selection to be made from the available choices)	#springFormRadioButtons($path $options $separator $attributes)	<@spring.formRadioButtons path, options separator, attributes/>
formCheckboxes (a set of check boxes allowing 0 or more values to be selected)	#springFormCheckboxes($path $options $separator $attributes)	<@spring.formCheckboxes path, options, separator, attributes/>
showErrors (simplify display of validation errors for the bound field)	#springShowErrors($separator $classOrStyle)	<@spring.showErrors separator, classOrStyle/>

Listing 8-25. *Example of the #formInput Macro*

```
<tr>
  <td>Depart From:</td>
  <td>#springFormInput("searchFlights.departFrom" "")</td>
  <td>Depart On:</td>
  <td>#springFormInput("searchFlights.departOn" "")
  <span style="font-size:smaller">(yyyy-MM-dd HH)</span></td>
</tr>
```

#springFormInput performs a #springBind on the path supplied as the first parameter and outputs an input field in HTML based on this bind. The second parameter, in the example an empty string, is used to convey additional attributes that the input field should have. This is useful for generating style or class attributes on the output. The preceding fragment will be rendered into the HTML in Listing 8-26 (assuming this form is not being shown after a validation failure).

Listing 8-26. *Rendered HTML from the Velocity Macro*

```
<tr>
  <td>Depart From:</td>
  <td><input type="text" name="departFrom" value="" ></td>
  <td>Depart On:</td>
  <td><input type="text" name="departOn" value="" >
  <span style="font-size:smaller">(yyyy-MM-dd HH)</span></td>
</tr>
```

When the form is shown after a validation failure, the value attributes of the input fields will contain any text entered by the user prior to submitting the form.

■**Tip** In Spring 1.2.6 the macros will also add an id attribute to the form fields that will have the same value as the name attribute. This makes the fields more accessible to JavaScript, for example.

#springFormHiddenInput and #springFormPasswordInput are basically similar to the standard #springFormInput macro. The only difference being that the input type is set to hidden or password, respectively. Note that for password fields, the value will never automatically be populated in the event that the form is redisplayed due to validation failure. This is for security reasons.

The next four macros are again all related to each other. They can all display groups of options either as a single select drop-down list, a multiselect list, radio buttons, or check boxes. With radio buttons and check boxes you must specify what the separator is between each element in the group—for example, <br> to show columns or   to show them in a row. Let's see an example of two of these in action. The actual options are created by the Controller and made available as part of the model. You might do this dynamically or perhaps through the referenceData() methods in your Controller.

In Listing 8-27 we show an example `Controller` that puts options for the grouped form input fields into a `Map` named `options`. Listing 8-28 shows a template that displays the same set of options as both a single select drop-down list and a group of check boxes. Lastly in Listing 8-29 we show the HTML that will be rendered from the template.

Listing 8-27. *Setting the Options Map in a Controller*

```
public ModelAndView handleRequest(...) {
    Map model = new HashMap();
    Map<String, String> options = new HashMap<String, String>();
    options.put("NYC", "New York City");
    options.put("LON", "London");
    options.put("PAR", "Paris");
    model.put("options", options);
    return new ModelAndView("cityForm", options);
}
```

Listing 8-28. *Displaying the Options in the Template*

```
<!-- can only select one here! -->
#springFormSingleSelect("command.city" $options "")


<br>


<!-- can select more than one here -->
#springFormCheckboxes("command.city" $options "<br>" "")
```

Listing 8-29. *HTML Output from the Grouped Input Macros*

```
<!-- can only select one here! -->
<select name="city" >
  <option value="LON"
>
London</option>
  <option value="NYC"
>
New York City</option>
  <option value="PAR"
>
Paris</option>

</select>

<br>

<!-- can select more than one here -->
<input type="checkbox" name="city" value="LON"
>     London <br>
```

```
<input type="checkbox" name="city" value="NYC"
>    New York City <br>
<input type="checkbox" name="city" value="PAR"
>    Paris <br>
```

■**Tip** By default, all of the Spring macros will close input field tags with the HTML 4–compliant tag closure `>`. If your templates should be XHTML compliant, you can instruct the macros to use XHTML tag closures `/>` by setting a variable in the template. For Velocity, place the line `#set($springXhtmlCompliant = "true")` in your template before calling any of the macros. For FreeMarker, use `<#assign xhtmlCompliant = true in spring>`.

As an added benefit, the example highlights how you can use codes for the values that will be submitted in the form fields, but present different text values to the user. In this example, we used city codes as the form field values and the full names of the cities in the presentation. This is a very common requirement in web applications.

Other Macros

There are a couple of macros in the table that we didn't discuss. They are

- `#springMessage`
- `#springMessageText`
- `#springUrl`

The two message macros can be used to specify localized messages based on text held in resource bundles. If your `ApplicationContext` defines a `MessageSource` bean (highly recommended), then its resource bundles will be searched to find the key that is passed as the parameter to the macro. The second of the two permits you to specify a default message value that will be used if the key cannot be found in the `MessageSources`.

`#springUrl` lets you use URLs in your templates that include the context root of the web application, without your template needing to know what the context root is. Having any part of your web application aware of the context root at which it is deployed makes it significantly less portable. For example, the fragment `#springUrl("/mycontroller.html")` will be rendered as `/myapp/mycontroller.html` if your application was deployed at a context root of `myapp`.

Number and Date Tools

Velocity makes available several useful tools from its supporting `velocity-tools-generic.jar` (you'll need to add these your `WEB-INF/lib` to take advantage of them). Two of these are the `NumberTool` and the `DateTool`. Both accept a `Locale` object in order to parameterize them for specific locales, but Spring offers a further benefit in that the `Locale` parameter can be retrieved using standard Spring `LocaleResolver` instances that we discussed earlier. That's great news, and Listing 8-30 shows how to do it in a `VelocityView` definition configured by

`ResourceBundleViewResolver`. You can also set these attributes on `VelocityViewResolver` to make them available to all of your Velocity Views.

Listing 8-30. *Adding a Number and Date Tool with Spring Locale Resolution*

```
home.class=org.springframework.web.servlet.view.velocity.VelocityView
home.url=/WEB-INF/velocity/home.vm
home.dateToolAttribute=date
home.numberToolAttribute=number
```

The names you give to the tools are the names you use to access them in your template files, as shown in Listing 8-31. We assume that the model contains an attribute of type `java.util.Date` with the name `flightDepartsOn`.

Listing 8-31. *Using the Date and Number Tools*

```
<h1>Flight details</h1>
<p>
  Flight departs: $date.format("E, MMMM d", $flightDepartsOn)
</p>
<p>
  Cost of flight: $number.format('currency', $flightCost)
</p>
```

When the template is rendered in the browser using the default locale (en_GB), we get the following response, shown in Figure 8-5.

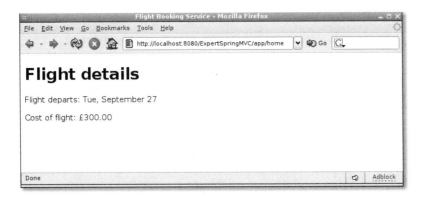

Figure 8-5. *Date and number formatting with a UK locale*

And if we switch the browser language to fr_FR (French) and reload the page, voilà! French formatting as shown in Figure 8-6.

Figure 8-6. *Locale-aware formatting, this time in French*

Additional Velocity Views

A final note on Velocity support: There are two additional views extending from `VelocityView` that you may recall from Figure 7-1 in Chapter 7.

- `VelocityToolboxView` offers the ability to load tools from a standard `toolbox.xml` configuration file (see the Velocity documentation for details of toolboxes). On your `View`, set the property `toolboxConfigLocation` to the location of `toolbox.xml`. You can optionally set this property on `VelocityViewResolver` too, in which case everything resolved by the resolver will be of type `VelocityToolboxView`.

- `VelocityLayoutView` further extends `VelocityToolboxView` and supports similar functionality to what you obtain by using the native `VelocityLayoutServlet` (part of the Velocity distribution, not Spring). A `VelocityLayoutView` consists of two distinct templates: the layout template and the main content template. When the model is rendered, initially the content template is merged with the model and placed in a Velocity variable named `screen_content`. The model is then merged again with the layout template, which has access to `$screen_content` in order to place it anywhere in the layout. `VelocityLayoutView` can be a good option if you want standard layouts for different content views, although you may be better served investigating other technologies such as SiteMesh (`http://www.opensymphony.com/sitemesh`) to achieve this.

Summary

In this section, we've covered Spring's support for two of the major open-source templating solutions available to you. We've shown how to set up your MVC application to enable a smooth integration, and we examined the significant value-added extras in the form of Spring's form-handling macros.

At this stage, you should be in a position to decide whether Velocity or FreeMarker is a suitable view tier technology for your applications, and how to go about writing that layer with confidence. If you decide upon Velocity, you might like to investigate *Pro Jakarta Velocity* by Rob Harrop (Apress, 2004).

In the next section we'll see how Spring enables seamless integration with another well-known presentation technology: XSLT.

XML and XSLT

XSLT is a popular view technology in many applications. It naturally and cleanly separates data from presentation and offers no opportunity to mix domain logic with the presentation, much as we've been advocating throughout this book.

However, despite tremendous advances in some XSLT engines, it can still be quite a heavyweight view layer in terms of processing power. Unless your application already deals with XML in some native form, then your model beans will also have to undergo an intermediate conversion to XML prior to transformation by XSLT. You could consider employing the W3C API, JDOM, or another XML API that you are familiar with to handle this conversion manually, but you really need to have a good reason for doing this. If you have to develop the stylesheets and you have only in-house expertise in JSP, Velocity, or similar, you may be best served switching your choice of view technology.

On the other hand, if you are creating `Source` objects in a more efficient format than XML DOM trees, or if your team already has in-house XSLT expertise (or better, a suite of existing stylesheets that you can take advantage of without having to develop them), then these may be mitigating reasons for considering XSLT as the view.

Defining an XSLT View

So having weighed up the pros and cons, let's see how to actually make use of XSLT for XHTML generation in your web applications. First off, we define a `View` and configure it. Listing 8-32 shows how using a definition in a `views.properties` file that will be resolved by our good friend `ResourceBundleViewResolver`.

Listing 8-32. *Defining an XSLT View*

```
home.class=com.apress.expertspringmvc.flight.web.view.HomePage
home.stylesheetLocation=/WEB-INF/xsl/home.xslt
```

Interestingly, the `View` class is obviously not provided by Spring but belongs to the application itself. Why? Well, as we mentioned in the introduction to this section, the native model (your `Map` of objects) probably has to be converted to an XML representation prior to transformation by your stylesheet. Although several libraries such as JAXB (`http://java.sun.com/webservices/jaxb`), Domify (`http://domify.sourceforge.net`), and Castor (`http://www.castor.org`) could potentially help automate this task, they may not offer the flexibility you need in generating your representation of the object graph. Your XML representation may even exist already in the model if you generated it in the `Controller` or obtained it from the service layer of your application.

■**Tip** If you find that something like Domify does provide what you need, then it would be a good idea to create a concrete `DomifyView` extending `AbstractXsltView` and use this for all your application needs.

Listing 8-33 shows the definition of the HomePage class that is our XSLT View. We're generating the XML representation manually as an example, but as we've seen, this may not be an ideal use of CPU cycles.

Listing 8-33. *HomePage XSLT View Class Definition*

```
public class HomePage extends AbstractXsltView {

    public HomePage() {
        super();
    }

    /**
     * @see AbstractXsltView#createXsltSource()
     */
    @Override
    protected Source createXsltSource(
        Map model,
        String root,
        HttpServletRequest request,
        HttpServletResponse response)
    throws Exception {

        // possibly not the best way to generate your
        // XML representation.  See discussion in the text
        List<SpecialDeal> specials =
          (List<SpecialDeal>) model.get("specials");
        Document doc =
            DocumentBuilderFactory
                .newInstance()
                .newDocumentBuilder()
                .newDocument();

        Element rootEl = doc.createElement(root);
        doc.appendChild(rootEl);

        for (SpecialDeal deal : specials) {
            Element dealEl = doc.createElement("deal");

            Element fromEl = doc.createElement("from");
            fromEl.appendChild(
                doc.createTextNode(deal.getDepartFrom().getName()));

            Element toEl = doc.createElement("to");
            toEl.appendChild(
                doc.createTextNode(deal.getArriveAt().getName()));
```

```
            Element costEl = doc.createElement("cost");
            costEl.appendChild(
                doc.createTextNode(String.valueOf(deal.getCost())));

            dealEl.appendChild(fromEl);
            dealEl.appendChild(toEl);
            dealEl.appendChild(costEl);

            rootEl.appendChild(dealEl);
        }

        return new DOMSource(doc);

    }

}
```

Hopefully you can begin to see the issue with generating the XML representation from the plain old Java object (POJO) model.

The concrete HomePage that we created, extends Spring's base AbstractXsltView and overrides the required createXsltSource() method. The processing in the abstract superclass will use this Source object as the source (of course) of the transformation.

■**Caution** In Spring 1.2, AbstractView.createXsltSource was not marked abstract, thereby not *requiring* you to implement it in your subclass and enforcing the desired contract. This method was added in Spring 1.2 to replace the legacy createDomNode method that returns a DOM object. Because only one of those methods should be implemented by subclasses, and backward compatibility was required for 1.1 subclasses, this wasn't possible and createDomNode was simply deprecated instead. In Spring 1.3, createDomNode has been removed and createXsltSource made abstract.

Transforming the XML Source

Listing 8-34 shows a textual representation of the DOM that we built up in the preceding method, assuming two special deals had been returned for our home page.

Listing 8-34. *The Raw XML Prior to Transformation*

```
<?xml version="1.0" encoding="UTF-8"?>
<specials>
  <deal>
    <from>London</from>
    <to>New York</from>
    <cost>300</cost>
  </deal>
  <deal>
    <from>Paris</from>
```

```
    <to>Moscow</from>
    <cost>100</cost>
  </deal>
</specials>
```

The name of the root element (`<specials>`) was in this case set by the `Controller` when it returned a single object as the model. The root name takes the name of a single model parameter in these cases.

If your model contains more than one object, though, you can set a root name in the `views.properties` file that we looked at in Listing 8-32. The value of a `home.root` property would be passed into our `createXsltSource` method as the second parameter (`String root`). If you don't set one, your XML will have a root element of `<DocRoot>`.

To complete the picture, our stylesheet that we instructed the `ViewResolver` to load from `/WEB-INF/xsl/home.xslt` is shown in Listing 8-35.

Listing 8-35. *Home Page Stylesheet*

```xml
<?xml version="1.0"?>

<xsl:stylesheet version="1.0"
  xmlns:xsl="http://www.w3.org/1999/XSL/Transform">

  <xsl:template match="/">

    <html>
      <head><title>Flight Booking Service</title></head>

      <body>
        <h1>Welcome to the Flight Booking Service</h1>
        <p>We have the following specials now:</p>

        <ul>
          <xsl:for-each select="/specials/deal">
          <li>
            <xsl:value-of select="./from"/> -
            <xsl:value-of select="./to"/> from
            <xsl:value-of select="./cost"/>
          </li>
          </xsl:for-each>
        </ul>

        <p><a href="search">Search for a flight.</a></p>

      </body>
    </html>

  </xsl:template>

</xsl:stylesheet>
```

Returning XML in the Raw

An interesting use case for the XSLT `View` is actually to avoid transforming the XML at all and simply return it raw. You can easily achieve this by opting *not* to specify a value for the `stylesheetLocation` property on your `View`.

Figure 8-7 shows the output of our home page after we comment out the `stylesheetLocation` property in `views.properties`.

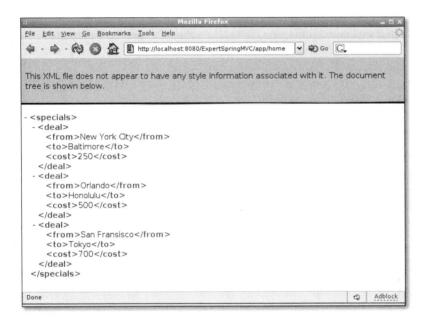

Figure 8-7. *XML output in the client*

Why would you want to do such a thing? It's possible that your application's clients are not humans but rather machines. In the simplest case, you could be providing something like an RSS feed for news clients.

Larger systems might use it as a decoupling strategy. The view layer from one part of the service emits a known XML variant so that it can be used as input by one or more content rendering engines (CREs). These CRE applications are then free to concentrate on generating the actual end product—probably for multiple device types and languages. Separation of concerns at a higher level!

Other Noteworthy XSLT Features

Before we move on, it's worth mentioning a couple of other features specific to Spring's XML/XSLT support. We'll take a brief glance at number and date formatting and stylesheet parameterization.

Number and Date Formatting

Unlike JSTL, Velocity, FreeMarker, and many other templating or web technologies, XSLT (to version 1.1) has relatively poor support for number and date formatting. To compensate, Spring provides a FormatHelper class which offers a number of locale-aware static utility methods.

Our example from earlier could be enhanced by formatting the cost value as a country-specific currency using the FormatHelper. Listing 8-36 shows how.

Listing 8-36. *Currency Formatting in XSLT*

```
for (SpecialDeal deal : specials) {
    ...

    String amt = FormatHelper.currency(
        (double) deal.getCost(), Locale.UK);
    Element costEl = doc.createElement("cost");
    costEl.appendChild(
        doc.createTextNode(amt);

    ...

}
```

XSL Parameters

Stylesheets can be parameterized through the <xsl:param/> directive. In your XSLT subclass a Map of name-value pairs can be created by overriding either the getParameters() or getParameters(HttpRequest) methods. The parameter names must match those defined in your XSLT template as declared with <xsl:param name="foo">default</xsl:param>. Listings 8-37 and 8-38 show how this works.

Listing 8-37. *Home Page View Setting Parameter Values*

```
@Override
protected Map getParameters() {
    Map p = new HashMap();
    p.put("imageOfTheDay", viewHelper.getImageLocation());
}
```

Listing 8-38. *Parameter Declaration in home.xslt*

```
<xsl:param name="imageOfTheDay">http://server/image.png</xsl:param>
```

Summary

In this section we've taken a close look at Spring's support for XML and XSLT. As before, we reviewed the pros and cons of applying XSLT as your view layer and introduced the concepts of the technology.

We've outlined the behavior of `AbstractXsltView`, shown how to extend this class to provide your own concrete implementations, and looked at the case for *not* transforming your generated XML. You should now have enough knowledge to know not just how to apply XSL in your Spring MVC applications, but when it is appropriate to consider it.

Next, we're going to move on to some of the lesser-known and -used view technologies.

PDF

Spring offers PDF support via Bruno Lowagie's iText library (http://www.lowagie.com/iText). The basic premise follows the same pattern as that for XSLT support. For each view that you wish to render as a PDF, you create a class that extends `AbstractPdfView` and fill in the required method `buildPdfDocument()`.

Listing 8-39 shows an example that can be used to display the home page of our sample application as a fairly simple PDF.

Listing 8-39. *Creating the PDF from the Model*

```
public class HomePagePdf extends AbstractPdfView {

  @Override
  protected void buildPdfDocument(
    Map model,
    Document document,
    PdfWriter writer,
    HttpServletRequest request,
    HttpServletResponse response)
  throws Exception {

    Paragraph header = new Paragraph(new Chunk(
      "FlightSearch Special Deals. ",
      FontFactory.getFont(FontFactory.HELVETICA, 24)));
    document.add(header);

    List<SpecialDeal> specials = (List<SpecialDeal>) model.get("specials");
    for (SpecialDeal deal : specials) {
      document.add(new Paragraph(
        deal.getDepartFrom().getName() + " - " +
        deal.getArriveAt().getName() + " from $" +
        deal.getCost()));
    }
  }
}
```

Configuring the Application to Use a PDF View

The last part of the setup involves simply telling Spring that you want to use your PDF generator class as the View. In views.properties (shown following in Listing 8-40) we simply set the home page View class to the one we just coded.

Listing 8-40. *views.properties Entries for the PDF Home Page*

```
homepage.class=com.apress.expertspringmvc.flight.web.view.HomePagePdf
```

Now when our home page is accessed, the PDF is generated on the fly, and your browser will either ask you what to do with the file or simply open your PDF viewer and display the results. Figure 8-8 shows the PDF.

Figure 8-8. *The home page rendered as a PDF*

Template PDFs with FOP

Creating anything other than trivial PDFs on the fly with iText is likely to be very time-consuming and code intensive, as can be seen from the preceding examples. You might like to investigate the Apache Formatting Objects Processor (FOP) driver, which can create the PDF from a template.

An example of how to get started is in the Spring sandbox, which contains an AbstractXslFoView class. The sandbox is available as part of the Spring source code available from the SourceForge project site (http://sourceforge.net/projects/springframework). You will also have to download the FOP library, which is large, from http://xmlgraphics.apache.org/fop.

■**Note** The AbstractXslFoView is actually an extension of Spring's XSLT support rather than its PDF support. The basic technology is XSLT, and PDF simply happens to be the output format from the transformation.

Excel

Spring supports two libraries for generating Excel spreadsheets as views: the Jakarta POI library and JExcel. Both are used in exactly the same way other than the choice of JAR file that you add to your WEB-INF/lib directory in the deployed application and the actual manner of manipulating the workbook in Java. We'll look at an example of how to use the POI library here.

Creating the Template

Creating an Excel spreadsheet is best done from a template, having your model values update certain cells within that template, which will perhaps be the subject of charts or formulae already built in to the XLS template file. Merging your model with the template is done in the same way as we've seen for XSLT and PDF Views—by coding a concrete extension to a Spring provided abstract class.

Figure 8-9 displays the template file that we've created for the basis for our view. Model data will be used to update this template, providing a nicely formatted view to our users. We'll store this template in our WAR file at WEB-INF/excel/home.xls.

Figure 8-9. *Excel template used to display flights*

Coding the View

Listing 8-41 shows the class `com.apress.expertspringmvc.flight.web.view.HomePageExcel`, which extends `AbstractExcelView`. The required method that you need to override is called `buildExcelDocument()`.

Listing 8-41. *Creating the Excel Spreadsheet from the Model*

```
public class HomePageExcel extends AbstractExcelView {

  @Override
  protected void buildExcelDocument(
    Map model,
    HSSFWorkbook workbook,
    HttpServletRequest request,
    HttpServletResponse response)
  throws Exception {

    HSSFSheet dataSheet = workbook.getSheet("FlightSearch");

    List<SpecialDeal> specials =
      (List<SpecialDeal>) model.get("specials");
    int row = 4;
    for (SpecialDeal deal : specials) {
      int column = 0;
      getCell(dataSheet, row, ++column)
        .setCellValue(deal.getDepartFrom().getName());
      getCell(dataSheet, row, ++column)
        .setCellValue(deal.getArriveAt().getName());
      getCell(dataSheet, row, ++column)
        .setCellValue(deal.getCost());
      row++;
    }
  }
}
```

This should all be starting to look quite familiar by now if you've read the XSLT and PDF sections earlier in this chapter.

The workbook is created for you by Spring and passed into this method as a parameter. You simply need to manipulate this object appropriately. In the preceding code, you can see that the model data is placed in particular cells of the spreadsheet in order to fit into the template. The `getCell()` method is a convenience method included with `AbstractExcelView` that just ensures the cell is available for you to set values on.

Configuring the Application

Lastly, it just remains to configure the View for use. In our views.properties file we need two entries specifying the class name that we want to use and the URL pointing to the template we want to use. Listing 8-42 has the details.

Listing 8-42. *views.properties Configuration for Excel Home Page*

```
home.class=com.apress.expertspringmvc.flight.web.view.HomePageExcel
home.url=/WEB-INF/excel/home
```

When we hit the home page of our application now, the spreadsheet is created on the fly from a combination of the model and the template. Either your browser will ask what to do with it, or it will just fire up your spreadsheet application (Excel or OpenOffice.org, for example) to display the output. Figure 8-10 shows how it looks.

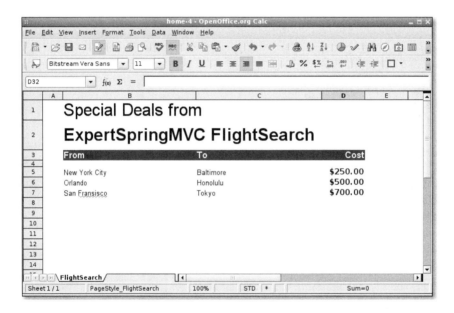

Figure 8-10. *Spreadsheet view of the home page*

JasperReports

JasperReports is an open-source reporting engine written in Java. Report designs are created in XML and can be output to several different formats. Jasper is a mature reporting engine now, and a commercial organization (JasperSoft) has recently been incepted to manage ongoing development and provide support.

We're not going to show an example of the report itself because of the verbose syntax, but we encourage you to take a look at the samples on the Jasper site (http://jasperreports. sourceforge.net), which has excellent documentation online. In this section we'll concentrate on showing how to integrate the reports with your application.

Spring's Jasper support consists of five concrete `View` implementations for each of the final output types available. These were shown in Figure 7-1 in the previous chapter and are recapped here.

- `JasperReportsCsvView`

- `JasperReportsHtmlView`

- `JasperReportsPdfView`

- `JasperReportsXlsView`

- `JasperReportsMultiFormatView`

The first four produce fixed format reports in CSV, HTML, PDF, and Excel format, respectively; the final one allows the format to be decided at runtime. A new, concrete type called `ConfigurableJasperReportsView` is likely to be available in Spring 1.3, which enables you to specify which `JRExporter` to use.

To use one of the Jasper `View` types, you specify the familiar configuration in the `ViewResolver`'s configuration file. Listing 8-43 shows an example that will display the home page model from our sample application as a Jasper PDF report.

Listing 8-43. *views.properties Settings for the Jasper Home Page*

```
home.class=org.springframework.web.servlet.view.jasperreports.JasperReportsPdfView
home.url=/WEB-INF/jasper/home.jrxml
```

The file `home.jrxml` is the report design itself. Jasper reports are natively XML, which is great if you need to get in and do low-level editing of a report, but coding one by hand can be quite laborious. A few GUI designers are available that will read and write Jasper's report design files, some of which are licensed commercially.

■**Tip** Although you can deploy the design file as a `.jrxml` just as we're showing here, Jasper needs to compile the report prior to use. Similar to JSPs, it will do this the first time it encounters a new report and then cache the resultant `.jasper` file. To do this, however, you need to make the `jdt-compiler.jar` available to your application and configure the JRCompiler accordingly. As such, it's recommended only for development environments. For production, you can precompile your reports using an Ant task provided with Jasper and deploy the compiled versions instead.

Multiformat View

The `JasperReportsMultiFormatView` is a thin wrapper that delegates to one of the other report types at runtime. A mapping key is specified that relates to the class name of the actual report type required.

In Listing 8-44, we show an example of how this can be used in the `Controller`. The `Controller` extracts the filename extension from the incoming request URI and uses it to tell Jasper which report format should be used.

Listing 8-44. *Using a URI Extension As a Mapping Key*

```
public ModelAndView handleMultiReport(
  HttpServletRequest request, HttpServletResponse response)
throws Exception {

  String uri = request.getRequestURI();
  String reportFormat = uri.substring(uri.lastIndexOf(".") + 1);

  Map model = getModel();
  model.put("format", reportFormat);

  return new ModelAndView("report", model);
}
```

With proper configuration of the request URIs in your dispatcher's context file, this method can now be used to serve multiple format reports. For example, a request of /ExpertSpringMVC/app/home.pdf will result in a PDF version of the report, and /ExpertSpringMVC/app/home.xls will generate an Excel spreadsheet–based report.

■**Note** The format key (format in the preceding example) is the name by which JasperReportsMultiFormatView will look up the actual format type (csv, xls, or whatever). If you need to change the name of the format key to something else, you can do so by setting the formatKey property on the View.

Populating the Report

A report isn't much to look at unless it has some data to show. In common with all Spring's supported view types, Jasper report Views extract their data from the model, and you can do this in two principal ways—differing slightly from other view types in this respect.

Jasper natively works with an instance of JRDataSource, which is an interface from the Jasper library. If your model contains a single attribute and it implements JRDataSource, then Spring will expose this object to the Jasper runtime. If your single model attribute is a java.util.Collection, this can also be used; Spring will convert the Collection to a JRDataSource and use this instead.

Should your model consist of more than one attribute, then you should configure the Jasper View to tell it which model attribute is the JRDataSource or Collection to use. Failing to do so means that Spring will expose the first attribute it finds that is one of those types—which may not be the data you wanted to see in your report! On the View configuration, set the reportDataKey value to the same name as your collection in the model. Listing 8-45 shows this setting.

Listing 8-45. *Specifying a Report Data Key for the Jasper Report*

```
home.class=org.springframework.web.servlet.view.jasperreports.JasperReportsPdfView
home.reportDataKey=jasperData
home.url=/WEB-INF/jasper/home.jrxml
```

In Listing 8-46, the `Controller` returns a model consisting of multiple objects, one of which is keyed under the name specified as the report data key in the `View`.

Listing 8-46. *A Model Containing the Report Data and Other Attributes*

```
public ModelAndView handleReport(
  HttpServletRequest request, HttpServletResponse response)
throws Exception {

  Map model = new HashMap();
  Collection reportData = getReportData();
  Collection otherData = getOtherData();
  model.put("jasperData", reportData);
  model.put("otherData", otherData);
  return new ModelAndView("home", model);
}
```

Summary

Jasper is another very flexible view technology that has myriad options not explored in this brief introduction. We've covered the basics of how to set up a JasperReport as a view and expose your data to it. We strongly recommend that you visit the JasperReports website to get a full rundown on what Jasper can do, safe in the knowledge that you can now apply all those great features to your Spring MVC applications.

Creating New Views

That pretty much concludes our tour of supported view technologies in Spring applications—and there was a lot of information to cover and take in. But what do you do in the unlikely event that Spring has no first-class support for your favorite view technology? Write it yourself, of course!

Spring is highly extensible in all departments, designed with thought in mind for the cases where additional support might be required for fringe cases. The view layer is no different.

If you need to implement a new view type, look through the JavaDoc and the source code to see if one of the existing hierarchy of classes offers suitable functionality first. `AbstractView` and `AbstractUrlBasedView` are prime candidates.

Should those classes really not do anything that you need, then implement the `View` interface directly and handle the response from the `render()` method.

Summary

In this chapter we've looked at the various technologies that can be used within your Spring Web MVC application, including JSP, templating technologies, XSLT, and document-based views. We also covered how to create your own view types that fit within the Spring architecture and that allow your application to display models in unusual ways.

We've presented a lot of information in this long chapter. The chances are that your applications will only ever use a small subset of the functionality and technologies that Spring supports in its view layer. If you have an application that uses all of it, please write in and let us know; we'd love to see it!

CHAPTER 9

■■■

Validation

Command objects that have been populated by DataBinder can be validated and report back errors when validation fails. Spring offers its own validation infrastructure as an add-on to core Spring. In fact, validation is not even considered part of Spring MVC.

Validators are implementations of the org.springframework.validation.Validator interface. They are stateless singleton classes that are configured in the Spring ApplicationContext and injected into your Controllers and test objects and their property values.

Validators are stateless objects just like Spring MVC Controllers. The Validator interface is designed to facilitate usage in a thread-safe manner; implementation classes should make sure they are thread-safe as well.

Two types of Validator implementations exist:

- Programmatic Validators where validation constraints are coded

- Declarative Validators that create validation constraints based on configuration

Programmatic Validators

The Validator interface has two methods that should be implemented. Refer to Listings 9-1 and 9-2.

Listing 9-1. *org.springframework.validation.Validator Interface*

```
public interface org.springframework.validation.Validator {
   public boolean supports(Class clazz);
   public void validate(Object target, Errors errors);
}
```

The validate() method implements the actual constraints on the target object. The supports() method defines which classes the Validator supports.

The org.springframework.validation.Errors interface is key to the Spring validation infrastructure. The Errors interface is discussed at the end of this chapter. Implementation classes of this interface register errors that occur when binding and validating objects. The instance received by the validate() method has to be populated with errors detected when testing the constraints on the target objects.

To reject a property value use one of the rejectValue() methods of the Errors interface.

Listing 9-2. *Validator Implementation for Address Objects*

```
package com.apress.expertspringmvc.validation;

import org.springframework.validation.Validator;
import org.springframework.validation.Errors;
import org.springframework.validation.ValidationUtils;

public class EasyAddressValidator implements Validator {
    public boolean supports(Class clazz) {
        Address.class.isAssignableFrom(clazz);
    }
    public void validate(Object target, Errors errors) {
        ValidationUtils.rejectIfEmtpy(errors, "location", "addressLocationEmpty");
    }
}
```

This Validator rejects the location property on the Address class if the property value is empty (null or a zero-length string). addressLocationEmpty is the error code that's looked up through an org.springframework.context.MessageSource instance; by default this is the ApplicationContext.

Let's extend the Address domain class Validator. See Listing 9-3.

Listing 9-3. *More Elaborate Validator for Address Objects*

```
package com.apress.expertspringmvc.validation;

import org.springframework.validation.Validator;
import org.springframework.validation.Errors;
import org.springframework.validation.ValidationUtils;

public class  AddressValidator implements Validator {
    public boolean supports(Class clazz) {
        return Address.class.isAssignableFrom(clazz);
    }
    public void validate(Object target, Errors errors) {
        ValidationUtils.rejectIfEmpty(errors, "city", "cityEmpty");
        ValidationUtils.rejectIfEmpty(errors, "location", "locationEmpty");
        ValidationUtils.rejectIfEmpty(errors, "postalCode", "postalCodeEmpty");
        ValidationUtils.rejectIfEmpty(errors, "country", "countryIsEmpty");
    }
}
```

As you can see, this `Validator` simply checks whether the required fields have been set. More complex constraints can be added as well. When a constraint is violated, the property value is rejected by means of specifying the property name and a message code.

Declarative Validators

Currently two declarative validation strategies are available for Spring:

- the Jakarta Commons `Validator`

- Valang

The Jakarta Commons `Validator` uses an XML configuration file to declaratively specify constraints. However, configuration is not intuitive, and its configuration format is very verbose.

Valang, which stands for *validation language*, is a language specifically designed for validating target objects. Its notation is concise and specifically targeted toward getting data validated.

Valang is an open-source project and is available from Spring Modules. Go to `https://springmodules.dev.java.net` to get a copy.

Rewriting the `EasyAddressValidator` in Valang syntax is very easy, as shown in Listing 9-4.

Listing 9-4. *Example of Declarative Constraint in Valang*

```
{
location : ? is not blank : 'Location must be specified' : 'addressLocationEmpty'
}
```

Each constraint written in Valang notation is enclosed in curly brackets ("{" and "}"). Multiple constraints can be combined to create one `Validator`. The fields in a constraint are separated with colons (":").

The first field in the constraint above is the property of the target object that's being validated, and the second field is the actual constraint. This particular constraint tests whether the location property is not blank. The question mark ("?") replaces the property name specified in the first field to reduce typing.

When the evaluation of the constraint returns `false`, the property specified in field one is rejected with the default message in field three. Field four contains the error code, which is optional. If the error code cannot be found for the locale of the user or the default locale, the default message will display.

A fifth optional field can contain error arguments. Note, though, that if error arguments are provided, then an error code must be provided.

To create a `Validator` from the constraint in Listing 9-5 Valang has to be configured in the Spring `ApplicationContext`.

`ValangValidatorFactoryBean` parses the Valang syntax once and creates a `Validator` instance. Any performance overhead resulting from replacing Java validators with Valang is thus limited to the one-time parsing of the syntax when the Spring `ApplicationContext` is loaded. See Listing 9-5.

Listing 9-5. *Valang Validator and Configuration for Address Objects*

```
<bean id="easyAddressValidator" ➥
class="org.springmodules.validation.ValangValidatorFactoryBean">
    <property name="syntax">
        <value><![CDATA[
{ location : ? is not blank : 'Location must be specified' : ➥
'addressLocationEmpty' }
        ]]></value>
    </property>
</bean>
```

Rewriting the address `Validator` with Valang is straightforward. Remember that the property in a constraint is rejected if the constraint evaluates to `false`. The constraint thus specifies which conditions must be matched for the object to be valid. Refer to Listing 9-6.

Listing 9-6. *Valang Validating Multiple Properties in One Validator*

```
{ city : ? is not blank : '' : 'cityEmpty' }
{ location : ? is not blank : '' : 'locationEmpty' }
{ postalCode : ? is not blank : '' : 'postalCodeEmpty' }
{ country : ? is not blank : '' : 'countryEmpty' }
```

When we want to extend the constraints for the address `Validator` in Valang it's important to take into account whether all constraints you specify are validated, as well as whether one or more constraints fail.

If we want to add a constraint that tests the length of the city name, we have to take into account that the previous constraint that tests whether the city name is blank may have failed. In other words we need to take into account that the city name may be `null`.

To achieve this, we let the second constraint succeed if city is blank. See Listing 9-7.

Listing 9-7. *Example of Cascading Constraints in Valang*

```
{ city : ? is not blank : '' : 'cityEmpty' }
{ city : ? is blank or length(?) <= 30 : '' : 'cityTooLong' }
```

The first constraint will reject the city property value if it's blank. The second constraint will only reject the city property value if it's not blank and it's more than 30 characters long.

We don't want to reject the city property in the second constraint if it's blank because the first constraint does this already. We do test whether the city property value is blank because we don't want a `NullPointerException` to be thrown when we test the length of the property value.

The example constraints shown in Listing 9-7 reveal that Valang supports complex logical tests. AND and OR logical operators are supported next to parentheses to define the order of prevailing.

Let's write a rather unrealistic constraint (Listing 9-8) to demonstrate complex tests.

Listing 9-8. *Example of Complex Boolean Logic in Valang*

```
{ postalCode :
    (? is blank or country is blank)
    or ((country in 'United States', 'France' and length(?) = 5)
    or (country = 'Belgium' and length(?) = 4)
    or country not in
    'United States', 'France', 'Belgium') :
    '' : 'postalCodeInvalid' : ?, country, length(?) }
```

This constraint will fail if the country and postal code are not blank; if the country is either the United States or France; if the length of the postal code is not 5 or the country is Belgium; and if the length of the postal code is not 4. Other combinations of postal code and country will be accepted as is by this constraint.

Also notice that the postal code, the country, and the length of the postal code are passed as error arguments.

Valang supports a wide range of operators to allow for extensive testing of target objects.

Table 9-1. *Operators Supported by Valang*

Operator	Types	Null Safe	Description
=, ==	Any	No	Tests equality of left and right values.
!=, <>, ><	Any	No	Tests inequality of left and right values.
<	N, D	No	Tests value to the left is less than value to the right. Only supports numbers and dates.
<=, =<	N, D	No	Tests value to the left is less than or equal to value to the right. Only supports numbers and dates.
>	N, D	No	Tests value to the left is more than value to the right. Only supports numbers and dates.
=>, >=	N, D	No	Tests value to the left is more than or equal to value to the right. Only supports numbers and dates.
IN <value> (, <value>)*	Any	No	Tests equality of value to the left with one of the values to the right.
NOT IN <value> (, <value>)*	Any	No	Tests inequality of value to the left with all of the values to the right.
BETWEEN <value> AND <value>	N, D	No	Tests value to the left is more than or equal to first value to the right and less than or equal to second value to the right. Only supports numbers and dates.
NOT BETWEEN <value> AND <value>	N, D	No	Tests value to left is less than first value to the right or more than second value to the right. Only supports numbers and dates.

Continued

Table 9-1. *Continued*

Operator	Types	Null Safe	Description
IS NULL, NULL	Any	Yes (`true`)	Tests value to the left is `null`.
IS NOT NULL, NOT NULL	Any	Yes (`false`)	Tests value to the left is not `null`.
HAS TEXT	Any (*)	Yes (`false`)	Tests `String` value to the left contains characters other than white space, has more than 0 characters and is not `null`.
HAS NO TEXT	Any (*)	Yes (`true`)	Tests `String` value to the left contains only white-space characters, contains no characters or is `null`.
HAS LENGTH	Any (*)	Yes (`false`)	Tests `String` value to the left is not `null` and has more than 0 characters.
HAS NO LENGTH	Any (*)	Yes (`true`)	Tests `String` value to the left is `null` or contains no characters.
IS BLANK	Any (*)	Yes (`true`)	Same as HAS LENGTH.
IS NOT BLANK	Any (*)	Yes (`false`)	Same as HAS NO LENGTH.
IS UPPERCASE, IS UPPER CASE, IS UPPER	Any (*)	No	Tests alpha characters in `String` value to the left are all uppercase.
IS NOT UPPERCASE, IS NOT UPPER CASE, IS NOT UPPER	Any (*)	No	Tests not all alpha characters in `String` value to the left are uppercase.
IS LOWERCASE, IS LOWER CASE, IS LOWER	Any (*)	No	Tests alpha characters in `String` value to the left are all lowercase.
IS NOT LOWERCASE, IS NOT LOWER CASE, IS NOT LOWER	Any (*)	No	Tests not all alpha characters in `String` value to left are lowercase.
IS WORD	Any (*)	Yes (`false`)	Tests `String` value to the left contains no white-space characters.
IS NOT WORD	Any (*)	Yes (`true`)	Tests `String` value to the left contains and least one white-space character.

N = number
D = date
* = takes value of the `toString()` *method*

Valang can test any value—either `String`, number, Boolean, and date literals or property values of any type. See Listing 9-9.

Listing 9-9. *Examples of Literal Values in Valang*

```
'a string example, next is a number example and after that a date example'
-10.5
[2005-07-30]
```

Internally Valang converts property number values to `java.math.BigDecimal`, while
`BigDecimal` also parses number literals. Valang's internal date parser parses date literals that
allow for powerful date constructs.

Valang uses `org.springframework.beans.BeanWrapperImpl` to read property values. The
property notation constructs of this class are supported in Valang. They include simple properties, nested properties, and access to `List` elements and `Map` entries. See Listing 9-10.

Listing 9-10. *Example of Property Accessors in Valang*

```
name
address.location
customers[0].name
salesParameters[seasonStartDate]
```

When accessing `Map` entries keys are expected to be `Strings`. Since `BeanWrapperImpl`'s
notation is reused in Valang the `String` values that represent key values are not quoted.

Valang supports mathematical expressions that can contain literal values of bean property values. Parentheses support proper mathematical prevailing. Valang considers the result
of mathematical expressions like the example in Listing 9-11 as values that can be tested.

Listing 9-11. *Example of Mathematical Expressions in Valang*

```
((10 - (5 + -3)) * (salesParameters[reduction] mod 3)) div 13
```

Supported mathematical operators are

- +
- −
- *
- / or div
- % or mod

Date literals deserve special attention when discussing Valang. They are always encapsulated in square brackets ("[" and "]"). Valang's internal date parser recognizes a limited
number of date formats, but you can add your own formats.

Its date operators are the real power of the Valang date parser. Suppose we want to test if a
date is today. It would be fairly trivial to write this in Java code, but it becomes more challenging when you have to provide a date value to test a property value in a validation language
notation.

To start discovering the functionalities of the Valang date parser we introduce the
`T` construct. `T` represents the current time, comparable to creating a new `java.util.Date()`
instance.

To test whether the value of the order timestamp property is earlier than the current timestamp with Valang, we use the constraint in Listing 9-12.

Listing 9-12. *Example of Using T As a Date Literal in Valang*

```
{ order.timestamp : ? < [T] : '' : 'order.timestamp.in_past' }
```

To make sure T represents the time of validation and not the time of parsing the syntax, Valang parses date literals every time the validation constraint is executed. These semantics make sure T is always now.

The Valang date parser supports two date operator types: shift operators and incremental operators.

Suppose we want to test whether the order timestamp property value is today (see Listing 9-13). To achieve this we have to create two limits: the start of the day and the end of the day. The date parser notation to create these two timestamps is [T<d] and [T>d]. The shift-down (<) and shift-up (>) operators take a one-character argument to determine how far back or forth to shift. Each shift operator affects a specific part of the timestamp. The d or day operator affects the time part of the timestamp. It resets the time to 00:00:00.000 for the shift-down operator and to 23:59:59.999 for the shift-up operator.

Listing 9-13. *Testing Whether a Date Value Is Today*

```
{ order.timestamp :

  ? between [T<d] and [T>d] :

  '' : 'order.timestamp.not_today' : ? }
```

Valang supports the shift operators shown in Table 9-2.

Table 9-2. *Shift Operators for Dates in Valang*

Notation	Description
>s	Shifts second to end of second (999 milliseconds).
<s	Shifts second to start of second (0 milliseconds).
>m	Shifts minute to end of minute (59 seconds, 999 milliseconds).
<m	Shifts minute to start of minute (0 seconds, 0 milliseconds).
>H	Shifts hour to end of hour (59 minutes, 59 seconds, 999 milliseconds).
<H	Shifts hour to start of hour (0 minutes, 0 seconds, 0 milliseconds).
>d	Shifts day to end of day (23 hours, 59 minutes, 59 seconds, 999 milliseconds).
<d	Shifts day to start of day (0 hours, 0 minutes, 0 seconds, 0 milliseconds).
>w	Shifts date to the end of the current week (next Sunday, 23 hours, 59 minutes, 59 seconds, 999 milliseconds).
<w	Shifts date to start of current week (previous Monday, 0 hours, 0 minutes, 0 seconds, 0 milliseconds).
>M	Shifts date to end of current month (last day of month, 23 hours, 59 minutes, 59 seconds, 999 milliseconds).
<M	Shifts date to start of current month (first day of month, 0 hours, 0 minutes, 0 seconds, 0 milliseconds).
>y	Shifts date to end of year (last day of year, 23 hours, 59 minutes, 59 seconds, 999 milliseconds).
<y	Shifts date to start of year (first day of year, 0 hours, 0 minutes, 0 seconds, 0 milliseconds).

Shift operators and incremental operators can be combined to create new timestamps. If we want to test whether the order timestamp lies between Monday 8 a.m. of this week and Friday 8 p.m. of this week we again have to create two new timestamps. [T<w+8H] shifts the current timestamp back to the start of the week (previous Monday at midnight) and adds 8 hours (previous Monday at 8 a.m.). [T>w<d-2d+20H] shifts the current timestamp forth to the end of the week (next Sunday evening just before midnight), shifts to the start of the day (start of Sunday at midnight), subtracts two days (start of Friday at midnight), and adds 20 hours (Friday 8 p.m.).

Valang supports the incremental date operators shown in Table 9-3. Any integer number above 0 can replace the incremented value.

Table 9-3. *Incremental Operators for Dates in Valang*

Notation	Description
+1S	Adds 1 millisecond to the date.
-1S	Subtracts 1 millisecond from the date.
+1s	Adds 1 second to the date.
-1s	Subtracts 1 second from the date.
+1m	Adds 1 minute to the date.
-1m	Subtracts 1 minute from the date.
+1H	Adds 1 hour to the date.
-1H	Subtracts 1 hour from the date.
+1d	Adds 1 day to the date.
-1d	Subtracts 1 day from the date.
+1w	Adds 1 week to the date.
-1w	Subtracts 1 week from the date.
+1M	Adds 1 month to the date.
-1M	Subtracts 1 month from the date.
+1y	Adds 1 year to the date.
-1y	Subtracts 1 year from the date.

In date expression T can also be replaced by a literal date value. [20050730<M] resolves to the start of Friday, 1 July 2005 at midnight.

Valang by default supports these date formats. The formats are in the notation supported by java.text.SimpleDateFormat.

Table 9-4. *Regular Expressions for Date Formats Valang Recognizes by Default*

Date Format	Regular Expression
yyyyMMdd	^\\d{8}$
yyyy-MM-dd	^\\d{4}\\-\\d{2}\\-\\d{2}$
yyyy-MM-dd HH:mm:ss	^\\d{4}\\-\\d{2}\\-\\d{2}\\s+\\d{2}:\\d{2}:\\d{2}$
yyyyMMdd HHmmss	^\\d{8}\\s+\\d{6}$
yyyyMMdd HH:mm:ss	^\\d{8}\\s+\\d{2}:\\d{2}:\\d{2}$
yyyy-MM-dd HHmmss	^\\d{4}\\-\\d{2}\\-\\d{2}\\s+\\d{6}$

Valang allows you to specify other date formats. For each custom date format you add to the date parser you need to provide a regular expression that matches the date format. Refer to Table 9-4 for examples of regular expressions. To make sure your regular expressions consume date literals entirely use "^" at the start of the regular expression and "$" at the end. In regular expressions "^" signifies the start of the literal, while "$" signifies the end.

Date formats are parsed by `java.text.SimpleDateFormat` and must use the notation implemented by this class. Look at the `SimpleDateFomat` javadoc for more details.

To configure Valang with custom date formats, inject them as a `Map` in the `dateParserRegistrations` property, as shown in Listing 9-14.

Listing 9-14. *Example of Registering Custom Date Formats with Valang*

```
<bean id="easyAddressValidator" class=➡
"org.springmodules.validation.ValangValidatorFactoryBean">
    <property name="syntax">
        <value><![CDATA[
{ order.timestamp : ? >= [200406] :
    'No orders dating before june 2004 can be  processed.' }
        ]]></value>
    </property>
    <property name="dateParserRegistrations">
        <props>
            <prop key="^\\d{6}$">yyyyMM</prop>
            <prop
              key="^\\d{4}\\-\\d{2}\\-\\d{2}\\s+\\d{2}:\\d{2}$">
yyyy-MM-dd HH:mm</prop>
        </props>
    </property>
</bean>
```

Valang has a number of built-in functions, as shown in Table 9-5. We've already discussed the length function in Listing 9-8.

Table 9-5. *Built-in Functions in Valang*

Function Name	Description
length	Returns the length of the return value of the `toString()` method of the target object.
len	See length.
size	See length.
upper	Returns the return value of the `toString()` method of the target object in uppercase characters.
lower	Returns the return value of the `toString()` method of the target object in lowercase characters.
!	NOT operation on `boolean` target objects.
resolve	Resolves a message code through a message source.

Custom functions can be registered with Valang to include in your constraints. To implement a custom function you need to extend org.springmodules.validation.functions. AbstractFunction. Custom function classes should implement the constructor of its parent class. The doGetResult method implements the actual function logic. Functions in Valang can have optional arguments, although most functions will probably expect a fixed number of arguments. The defineMinNumberOfArguments and definedMaxNumberOfArguments methods check whether the number of arguments passed to the function is within the accepted range. See Listing 9-15.

Listing 9-15. *Custom Function That Alters the Case of a String Value*

```
package com.apress.expertspringmvc.validation;

import org.springmodules.validation.functions.AbstractFunction;
import org.springmodules.validation.functions.Function;
import org.apache.commons.lang.WordUtils;

public class AlterCaseFunction extends AbstractFunction {
   public AlterCaseFunction(Function[] functions, int line, int column) {
      super(functions, line, column);
      defineMinNumberOfArguments(1);
      defineMaxNumberOfArguments(1);
   }
   protected Object doGetResult(Object target) {
      String value = getArguments()[0].getResult(target).toString();
      return WordUtils.swapCase(value);
   }
}
```

AlterCaseFunction swaps the case for the value of its argument. Its constructor is required by Valang to instantiate the function. To register this function with Valang we have to configure it in ValangValidatorFactoryBean, as shown in Listing 9-16.

Listing 9-16. *Registering the alterCase Function with Valang*

```
<bean id="caseSwappingValidator"
   class="org.springmodules.validation.ValangValidatorFactoryBean">
   <property name="syntax">
      <value><![CDATA[
{ name : alterCase(?) = 'sTEVEN' : 'Name must be Steven' }
      ]]></value>
   </property>
   <property name="customFunctions">
      <map>
         <entry key="alterCase"
            value="com.apress.expertspringmvc.validation.AlterCaseFunction"/>
      </map>
   </property>
</bean>
```

Custom Valang function classes often need collaborating objects to do their work. These objects can be autowired by name or by type. To get collaborating objects, add JavaBean properties to the function class and overwrite either the isAutoWireByName() or isAutoWireByType() methods defined in AbstractFunction. The init() method that's also defined in AbstractFunction can be overwritten to make sure mandatory properties have been set.

The init() method will be called by Valang after the properties have been autowired. Autowiring by type will fail if more than one bean definition of the same type is found in the Spring container. See Listing 9-17.

Listing 9-17. *Example of Autowiring in Custom Valang Functions*

```
package com.apress.expertspringmvc.validation;

import org.springmodules.validation.functions.AbstractFunction;
import org.springmodules.validation.functions.Function;
import org.springframework.jdbc.core.JdbcTemplate;
import org.springframework.util.Assert;

public class SqlQueryForIntFunction extends AbstractFunction {
   private JdbcTemplate jdbcTemplate = null;

   public SqlQueryForIntFunction(Function[] functions, int line, int column) {
      super(functions, line, column);
      defineMinNumberOfArguments(1);
      defineMaxNumberOfArguments(2);
   }

   public boolean isAutowireByName() {
      return true;
   }

   public void setJdbcTemplate(JdbcTemplate jdbcTemplate) {
      jdbcTemplate = jdbcTemplate;
   }

   public void init() throws Exception {
      Assert.notNull(jdbcTemplate, "JdbcTemplate is required!");
   }

   protected Object doGetResult(Object target) {
      String sql = getArguments()[0].getResult(target).toString();
      return new Integer(jdbcTemplate.queryForInt(sql));
   }
}
```

The SqlQueryForIntFunction takes a SQL statement that returns an integer value like a count on a database table. The SQL statement is executed on an instance of JdbcTemplate that has to be injected. The isAutowireByName() method returns true, so a bean definition named jdbcTemplate needs to be configured in the Spring container (see Listing 9-18). The init() method verifies whether a JdbcTemplate instance has been properly injected.

Listing 9-18. *Configuring JdbcTemplate to Be Injected in a Custom Valang Function*

```
<bean id="jdbcTemplate" class="org.springframework.jdbc.core.JdbcTemplate">
   <property name="dataSource" ref="dataSource"/>
</bean>
```

Next, as shown in Listing 9-19, we have to register this function with ValangValidatorFactoryBean to use it in our constraints.

Listing 9-19. *Registering queryForInt Custom Function with Valang*

```
<bean id="validator" class=➥
" org.springmodules.validation.ValangValidatorFactoryBean">
   <property name="valang">
      <value><![CDATA[
{ userId : 1 == queryForInt('select count(0) from users where userId = ' + ➥
userId) : 'User not found in database' }
      ]]></value>
   </property>
   <property name="customFunctions">
      <props>
        <prop
           key="queryForInt"
           >com.apress.expertspringmvc.validation.SqlQueryForIntFunction</prop>
      </props>
   </property>
</bean>
```

Custom Valang function classes can implement a number of Spring callback interfaces to get hold of the ApplicationContext or resource loader. Supported interfaces are

- org.springframework.context.ApplicationContextAware

- org.springframework.context.ApplicationEventPublisherAware

- org.springframework.beans.factory.BeanFactoryAware

- org.springframework.context.MessageSourceAware

- org.springframework.context.ResourceLoaderAware

- org.springframework.web.context.ServletContextAware

If any of these interfaces are implemented by a registered custom function, Valang will inject the related object. If your function implements ApplicationContextAware or BeanFactoryAware, consider using autowiring to get hold of collaborating services instead of dependency lookup.

Message Sources

The Spring ApplicationContext implements the org.springframework.context.MessageSource interface used to resolve messages based on the locale of the user. When error codes are used to reject property values or entire objects, Spring MVC asks the ApplicationContext for a message for a given locale.

The ApplicationContext checks if a local bean named messageSource has been defined. If no such bean is available, control is delegated to the parent ApplicationContext. If the parent ApplicationContexts have no messageSource defined an exception is thrown.

To set up internationalization for validation error messages, configure org.springframework.context.support.ResourceBundleMessageSource with bean name messageSource.

ResourceBundleMessageSource takes one or more base names to look up localized messages. These base names are appended with an underscore ("_"), the locale code ("NL", "FR", "ES", ...) and ".properties", resulting in a filename that's loaded from the classpath. These files will be checked sequentially to resolve error codes, giving priority to the last message found.

ResourceBundleMessageSource uses java.util.ResourceBundle internally to load the message files from the classpath. ResourceBundle instances are cached to improve performance.

org.springframework.context.support.ReloadableResourceBundleMessageSource reloads message files dynamically when they have changed. Set the cacheSeconds property to define the delay between refresh attempts (-1 being the default to cache forever). This message source uses Spring resource loaders to find message files defaulting to the default resource loader of the ApplicationContext. When loading message files from the classpath it should be noted that many application servers cache resources in the classpath. Changes made to message files may thus not be refreshed; put your files in the /WEB-INF folder to circumvent this. Do not set cache seconds to 0 in production environments, as this will check the modification timestamp of the message files on every message request.

Both ResourceBundleMessageSource and ReloadableResourceBundleMessageSource extend the AbstractMessageSource that implements message handling. When error arguments are passed, MessageFormat replaces tokens in the message. A message example with tokens supported by MessageFormat is:

```
Your company name {0} is too long.
```

AbstractMessageSource supports MessageSourceResolvable instances as error arguments that will be resolved by AbstractMessageSource. See Listing 9-20.

Listing 9-20. *Example of Message File Using Java Property Notation*

```
cpyNameToLong=Your {0} {1} is too long.
cpyName=Company name

errors.rejectValue("name", "cpyNameTooLong", new Object[] { new
DefaultMessageSourceResolvable("cpyName"), company.getName() }, null)
```

Validators and Business Logic

Validators are related to the presentation layer. However, if objects that are validated by a Validator are passed on to the business logic, this Validator can also be considered as part of the business logic layer.

Constraints can be called or implemented in three places:

- Validators

- service objects

- a validation method on domain classes

Validators are the only truly pluggable option. They can be injected into Controllers that call the business logic. Business logic has to implement second-level coarse-grained constraints, probably by throwing business exceptions. Validators handle the first-level validation that's more fine-grained, supports internalization, and is fully integrated with the presentation layer through the Errors interface. These are the most important advantages Validators offer over other alternatives.

Errors Interface

The Errors instance received by the validate method of the Validator interface is actually an instance of BindException. These two classes serve to report validation errors on the target being validated.

Two error types can be distinguished:

- Errors related to the object itself

- Errors related to missing or invalid property values

To reject an object as a whole, use the reject() methods (see Listing 9-21).

Listing 9-21. *reject() Methods in the org.springframework.validation.Errors Interface*

```
public void reject(String errorCode);
public void reject(String errorCode, String defaultMessage);
public void reject(String errorCode, Object[] errorArguments, String
defaultMessage);
```

Rejecting an object as a whole is called a *global error*, because though no specific property value is invalid, the form values cannot be processed. An example could be a customer who is underage.

When property values are invalid or required properties are missing, the rejectValue() methods can be used, as shown in Listing 9-22.

Listing 9-22. *rejectValue() Methods in the org.springframework.validation.Errors Interface*

```
public void rejectValue(String propertyName, String errorCode);
public void rejectValue(String propertyName, String errorCode, ➡
String defaultMessage);
public void rejectValue(String propertyName, String errorCode, Object[] ➡
errorArguments, String defaultMessage);
```

Rejecting a property value is called a *field error*. Types of field errors include invalid values of any kind, null values for required properties, and String values containing only white-space characters.

Global errors typically appear on top of a form in the view, while field errors typically appear next to the input fields they are related to.

The Errors interface supports nested Validators. This allows you to reuse Validators for a single class to validate object graphs. Two methods on the Errors interface allow you to manage the nested path. The nested path defines the path to the object that is rejected (or its property values).

CustomerValidator dispatches control to the AddressValidator to validate the address property. Before delegating, the CustomerValidator changes the nested path. Refer to Listing 9-23.

Listing 9-23. *Example of Using Nested Path to Delegate to Other Validator*

```
package com.apress.expertspringmvc.validation;

import org.springframework.validation.Validator;
import org.springframework.validation.Errors;
import com.apress.expertspringmvc.Customer;
import org.apache.commons.lang.StringUtils;

public class  CustomerValidator implements Validator {
    public boolean supports(Class clazz) {
        return Customer.class.isAssignableFrom(clazz);
    }
    public void validate(Object target, Errors errors) {
        Customer customer = (Customer)target;
        // other constraint checks
        errors.pushNestedPath("address");
        getAddressValidator(customer.getAddress(), errors);
        errors.popNestedPath();
    }

    private Validator addressValidator = null;
    public void setAddressValidator(Validator addressValidator) {
        this.addressValidator = addressValidator;
    }
    private Validator getAddressValidator() {
        if (this.addressValidator = null) {
            throw new IllegalStateException("Address validator is not available");
```

```
    }
        return this.addressValidator;
    }
}
```

pushNestedPath adds the path to the existing nested path if one is set; otherwise, the nested path is set to the value being pushed. popNestedPath removes the last nested path that has been added to restore the nested path to the previous value.

Notice CustomerValidator manages the nested path by means of pushing and popping on the Errors instance. The AddressValidator instance is clueless that its caller is another Validator; it is injected in CustomerValidator.

Testing Validators

Testing your validators—both declarative and programmatic validators—is important to verify that they validate only *valid* objects. Declarative validators like those created with Valang should be tested to verify the syntax and configuration work correctly. We only have to pass in an object to validate, and an Errors instance so calling a Validator from a test case is straightforward.

More challenging is verifying whether the correct error codes have been registered with the Errors instance for specific validation errors. Spring 2.0 offers a convenience class to check whether an Errors instance has only the error codes we expect. ErrorsVerifier can be found in the spring-mock.jar and offers methods to check the content of an Errors instance.

The test case in Listing 9-24 demonstrates the use of ErrorsVerifier. The testEmptyPersonValidation() method validates a Person object that has no values for its properties and verifies whether the Errors instance contains the expected errors.

Listing 9-24. *Using the ErrorsVerifier Class to Test the State of an Errors Instance*

```
public class PersonValidatorTests extends TestCase {
    public void testEmptyPersonValidation() {
        Person person = new Person();
        Validator validator = new PersonValidator();
        BindException errors = new BindException(person, "target");
        validator.validate(person, errors);

        new ErrorsVerifier(errors) {
            {
                forProperty("firstName").hasErrorCode("person.firstName.required")
                .forProperty("lastName").hasErrorCode("person.lastName.required")
                .otherwise().noErrors();
            }
        }
    }
}
```

The ErrorsVerifier class uses a special notation. First of all we create an anonymous class by calling new ErrorsVerifier(errors) {}. We pass in the Errors instance we want to verify in the constructor and in the constructor body—which is again enclosed in curly brackets—and we call the forProperty method and pass firstName as property name. Next we call the hasErrorCode method and pass in the error code we expect to be present in the Errors instance. If this error code cannot be found for the firstName property, an exception will be thrown. This notation is repeated for the lastName property. The hasErrorCode can be called more than once for a property and can also be used to check for global errors.

Lastly the otherwise and noErrors() methods are called. These methods verify if no other errors than the one we expect are present in the Errors instance. The ErrorsVerifier class is very convenient to quickly test if your Errors instance contains the correct error codes after being passed to a Validator. Imagine the Java code you would have to write otherwise to test that the content of the Errors instance is as expected!

Summary

Spring offers an excellent validation framework. The Validator and Errors interface form the backbone and allow you to write your own Validator implementations. If you'd rather use declarative validation, have a look at Valang. This framework creates a Spring Validator instance based on a set of constraints defined in its proper validation language. Valang is very convenient to quickly write constraints for your command classes. Its operators, functions, and date parser functionalities offer more power and flexibility than Validators written in Java. Whether you write your Validators in Java or Valang, you should always test them to check whether all error conditions are rejected properly.

Next to validation Spring also offers support for internationalization through its MessageSource interface. This interface will resolve messages for the locale of your users so that you can offer your applications in their languages.

CHAPTER 10

■■■

Testing Spring MVC Applications

By writing applications that are modular, pluggable, and loosely decoupled you are also creating applications that are extremely testable. The Spring Framework encourages you to build applications in such a way that creating both unit tests and integration tests is fast, easy, and rewarding. In this chapter, we will look at strategies and techniques for writing tests (both unit and integration) for your Spring MVC components.

We will build upon the JUnit testing framework and use Spring's built-in testing stubs (found in `spring-mock.jar`), as well as introduce mock objects (with the jMock library) for use with integration tests. One of the main selling points for building applications the Spring way is that tests become feasible to create, and we'll show you how to do it in this chapter.

Overview

When we say *testing*, what do we mean exactly? By testing, we specifically mean both unit tests and integration tests. These types of tests are focused on the actual methods of classes and the interactions between software components, respectively. What we won't cover is user acceptance testing, which is testing performed by users interacting with the interface of the application. We certainly aren't diminishing the usefulness of user acceptance tests, but unit and integration tests should locate most of the issues before they ever reach the users.

Unit Tests

A tremendous amount of literature is already available about unit tests, so we won't rehash it all here. However, we will spend time discussing what a unit test is—and isn't—to contrast it with an integration test.

■**Tip** Looking for more information on unit testing? We'd like to recommend both *JUnit Recipes* by J.B. Rainsberger and Scott Stirling (Manning Publications, 2004), and *Pragmatic Unit Testing in Java* (The Pragmatic Programmer, 2003) by Andrew Hunt and David Thomas.

The basic definition of a *unit test* is "a discrete test condition to check correctness of an isolated software module." Although we believe that this statement is correct, there is perhaps a better way to define a unit test. We argue that a test should strive to follow these tenets if it is *truly* to be called a unit test:

- *Run fast*: A unit test must run extremely fast. If it needs to wait for database connections or external server processes, or to parse large files, its usefulness will quickly become limited. A test should provide an immediate response and instant gratification.

- *Zero external configuration*: A unit test must not require any external configuration files—not even simple text files. The test's configurations must be provided and set by the test framework itself by calling code. The intent is to minimize both the runtime of the test and to eliminate external dependencies (which can change over time, becoming out of sync with the test). Test case conditions should be expressed in the test framework, creating more readable test conditions.

- *Run independent of other tests*: A unit test must be able to run in complete isolation. In other words, the unit test can't depend on some other test running before or after itself. Each test is a stand-alone unit.

- *Zero external resources*: A unit test must not depend on any outside resources, such as database connections or web services. Not only will these resources slow the test down, but they are outside the control of the test and thus aren't guaranteed to be in a correct state for testing.

- *Leave external state untouched*: A unit test must not leave any evidence that it ever ran. Unit tests are written to be repeatable, so they must clean up after themselves. Obviously, this is much easier when the test doesn't rely on external resources (which are often harder to clean up or restore).

- *Test smallest unit of code*: A unit test must test the smallest unit of code possible in order to isolate the code under test. In object-oriented programming, this unit is usually a method of an object or class. Writing unit tests such that a method is tested independently of other methods reduces the number of code lines that could contain the potential bug.

■**Caution** Obviously, Spring applications rely heavily upon the `ApplicationContext` and its XML configuration files at runtime. Your unit tests, however, should not rely on these facilities. Many if not all of Spring's practices promote the ability to run your code outside of Spring itself. Your code should always be able to be unit tested without the `ApplicationContext`'s involvement. To test the wiring and configuration of your system, see "Integration Tests" later in this chapter.

Tools

For all of the unit tests in this book, we have used the ubiquitous JUnit (http://www.junit.org) library. It is the de facto standard for writing unit tests in Java, with wide industry support and many add-ons. The Spring Framework uses JUnit for its tests, so there are plenty of excellent examples available if you want to see how unit tests are created in the wild. You can find the framework's tests in the test directory of the downloaded release.

Example

We will quickly illustrate an example of a unit test to provide some perspective and to give our discussions some weight. The Flight class from Chapter 4 is the perfect candidate for a unit test, as it doesn't require external resources and contains business logic statements.

Listing 10-3 is the complete test case for the Flight class. We begin by using setUp() to create and initialize an instance of Flight, complete with a single FlightLeg between two cities. Having one commonly configured Flight instance makes each test easier to write because of the consistency of data across test methods.

As you can see, we like to place each situation being tested inside its own test method. This technique is different than many of the tests you'll find in the Spring source code distribution, where you'll commonly find one test method containing many different actions and assertions. We believe that tests should run in isolation, so we sacrifice brevity for more explicit test separation. Another benefit of this type of test method separation is that the risk of orthogonal code affecting the real method under test is reduced.

Some tests are very simple, testing mere getters or read-only accessor methods. For instance, Listing 10-1 is verifying that the total cost returned by getTotalCost() happens to be the same cost specified when the Flight instance was created. These simple-looking methods are just as important to test as the seemingly more complicated methods. Not only does it increase the test coverage, but it is providing a very helpful safety net once the refactoring begins (which will happen sooner or later).

Listing 10-1. *testGetTotalCost Method*

```
public void testGetTotalCost() {
    assertEquals(40, flight.getTotalCost());
}
```

Other test methods, like the one shown in Listing 10-2, require more configuration than is provided by the setUp() method. Here we create test local parameters that are controlled to give our tests precise outcomes, such as a nonstop FlightLeg with valid start and end times.

Notice that the assertEquals() method calculates the expected value independently from the start and end objects set up at the beginning of the test. Why not just use assertEquals ((end.getTime()-start.getTime()), flight.getTotalTravelTime())? The expected value (the first parameter to the assertEquals() method) should never be calculated from parameters that participate in the test, in order to ensure the test itself doesn't modify any data that would affect its validity.

It's possible, however unlikely, that getTotalTravelTime() could alter the values of the start and end objects. If it did manage to alter the values, the test might appear to succeed even though it would not return the value you expected when you wrote the test method. In other words, you would get a false positive.

Listing 10-2. *testGetTotalCost Method*

```
public void testGetTotalTravelTimeOneLeg() throws Exception {
    Date start = sdf.parse("2005-01-01 06:00");
    Date end = sdf.parse("2005-01-01 12:00");

    List<FlightLeg> legs = new ArrayList<FlightLeg>();
    legs.add(new FlightLeg(fooCity, start, barCity, end));
    flight = new Flight(legs, new BigDecimal(40));

    assertEquals((6*60*60*1000), flight.getTotalTravelTime());
}
```

To put it all together, Listing 10-3 contains the entire FlightTest.

Listing 10-3. *Unit Test for Flight Class*

```
public class FlightTest extends TestCase {

    private Flight flight;
    private SimpleDateFormat sdf = new SimpleDateFormat("yyyy-MM-dd HH:mm");
    private Airport fooCity;
    private Airport barCity;

    public void setUp() throws Exception {
        super.setUp();
        fooCity = new Airport("foo", "F");
        barCity = new Airport("bar", "B");

        List<FlightLeg> legs = createSingleLeg();
        flight = new Flight(legs, new BigDecimal(40));
    }

    public void testGetTotalCost() {
        assertEquals(40, flight.getTotalCost());
    }

    public void testGetDepartFrom() {
        assertEquals(fooCity, flight.getDepartFrom());
    }

    public void testGetArriveAt() {
        assertEquals(barCity, flight.getArrivalAt());
    }
```

```
public void testGetNumberOfLegs() {
    assertEquals(1, flight.getNumberOfLegs());
}

public void testIsNonStopOneLeg() {
    List<FlightLeg> legs = createSingleLeg();
    flight = new Flight(legs, new BigDecimal(40));
    assertTrue(flight.isNonStop());
}

public void testIsNonStopTwoLegs() {
    List<FlightLeg> legs = createSingleLeg();
    flight = new Flight(legs, new BigDecimal(40));
    legs.add(new FlightLeg(fooCity, new Date(), barCity, new Date()));
    assertFalse(flight.isNonStop());
}

public void testGetTotalTravelTimeOneLeg() throws Exception {
    Date start = sdf.parse("2005-01-01 06:00");
    Date end = sdf.parse("2005-01-01 12:00");

    List<FlightLeg> legs = new ArrayList<FlightLeg>();
    legs.add(new FlightLeg(fooCity, start, barCity, end));
    flight = new Flight(legs, new BigDecimal(40));

    assertEquals((6*60*60*1000), flight.getTotalTravelTime());
}

public void testGetTotalTravelTimeTwoLegs() throws Exception {
    Date start = sdf.parse("2005-01-01 06:00");
    Date end = sdf.parse("2005-01-01 12:00");

    List<FlightLeg> legs = new ArrayList<FlightLeg>();
    legs.add(new FlightLeg(fooCity, start, barCity, end));
    flight = new Flight(legs, new BigDecimal(40));

    Date secondStart = new Date(end.getTime());
    Date secondEnd = sdf.parse("2005-01-01 14:30");
    legs.add(new FlightLeg(new Airport("secondFoo", "F2"), secondStart,
            new Airport("secondBar", "B2"), secondEnd));

    assertEquals((8*60*60*1000)+(30*60*1000), flight.getTotalTravelTime());
}

public void testWrongEndTime() throws Exception {
    Date start = sdf.parse("2005-02-01 06:30");
    Date end = sdf.parse("2005-02-01 04:00");
```

```
        List<FlightLeg> legs = new ArrayList<FlightLeg>();
        legs.add(new FlightLeg(fooCity, start, barCity, end));
        flight = new Flight(legs, new BigDecimal(40));

        try {
            flight.getTotalTravelTime();
            fail("Should have thrown exception");
        } catch(IllegalArgumentException e) {
            assertEquals("Start date must be before end date", e.getMessage());
        }
    }

    private List<FlightLeg> createSingleLeg() {
        List<FlightLeg> legs = new ArrayList<FlightLeg>();
        legs.add(new FlightLeg(fooCity, new Date(), barCity, new Date()));
        return legs;
    }

}
```

Private Methods

As you may have noticed, we didn't write any tests that explicitly test private methods of the class. Certainly private methods are internal implementation-specific methods and are not part of the public API of the class. We write tests to test how the object behaves, from the perspective of a client of the class. This is an important point about unit tests, because they force the test writer (who should be the same person who creates the class) to think like a client of the class. The test author quickly begins to ask questions such as, How would I want to use this class? and What do I need from this class to get the job done? Writing unit tests can quickly expose any weaknesses of the class in terms of usability, which can be very beneficial.

How Do I Know When the Test Is Done?

A common question that pops up when writing unit tests is "How do I know If I've written enough tests?" There isn't a quick and easy answer to this, but a few guidelines and tools can help you determine how much of the code is actually tested.

The first guideline: Test your methods with values you don't expect to receive. To begin, test your methods with zeros and nulls as input values. Your method should gracefully handle this case, which we will call an *edge case*. Edge cases are conditions that might expose a problem because they are near or at the edge of acceptable values. Examples of this are zero, null, infinity, and conditions that are defined by your business logic as maximum or minimum. Creating tests for all of these edge cases is a good start toward completeness.

Once you have tests for the edge cases, simply write tests for the common cases. These test scenarios should use values that are representative of conditions that will occur most frequently. You do not need to test every single value (a lot of real numbers are out there), so use your best judgment here. The edge cases are certainly more important to test, because they are most often forgotten or neglected by the code, but the common case(s) should always be tested as well.

With the common cases out of the way, take a look at the algorithm you are testing and identify all the branches and decision points. To have a complete set of tests, each branch and condition that fires the branch must be tested. For instance, if you have a `switch` statement, make sure your tests use values that will exercise each condition of the statement including the `default` statement. This also applies to anywhere an exception might be thrown (see `testWrongEndTime()` in `FlightTest` (Listing 10-3) for an example).

Of course, any software other than the most trivial will have numerous branches, exception cases, and execution paths. To ensure that your tests have exercised all of the potential situations, you can use special tools to track which code is tested and which code isn't. These are called *code coverage tools*, and they work hand-in-hand with testing frameworks (though they don't require them) to give you an idea of how much of the system is actually tested.

Code coverage utilities, such as Clover (`http://www.cenqua.com/clover`) and EMMA (`http://emma.sourceforge.net`), instrument the code under test by wrapping each line and condition with a flag. These flags are set when the active test actually runs the particular line of code. When the tests complete, the utilities generate a detailed report of which lines of source code were exercised by the unit tests. The report, as shown in Figure 10-1, provides an excellent visual way to see how much of the system is actually tested by your unit and integration tests.

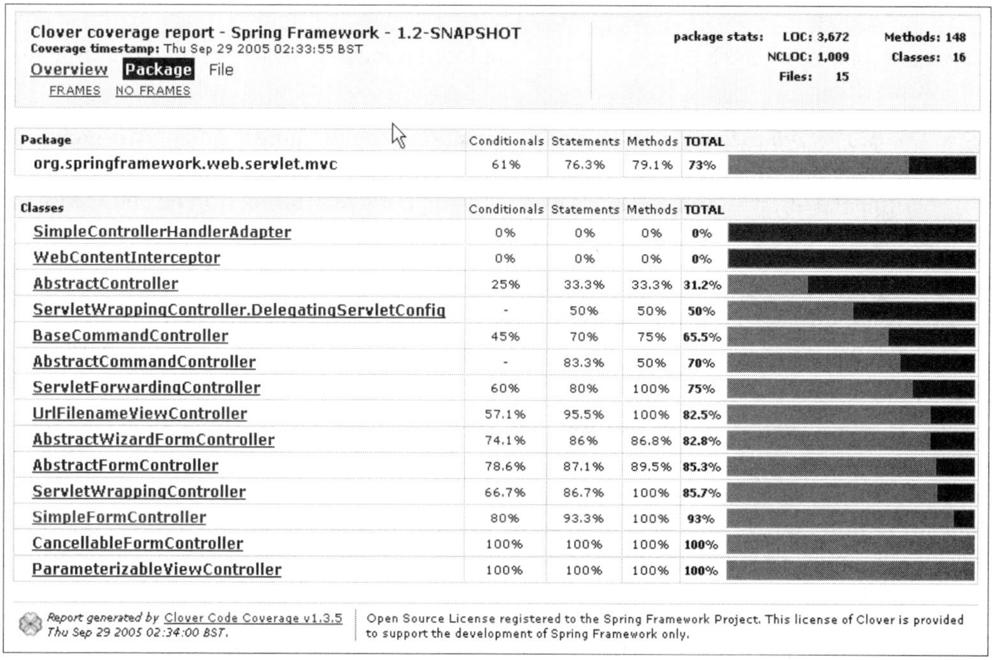

Figure 10-1. *HTML report from Clover*

■**Tip** Spring uses Clover for code coverage, and you can generate and view up-to-the-minute coverage reports yourself with the Ant build included with the source code.

Even if you have managed to obtain 100% code coverage from your tests, you're not necessarily finished writing tests. Code coverage utilities are very helpful, but they cannot indicate whether you have sufficiently covered the edge cases. For example, they may tell you if you tested a hypothetical `addition()` method, but they don't know if you tried it with `nulls`, zeros, negative numbers, or infinity. You must use a combination of code coverage reporting plus edge case tests to really begin to feel like you have a complete set of tests.

When Do I Write Tests?

Another common question when writing tests is "When in the process of building the system are tests created?" The answer to this depends a lot on what software development methodology you subscribe to.

Extreme Programming (`http://www.extremeprogramming.org`), or *XP*, was one of the first methodologies to popularize the Agile (`http://agilemanifesto.org`) movement. One of XP's main tenets is a technique named *test-driven development*, or *TDD*. It says that before any code is created, a unit test must first be written. At a very basic level, this means that if strictly followed, all code will have corresponding tests. However, if the proponents of TDD are correct, this technique has much broader implications.

- *You will always have tests for the system if you create them first.* When crunch time comes, unit tests are often left by the wayside. This can be a dangerous decision, especially because crunch time is when development is moving the fastest (and thus is at its most risky).

- *You will get immediate feedback for all code additions and changes.* As software grows and refactoring becomes more important, the safety net of unit tests is essential. By writing the test first, you will know instantly whether a refactoring worked and regression bugs were introduced.

- *The system design will emerge in the simplest possible form.* TDD proponents argue that because the code is created in response to tests, the system will emerge with only the code that allows the tests to pass. By focusing on passing tests, the code won't have a chance to expand into areas not originally intended or required.

The *Rational Unified Process (RUP)* merely defines a "construction" phase, where the software code and tests are created in no specified order.

Feature Driven Development (FDD) declares that unit testing occurs in the fifth process, "Build by Feature." FDD does not define exactly when in the process the unit tests are created, only that they must be created.

Our personal feelings on the subject are these: Test as early as you can. Although strictly following TDD can be a bit dogmatic, writing tests first really does help to drive a more simple design (of course, it helps to know where you are going). Writing the tests during software construction—especially at the same time the module under test is being created or updated—is an excellent idea. We've noticed that any initial slowdown in coding velocity is greatly outweighed by the confidence you will have in the system plus the natural robustness from the tests themselves. Bottom line is, don't delay writing those unit tests.

It's important to note that the advice to write tests as early as possible is specific to unit tests. Integration tests are naturally created later in the process, as more pieces of the system have been built.

What If the Code Has Dependencies?

The unit test suggestions, such as testing the smallest amount of code, are quite reasonable when testing the domain object model, because it is easy to create and control instances of dependencies. As shown in Listing 10-3, the FlightTest simply creates new objects such as FlightLeg in order to create certain test conditions. However, if the code requires dependencies that are heavyweight or tied to external resources, writing unit tests becomes more difficult.

For example, consider how one would write a unit test for the following service layer class. We've created a simple AccountService interface, implemented by AccountServiceImpl, shown in Listing 10-4. The service class delegates to an AccountDao for loading Account instances from persistence. The Account class implements the business logic for its activation.

Listing 10-4. *AccountServiceImpl*

```
public class AccountServiceImpl implements AccountService {

    private AccountDao accountDao;

    public void setAccountDao(AccountDao accountDao) {
        this.accountDao = accountDao;
    }

    public void activateAccount(Long accountId) throws AccountNotFoundException {
        Assert.notNull(accountId, "accountId must not be null");
        Account account = accountDao.getAccount(accountId);
        if (account == null) {
            throw new AccountNotFoundException(accountId);
        }
        account.activate();
    }

}
```

We can already see some of the conditions the unit test must test, including:

- What if the Data Access Object (DAO) returns a null account?

- What if the method parameter is null?

- How do we ensure that the account returned by the DAO is the one that is activated?

To successfully test those conditions, the service object requires a functioning DAO. However, to keep from violating our unit test rules, we must not actually interact with the database. Therefore, the AccountDao instance that the AccountServiceImpl uses can't be the real implementation. We need to somehow replace the AccountDao with an object that looks and feels like the real thing, but instead of pulling objects from the database it returns objects from memory.

To solve this problem, dependencies such as the DAO layer can be replaced by stand-ins called *mock objects*. Instead of the real thing, we will create a mock replacement for the AccountDao, which we will set into the AccountServiceImpl object before the test is run. This way we will have full control over any dependencies, isolating the service object to be the variable under test, as well as avoiding any interaction with external resources.

■**Note** Dependency Injection plays a big part in allowing for easy testing through mock objects. Because the dependency is set into the class via a simple setter, the dependency can easily be substituted with a mock object at test time.

Mock Objects

Mock objects add intelligence and programmability to stub classes, making them in essence scriptable stubs. Think of mock objects as smart placeholders for dependencies. Mock objects are created dynamically, inside the tests that utilize them. They typically are implemented using JDK java.lang.reflect.Proxy objects, implementing the interface of the dependency while replacing the behavior. More advanced mock object libraries also support creating mocks for classes that do not implement interfaces.

Mock objects allow you to script the behavior of the mock in order to create different situations for testing. For instance, you can control which objects are returned from a method call, or you can instruct the mock object to throw an exception instead of returning a value. This technique allows you to essentially inject objects into tests that are the results from method calls.

Mock objects also let you specify exactly which methods should be called on the mock, and in what order. This is a type of *inside-out* testing, as you can ensure that only the expected methods on a dependency are called. Once configured, you can instruct the mock object to fail the test if an expected method was never called or if a method was called on the mock that was never expected.

There are three main mock object libraries, each with their own pros and cons. Refer to Table 10-1.

Table 10-1. *Mock Object Libraries*

Title	URL	Documentation	Notes
MockObjects	http://www.mockobjects.com	Minimal, lacking.	One of the first mock object libraries.
jMock	http://www.jmock.org	Good, included Getting Started Guide and tutorials.	Rewrite of MockObjects, handles mocking interfaces and classes.
EasyMock	http://www.easymock.org	Good, many examples.	Used by Spring for testing.

We can recommend either jMock or EasyMock for your mock object needs. As noted, Spring uses EasyMock for testing, so you may want to choose this package due to the number of examples available in the Spring source code. However, we have the most experience with jMock, so we will use it for the examples in this chapter.

With the mock object library chosen, it's time to write the unit test for `AccountServiceImpl`.

Mock Object Techniques

We use mock objects during testing for two main reasons: to isolate the class under test from outside influence and to control dependencies.

While unit tests should test a single unit of code in isolation, it's rare to find a class or a method that is completely void of dependencies in one form or another. If the dependency is a simple POJO, using the `new` operator is an easy way to create an instance used just for the test. However, if the dependency is not easily created or requires heavyweight resources such as database connections, using the `new` operator isn't often possible. Mock objects step in to "mock" the dependency, thus allowing the code under test to operate without invoking outside resources.

Real mock objects, and not just simple stubs, allow you to control their behavior. This is extremely important when mocking heavyweight resources such as DAOs. Because you are testing against a mock DAO, there is no database, so how does the DAO retrieve any objects? Mocks can be told not only how to look (what interface to appear as) but how to act. In other words, you instruct a mock object what to do when certain methods are called. When mocking a DAO, for instance, you can easily say, "When the method `loadFoo()` is called, return this instance of `Foo`."

To summarize, mock objects are used when you need to either replace a heavyweight dependency with a lightweight instance just for testing, or when you need to use an intelligent stub. Those two situations often occur simultaneously, making mock objects a perfect addition to any testing tool belt.

Let's move on to some concrete examples showing off how mock objects work with real tests.

Unit Tests with jMock

For the `AccountServiceImpl` test we will create a mock for `AccountDao` in order to return an `Account` instance we can control. To begin, the superclass for the test will be `org.jmock.MockObjectTestCase` instead of `junit.framework.TestCase`. This is not required; however, it makes using jMock much easier and is recommended. The `MockObjectTestCase` class provides helper methods used when creating the mock instance, and not using it simply means that configuring mocks will be more verbose.

Let's begin by setting up the test class, creating an instance of `AccountServiceImpl` and a mock `AccountDao`, shown in Listing 10-5.

Listing 10-5. *AccountServiceImplTest Setup*

```
public class AccountServiceImplTest extends MockObjectTestCase {

    private AccountService accountService;
    private Mock mockAccountDao;
    private AccountDao accountDao;

    protected void setUp() throws Exception {
        super.setUp();
        accountService = new AccountServiceImpl();
        mockAccountDao = mock(AccountDao.class);
        accountDao = (AccountDao) mockAccountDao.proxy();
        ((AccountServiceImpl)accountService).setAccountDao(accountDao);
    }
```

Notice how we require two distinct objects for the mock: an instance of mock and its proxy. The mock is the object the test configures and controls, while the proxy is the stand-in we provide to the service object.

The setup() method introduces the mock() method, the first helper method provided by the MockObjectTestCase class. This method is a builder, accepting an interface and returning an instance of its mock.

■**Tip** Programming with interfaces allows you to easily work with mock object libraries.

With the mock created, let's now create the first unit test for this class (Listing 10-6). We will test that the service object will throw an AccountNotFoundException if the DAO returns a null Account. This will require the mock to be instructed to expect a single call to getAccount() with a parameter equal to what we provide to the service object, and to return a value of null.

Listing 10-6. *testActivateAccountWithNoAccountFound*

```
    public void testActivateAccountWithNoAccountFound() {
        mockAccountDao.expects(once())
                .method("getAccount")
                .with(eq(new Long(1)))
                .will(returnValue(null));

        try {
            accountService.activateAccount(new Long(1));
            fail("Should have thrown AccountNotFoundException");
        } catch(AccountNotFoundException e) {
            assertTrue(e.getMessage().contains("1"));
        }
```

```
        mockAccountDao.verify();
}
```

Notice how the initialization of the mockAccountDao reads very much like the previous description of the test. You can read the mock object configuration as, "The mockAccountDao should expect a single call to the getAccount() method with a parameter equal to 1L and will return the value of null."

After the configuration, the service method activateAccount() is called with the correct parameter. When the service method delegates to the accountDao, the mock object will return null as instructed. The service object, never the wiser, continues on with its logic and throws the exception.

If a method was called on the mock that it was not expecting, the mock will cause the test to fail immediately. However, because there is no immediate failure on expectations never met (for instance, if a mock method was never called), the verify() method is required to ensure that the mock will cause a failure if an expectation was never met.

Tip Always place a call to verify() for every mock you configure in your test case.

Another test we wish to write for the AccountServiceImpl object is the optimistic case of everything working smoothly. We want to ensure that the Account object returned by the accountDao is correctly activated. For this test, shown in Listing 10-7, instead of returning null we will return an instance of Account that we control. After the service method runs, it will be easy to check the state of the Account object to see whether it was correctly activated.

Listing 10-7. *testActivateAccountWithAccount*

```
public void testActivateAccountWithAccount() {
    Account account = new Account();
    assertFalse(account.isActivated());

    mockAccountDao.expects(once())
        .method("getAccount")
        .with(eq(new Long(1)))
        .will(returnValue(account));

    accountService.activateAccount(new Long(1));

    assertTrue(account.isActivated());

    mockAccountDao.verify();
}
```

The setup for the mock object is very similar to the previous test case. However, for this test we return a real instance of Account, one that we have created. After the service method completes, we check that the account was activated.

While this test is checking that the correct account was activated, it is also subtly checking that the parameter passed to `activateAccount()` is correctly passed to the `getAccount()` method of the DAO. When we instruct the mock object to expect a call "with a parameter equal to `new Long(1)`", we are telling the mock to throw an exception if it receives a different value. Therefore, we are also testing that we are calling the DAO with the correct information.

If the wrong or unexpected value is passed to the mock (for this example, the value of 2), the mock will throw an exception looking much like the following the one in Listing 10-8.

Listing 10-8. *Incorrect Value Passed to Mock*

```
org.jmock.core.DynamicMockError: mockAccountDao: no match found
Invoked: com.apress.expertspringmvc.testing.AccountDao.getAccount(<2>)
Allowed:
expected once: getAccount( eq(<1>) ), returns
<com.apress.expertspringmvc.testing.Account@1a05308>

  at org.jmock.core.AbstractDynamicMock.mockInvocation(Unknown Source)
  at org.jmock.core.CoreMock.invoke(Unknown Source)
  at $Proxy0.getAccount(Unknown Source)
  at com.apress.expertspringmvc.testing.AccountServiceImpl.activateAccount(
AccountServiceImpl.java:15)
```

Mock Objects Summary

Mock objects are an excellent way to write unit tests for components that rely on dependencies that would otherwise be heavyweight or difficult to test. Mocks are intelligent stubs, able to be scripted to expect certain inputs and respond with certain outputs. You should use mocks when the dependency would violate some of the unit test guidelines, most importantly "run fast" and "zero external resources."

Mocks can be scripted to expect one or more methods, called in a particular order, and with a particular set of parameters. Mocks can return any preset value, throw an exception instead of returning a value, or simply return void.

Mocks will fail a test if the code under test uses the mock in unexpected way, or doesn't exercise the mock at all. If using jMock, remember to call `verify()` on your mock objects at the end of the test case to ensure all expectations are met.

Mocks don't have to be used for replacements of heavyweight objects such as DAOs. They can be used anywhere dependencies are found, making it easy to isolate the class under test by ensuring that all other participants in the test perform and behave exactly as specified.

Testing Controllers

Up to this point, we've discussed testing both the domain object model as simple JUnit tests and testing the service layer with the help of mock objects. The web layer has its own set of testing tips and tricks, as it requires both the service layer and Servlet API classes. Testing `Controllers` requires both mock objects and a set of stubs for classes such as `HttpServletRequest` and `HttpSession`. Tests for `Controllers` can be written just as easily as service layer tests and can be run just as fast.

The Spring Framework provides a `spring-mock.jar` that includes classes useful for writing both unit tests and integration tests. We will focus on a very useful set of stubs for testing web components in the `org.springframework.mock.web` package, including classes such as `MockHttpServletRequest`, `MockHttpServletResponse`, and `MockServletContext`. These are lightweight classes and can be used in any unit test, not just tests for `Controllers`.

Stubs vs. Mocks

While the names for the classes in `spring-mock.jar` begin with *mock*, we argue that they are in fact *stubs*. The term *stub* indicates that the class is unintelligent with no scripting or control abilities. While mocks can be configured with expectations and programmable behavior, a stub is merely a placeholder with simple predefined behavior.

In no way does this mean that the provided classes such as `MockHttpServletRequest` are less than useful. These classes play a valuable role in testing web components, and the fact that they are predefined saves plenty of time when writing tests.

Stubs are useful not only in testing situations, but also when integrating application layers. Stubs can help development teams deliver slices faster by allowing each layer to develop at an independent rate. As layers are built out, they can use stubs as stand-ins for the dependent layers. As layers complete their functionality, the stubs are replaced and testing continues.

Servlet API Stubs

The `spring-mock.jar` provides a full array of stubs for the Servlet API, among other things. These classes are simple to create, and for the most part behave exactly like their real-life counterparts.

- `MockHttpServletRequest`
- `MockHttpServletResponse`
- `MockHttpSession`
- `MockServletConfig`
- `MockServletContext`
- `MockPageContext`
- `MockRequestDispatcher`
- `MockFilterConfig`
- `MockExpressionEvaluator`: Useful for testing JSP 2.0 components; requires `jstl.jar` on the classpath

Controller Test Example

Let's put these stubs to work testing a `Controller` that will expose the `activateAccount()` method to the web. A client wishing to activate an account will use the HTTP POST method and provide a request parameter named `id`. For simplicity's sake, we will assume that an aspect of the system has taken care of the security checks for user credentials and permissions.

The `Controller` code is shown in Listing 10-9.

Listing 10-9. *ActivateAccountController*

```
public class ActivateAccountController extends AbstractController {

    private AccountService accountService;

    public ActivateAccountController() {
        setSupportedMethods(new String[]{"POST"});
    }

    public void setAccountService(AccountService accountService) {
        this.accountService = accountService;
    }

    @Override
    protected ModelAndView handleRequestInternal(HttpServletRequest request,
            HttpServletResponse response) throws Exception {
        String idParam = request.getParameter("id");
        if (! StringUtils.hasText(idParam)) {
            response.sendError(HttpServletResponse.SC_BAD_REQUEST,
                    "Missing id parameter");
            return null;
        }
        Long id = null;
        try {
            id = Long.valueOf(idParam);
        } catch(NumberFormatException e) {
            response.sendError(HttpServletResponse.SC_BAD_REQUEST,
                    "ID must be a number");
            return null;
        }

        accountService.activateAccount(id); // let the infrastructure handle
                                            // the business exception of
                                            // AccountNotFoundException

        return new ModelAndView("success"); // this should redirect somewhere
    }

}
```

We introduced a few conditions in this Controller that are ripe for testing. First, the id parameter could be missing or empty. Second, the id parameter could have an incorrect format. Third, the activateAccount() method itself could throw an exception. Fourth, the client could attempt to access this Controller with a HTTP GET.

That's a lot to test, but as you'll see it's quite easy with the Servlet API stubs in tandem with mock objects. Let's first set up the test, including the creation of the Controller, the mock for the AccountService object, and the stubs. See Listing 10-10.

Listing 10-10. *ActivateAccountControllerTest Setup*

```
public class ActivateAccountControllerTest extends MockObjectTestCase {

    private ActivateAccountController controller;
    private Mock mockAccountService;
    private AccountService accountService;

    private MockHttpServletRequest request;
    private MockHttpServletResponse response;

    protected void setUp() throws Exception {
        super.setUp();
        controller = new ActivateAccountController();
        mockAccountService = mock(AccountService.class);
        accountService = (AccountService) mockAccountService.proxy();
        controller.setAccountService(accountService);
        request = new MockHttpServletRequest();
        response = new MockHttpServletResponse();
    }
```

Next, let's create a test for the very simple case of a client attempting to use HTTP GET instead of HTTP POST. For this test, shown in Listing 10-11, we will configure our HttpServletRequest stub to report the GET method, and we will call the Controller's handleRequest() method. We choose to call this method, even though our controller only implements handleRequestInternal(), because handleRequest() implements the logic for checking request methods. We are really testing whether we configured the Controller to accept only the POST method, not necessarily the logic that checks the request methods (since we generally trust the Spring code, but if not, feel free to run the framework's tests locally).

Listing 10-11. *testGet Method*

```
    public void testGetMethod() throws Exception {
        request.setMethod("GET");

        try {
            controller.handleRequest(request, response);
            fail("Should have thrown RequestMethodNotSupportedException");
        } catch (RequestMethodNotSupportedException e) {
            // ok
        }
    }
}
```

As you can see, using the stubs is more straightforward than that working with mock objects. If this test passes, it means that we've configured the Controller to reject GET methods.

For the second test (Listing 10-12), we will use the correct HTTP method, but we will forget the id parameter. This should not throw any exceptions, but it should set the HttpServletResponse for an error state with the correct error message.

Listing 10-12. *testMissingIdParam Method*

```
public void testMissingIdParam() throws Exception {
    request.setMethod("POST");

    ModelAndView mav = controller.handleRequest(request, response);

    assertNull(mav);
    assertEquals(HttpServletResponse.SC_BAD_REQUEST, response.getStatus());
    assertEquals("Missing id parameter", response.getErrorMessage());
}
```

Notice that we are using methods provided by the MockHttpServletResponse object to manually check the state of the response object. The values that were set in the Controller via response.sendError() are then checked with getStatus() and getErrorMessage(). The ability to introspect the request and response objects is part of the value add the stubs provide, as the native API interfaces don't provide this functionality.

For completeness, we've included the rest of the tests for the possible error conditions in the Controller. The last two test cases (Listing 10-13) use both mock objects and stubs to test the interaction of the Controller with the service layer. Fundamentally, it's no different than using mocks to replace the DAO layer.

Listing 10-13. *Additional Test Cases for ActivateAccountController*

```
public void testBlankIdParam() throws Exception {
    request.setMethod("POST");
    request.addParameter("id", "    ");

    ModelAndView mav = controller.handleRequest(request, response);

    assertNull(mav);
    assertEquals(HttpServletResponse.SC_BAD_REQUEST, response.getStatus());
    assertEquals("Missing id parameter", response.getErrorMessage());
}

public void testIdNotANumber() throws Exception {
    request.setMethod("POST");
    request.addParameter("id", "fwewefas");

    ModelAndView mav = controller.handleRequest(request, response);

    assertNull(mav);
    assertEquals(HttpServletResponse.SC_BAD_REQUEST, response.getStatus());
    assertEquals("ID must be a number", response.getErrorMessage());
}
```

```
public void testOK() throws Exception {
    request.setMethod("POST");
    request.addParameter("id", "1");
    mockAccountService.expects(once())
            .method("activateAccount")
            .with(eq(new Long(1)));

    ModelAndView mav = controller.handleRequest(request, response);

    assertNotNull(mav);
    assertEquals("success", mav.getViewName());
}

public void testMissingAccountPropogatesException() throws Exception {
    request.setMethod("POST");
    request.addParameter("id", "1");
    mockAccountService.expects(once())
            .method("activateAccount")
            .with(eq(new Long(1)))
            .will(throwException(new AccountNotFoundException(1L)));

    try {
        controller.handleRequest(request, response);
        fail("Should have propogated the AccountNotFoundException");
    } catch (AccountNotFoundException e) {
        // ok
    }
}
```

Testing Controllers Summary

Testing Controllers is a natural component of a full suite of unit tests for your system. Controllers written for Spring MVC are easily testable because their dependencies are set via Dependency Injection, and in general they do not require any facilities from a running container. The framework code is easily stubbed or mocked so that tests can be written and verified quickly.

The Spring Framework provides a rich set of testing stubs inside spring-mock.jar, including classes to make writing unit tests for web components very simple. These Servlet API stubs are not specific to Spring, so you may find them useful for any tests you create for your web components.

When testing components such as Controllers, you should create mock objects for dependent objects such as the service layer.

Above all, testing web components should not be any different than testing your domain object model. A combination of stubs and mocks can make writing and running unit tests for Controllers simple, effective, and productive.

Unit Test Summary

Unit tests are meant to be created quickly and run quickly, providing you with a safety net for eventual refactorings and helping to design a simpler system. Writing tests for the obvious situations isn't enough; make sure to consider the edge cases of the code and to test all logic branches and exceptional conditions. A code coverage utility can help in tracking which code is actually tested.

It's important to view the list of unit test tenets not as hard and fast rules, but as guidelines to help you write the most effective unit tests possible. The important elements of unit tests, running fast and independently, should permeate all the tests you create. Remember that unit tests are written by you, for you. Keep them easy to create and easy to run, and they will continue to be useful for you.

We recommend that unit tests should be created as early as possible, ideally concurrently with the module's creation.

Using mock objects will isolate the class under test to ensure that external variables are removed from the test. Mock objects also allow a unit test to run without the presence of the dependency so that the test can run quickly and without risk of affecting the outside world. Mocks are also a very good way, and sometimes the only way, to test how your code will react when the dependency behaves under edge cases or in unexpected ways.

Spring provides stubs for easy testing with J2EE APIs such as the Servlet API. You should use these classes, such as `MockHttpServletRequest` and `MockHttpServletResponse`, when writing tests for `Controllers` or other web components. These stubs are very easy to use, and make writing tests for `Controllers` as easy as testing any other Java class. As with writing all other unit tests, when testing `Controllers` be sure to adhere to the principles of "run fast" and "zero external configuration."

Some test situations and scenarios, however, simply do not fit into the criteria for a unit test. If you find you need to write tests that test the interaction between components, you are writing what is called an *integration test*. We will discuss integration tests throughout the rest of the chapter. Let's define them now.

Integration Tests

We have painted a picture of unit tests as fast, small, lightweight tests that are quick to write and run. Unit tests are designed to test the smallest elements of your system, isolating each element and module from the rest of the system. These types of tests not only help ensure correctness for your system, but also help direct the design of your code—that is, your code needs to become modular if unit tests can be written effectively in the first place.

Unit tests are excellent for the components of the system that comprise the business logic. However, there is a lot of code in the system that isn't necessarily business logic, usually in the form of database interaction code (the DAOs). Testing these components can quickly break the rules that we try to follow for unit tests. For example, a unit test shouldn't interact with external systems such as the database, but how are you supposed to test your DAO classes? Also, a unit test should test a component in isolation, but how are you supposed to test that your entire system is wired together properly inside the `ApplicationContext`?

Enter integration tests: tests written with the same testing framework as your unit tests, but created specifically to test the interaction between the components of your system. Integration tests look a lot like unit tests, but they differ on their scope and intention. We're also allowed to bend the rules mentioned above, while keeping with the main themes of quickness, repeatability, and isolation.

Bend, Don't Break

When you create an integration test, you are openly acknowledging that you are testing the interaction between two components of the system. Many times, this might mean you are even writing tests that interact with the database. As you create these tests, keep in mind the tenets that make unit tests so successful.

- *Leave external state untouched*: Even though an integration test might interact with the database, when the test is finished it must leave that database in a clean state. The database, or any external resource, must be left in the same state it was in before the test ran. For example, this means you must roll back the database transaction after each test run. It's a safe and simple way to ensure the database is not changed.

- *Isolated external resources*: We argued that for unit tests, there should be no external resources involved. For an integration test, though, testing the interaction with the external resource is the whole point. However, the test should exercise only one external resource at a time to minimize the areas affected and to keep the test run times as low as possible.

- *Run fast*: Still as important for integration tests as it is for unit tests, all of your tests should run extremely fast. This is related to keeping each test dependent on only one external resource, as well as smart resource management. For instance, if your integration test requires a Spring `ApplicationContext`, caching the context instance across test runs can greatly speed up the test runs. Of course, if your test alters the `ApplicationContext`, you will want to recreate the context for every test run.

- *Test smallest unit of code*: Even though integration tests are written testing two components of the system, each individual test must still exercise a single method of the class under test. Keeping the amount of code under test to a minimum is extremely helpful when a bug is inevitably found, as it minimizes the amount of code you have to search through.

As you can see, the basic guidelines for integration tests mesh well with unit tests. However, with integration tests, we are explicitly testing the interaction of two or more components in the system. With Spring applications, this type of testing becomes quite important because of the amount of configuration and the extent it reaches into the system.

If we take a step back and look at the range of testing types, we might consider the compiler itself to be a type of test. It is ensuring that access modifiers are obeyed, that the correct number of parameters is used, and that you are returning the correct type of object from a method. These are fundamental checks we must perform before the system is ever run, and the compiler is performing these syntactical tests for use before compilation. Moving up the scale in terms of scope, we then encounter unit tests, mentioned earlier in this chapter. Here we are testing small units of code, such as methods. So far, though, we've only essentially tested Java code. External system-level configurations have yet to be tested, and yet they are as important as any Java code we write.

This is why we must write integration tests, because there are neither any compiler checks for the system's configuration (short from simple DTD validity, non-semantic checks) nor unit tests for exercising the configuration. The integration tests perform this crucial role for Spring applications, and as you'll see they are nearly as simple to create and run as unit tests.

Overview

The Spring Framework ships with a set of classes designed to enable effective and simple integration tests. Also found in `spring-mock.jar`, but unlike the Servlet API stubs, these classes are specifically intended for Spring applications.

The intent of integration tests is to ensure the configuration of the components with the Spring Framework is correct and functioning; therefore, it makes sense to begin the test with a real `ApplicationContext`. In contrast, during unit tests we created every object and dependency by hand, completely divorced from the container. During integration tests, all objects and their dependencies will come from the `ApplicationContext`, just like they will during a running application.

As you might imagine, if we are trying to keep all tests running extremely quickly, how to we accomplish this while creating an `ApplicationContext` for every test? To solve this problem, the `ApplicationContext` is cached between test methods and loaded only once. This is a trade-off to keep tests running quickly, especially when heavyweight objects exist such as `DataSources` or connection pools.

The main base class for integration tests is `org.springframework.test.AbstractSpringContextTests`. It is a subclass of JUnit's TestCase, and it is responsible for caching the `ApplicationContext` after load and providing methods to reload the context if required. However, its subclass, `AbstractDependencyInjectionSpringContextTests`, is what most of your non-transactional tests will subclass. This class will use Dependency Injection to populate the test class itself with required objects before the test methods are run. What better way to retrieve dependencies for your test than through Dependency Injection itself!

Most integration tests will eventually run into the database, so tight control over transaction demarcation is required inside integration tests. Normally we want to perform all of our work under a transaction, but at the end of the test roll back the transaction to ensure that the external world will be left in a clean state. Not only does this technique save us in the event we have a test accidentally delete the entire database, but it allows future tests to run with expected data available.

To help with database integration tests, Spring provides the handy `AbstractTransactionalSpringContextTests` class, which is injected with an instance of a `PlatformTransactionManager` during initialization. By default, this test class will begin a transaction before every test method and then roll it back during the teardown phase. If you do wish to commit the transaction after your test run, you may call `setComplete()` before your tests completes.

The main themes repeated in these classes are quickness and safety. Because integration tests interact with the database, the potential for damage is much greater than with a simple unit test. The classes provided by Spring allow for easy creation of tests that run quickly and will, by default, clean up after every test method. If your tests do not require any database interaction, then `AbstractDependencyInjectionSpringContextTests` is the class to choose. If your tests do touch the database, we recommend `AbstractTransactionalSpringContextTests` for simplified control over the transaction between and during test methods.

Example

As always, code examples speak louder than words, so let's create an example of a transactional integration test. We will test the configuration and wiring of the typical components of a Spring MVC application, including the `Controller`, service layer, and DAO.

For the example in Listing 10-14, we will create a test for the `HomeController` we introduced in Chapter 4.

Listing 10-14. *HomeControllerIntegrationTest*

```
public class HomeControllerIntegrationTest extends
        AbstractTransactionalSpringContextTests {

    private HomeController homeController;
    private MockHttpServletRequest request;
    private MockHttpServletResponse response;

    public void setHomeController(HomeController homeController) {
        this.homeController = homeController;
    }

    @Override
    protected void onSetUpBeforeTransaction() throws Exception {
        super.onSetUpBeforeTransaction();
        request = new MockHttpServletRequest();
        response = new MockHttpServletResponse();
    }

    @SuppressWarnings("unchecked")
    public void testRequest() throws Exception {
        request.setMethod("GET");
        ModelAndView mav = homeController.handleRequest(request, response);
        assertNotNull(mav);
        List<SpecialDeal> specials = (List<SpecialDeal>)
                mav.getModel().get("specials");
        assertNotNull(specials);
        assertTrue(specials.size() > 0);
    }

    @Override
    protected String[] getConfigLocations() {
        return new String[]{"classpath:applicationContext.xml",
                "classpath:spring-servlet.xml"};
    }
}
```

It's very important that whenever you use the AbstractTransactionalStringContextTests class that a PlatformTransactionManager can be found, by type, in the ApplicationContext created for the test. This class is able to run without a transaction manager; however, this will likely lead to unwanted behavior, and most likely behavior that is different than production deployment.

If you wish to ignore the fact that no transaction manager exists, you must turn off dependency checking, as shown in Listing 10-15. The AbstractDependencyInjectionSpring➥ ContextTests by default will attempt to account for all dependencies by type, but you can change this behavior with the setDependencyCheck() method called from the constructor of your test class.

Listing 10-15. *Turning Off Dependency Checking If No Transaction Manager Exists*

```
public HomeControllerIntegrationTest() {
    setDependencyCheck(false);
}
```

The ApplicationContext is configured from the list of resource names returned by the getConfigLocations() abstract method. All of your test classes must implement this method and return one or more resource names pointing to ApplicationContext configuration files. All of these files will be combined into a single ApplicationContext to be used during testing. Any Dependency Injection is performed using this ApplicationContext as a source.

Tip In our experience, it's best to use resource names relative to the classpath, as that makes it easier to run the tests in different environments and IDEs.

The Spring integration test base classes override the setUp() method and mark it as final, but do provide life cycle callback methods for subclasses that require per-test method initialization. For transactional tests, two methods are provided: onSetupBeforeTransaction() to be called before the transaction is started, and onSetupAfterTransaction() to be called after the transaction is started. Both callbacks are called inside setUp(), and thus before every single test method.

For our example, we have implemented onSetupBeforeTransaction() in order to simply initialize any required testing stubs.

Because the transactional test cases are subclasses of AbstractDependencyInjection➥ SpringContextTests, we provide a setHomeController() method so that our test class can avoid the manual lookup of dependencies from the ApplicationContext. The dependencies are resolved by type via the autowiring algorithm, and will be re-injected before every test method. Of course, because the Controller class originates from the ApplicationContext, all of its dependencies will be injected as well. The assumption at this point is that the class under test should be fully initialized as if it were running in production.

The actual test method, testRequest(), is written and run just like any other JUnit test method. However, during the method a transaction is live, and unless setComplete() is called, at the end of testRequest() the transaction will be rolled back.

Create and Use a Special ApplicationContext for Tests Only?

A common question regarding Spring's integration test support classes is, "Should I create a custom `ApplicationContext` configuration for my tests?" Our initial answer to this question is no, for a good reason. We feel that much of the purpose for integration tests is to test the configuration of the application as it will run in production. There's rarely another good opportunity to test all that XML, including external configurations such as Hibernate mapping files, before a deployment.

It is possible that your configuration will require extra bean definitions to replace objects found only inside your J2EE container, such as connection pools or transaction managers. If your application requires these container-provided resources, you can create a `testOnlyApplicationContext.xml` configuration with bean definitions for those external resources. Spring can easily host connection pools and transaction managers, which you can use when running the code outside of the container.

Through intelligent modularization of the configuration files, you will find it easy to swap bean definitions at test runtime.

Role of the Application Server

It's important to mention that integration tests are still intended to be run outside of the application server. Even though the full Spring `ApplicationContext` is constructed, the test should still run without being deployed. Both unit tests and integration tests must still run as quickly as possible, and testing outside the application server is the only way to run the tests and get immediate feedback.

Testing inside the container is another way to perform integration tests, but should be avoided due to the time it takes to run the tests. Any test that becomes a hassle to run will quickly fall out of fashion and thus usefulness. We discourage requiring an application server for tests.

If your application requires the application server to run, it's possible that it is not taking advantage of the configuration options provided by Spring. As mentioned, even if you are using the server's connection pool during deployments, you can use Spring to create a connection pool for test runs.

Summary

Integration tests ensure that the application is wired and configured correctly by creating a full Spring `ApplicationContext` for the test class. Spring provides base classes for easy implementation of dependency injected and transactional tests, making it easy and safe to create tests that exercise multiple layers of the system, including the database.

These types of tests follow the basic guidelines of unit tests, except they explicitly are testing how multiple components of the system interact. This is an important testing step, as it checks that all the XML is configured correctly, and usually that the database mappings are correct as well.

Spring's `AbstractDependencyInjectionSpringContextTests` class performs autowiring by type on the test class itself to populate it with all of its dependencies. These dependencies are normally the classes under test, and thus enter the test fully wired and configured.

The `AbstractTransactionalSpringContextTests` extends the Dependency Injection test by managing a transaction for each test method. By default, a transaction is created before each test method and then rolled back afterward, to ensure that the outside "world" was not permanently changed. This class, however, requires a `PlatformTransactionManager` in the `ApplicationContext` to be able to manage the transactions.

Testing Summary

Spring MVC applications are highly testable, due to their use of interfaces, Dependency Injection techniques, and decoupled designs. Both unit and integration tests can easily be written to test not only the domain model, but all layers of the application. The Spring Framework provides many classes inside `spring-mock.jar` to help with test creation and management. In combination with mock objects, the tests for your web components and other layers can provide immediate feedback for new features and refactorings. This leads to higher confidence in the system, and thus a greater ability to adapt the system to growing needs and requirements.

Above all, remember that tests should always run fast, whether you are testing a simple POJO or a complex web `Controller`. Tests that run fast are tests that are built and run during development, when they can catch issues earliest.

CHAPTER 11

■■■

Introduction to
Spring Web Flow

This chapter will provide a high-level introduction to Spring Web Flow, a framework for managing complex page navigation and conversational scope within web applications. At the end of this chapter you will

- Understand the motivation for Spring Web Flow

- Be familiar with the terms and concepts within Spring Web Flow

What Itch Does Spring Web Flow Scratch?

Today, the Java Servlet specification (http://www.jcp.org/aboutJava/communityprocess/final/jsr154) provides developers with a standard for processing HTTP requests within a web application.

The specification defines three different scopes that dictate the visibility and location of objects and attributes that are associated with request processing. Table 11-1 lists the existing scopes from the server's perspective as we know them today.

Table 11-1. *Servlet Scopes*

Name	Lifetime	Typically Used For
Request	Has the smallest lifetime, is unique to each request from a browser, and will be discarded when the view is returned to the browser.	Contains data sent from the browser (e.g., browser headings and request parameters).
Session	Starts as soon as each unique browser accesses the server, and ends if the server hasn't received a request from that browser within a specified timeout (default of 30 minutes) or if explicitly destroyed. This scope allows objects to live across requests.	Information about the current user (user details, authentication) is usually stored in this scope.
Application	Lives for the duration of the web application deployment.	Contains shared application components and configuration elements.

For many problems these existing scopes are sufficient. A page can access the request scope for data specific to a single request and session scope can be used to hold objects that are required for the user's entire session such as authentication information.

The Problem with the Servlet Specification

Many web applications have use cases that do not naturally fit into the scopes provided by the Servlet specification. These use cases often span more than one page but do not require the longevity of the session. Users may also perform different use cases per browser session or even execute the same use case over and over. In this scenario, data associated with one use case execution needs to be cleaned up before a new execution can begin, which is something the session cannot do. In essence, the Servlet specification is missing the concept of a *conversational* scope to support the execution of use cases that span multiple pages.

■**Note** In Spring Web Flow, the name for a conversation is *flow*. We will use the two words interchangeably throughout the next two chapters.

Figure 11-1 illustrates these different types of interactions.

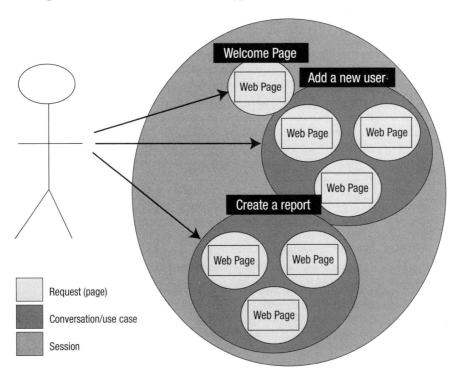

Figure 11-1. *Example use cases and corresponding scopes*

This means for any nontrivial web application, request scope is too fine grained and session scope is not fine grained enough.

Why not store everything in the session and manually perform cleanups when the conversation ends? To begin, there are many well-documented issues associated with storing context within the session, including (but not limited to):

- *Server affinity.* If your application is to be deployed into a clustered environment, then your clients will suffer from server affinity. This occurs because a user's session is unique to each server, so if a user connects to another server, he will receive a whole new session. Server affinity prevents failover (http://en.wikipedia.org/wiki/Failover), thus reducing your ability to load balance within a cluster.

■**Note** There are solutions for session replication in clustered environment, but they are typically very expensive and complex, and they always incur some performance overhead.

- *Greatly increased memory footprint per user.* Because each user's session is stored in memory, the serving capacity of each server is reduced. This is compounded by the fact that out-of-date context (e.g., ended or expired conversations) still exists in the session and needs to be manually removed.

- *Name space clashes.* Assuming context for a user registration use case is stored in the session under the name "registration," what happens if any given user tries to register more than one user at the same time using multiple browser windows or tabs? The data will overwrite itself. In summary, the concept of a conversation scope is a missing piece of the Servlet specification. The life span of conversational scope is longer than a request but shorter than a session. It has an explicit beginning and an end that corresponds to the time to complete or cancel an application transaction that spans one or more requests into the server.

- *No vocabulary for process modeling.* The absence of conversational scope introduces a mismatch between modeling and implementation. Process modeling is not concerned with individual pages or the concept of a session that encapsulates the browser's entire interaction with the server. Instead, it focuses on modeling one or more business goals of a system. The current Servlet specification (and modern MVC implementations) do not provide implementation constructs, or vocabularly that engineer naturally to and from a process model.

The Solution

So how does Spring Web Flow help?

The Flow Is King

Firstly, Spring Web Flow treats conversational scope as a first-level citizen. It was designed from the ground up with that as the centerpiece. The core artifact within Spring Web Flow is the *flow* (or conversation). It is this *flow definition* that defines a blueprint for a conversation with the user. Conversations can execute in parallel without intruding on each other, and when the conversation has finished, all allocated resources are automatically cleaned up.

Implementation Agnostic

Secondly, Spring Web Flow is deliberately abstracted away from the Servlet specification. The core artifacts within Spring Web Flow are flows, states, actions, and views. As you will see, there is nothing web-specific about a flow definition; the flow itself could be describing a set of web pages, a set of windows in a GUI, or even the communication between disparate systems. At no point within Spring Web Flow are you presented with an HttpServletRequest or an HttpServletResponse.

Accessible Lexicon

Thirdly, Spring Web Flow enables communication. You will find the core model simple, and the terminology used is readily accessible to nontechnical people. Tools already exist (like the Spring IDE Web Flow editor for Eclipse (http://www.springide.org/project)) that make XML-based flow definitions easily understood, thus bridging the gap between design and implementation.

Figure 11-2 shows a screenshot of the Spring Web Flow plugin for Eclipse.

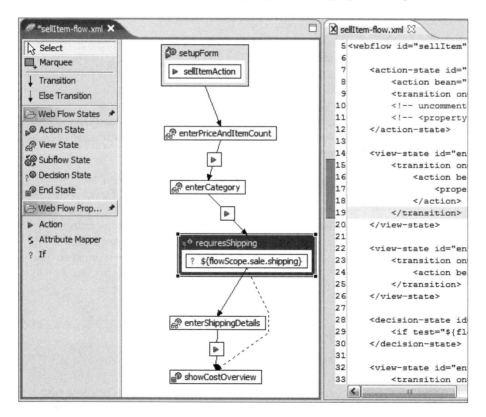

Figure 11-2. *Spring Web Flow plugin for Eclipse*

■**Note** The actual flow displayed here is a slight variation on the use case we will be implementing later in this chapter.

Because the terminology used within Spring Web Flow is implementation agnostic, flow definitions provide a valuable source of documentation that is understandable by all parties involved in the development process, and best of all, it is never out of date.

Best Practices

Drawing from its roots within the Spring community, Spring Web Flow adheres to established best practices:

- Develop against interfaces to allow you to plug in the most appropriate implementation. A fine-grained life cycle event listener infrastructure provides further customization points.

- Favor integration with established technologies over reinventing the wheel. Spring Web Flow ties into much of the same foundational infrastructure Spring MVC does. This includes Spring's `BeanFactory` for configuration, Spring's `Data Binder` and `Validator` concepts, and Spring MVC's `DispatcherServlet` and `View` resolution subsystems.

- Allow reusablility from within other established web frameworks, to provide a choice in product configuration. As an embeddable "page flow engine," Spring Web Flow integrates out of the box with Struts, JavaServer Faces (JSF), and Portlet MVC environments.

- Facilitate test-driven development (TDD) by removing coupling between components, collaborators, and the deployment environment. Flow executions are easy to test both in isolation and as part of an end-to-end integration test.

Low Adoption Overhead

Because Spring Web Flow is self-contained, there is little impact when introducing it on existing projects. There is no requirement or suggestion that Spring Web Flow should be the only player in the project. It should simply be used when it is appropriate.

Spring Web Flow is another `Controller` tool in the MVC toolbox. It does not require exclusivity, it does not impose any restrictions on your domain model, and it fits very easily into the existing Spring MVC architecture. In fact, a major design goal of Spring Web Flow was to do one thing and do it well.

The final aspect of adoption is modifications to existing code. Because artifacts within Spring Web Flow are interfaces as opposed to abstract classes, your cost of modifying your existing artifacts is very low. In all likelihood there would be very little impact on your existing code base; integration is usually a case of configuring one of the provided `Controller` implementations.

Not a Golden Hammer

Although Spring Web Flow is very powerful, flexible, and well architected, it is a solution to a specific problem—that of conversation scope. The definition of a conversation (for our purposes) is a logical progression through a predetermined set of steps to complete a business goal.

Is Spring Web Flow suitable for all web applications? No. Is it suitable for sites that are effectively static resources, each page disconnected from others where the user can jump from one page to another? No.

It is tempting when using Spring Web Flow to start thinking of it as the only weapon in your toolbox, the proverbial golden hammer (you only have a hammer, so everything looks like a nail), but this would be a misuse of the tool.

There are very few absolutes in web development, however, we offer Table 11-2 simply as a pragmatic guide.

Table 11-2. *When to Use Spring Web Flow*

Solution	When to Use
Spring MVC `Controller`	The page exists in isolation, not as part of a flow, and requires very little logic to generate it.
Spring MVC `SimpleFormController`	The page is part of a simple form-submission flow, such as a simple search box.
Spring MVC `AbstractWizardFormController`	A process is represented by a set of sequential pages through which the user is guided.
Spring Web Flow	Any nontrivial, stateful, guided multipage navigation is required.

■**Note** Even simple use cases may be better implemented in Spring Web Flow if they can be reused as subflows by larger flows. We will cover this in Chapter 12.

The key point is that Spring Web Flow isn't a replacement for Spring MVC; it is a complement to it.

The Big Picture

So what makes up Spring Web Flow? What does it look like? How does it fit into your application architecture?

Architectural Overview

As Figure 11-3 illustrates, Spring Web Flow integrates with Spring MVC, Spring Portlet MVC, Struts, and JavaServer Faces (JSF). Because Spring Web Flow is very self-contained, the entry points to all these frameworks are consistent, and therefore the cost of integration is minimal.

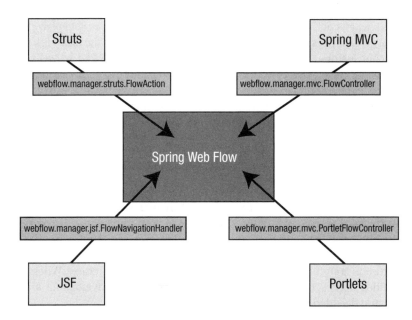

Figure 11-3. *Overview of integration options*

Integration with other frameworks is done by way of a Front Controller (`http://java.sun.com/blueprints/corej2eepatterns/Patterns/FrontController.html`)—associating a flow with a URL that is backed by a `Controller`.

Inside the Spring Web Flow System

Inside Spring Web Flow a central `FlowExecutionManager` façade is responsible for launching executions of flows on behalf of clients. These flow executions represent new user conversations with the server. Each conversation is given its own local data structure, called *flow scope*, allowing for storage of conversational state. Spring Web Flow fully manages the storage and restoration of these `FlowExecution` objects in a repository, and automatically discards them when a conversation ends.

Different Scopes

As previously discussed, information (or context) created during a user's interaction with the server is stored in a request, session or conversational scope.

The Servlet API provides infrastructure for accessing request and session scope, and Spring Web Flow provides access to conversational scope/flow scope.

The primary concern when considering scopes is that of storage: where does data placed in a scope actually live? Request scope is stored in the request (the data sent from the browser); session (and application) scope is stored on the server. Where is flow scope stored? The answer is in a repository. More specifically, Spring Web Flow delegates this responsibility to implementations of `org.springframework.webflow.execution.FlowExecutionRepository`. As you would expect, Spring Web Flow provides a number of implementations to support different usage scenarios:

- `SimpleFlowExecutionRepository`

- `ContinuationFlowExecutionRepository`

- `ClientContinuationFlowExecutionRepository`

The first two repository implementations are stateful and are managed in server-side data structures, typically the session. In this case, putting attributes in flow scope directly increases server-side memory requirements, as it increases the size of a flow execution stored in a repository that is managed in a user's session.

The last implementation is stateless and requires no server-side data structures. When using this strategy, encoded flow executions representing the state of user conversations are serialized out to clients and decoded on each request into the server.

You will learn much more about the different repository implementations in Chapter 12, including how `ContinuationRepositories` allow browser navigational buttons to behave in a sensible way within Spring Web Flow. For now it is important to understand that Spring Web Flow represents the concept of an ongoing conversation with a user in an object called a `FlowExecution` and is fully responsible for the management of those executions within a repository.

Building Blocks

Before Spring Web Flow can *execute* flows, there must be at least one flow *defined*. As discussed, the key artifact in Spring Web Flow is the flow definition. The primary challenge for developers becomes the design and implementation of a flow definition, a blueprint for user conversations that drives the execution of a business process.

■**Note** With Spring Web Flow, the primary challenge for developers is the design and implementation of a flow definition.

To demonstrate the process of designing and implementing a flow definition, we'll show a use case of purchasing a product (graphically represented in Figure 11-4). For our purposes, let's simplify and assume the user has already logged in and already chosen the type of product she wishes to purchase.

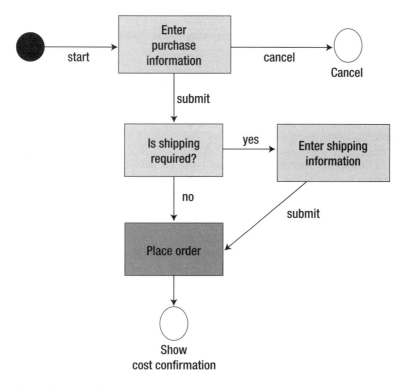

Figure 11-4. *Purchase Product use case*

The preceding flow is very simple, consisting of two steps the user must complete. These include:

1. Entering the product purchase information

2. Optionally entering product shipping information

There are also two additional steps that perform back-end processing—the first determining whether shipping is required and the second for submitting the order for processing. The user never "sees" these steps, as they are carried out by application code.

Finally, there is a single end step called "Show cost confirmation." When that step is reached, the user can review the result of order processing but cannot go back and resubmit.

As you will see, one of the architectural strengths of SWF is that it composes logical user interactions into discrete, self-contained components called flows. This brings several benefits. When an execution of a flow starts, the user can participate in it, but once it ends the user cannot go back; she can only start a new execution. In addition, the user can only participate in a very controlled manner, with the flow fully determining how to handle user events.

As a self-contained component, the Purchase Product flow can be made independent of the other work flows in the system, such as Authenticate User or Browse Catalog, and be reused in other contexts. This leads to a highly composable application, with the ability to mix and match flows to create larger and more complex applications.

■**Note** A flow that is called from another flow is referred to as a *subflow*. See Chapter 12 for more details.

Before walking through the implementation of the example flow, we'll use the following sections to define some important terminology and concepts.

Flows

Within Spring Web Flow, a flow defines a conversation, or dialogue, between users and the server. It serves as a blueprint for a use case or business process. The Purchase Product use case is one example of a flow.

States

The steps of a flow are called *states*. A state encapsulates behavior that executes when the state is entered. The exact behavior is a function of the state's type. Spring Web Flow provides five core types of states, shown in Table 11-3.

Table 11-3. *Types of States*

Name	Description
Action state	Executes your application code, typically delegating to a business service in the middle tier.
View state	Renders a view allowing the user to participate in the flow by entering data or viewing a message.
Subflow state	Spawns another flow as a subflow. The spawning flow is suspended until the subflow reaches an end state, at which point the subflow will end and the spawning flow will resume.
Decision state	Evaluates a condition to drive a transition to a new state.
End state	Terminates a flow.

Every flow definition must contain exactly one start state and at least one end state.

Transitions

All states except end states are transitionable and maintain a set of one or more transitions that define "allowed paths" to other states. A transition is triggered on the occurrence of an *event*.

Events

An event is nothing more than "something that happens" within a state. An event is treated as a state outcome that captures the logical result of a state's execution.

From Figure 11-4, you can see the event names such as "submit" and "yes" driving state transitions (the arrows between states). The "submit" event communicates that a submit button was pressed as the outcome of a view state, and the "yes" event communicates that a true result was returned when evaluating a conditional expression as the outcome of a decision state.

So with knowledge of these basic building blocks in place, the challenge of implementing a flow definition becomes:

1. defining the states of the flow

2. defining the possible transitions between states and the event-driven criteria for those state transitions.

Your First Flow

In this section you will implement the example Purchase Product use case using Spring Web Flow. Chapter 12 will cover many of the decisions that the author has made and reevaluate some of those decisions regarding how this example works within Spring MVC. This section will not cover Spring MVC itself, as that is sufficiently covered elsewhere in this book. For now, let's assume you have a working Spring MVC project that can be built and deployed onto a servlet container.

Installing Spring Web Flow

Instructions for downloading and installing Spring Web Flow can be found at http:// opensource2.atlassian.com/confluence/spring/display/WEBFLOW/Home.

Proposed Flow Directory Structure

From our experience it is best to partition your Spring Web Flow configuration information into file fragments that are responsible for their own concerns. Figure 11-5 is an example of a prudent directory structure for managing Spring Web Flow configuration artifacts.

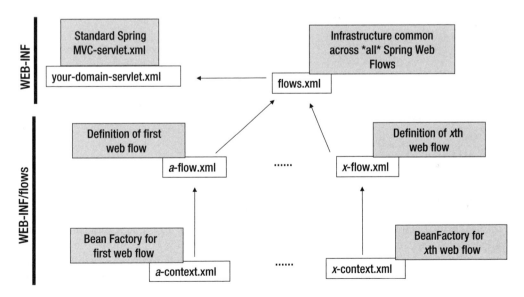

Figure 11-5. *Suggested directory layout*

The Purchase Product Flow Definition

A flow definition can be engineered in a number of ways. Many users use XML to define their flows, as XML is a human readable and highly toolable format. However, you may also define flows in Java (by extending `AbstractFlowBuilder`) or with your own custom format by implementing a custom `FlowBuilder`.

For the Purchase Product example web flow, you will use XML. Recall the graphical depiction of the flow definition in Figure 11-4.

Implementing the First Step: View States

The first step of this flow is to enter the purchase information, which requires the user to participate in the flow by providing the following bits of information:

- The price at which the product should be sold

- The quantity of products that are to be sold for this order

Since this is the first step of the flow, it is designated as the start state. Since it is a step where the user is involved, it is a view state. A view state will select a view to render to allow the user to participate in the flow. See Listing 11-1.

Listing 11-1. `/WEB-INF/flows/purchase-flow.xml`

```xml
<?xml version="1.0" encoding="UTF-8"?>
<!DOCTYPE flow PUBLIC "-//SPRING//DTD WEBFLOW 1.0//EN"
"http://www.springframework.org/dtd/spring-webflow-1.0.dtd">

<flow start-state="enterPurchaseInformation">
    <view-state id="enterPurchaseInformation" view="purchaseForm">
    …
    </view-state>
</flow>
```

The preceding instruction means, "When an execution of this flow starts, enter the `enterPurchaseInformation` state. Then select the `purchaseForm` view for display to the user, and pause the flow execution until a user event is signaled."

Transitions

As it stands, the preceding view-state definition is incomplete. Recall that all transitionable state types, which include the view state, must define at least one transition that leads to another state.

Also recall that a transition is triggered by the occurrence of an event. A view-state event is triggered by the user to communicate what action the user took. For example, the user may press the "submit" or "cancel" button. So for a view state, the set of transitions define the supported user events you wish to respond to for that state and how you wish to respond to them, as defined in Listing 11-2.

Listing 11-2. /WEB-INF/flows/purchase-flow.xml *Containing Transitions*

```
<flow start-state="enterPurchaseInformation">
    <view-state id="enterPurchaseInformation" view="purchaseForm">
        <transition on="submit" to="requiresShipping">
        <transition on="cancel" to="cancel"/>
    </view-state>
</flow>
```

The preceding transition instructions can be read, "On the occurrence of the submit event, transition to the requiresShipping state; on the occurrence of the cancel event, transition to the cancel state."

Actions

At this point you have defined a simple view state that will display a form and respond to "submit" and "cancel" events. You have yet to define the target states of the above transitions, which is the next logical step.

Before continuing, however, consider some requirements typical of most form views. Forms usually need to be prepared before their display; that is, it is often the case that view prerender logic needs to be executed. This logic might load the "backing form object" that will be edited in the form, or it might load a collection of objects from the database for display in a drop-down menu or select box.

Similarly, when a form is submitted, there is typically submit or postback logic that needs to execute. This logic is usually concerned with data binding (the process of copying form input parameters into properties of the "backing form object") and data validation (the process of validating the new state of the form object).

In Spring Web Flow, you invoke arbitrary command logic such as prerender and postback logic by executing an action that implements the core org.springframework.webflow.Action interface, as shown in Listing 11-3.

Listing 11-3. org.springframework.webflow.Action

```
public interface Action {
    Event execute(RequestContext context);
}
```

The interface is simple, consisting of a single method. An Action is expected to execute arbitrary logic when invoked in the context of a request. Once execution has completed, a result event (or outcome) is returned which the calling flow may respond to.

An Action can do whatever you want it to do, and we'll cover a number of out-of-the-box implementations in this book. What is important to understand now is the Action is the core construct for executing application code from a flow, and there are many opportunities to execute Actions within the life cycle of a flow. Table 11-4 provides the available execution points within a flow life cycle.

Table 11-4. *Action Execution Points Within the Flow Life Cycle*

Point	Description
On flow start	Execute one or more "start actions" when a flow starts.
On flow end	Execute one or more "end actions" when a flow ends.
On state enter	Execute one or more "entry actions" when a state is entered.
On state exit	Execute one or more "exit actions" when a state is exited.
Before transition	Execute one or more "transition actions" before executing a transition.

In this case, you are interested in executing view prerender logic when the enterPurchaseInformation state is entered. Then, on execution of the submit transition you are interested in executing data binding and validation postback logic. See Listing 11-4.

Listing 11-4. /WEB-INF/flows/purchase-flow.xml *Containing Entry Actions*

```
<flow start-state="enterPurchaseInformation">
    <view-state id="enterPurchaseInformation" view="purchaseForm">
        <entry-actions>
            <action bean="formAction" method="setupForm"/>
        </entry-actions>
        <transition on="submit" to="requiresShipping">
            <action bean="formAction" method="bindAndValidate"/>
        </transition>
        <transition on="cancel" to="cancel"/>
    </view-state>
</flow>
```

The preceding instruction now reads, "When an execution of this flow starts, enter the enterPurchaseInformation state. When the state is entered, first execute the setupForm() method on the formAction. Then select the purchaseForm view for display to the user, and pause the flow execution until a user event is signaled."

The submit transition instruction now reads, "On the occurrence of the submit event, transition to the requiresShipping state if the bindAndValidate() method on the formAction executes successfully."

This gives you behavior typical of a form view state, executing prerender logic as part of a state entry action, and postback logic as part of a specific transition action. If the transition action returns a result other than success, the transition will not be allowed, and the state will be reentered. This allows us to respond to data binding and validation errors correctly by redisplaying the view so the user can review the errors and revise his edits.

Action Bean Definitions

At this point you have referenced an Action bean from the flow definition with the formAction identifier (<action bean="formAction" method="setupForm"/>).

However, you have not defined the mapping between that identifier and a specific `Action` implementation. This is where the existing Spring infrastructure comes in, as Spring Web Flow uses Spring to drive configuration of flow artifacts such as `Action`. Refer to Listing 11-5.

Listing 11-5. `/WEB-INF/flows/purchase-flow.xml` *Importing Spring Beans*

```
<flow start-state="enterPurchaseInformation">
    <view-state id="enterPurchaseInformation" view="purchaseForm">
        <entry-actions>
            <action bean="formAction" method="setupForm"/>
        </entry-actions>
        <transition on="submit" to="requiresShipping">
            <action bean="formAction" method="bindAndValidate"/>
        </transition>
        <transition on="cancel" to="cancel"/>
    </view-state>

    <import resource="purchase-flow-context.xml"/>
</flow>
```

Listing 11-6 is the contents of `/WEB-INF/flow/purchase-flow-context.xml`.

Listing 11-6. `/WEB-INF/flow/purchase-flow-context.xml`

```
<?xml version="1.0" encoding="UTF-8"?>
<!DOCTYPE beans PUBLIC "-//SPRING//DTD BEAN//EN"
"http://www.springframework.org/dtd/spring-beans.dtd">
<beans>
    <bean id="formAction" class="org.springframework.webflow.action.FormAction">
        <property name="formObjectName" value="purchase"/>
        <property name="formObjectClass" value="purchase.domain.Purchase"/>
        <property name="formObjectScope" value="FLOW"/>
        <property name="validator">
            <bean class="purchase.domain.PurchaseValidator"/>
        </property>
    </bean>
</beans>
```

By using the `import` element, you can pull in any number of files containing bean definitions that define artifacts local to the flow definition. These imported bean definitions also have full access to the beans defined in the parent `WebApplicationContext`, typically the `DispatcherServlet` context.

In this case `formAction` corresponds to a singleton instance of `org.springframework.webflow.action.FormAction`. This action is a `MultiAction` implementation that provides a number of action methods related to form processing, including `setupForm` for executing form prerender logic and `bindAndValidate` for executing form postback logic.

When invoked, `setupForm` will create an instance of the `purchase.domain.Purchase` form object class and place it in `flow` scope under the name `purchase`. This automatically exposes the `Purchase` object to the views by that name, which will allow correct prepopulation fields based on default values.

When `bindAndValidate` is invoked it will bind incoming request parameters to the existing `purchase` bean managed in flow scope. After successful data binding, the configured `Validator` will then validate the new state of the bean.

■**Note** `FormAction` is a very rich object and will be investigated further in Chapter 12.

Testing the Flow Execution

At this point you nearly have a syntactically correct flow definition whose execution can be unit tested outside of the container. By filling in temporary state "placeholders" for the undefined states, you'll correct the remaining syntax errors. Refer to Listing 11-7.

Listing 11-7. `/WEB-INF/flows/purchase-flow.xml` *Adding End State placeholders*

```
<flow start-state="enterPurchaseInformation">
    <view-state id="enterPurchaseInformation" view="purchaseForm">
        <entry-actions>
            <action bean="formAction" method="setupForm"/>
        </entry-actions>
        <transition on="submit" to="requiresShipping">
            <action bean="formAction" method="bindAndValidate"/>
        </transition>
        <transition on="cancel" to="cancel"/>
    </view-state>

    <end-state id="requiresShipping"/>
    <end-state id="cancel"/>
    <import resource="purchase-flow-context.xml"/>
</flow>
```

With the `requiresShipping` and `cancel` placeholder, when either the `submit` or `cancel` transitions are executed, the flow terminates. Once a test verifies that the `enterPurchaseInformation` controller logic executes successfully, you'll properly implement the `requiresShipping` state, as well as the remaining states of the flow.

Extending AbstractFlowExecutionTests

How do you test the execution of the flow defined so far? Spring Web Flow ships support classes within the `org.springframework.webflow.test` package. This support includes convenient base classes for implementing flow execution tests, as well as mock implementations of core Web Flow constructs such as the `RequestContext` to support unit testing flow artifacts such as `Actions` in isolation.

In this case, execution of the preceding purchase flow needs testing. Specifically, the following can be asserted:

- When the flow starts, it transitions to the correct start state: enterPurchaseInformation.

    - After the enterPurchaseInformation state has entered:

        - The correct View is selected (purchaseForm).

        - The model data the View needs is provisioned correctly (an instance of a purchase bean is present).

- On the occurrence of the cancel event, the flow execution ends.

- On the occurrence of the submit event data binding and validation logic executes correctly.

This is accomplished by writing a test that extends AbstractFlowexecutionTests. Refer to Listing 11-8.

Listing 11-8. *Test Class to Test the Example Flow*

```
public class PurchaseFlowExecutionTests extends AbstractXmlFlowExecutionTests {
    @Override // the location of the flow definition in the file system
    protected Resource getFlowLocation() {
        File flowDir = new File("src/webapp/WEB-INF");
        return new FileSystemResource(new File(flowDir, "purchaseflow.xml"));
    }
    .....

    @Override // the location of the flow definition in the file system
    protected Resource getFlowLocation() {
        File flowDir = new File("src/webapp/WEB-INF");
        return new FileSystemResource(new File(flowDir, "purchase-flow.xml"));
    }

    // test that the flow execution starts as expected
    public void testStartFlow() {
        ViewSelection selectedView = startFlow();
        assertCurrentStateEquals("enterPurchaseInformation");
        assertModelAttributeNotNull("purchase", selectedView);
        assertViewNameEquals("purchaseForm", selectedView);
    }

    // test a successful submit, including data binding
    public void testSubmitPurchaseInformation() {
        testStartFlow();
        Map parameters = new HashMap(2);
        parameters.put("price", "25");
        parameters.put("quantity", "4");
```

```
        ViewSelection selectedView = signalEvent("submit", parameters);
        Purchase purchase = (Purchase)selectedView.getModel().get("purchase");
        assertEquals("Wrong price" new MonetaryAmount("25"), purchase.getAmount());
        assertEquals("Wrong quantity", 4, purchase.getQuantity());
        assertFlowExecutionEnded();
    }
}
```

The preceding test ensures that the controller logic implemented thus far within the flow definition works as expected. The test can also serve as a convenient way to test the execution of the use case from the web tier down. As additional states are added to the flow, you simply add additional test methods that signal events that drive transitions to those states and verify that the respective state behavior executes correctly.

Decision States

Recall that the next step in this sample flow is to optionally allow the user to enter product shipping information. In other words, there exists some condition that determines whether or not shipping information is required for a given flow execution.

The decision state (see Listing 11-9) is designed to handle this type of situation, where a condition needs to be evaluated to drive a state transition. A decision state is a simple, indempotent routing state.

Listing 11-9. `/WEB-INF/flows/purchase-flow.xml` *Containing a Decision State*

```xml
<flow start-state="enterPurchaseInformation">
    <view-state id="enterPurchaseInformation" view="purchaseForm">
        <entry-actions>
            <action bean="formAction" method="setupForm"/>
        </entry-actions>
        <transition on="submit" to="requiresShipping">
            <action bean="formAction" method="bindAndValidate"/>
        </transition>
        <transition on="cancel" to="cancel"/>
    </view-state>
    <decision-state id="requiresShipping">
        <if test="${flowScope.purchase.shipping}" then="enterShippingDetails" ➥
else="placeOrder"/>
    </decision-state>
    <view-state id="enterShippingDetails" view="shippingForm">
        <transition on="submit" to="placeOrder">
            <action bean="sellItemAction" method="bindAndValidate"/>
        </transition>
    </view-state>
    <import resource="purchase-flow-context.xml"/>
</flow>
```

As you can see, if the `shipping` property of the `purchase` bean in `flow scope` evaluates to true, the flow will transition to the `enterShippingDetails` state; otherwise, the flow will transition to the `placeOrder` state.

In this scenario the decision-state evaluation criteria is an expression defined within the flow definition. Had the decision criteria been more complex, it could have been made in Java application code. You'll see how to do this in Chapter 12.

■**Note** You'll learn how to invoke methods on business objects to drive decision-state decisions in Chapter 12.

Action States

Once all information about the product purchase has been collected from the user and validated, the purchase order can be submitted. The processing of the purchase order is the first time in this flow where the business tier needs to be invoked, within a transactional context.

The action state is designed to invoke application code, and perhaps code that is non-indempotent (it should not be repeated). When an action state is entered, one or more actions are invoked. What these actions do is up to you. In this case, you are interested in calling the `placeOrder()` method on an existing `OrderClerk` business façade. See Listing 11-10.

Listing 11-10. *OrderClerk Interface*

```
@Transactional
public interface OrderClerk {
    void placeOrder(Purchase purchase);
}
```

To do this, you simply instruct the flow to call the `placeOrder()` method for you when the action state is entered, as shown in Listing 11-11.

Listing 11-11. `/WEB-INF/flows/purchase-flow.xml` *Containing placeOrder Action State*

```
<flow start-state="enterPurchaseInformation">
    <view-state id="enterPurchaseInformation" view="purchaseForm">
        <entry-actions>
            <action bean="formAction" method="setupForm"/>
        </entry-actions>
        <transition on="submit" to="requiresShipping">
            <action bean="formAction" method="bindAndValidate"/>
        </transition>
        <transition on="cancel" to="cancel"/>

    </view-state>
```

```
    <decision-state id="requiresShipping">
        <if test="${flowScope.purchase.shipping}" then="enterShippingDetails" ➥
else="placeOrder"/>
    </decision-state>

    <view-state id="enterShippingDetails" view="shippingForm">
        <transition on="submit" to="placeOrder">
            <action bean="sellItemAction" method="bindAndValidate"/>
        </transition>
    </view-state>

    <action-state id="placeOrder">
        <action bean="orderClerk" method="placeOrder(${flowScope.purchase})"/>
        <transition on="success" to="showCostConfirmation"/>
    </action-state>
    <import resource="purchase-flow-context.xml"/>
</flow>
```

In this case the action referenced is the orderClerk, which is simply a plain old Java object (POJO). The referenced OrderClerk implementation has no dependency on SWF and does not implement the Action interface—Spring Web Flow will adapt the placeOrder method to the Action interface automatically. As you can see, method argument expressions can also be specified.

The preceding action-state definition means, "When the placeOrder state is entered, invoke the placeOrder() method on the orderClerk façade, passing it the purchase object from flow scope as an input argument; then, on a successful return (when no exception is thrown) transition to the showCostConfirmation state."

Action states are not limited to invoking just one action; you may invoke any number of actions as part of a chain. You will see how and when to do this in Chapter 12.

Note You'll learn more about Chain of Responsibility and Spring's POJO-method-binding capability in Chapter 12.

End States

The last core state type needed to complete the example flow is the end state. End states simply terminate the executing flow when entered. Once the execution of a flow is terminated, any allocated resources in flow scope are automatically cleaned up. The execution cannot "come back;" it is only possible to start a new, completely independent execution.

Note The exception to this is if the ending flow is being used as a subflow, in which case the flow that spawned the subflow is expected to resume execution. For more information on subflows, consult Chapter 12.

End states effectively define possible flow outcomes (see Listing 11-12). In the Purchase Product flow there are two possible outcomes: cancel and showCostConfirmation.

Listing 11-12. /WEB-INF/flows/purchase-flow.xml *Containing End States*

```
<flow start-state="enterPurchaseInformation">
    <view-state id="enterPurchaseInformation" view="purchaseForm">
        <entry-actions>
            <action bean="formAction" method="setupForm"/>
        </entry-actions>
        <transition on="submit" to="requiresShipping">
            <action bean="formAction" method="bindAndValidate"/>
        </transition>
    <view-state>

    <decision-state id="requiresShipping">
        <if test="${flowScope.purchase.shipping}" then="enterShippingDetails" ➡
else="placeOrder"/>
    </decision-state>

    <view-state id="enterShippingDetails" view="shippingForm">
        <transition on="submit" to="placeOrder">
            <action bean="sellItemAction" method="bindAndValidate"/>
        </transition>
    </view-state>

    <action-state id="placeOrder">
        <action bean="orderClerk" method="placeOrder(${flowScope.purchase})"/>
        <transition on="success" to="showCostConfirmation"/>
    </action-state>
    <end-state id="showCostConfirmation" view="costConfirmation"/>
    <end-state id="cancel" view="home"/>
    <import resource="purchase-flow-context.xml"/>
</flow>
```

End states can optionally select ending or confirmation views that should be rendered when they are entered. In this scenario, the showCostConfirmation state selects the costConfirmation view, which will display a summary of the purchase order cost after order placement.

End states may also be used to trigger redirects after flow, which is a common pattern to further restrict accidental Back button usage by redirecting the user to a new browser URL.

The Purchase Product Flow: What's Next

At this point, the purchase order flow has been fully implemented. Listing 11-12 contains a human-readable, self-contained definition that fully encapsulates the navigation rules for the purchase product use case—allowing you to change navigation rules without impacting anything else in the system. This module can now be fully tested out of the container and readied for deployment within the container.

Spring MVC Deployment

To deploy the flow for execution within a Spring MVC environment, you need to define a
`FlowController` which is a special type of `org.springframework.web.servlet.mvc.Controller`.
One `FlowController` will typically manage the execution of all flows within an application.

The FlowController

A `FlowController` serves as an Adapter (http://en.wikipedia.org/wiki/Adapter_pattern)
between Spring MVC and Spring Web Flow (it has knowledge of both systems). A
`FlowController` exposes a set of managed flow executions for execution at a specific
request URL.

Listing 11-13. *Spring MVC DispatcherServlet Configuration*

```
<bean name="/purchase.htm" class="org.springframework.webflow.manager.mvc.
FlowController">
    <constructor-arg ref="flowRegistry"/>
</bean>
```

Spring MVC will now route requests for the `/purchase.htm` URL to the `org.springframework.`
`webflow.mvc.FlowController`. As you can see, the `Controller` needs a reference to a
`flowRegistry`, which contains the flow definitions that are eligible for execution.

FlowRegistry

A `FlowRegistry` (see Listing 11-14) is a dictionary of flow definitions eligible for execution. Flow
definitions placed in a registry are indexed by their identifiers. By default, the filename of the
flow definition, minus the file extension, is treated as the flow `id`.

Listing 11-14. `/WEB-INF/flow.xml` *Including the purchaseFlow*

```
<bean name="flowRegistry"
class="org.springframework.webflow.registry.XmlFlowRegistryFactoryBean">
    <property name="flowLocations">
        <list>
            <value>/WEB-INF/flow/purchase-flow.xml</value>
        </list>
    </property>
</bean>
```

As you define new flow definitions, you simply add them as new flow locations. Wildcard
matches are also supported, building on Spring's `ResourceArrayPropertyEditor`. See Listing 11-15.

Listing 11-15. /WEB-INF/flow.xml *Including All Available Flows*

```
<bean name="flowRegistry"
class="org.springframework.webflow.registry.XmlFlowRegistryFactoryBean">
    <property name="flowLocations" value="/WEB-INF/flows/**/*-flow.xml">
</bean>
```

If needed, flow definitions may also be explicitly assigned identifiers and additional, custom properties when registered.

Additional Configuration

A FlowController plus a FlowRegistry are the only required deployment artifacts for executing flow definitions within a Spring MVC environment. If you need more power—for example, you wish to control the way in which flow executions are stored or observe the life cycle of certain flows—there are additional objects that may be configured, but that configuration is entirely optional.

■**Tip** Spring Web Flow provides meaningful defaults, but still gives you the power to customize and extend when you need to. You'll learn how to configure more advanced options in Chapter 12.

View Template Resolution

There is still one important topic that we have not yet discussed: How are logical view names selected by view states translated to physical view templates that render responses? The answer is Spring MVC's built-in ViewResolver infrastructure. Spring Web Flow does not care for this concern; as a controller framework, it simply makes logical view selections. It is the job of the calling framework (i.e., Spring MVC) to care for mapping those logical view selections to renderable templates.

View Template Requirements

There are a few requirements placed upon view templates that participate in flow executions. It should be noted however, that there are not many, and they do not prevent views from being used "outside" a web flow environment.

- To signal an event in an executing flow, the view must submit back a parameter that associates the request with the correct flow execution. By default, this is the _flowExecutionId parameter.

- To tell the flow what user event occurred, the view must submit back a parameter that identifies the event. By default, this is the _eventId parameter.

Those are the only two requirements: each view wishing to participate in an executing flow must submit the _flowExecutionId parameter to associate itself with the correct flow execution and _eventId parameter to tell that execution what happened in the resuming view state.

Listing 11-16 contains an example of a view participating in a flow execution by submitting back the necessary parameters via hidden form parameters.

Listing 11-16. *Example JSP to Continue an Existing Flow*

```
<html>
  <head><title>Example page to continue a flow</title></head>
  <body>
    <form method="POST" action="/purchase.htm">
        …
      <input type="hidden" name="_flowExecutionId" value="${flowExecutionId}"/>
      <input type="button" name="_eventId_submit" value="Submit"/>
    </form>
  </body>
</html>
```

This example shows use of the special eventId button name prefix, which allows Spring Web Flow to obtain the_eventId without JavaScript when using multiple submit buttons within a single form.

Launching the Flow from the Browser

With the knowledge you have now, you are ready to execute an instance of the Product Purchase flow from your web browser. To launch a new flow execution, simply point it at the URL of the FlowController, parameterizing the URL with the flow to execute:

```
http://localhost:8080/purchase.htm?_flowId=purchase-flow
```

Each time you hit that URL, a new flow purchase-flow execution will be launched and transitioned to its start state. When the execution reaches a view state, control will be returned to the client to allow the user to participate in the flow. Subsequent requests to the server must provide the _eventId and the_flowExecutionId to specify what happened in what conversation.

▪**Tip** You can think of the flowId as analogous to the name of a class, while the flowExecutionId is analgous to an object reference.

This ping-pong between the view and Spring Web Flow can be visualized as shown in Figure 11-6.

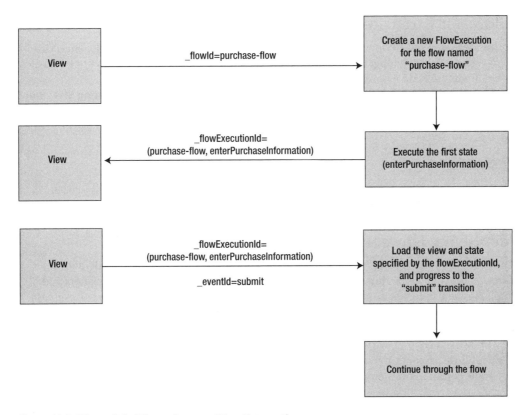

Figure 11-6. *View of the View->Server->View Interaction*

Summary

Spring Web Flow was designed from the outset to manage the definition and execution of a dialogue between a user and the server. It is not an extension to Spring MVC, but rather a stand-alone (and very well-integrated) tool for developing self-contained application controller modules.

Model Conversations

Developers now have a tool kit that explicitly models the conversational flow, in addition to providing access to the existing servlet (or portlet) infrastructure.

Conversation scope is not just a subset of session scope; it is the ability to assign each new conversation its own new data set. Request scope is unique per page request, session scope is unique per browser, and conversation scope is unique per conversation. Conversations can actually span sessions (more on this in Chapter 12) or exist multiple times within the same session.

Allows for Extension

Spring Web Flow was designed from the ground up to be as extensible as possible. This is achieved through providing well-documented extension points and its ability to hook into a rich domain model in a noninvasive manner.

Another driving factor for Spring Web Flow was that of integration with existing MVC tool kits. Because Spring Web Flow is self-contained, integration is usually a case of configuring one of the provided adapters and requires very little, if any manipulation of your existing code.

Testable

Spring Web Flows allows for the development of externalized, self-contained `Controller` modules that are fully testable out of the container.

Identifying Flows (Easy, Natural Language)

The vocabulary that Spring Web Flow uses is sensibly not tied to a web tier; it talks about flows, states, and views, thus reducing the inherent conceptual gap between designers and implementers. In fact, it is not too much of a stretch to imagine a nirvana where the use-case models are manipulated in your favorite UML tool that Spring Web Flow then interrogates via an implementation of `org.springframework.webflow.config.FlowBuilder`.

In the next chapter, we will delve into the more advanced aspects of Spring Web Flow (e.g., subflows, exception handling, continuations, long-living transactions) and detail how to handle common problems like Back button navigation and double submissions.

CHAPTER 12

Advanced Spring Web Flow

This chapter builds on the introduction we presented in Chapter 11 and covers some of the more advanced problems that Spring Web Flow solves. You will see how Spring Web Flow simplifies web application development by elegantly solving the Back button problem, as well as the duplicate form submission problem.

After reading this chapter you will have a deeper understanding of how Spring Web Flow works and be able to extend the framework to meet your needs.

Business Logic and Flows

Chapter 11 introduced the Spring Web Flow framework and walked through the implementation of an example flow. It also discussed how Spring Web Flow should not be treated as a golden hammer. One area where you need to be especially considerate of this point is that of logic; how much and what type of logic is appropriate in a web flow definition?

Business Logic

Let's reconsider the problem Spring Web Flow solves, that of modeling conversations and executing complex page navigation rules. It is neither a business rules engine nor a generic work flow engine, and it does not claim to be. Spring Web Flow fits very firmly in the presentation layer of the layered architecture discussed in Chapters 2 and 3. Because of its power and the fact a flow definition "feels" somewhat like a work flow document, it can be tempting to allow business logic to creep into the flow definition, but it really doesn't belong there.

Why does this matter? Well, primarily because your business rules are no longer *isolated* or *explicit*. As an example, one of us was responsible for developing a web application that allowed nontechnical users to maintain their own web site content. Part of the business rules stated that users could only edit pages for which they had both exclusive access and appropriate permissions. To meet these requirements the author produced the flow fragment shown in Listing 12-1.

Listing 12-1. *Spring Web Flow Fragment Enforcing Business Rules*

```
<action-state id="lockPage">
  <action name="lock" bean="lockAction" method="lock"/>
  <action name="checkPermissions" bean="securityAction" ➥
method="checkPermissions"/>
  <transition on="lock.error" to="concurrentEditError.view"/>
```

```
    <transition on="checkPermissions.error" to="accessDenied.view"/>
    <transition on="checkPermissions.success" to="nextAction"/>
  </action-state>
```

■**Note** Both lockAction and securityAction were trivial adapters between Spring Web Flow and the business tier and hence are not shown. In the "POJO Actions" section later in this chapter you will see how to do away with such objects.

Although this worked, it was not ideal; the business rule was only enforced in the flow definition. If the business rule was changed (e.g., they only had to have exclusive access) then the web flow definition would have to change, even though the affected logic has nothing to do with presentational or navigational logic.

Many enterprise applications have multiple entry points into the system, including not only the XHTML interface, but also web services, batch updates, and even rich clients. When business logic resides only in web flow artifacts, all other systems either lack that logic or need to reimplement it. For this reason, keep the business logic of the system out of the web flow layer and inside the business (or service) layer and domain model.

■**Tip** Asking the question "what needs to change if I change *x*?" is a good way of determining whether *x* belongs or not. If changing *x* requires changing multiple layers or a seemingly irrelevant layer (as in this case), then there is something wrong with the application design. In this case, a change to the business logic resulted in a change to the flow definition, indicating the flow definition is not the right place for this logic.

So what is the solution? Simple: Move the business rule out of the web flow. Does this prevent the web flow from referencing the business rule? Of course not, it simply means that the web flow does not *implement* the business rule. Refactoring might lead to something like Listing 12-2.

Listing 12-2. *Spring Web Flow Fragment Referencing Business Rules*

```
  <action-state id="checkRights ">
    <action bean="checkRightsAction"/>
    <transition on="error" to="rightsViolation.view"/>
    <transition on="success" to="nextAction"/>
  </action-state>
```

The flow now drives the *execution* of the business rule, but does not *define* it. When implementing Spring Web Flow, be sure to avoid inadvertently coding business logic inside of your flow.

Flow Granularity

Flows come in varying granularities, from large top-level flows composed of many smaller subflows to self-contained flows with no dependencies. Spring Web Flow gains much of its power from its ability to compose multiple flows together, creating modular and reusable application components.

Up to this point, you have seen flow definitions that are self-contained with no composition. In this section we will show you how to create modular flow definitions with subflows and inner flows.

Subflows

A *subflow* is simply a flow called by another flow. Any flow can be a subflow, and any subflow is a flow. This is possible because a flow is a coarse-grained component with a well-defined contract that acts as a self-contained black box. What happens inside a flow is hidden from any other flows, including the calling flow.

■**Note** When a flow is spawned by another flow, the spawning flow is often referred to as the *parent flow* or *calling flow*, while the flow being spawned is often referred to as the *subflow* or *child flow*.

Architecturally, subflows are a powerful mechanism that enable the definition of complex flows composed of one or more subflows. Subflows can themselves contain subflows (there is no limit to the depth of subflow nesting). Subflows are best used to model logical sequences of steps when reuse is possible.

Consider the Purchase Product use case from Chapter 11; it contained a step to capture product shipping information. In a real application this step could be quite complex, consisting of different screens dependent upon the mechanism used to ship the product (air, sea, land, and so on). You can imagine this step being reused elsewhere in the application (wherever shipping information is required), and therefore this self-contained and reusable component is a good candidate for refactoring into its own flow. The steps involved in refactoring logic out of an existing flow and into a subflow are as follows:

1. Isolate the web flow fragment and dependent beans to be modeled as a subflow.

2. Move the fragment and the dependent beans into their own flow definition.

3. Within the new flow definition, define an end state for every logical flow outcome. Each end state should expose any flow attributes that are "returned" by that outcome (in this case, the shipping information).

4. Replace the factored-out fragment in the original flow with a call to the subflow using the subflow state.

Recall the flow definition from Chapter 11. The isolated fragment related to entering shipping information is boldface. See Listing 12-5.

Listing 12-3. *The Purchase Product Flow Definition*

```
<flow start-state="enterPurchaseInformation">
  <view-state id="enterPurchaseInformation" view="purchaseForm">
    <entry-actions>
      <action bean="formAction" method="setupForm"/>
    </entry-actions>
    <transition on="submit" to="requiresShipping">
      <action bean="formAction" method="bindAndValidate"/>
    </transition>
    <transition on="cancel" to="cancel"/>
  </view-state>

  <decision-state id="requiresShipping">
    <if test="${flowScope.purchase.shipping}" then="enterShippingDetails" ➥
    else="placeOrder"/>
  </decision-state>

  <view-state id="enterShippingDetails" view="shippingForm">
    <transition on="submit" to="placeOrder">
      <action bean="sellItemAction" method="bindAndValidate"/>
    </transition>
  </view-state>

  <action-state id="placeOrder">
    <action bean="orderClerk" method="placeOrder(${flowScope.purchase})"/>
    <transition on="success" to="showCostConfirmation"/>
  </action-state>
  <end-state id="showCostConfirmation" view="costConfirmation"/>
  <end-state id="cancel" view="home"/>
  <import resource="purchase-flow-context.xml"/>
</flow>
```

The preceding fragment uses the purchase bean, which contains all the shipping information as member variables. Since subflows are independent and isolated from their calling flows, the shipping information will be extracted into its own class called Shipping. This new Shipping class will be managed by its own FormAction.

Thus, a new flow (as listed in Listing 12-4) is created in /WEB-INF/flows/shipping-flow.xml.

Listing 12-4. *New Spring Web Flow Subflow*

```
<flow start-state="requiresShipping">
  <decision-state id="requiresShipping">
    <if test="${flowScope.requiresShipping}" then="enterShippingDetails"
    else="finish"/>
  </decision-state>
```

```
<view-state id="enterShippingDetails" view="shippingForm">
  <entry-actions>
    <action bean="formAction" method="setupForm"/>
  </entry-actions>
  <transition on="submit" to="finish">
    <action bean="formAction" method="bindAndValidate"/>
  </transition>
</view-state>

<end-state id="finish">
  <output-attribute name="shipping"/>
</end>

<import resource="shipping-flow-context.xml"/>
</flow>
```

■**Note** Deciding whether to put the requiresShipping guard into the subflow or keep it in the calling flow is an interesting exercise. On the one hand you could argue that the decision is part of the enterShipping logic (and hence be part of the subflow); on the other you could argue that the subflow should only be called when needed (and hence be part of the calling flow).

When a subflow ends (by reaching an end state), the subflow signals an ending result event with the id of the end state. The resuming subflow state in the calling flow is responsible for executing a transition on the occurrence of that event, as well as mapping any output attributes (which you can think of as return values).

■**Tip** If the flow will only ever be called as a subflow, then there is no need to specify views on the end state.

In this example the new shipping subflow is "returning" the shipping bean to the calling flow, or at least making the shipping information available to the calling flow. The <output-attribute name="shipping"/> declaration informs Spring Web Flow to expose the shipping object once the subflow has finished. As you will see later, the calling flow can then retrieve this and map it into its scope.

Listing 12-5 contains the definition of the shipping flow's formAction bean.

Listing 12-5. /WEB-INF/flows/shipping-flow-context.xml *Bean Factory for the shippingInformation Subflow*

```
<beans>
  <bean id="formAction" class="org.springframework.webflow.action.FormAction">
    <property name="formObjectName" value="shipping"/>
```

```
    <property name="formObjectClass" value="purchase.domain.Shipping"/>
    <property name="formObjectScope" value="FLOW"/>
    <property name="validator">
      <bean class="purchase.domain.ShippingValidator"/>
    </property>
  </bean>
</beans>
```

Finally the `flowRegistry` bean in `/WEB-INF/flows.xml` is updated to include the new subflow, as shown in Listing 12-6.

Listing 12-6. *Modified flowRegistry Definition*

```
<bean name="flowRegistry"➥
class="org.springframework.webflow.registry.XmlFlowRegistryFactoryBean">
    <property name="flowLocations">
      <list>
        <value>/WEB-INF/flows/purchase-flow.xml</value>
        <value>/WEB-INF/flows/shipping-flow.xml</value>
      </list>
    </property>
</bean>
```

The subflow is now ready to be used. The next step is to replace the extracted fragment in `/WEB-INF/flows/purchase-flow.xml` with a new subflow-state definition that instructs the flow to spawn the shipping flow as a subflow. The refactored purchase flow is shown in Listing 12-7.

Listing 12-7. *Modified /WEB-INF/flows/purchase-flow.xml*

```
<flow start-state="enterPurchaseInformation">
  <view-state id="enterPurchaseInformation" view="purchaseForm">
    <entry-actions>
      <action bean="formAction" method="setupForm"/>
    </entry-actions>
    <transition on="submit" to="enterShippingInformation">
      <action bean="formAction" method="bindAndValidate"/>
    </transition>
    <transition on="cancel" to="cancel"/>
  </view-state>

  <subflow-state id="enterShippingInformation" flow="shipping-flow">
    <attribute-mapper>
      <input-mapping name="purchase.requiresShipping" as="requiresShipping"/>
      <output-mapping name="shipping" as="purchase.shipping"/>
    </attribute-mapper>
    <transition on="finish" to="placeOrder"/>
  </subflow-state>
```

```
<action-state id="placeOrder">
  <action bean="orderClerk" method="placeOrder(${flowScope.purchase})"/>
  <transition on="success" to="showCostConfirmation"/>
</action-state>
<end-state id="showCostConfirmation" view="costConfirmation"/>
<end-state id="cancel" view="home"/>
<import resource="purchase-flow-context.xml"/>
</flow>
```

Tip Remember, by default the name of the flow is derived from the name of the file it is defined in. Because the file is `/WEB-INF/flows/shipping-flow.xml`, the name (by default) is `shipping-flow`.

The subflow state defines a number of instructions including

- the flow to spawn as a subflow(`shipping-flow`);

- a set of attribute mappings (explained in the following section);

- one or more transitions eligible for execution when the subflow ends.

When calling a subflow a transition is typically defined for every end state within the subflow. When the subflow reaches an end state, the subflow will end, and control will return back to the subflow state in the calling flow. If the subflow state does not contain a transition matching the ending result of the subflow, a `NoMatchingTransitionException` will be thrown.

Attribute Mappings

A new element has been introduced within the `<subflow-state>` element: `<attribute-mapper>`. The `<attribute-mapper>` element, covered in the following section, plays a significant role when calling subflows, providing the integration between a parent flow and a child flow.

Subflows acting as self-contained black boxes are a very powerful concept, but are somewhat limited if there is no communication at all between the calling flow and the subflow. This is where `AttributeMappers` come in. Remember, subflows are independent of the parent flow and do not share the parent flow's context. Any information the parent needs to pass into the subflow, or the subflow needs to return back to the parent, must be explicitly mapped.

Note The `attribute-mapper` fragment from Listing 12-7 contains both an `input-mapping` and an `output-mapping`; however, `input-mapping`, `output-mapping`, and even `attribute-mapper` are not required.

AttributeMappers

The org.springframework.binding.AttributeMapper, shown in Listing 12-8, is a generic service interface for mapping attributes from one source to another. Spring Web Flow uses it to map objects and properties from one flow to another.

Listing 12-8. *AttributeMapper Interface*

```
public interface AttributeMapper {
    void map(Object source, Object target, Map context);
}
```

Example

Let's look again at the subflow state and attribute mappings from Listing 12-7:

```
<subflow-state id="enterShippingInformation" flow="shipping-flow">
  <attribute-mapper>
    <input-mapping name="purchase.requiresShipping" as="requiresShipping"/>
    <output-maping name="shipping" as="purchase.shipping"/>
  </attribute-mapper>
  <transition on="end" to="placeOrder"/>
</subflow-state>
```

The <input-mapping> element instructs Spring Web Flow to map the value of the requiresShipping property of the purchase object in the *parent flow scope* to an attribute in the subflow scope with the name requiresShipping.

The <output-mapping> element instructs Spring Web Flow to map the result of the shipping *subflow output attribute* to the shipping property on the purchase object in the *parent flow scope*.

Figure 12-1 graphically represents this.

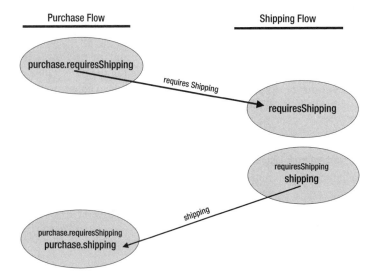

Figure 12-1. *Graphical representation of mapping attributes to and from a subflow*

Custom AttributeMappers

If the default implementation (`org.springframework.webflow.support.`
`ParameterizableFlowAttributeMapper`) is not sufficient, you can provide your own implementation of `org.springframework.webflow.FlowAttributeMapper`. Listing 12-9 provides a listing for a custom implementation of `FlowAttributeMapper`, which performs the same function.

Listing 12-9. *Implementation of ShippingAttributeMapper*

```
public final class ShippingAttributeMapper implements FlowAttributeMapper {
    public Map createSubflowInput(RequestContext requestContext) {
        Map map = new HashMap();
        Purchase purchase = (Purchase)➥
requestContext.getFlowScope().get("purchase");
        map.put("requiresShipping", purchase.isRequiresShipping());
        return map;
    }

    public void mapSubflowOutput(Map subflowOutput, RequestContext requestContext) {
        Shipping shipping = (Shipping) subflowOutput.get("shipping");
        Purchase purchase = (Purchase)➥
requestContext.getFlowScope().get("purchase");
        purchase.setShipping(shipping);
    }
}
```

The attribute mappings in the subflow state in `/WEB-INF/flows/purchase-flow.xml` would now change to `<attribute-mapper bean="shippingAttributeMapper"/>`.

■Tip You can plug in a custom `AttributeMapper` using the `bean` attribute. Many other constructs support pluggability in this fashion. Search for the `bean` attribute within the `spring-webflow` DTD to review them.

Inline Flows

Subflows are a very powerful construct within Spring Web Flow; they allow you to encapsulate and reuse page navigation logic in multiple contexts. One consequence of extracting a flow to be used as a subflow is that the extracted flow becomes usable as a top-level, or first-class, flow. This level of exposure may not always be desirable. For example, a particularly complex process that is composed of multiple logical subprocesses may benefit from being partitioned into separate flows, even if those flows will never be needed outside of the parent flow. The appropriate construct for this scenario is an *inline* flow.

An inline flow has the exact same behavior as a subflow; they are both flows, but inline flows exist entirely within the containing flow definition and are local to that definition. The general strategy for extracting an inline flow is as follows:

1. Move the flow fragment into an `<inline-flow>` element within the parent flow.

2. If the fragment was previously a top-level flow, remove the flow from the `flowRegistry`.

Applying step 1 to `/WEB-INF/flows/purchase-flow.xml` makes the shipping flow an inline flow, as shown in Listing 12-10. Notice how the parent subflow state doesn't change. There is no difference between calling either a top-level flow or an inline flow as a subflow. An inline flow by definition must simply be declared (and fully contained) within the calling flow.

■**Tip** Subflows are retrieved via the `flowRegistry` mechanism, while inline flows are declared within the same flow.

Listing 12-10. `/WEB-INF/flows/purchase-flow.xml` *with the Shipping Flow As an Inline Flow*

```
<flow start-state="enterPurchaseInformation">
<view-state id="enterPurchaseInformation" view="purchaseForm">
  <entry-actions>
    <action bean="formAction" method="setupForm"/>
  </entry-actions>
  <transition on="submit" to="enterShippingInformation">
    <action bean="formAction" method="bindAndValidate"/>
  </transition>
  <transition on="cancel" to="cancel"/>
</view-state>
<subflow-state id="enterShippingInformation" flow="shipping-flow">
  <attribute-mapper>
    <input-mapping name="purchase.requiresShipping"➥
as="requiresShipping"/>
    <output-mapping name="shipping" as="purchase.shipping"/>
  </attribute-mapper>
  <transition on="finish" to="placeOrder"/>
</subflow-state>
<action-state id="placeOrder">
  <action bean="orderClerk" method="placeOrder(${ flowScope.purchase})"/>
  <transition on="success" to="showCostConfirmation"/>
</action-state>
<end-state id="showCostConfirmation" view="costConfirmation"/>
<end-state id="cancel" view="home"/>
<import resource="purchase-flow-context.xml"/>
```

```
<inline-flow id="shipping-flow">
  <flow start-state="requiresShipping">
    <decision-state id="requiresShipping">
      <if test="${flowScope.requiresShipping}" then="enterShippingDetails"↩
else="finish"/>
    </decision-state>
    <view-state id="enterShippingDetails" view="shippingForm">
      <entry-actions>
        <action bean="formAction" method="setupForm"/>
      </entry-actions>
      <transition on="submit" to="finish">
        <action bean="formAction" method="bindAndValidate"/>
      </transition>
    </view-state>
    <end-state id="finish">
      <output-attribute name="shipping"/>
    </end>
    <import resource="shipping-flow-context.xml"/>
  </flow>
</inline-flow>

</flow>
```

Summary

Flow definitions have two levels of granularity, shown in Table 12-1.

Table 12-1. *Flow Definition*

Flow Artifact	Appropriate Use
Top-level flow	Defines an entire use case that can be reused in other contexts as a subflow. Responsible for completing a logical application transaction.
Inline flow	Defines an application transaction that is encapsulated within a larger use case and is fully contained within the larger flow.

The key point to take away is that a flow always represents a controlled navigation that accomplishes a logical unit of work for a single user. Whether it should be a top-level flow or inline flow is dependent upon whether the flow logic should be reused in other contexts.

At the start of a flow definition process it is best not to worry too much about whether a flow should be a top-level flow or an inline flow. The need for extracting flows has a tendency to identify itself in the same way a method, or an interface naturally manifests itself as development progresses. The key point is to ensure that a flow models a cohesive application transaction.

■Tip It may be helpful to think of a flow as a method call, just one that can span many requests into the server. Following this analogy, top-level flows would be public, while inline flows would be private.

Managing FlowExecutions

In this section we will look in detail at the life cycle of a FlowExecution from start to end and learn how that life cycle is managed. Before discussing how a FlowExecution is created, it is worth reviewing how Spring Web Flow is integrated into the various web frameworks.

Integration with Web Frameworks

Chapter 11 introduced the definition of a flow and discussed briefly how FlowExecutions are managed. In this section we will delve into the FlowExecutionManager, the central façade for driving the execution of flows, and examine what happens behind the scenes.

Essentially, the FlowExecutionManager is the primary façade through which other systems like Spring MVC communicate with Spring Web Flow. If Spring Web Flow is a proverbial black box, then FlowExecutionManager is the lid.

This "handover" to Spring Web Flow is accomplished by calling either the FlowExecutionManager.launch() or FlowExecutionManager.signalEvent() method, which instructs Spring Web Flow to initiate processing of an external user event. The launch operation instructs Web Flow to launch an entirely new flow execution (or user conversation), and the signalEvent operation instructs Web Flow to signal a user event against the current state of an existing flow execution. Both methods accept org.springframework.webflow. ExternalContext and return org.springframework.webflow.ViewSelection. Listing 12-11 shows the ExternalContext interface façade.

Listing 12-11. *Implementation of org.springframework.webflow.ExternalContext*

```
public interface ExternalContext {
    Map getRequestParameterMap();
    Map getRequestMap();
    SharedMap getSessionMap();
    SharedMap getApplicationMap();
    public interface SharedMap extends Map {
        public Object getMutex();
    }
}
```

The ExternalContext interface enables Spring Web Flow artifacts such as actions to access information about the calling environment in a standard, normalized fashion, without coupling those artifacts to a specific deployment environment. It is up to a system calling into Spring Web Flow to provide an appropriate ExternalContext implementation. This implementation may provide access to environment-specific constructs; for example, the servlet-specific ExternalContext (org.springframework.webflow.context.servlet.ServletExternalContext) provides access to the native HttpServletRequest and HttpServletResponse Servlet artifacts.

Table 12-2 provides a list of ExternalContext adapters provided by Spring Web Flow.

Table 12-2. *Provided Adapters for ExternalContext*

Adapter Class	Description
`org.springframework.webflow.context.` `portlet.PortletExternalContext`	Provides information about a request into Spring Web Flow from a JSR-168 Portlet environment.
`org.springframework.webflow.context.` `servlet.ServletExternalContext`	Provides information about a request into Spring Web Flow from within an HTTP Servlet environment. A StrutsExternalContext subclass exists for integration with the Struts framework.
`org.springframework.webflow.manager.` `jsf.JsfExternalContext`	Provides information about a request into Spring Web Flow from JavaServer Faces (JSF).

After processing an external event, the `FlowExecutionManager` returns a `ViewSelection`. A `ViewSelection` is a `ValueObject` (`http://java.sun.com/blueprints/corej2eepatterns/ Patterns/TransferObject.html`) that selects a view to be rendered after event processing and any model data to be rendered with it. Refer to Table 12-3.

Table 12-3. *Overview of org.springframework.webflow.ViewSelection*

Property	Description
`viewName`	Logical name of the `View`.
`model`	Map containing data that may be rendered by the view.
`redirect`	Boolean value indicating whether the view should trigger a redirect.

You may wonder why `ViewSelection` is a class but `ExternalContext` is an interface. `ExternalContext` is a contract for behavior, but a `ViewSelection` is a concrete object—a value object. Spring Web Flow does not make assumptions about the environment it is executing within, so it cannot determine which *implementation* of `ExternalContext` to instantiate. It is up to the external system to instantiate an appropriate `ExternalContext` when calling into Spring Web Flow. Similarly, Spring Web Flow makes logical view selections when executing flows but does not care for response rendering. It is also the responsibility of the calling system to locate the appropriate view template to render using a returned `ViewSelection` as a pointer. This is why a `ViewSelection` and not `View` is returned.

The FlowExecutionManager

As mentioned in the previous section, the `FlowExecutionManager` is responsible for managing the creation and resuming of `FlowExecutions`. It defines two methods, as shown in Listing 12-12.

Listing 12-12. *org.springframework.webflow.manager.FlowExecutionManager*

```
public interface FlowExecutionManager {
    public ViewSelection launch (
                             String flowId,
                             ......
                          ) throws FlowException;
```

```
    public ViewSelection signalEvent(
                          String eventId,
                          String flowExecutionId,
                          ExternalContext context
                   ) throws FlowException;
}
```

Note You will notice that the `FlowExecutionManager` isn't responsible for ending a flow. It is the responsibility of the flow itself to determine when it has finished.

When a request is sent from a browser to launch a new flow execution or signal an event in an existing execution, that request is expected to provide the appropriate parameters. The initial request handler (or "Front Controller"), typically an adapter between a web framework like Spring MVC and Spring Web Flow, is then expected to extract those parameters and invoke this `FlowExecutionManager` façade. To launch a new flow execution, the _flowId parameter is required. To signal an event in an existing flow execution, the _flowExecutionId and _eventId parameters are required.

The default names by which these logical `FlowExecutionManager` request parameters are defined are sensible (_flowId, _flowExecutionId, and _eventId). If you wish to change them, however, you can configure the controller adapters such as the Spring MVC `FlowController` with a custom `org.springframework.webflow.manager.support.` `FlowExecutionManagerParameterExtractor`.

FlowExecutions

A single execution of a flow definition is a core concept within Spring Web Flow. This concept is realized by the `org.springframework.webflow.execution.FlowExecution` interface. A single flow definition may have any number of active `FlowExecutions` executing in parallel, where each `FlowExecution` represents a unique instance of that flow, for a given user at a point in time.

Tip It may help to think of a Flow as being analgous to a class, a definitional construct, whereas a `FlowExecution` is an instance of that class, an active construct.

You might assume a `FlowExecution` implementation is simply a glorified `Map` representing a snapshot of conversational state, but it is actually a much richer object. A `FlowExecution` encapsulates not only the state of an executing flow including the current state, the flow scope, and the stack of flow sessions, but also the behavior necessary to respond to external events. See Listing 12-13.

Listing 12-13. `org.springframework.webflow.execution.FlowExecution`

```
public interface FlowExecution extends FlowExecutionContext {
    ViewSelection start(ExternalContext externalContext)
                                throws StateException;

    ViewSelection signalEvent(String eventId, ExternalContext externalContext)
                                throws StateException;


    void rehydrate(
                    FlowLocator flowLocator,
                    FlowExecutionListenerLoader listenerLoader);
}
```

The interface that is extended (`org.springframework.webflow.FlowExecutionContext`, see Listing 12-14) provides contextual information about the executing flow.

Listing 12-14. `org.springframework.webflow.FlowExecutionContext`

```
public interface FlowExecutionContext extends FlowExecutionStatistics {
    Flow getRootFlow();
    Flow getActiveFlow() throws IllegalStateException;
    State getCurrentState() throws IllegalStateException;
    FlowSession getActiveSession() throws IllegalStateException;
}
```

You can see that `FlowExecutionContext` provides information about the root (or top level) flow definition, the active flow definition, the current state, and the `activeSession`.

It is important to understand that a `FlowExecution` lasts for the entire execution of the flow *including* the spawning of subflows. The root flow will always be the top-level flow for which the `FlowExecution` is created (in our example this would be `purchase-flow`). If the flow spawns a subflow (e.g., `shipping-flow`) the root flow remains the same, but `getActiveFlow()` now returns the subflow definition (`shipping-flow`).

FlowSessions

This distinction between the root flow and the active flow is modeled by `org.springframework.webflow.FlowSession`. A stack of `FlowSessions` are maintained by `FlowExecutionImpl`.

In the simple case of a flow without any subflow states, there will only ever be a single `FlowSession`. If a flow does contain a subflow state, then each time a subflow is spawned, the top (active) `FlowSession` is suspended, and a new `FlowSession` is created and pushed onto the stack (shown in Figure 12-2).

As you can see, there is a single `FlowExecution` representing the entire conversation, but each flow that is spawned (including the parent) receives its own `FlowSession`. Each instance of `FlowSession` has its own local data structure that is the basis for "flow scope." Figure 12-2 also shows some of the statuses that a `FlowSession` can have. Table 12-4 lists all of the possible statuses and their relevance or meaning (the statuses are defined in `org.springframework.webflow.FlowSessionStatus`).

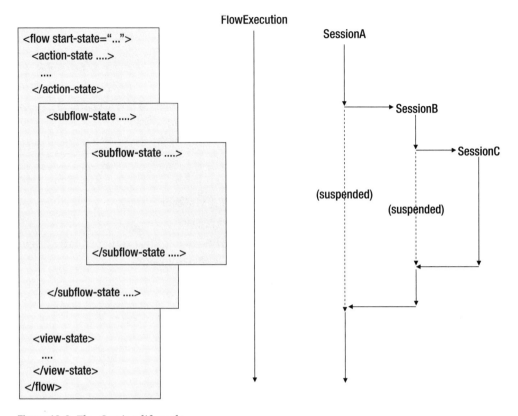

Figure 12-2. *FlowSession life cycle*

Table 12-4. *Status of the FlowSession*

Status	Meaning	Event
Created	The FlowSession has been created, but is not yet active.	Creation of a new FlowExecution.
Active	The FlowSession is currently executing.	When a flow is resumed.
Paused	The FlowSession is awaiting user input.	When the view is rendered.
Suspended	The FlowSession is still valid, but not active.	When a new subflow is created, the existing FlowSession is suspended.
Ended	The FlowSession is no longer active.	When the end state has been reached.

RequestContext

So far we have looked at FlowExecution which represents the execution of an entire top-level flow including any subflows that are spawned, and FlowSession which represents the execution of a single flow definition. There is one final *lifetime* that hasn't yet been covered, the lifetime of a request to *manipulate* a FlowExecution. This is modeled by org.springframework. webflow.RequestContext. You may recognize this as the parameter that is passed into the org.springframework.webflow.Action.execute() method. This object is the one that you will probably be most familiar with if you have implemented a custom Web Flow artifact such as an `Action` or a `FlowAttributeMapper`. It is a convenient façade that allows you to access information about the currently executing request and the environment in which it is executing. See Listing 12-5.

Listing 12-15. `org.springframework.webflow.RequestContext`

```
public interface RequestContext {
    ExternalContext getExternalContext();
    FlowExecutionContext getFlowExecutionContext();
    Scope getRequestScope();
    Scope getFlowScope();
    Map getProperties();
    Event getLastEvent();
    Transition getLastTransition();
    void setProperties(Map properties);
    Map getModel();
}
```

As you can see, you can access the `ExternalContext`, different levels of data scope, the state of the conversation, and so on. The key point is that the `RequestContext` represents context about the current request.

Table 12-5 summarizes the *key* artifacts that provide information about the execution of a flow.

Table 12-5. *Main Artifacts Used for the Execution of a Flow*

Artifact	Description
`org.springframework.webflow.ExternalContext`	Provides access to the external environment in which Spring Web Flow is executing.
`org.springframework.webflow.ViewSelection`	Defines a logical view selected for rendering.
`org.springframework.webflow.execution.FlowExecution`	Represents the entire execution of a top-level flow, including any spawned subflows.
`org.springframework.webflow.FlowSession`	Represents the execution of a single flow definition (not including subflows).
`org.springframework.webflow.RequestContext`	Represents the execution of a single request into Spring Web Flow triggered by the occurrence of an external event.

FlowExecutionListener

Spring Web Flow defines a rich event model that allows you to observe the life cycle of an executing flow. You can write your own observer by implementing the `org.springframework.webflow.execution.FlowExecutionListener` interface. See Listing 12-16.

Listing 12-16. `org.springframework.webflow.execution.FlowExecutionListener`

```
public interface FlowExecutionListener {
    void requestSubmitted(RequestContext context);
    void requestProcessed(RequestContext context);
    void sessionStarting(RequestContext context, State startState, Map input)
                            throws EnterStateVetoException;
    void sessionStarted(RequestContext context);
    void eventSignaled(RequestContext context, State state);
    void stateEntering(RequestContext context, State nextState)
                            throws EnterStateVetoException;
    void stateEntered(RequestContext context, State previousState, State state);
    void resumed(RequestContext context);
    void paused(RequestContext context, ViewSelection selectedView);
    void sessionEnding(RequestContext context);
    void sessionEnded(RequestContext context, FlowSession endedSession);
}
```

Implementing a `FlowExecutionListener` allows you to weave in behavior in an interceptor-like way. For example, you could provide a `SecurityFlowExecutionListener` implementation that throws an `EnterStateVetoException` preventing a state from entering if the user does not have the necessary permissions. You might develop listeners to apply custom auditing, breadcrumbs (navigation history), or transactional behavior and so on.

■**Tip** For convenience Spring Web Flow provides an empty `FlowExecutionListener` implementation, `org.springframework.webflow.execution.FlowExecutionListenerAdapter`.

Listeners are attached to a `FlowExecution` via an `org.springframework.webflow.execution.FlowExecutionListenerLoader`. The `FlowExecutionListenerLoader` infrastructure allows you to define which `FlowExecutionListeners` apply to which flow definitions. Spring Web Flow provides an `org.springframework.webflow.manager.ConditionalFlowExecutionListenerLoader` implementation for convenience, which is registered with the `FlowExecutionManager` implementation.

Listing 12-17 shows how to amend the `flowExecutionManager` declaration to attach a collection of listeners to executions of all flow definitions.

Listing 12-17. *XML Fragment to Register a Number of* `FlowExecutionListeners`

```
<bean id="flowExecutionManager"➥
class="org.springframework.webflow.manager.FlowExecutionManagerImpl">
  <constructor-arg ref="flowRegistry"/>
  <property name="listenerLoader">
    <bean
class="org.springframework.webflow.manager.ConditionalFlowExecutionListenerLoader">
      <property name="listeners">
```

```
        <list>
            <bean class="purchase.webflow.PurchaseItemFlowExecutionListener"/>
            <bean class="purchase.webflow.AnotherPurchaseItemFlowExecutionListener"/>
        </list>
      </property>
    </bean>
  </property>
</bean>
```

FlowExecution Repositories

When an active FlowExecution needs to be persisted (saved before a page is displayed) or loaded (resumed after a page is submitted), it is moved to and from a repository. This is taken care of within Spring Web Flow by implementations of org.springframework.webflow. execution.repository.FlowExecutionRepository (see Listing 12-18).

Listing 12-18. org.springframework.execution.repository.FlowExecutionRepository

```
public interface FlowExecutionRepository {
    public FlowExecutionContinuationKey generateContinuationKey(
                                    FlowExecution flowExecution
                                    ) throws FlowExecutionRepositoryException;

    public FlowExecutionContinuationKey generateContinuationKey(
                                    FlowExecution flowExecution,
                                    Serializable conversationId
                                    ) throws FlowExecutionRepositoryException;

    public FlowExecution getFlowExecution(
                                    FlowExecutionContinuationKey key
                                    ) throws FlowExecutionRepositoryException;

    public void putFlowExecution(
                                    FlowExecutionContinuationKey key,
                                    FlowExecution flowExecution
                                    ) throws FlowExecutionRepositoryException;

    public void invalidateConversation(
                                    Serializable conversationId
                                    ) throws FlowExecutionRepositoryException;
}
```

When saved in a repository, a FlowExecution object is indexed under a unique key, called a *continuation key*. This continuation key provides enough information to track a single *logical* user conversation that is still ongoing, as well as an index into a snapshot of the conversation taken at a point in time (relative to the user) that can be restored. This deserves more explanation, so let's look at the concept of continuations in detail.

Continuations

Continuations (http://www-128.ibm.com/developerworks/java/library/j-contin.html, http://en.wikipedia.org/wiki/Continuation) allow you to capture the entire state of a system at a point in time and isolate that state in a form that can be resumed at a later point. They effectively allow you to go back in time and restore a system as it was at that time, "continuing" from there.

Tip Remember, Spring Web Flow already has an object that represents the execution of a flow at a specific point in time, the FlowExecution.

The Problem of Back Buttons and New Browser Windows

You'll see that a continuation-based approach is a powerful concept that, when applied to the domain of web applications, helps solve many problems that plague web developers, including the well-known Back button problem.

Recall in Spring Web Flow that the state of a user conversation at a point in time is held by a FlowExecution object, which is stored in a repository between requests. The source of a repository is configurable, and Spring Web Flow provides both server-side and client-side solutions. If the repository is stored server-side in the user's session and there is only a *single* copy of a FlowExecution per user conversation, the following issues start to arise:

- What if during the conversation the user goes back in his local history without telling the server? The browser is now "out of sync" with the state of the FlowExecution on the server. This could result in signaling an event in the wrong state or even the wrong flow (when using subflows).

- What if the user launches a new window? Both windows will reference the same FlowExecution. Doing work in either window will cause problems, as the other window will then be out of sync with the server.

Clearly, a trivial form of FlowExecution storage is not good enough when browser navigational button support is a requirement. Continuations provide a good solution to this problem.

With a continuation-based approach, instead of storing a single copy of a FlowExecution for a logical conversation, you store multiple copies, where each copy represents the state of the conversation at a point in time that is restorable. Given this, consider the case of going back within local browser history. When you click Back, you go back to a page that references a specific FlowExecutionContinuation, which represents a restorable snapshot of the conversation at that time. When you click a submit button, the FlowExecution is restored at that point and continued from there. It is always restored in the correct state, so the client always remains in sync with the server.

Like anything, however, there are trade-offs. And continuations are no exception. Specifically:

- Creating copies of a `FlowExecution` to support restoration increases memory requirements. There is also some CPU overhead, as copies are created (based on serialization by default, which also requires objects in flow scope to be serializable).

- A copy is a snapshot of the `FlowExecution` at a point in time. If you go back to a previous snapshot, you lose data collected by later snapshots. This "undo" behavior may not be what users expect.

- Sometimes you don't want to allow back under any circumstances. For example, consider a step in a flow that inserts a token in a database table. You want to make sure that step executes once, and only once in the logical conversation. If a continuation is created for every view state, nothing is stopping the user from going back in history and reexecuting that step.

These trade-offs are manageable, but it is important to note that implementing a robust continuation server is not a trivial undertaking.

To address memory concerns, continuations can be expired after a configurable idle period, and the maximum number of continuations allowed per conversation can be capped.

As for the second "undo" issue, this in large part requires exercising caution on the part of the web developer. Data placed in flow scope is really associated with a continuation. So if you go back and reference a continuation created at a previous point in time before the data was created, the data will no longer be there when you continue from that point. Likewise, if the data was created during the execution of a subflow, going back to a previous continuation may restore to a point before the subflow was even launched!

To deal with this, Spring Web Flow provides access to more globally scoped data structures like conversational and session scope, which are shared by all continuations associated with a logical conversation. Data placed in these scopes remains there even if you go back and restore a previous continuation. It is very important to understand the semantic differences here.

To the third point, continuations can be explicitly invalidated. For example, assume after view state number three of a ten-view-state flow, all previous `FlowExecutionContinuations` should be invalidated, preventing use of the Back button for those steps from that point on. This can be metadata driven, for example by marking a view state as "nonrepeatable." In addition, all continuations associated with a logical conversation can be automatically invalidated after it is determined the conversation "ends" (by one of the continuations reaching an end state).

■**Note** The memory expense of using a continuations-based implementation depends somewhat upon where the continuations are stored. If they are stored on the client (as you will see), there is actually no server-side state at all.

FlowExecutionRepository Implementations

As discussed, Spring Web Flow represents an execution of a flow in the `FlowExecution` object, and a `FlowExecution` is loaded and saved from a repository while a logical conversation remains active between requests. In a continuation-based repository, each conversation "snapshot" is captured by an `org.springframework.webflow.execution.repository.continuation.FlowExecutionContinuation` which represents a `FlowExecution` at a single point in time.

An `org.springframework.webflow.execution.repository.continuation.FlowExecutionContinuation` is identified by a unique `org.springframework.webflow.execution.repository.FlowExecutionContinuationKey`, which consists of two logical parts, defined in Table 12-6.

Table 12-6. *The Parts of a FlowExecutionContinuationKey*

Name	Description
ConversationId	A unique id that identifies a logical conversation or dialog between a user and the server. This id remains the same for the duration of the logical conversation.
ContinuationId	A "pointer" to a single instance of a FlowExecutionContinuation associated with a logical conversation.

Recall that in Chapter 11 the unique key submitted by the view back to the server to participate in an ongoing conversation was called the `_flowExecutionId` by default. This is a `String`-encoded representation of the previously mentioned `FlowExecutionContinuationKey` and consists of two delimited parts. The first part identifies the active, logical conversation (in a repository), and the second part identifies the continuation (or restorable snapshot) to restore. The `_flowExecutionId` that is submitted by a view is parsed into a `FlowExecutionContinuationKey` object, which is then used to load the correct `FlowExecution` from the repository.

Spring Web Flow provides a number of stateful implementations of `FlowExecutionRepository` and a single, stateless, client-side implementation, as described in the following sections.

Stateful FlowExecution Repositories

Stateful repositories manage their own state and are typically stored in server-side data structures such as the HTTP session. Two implementations exist: `org.springframework.webflow.execution.repository.continuation.ContinuationFlowExecutionRepository` and `org.springframework.webflow.execution.repository.SimpleFlowExecutionRepository`.

ContinuationFlowExecutionRepository

This implementation provides a stateful server-side solution that supports browser navigational button use.

It stores snapshots of FlowExecutions that represent a stateful user conversation in an in-memory map. Each map entry key is a conversationId, uniquely identifying a single ongoing conversation between a client and the Spring Web Flow system. Each map entry value is an org.springframework.webflow.execution.repository.continuation.Conversation object, providing the details about one ongoing logical conversation. Each Conversation object maintains a stack of org.springframework.webflow.execution.repository.continuation. FlowExecutionContinuations, each continuation representing a restorable state of a conversation at a point in time. These continuations allow users to go back in their browser successfully to continue a conversation from a previous point.

SimpleFlowExecutionRepository

This is a trivial implementation that stores single instances of FlowExecutions in an in-memory map with a much simpler structure than the ContinuationFlowExecutionRepository. It requires minimal resource requirements, designed to be used when supporting browser navigation button use is not necessary (as is the case for many intranet applications that lock down the browser).

In this repository, each map entry key is a conversationId and each map entry value is a FlowExecutionEntry object. The FlowExecutionEntry (which is internal to SimpleFlowExecutionRepository) consists of the FlowExecution and a unique continuationId that acts as a token required for accessing the conversation. Because the continuationId is changed after every transition, Back button use and duplicate form submission are not supported and will result in a NoSuchConversationContinuationException being thrown consistently each time.

Note This is the default implementation used by RepositoryFlowExecutionStorage.

Stateless FlowExecution Repositories

Stateless repositories do not maintain any internal state, but instead rely on conversational state to be stored externally—for example, in the database or in a serialized structure sent from the client. Currently there exists one stateless implementation, org.springframework. webflow.execution.repository.continuation.ClientContinuationFlowExecutionRepository.

ClientContinuationFlowExecutionRepository

This repository implementation encodes the state of the FlowExecutionContinuation into the continuationId, which is written out to the browser in the _flowExecutionId parameter. On a subsequent request, that encoded FlowExecutionContinuation is deserialized and resumed. This implementation requires no server-side state whatsoever, but still reaps all the benefits of continuations, including proper browser navigational behavior.

There are trade-offs to consider when evaluating this strategy:

- If the `flowExecution` is large then it becomes more expensive to send to the client and back on every request. You may be limited to POSTs only.

- There is a security risk when storing all the information on the client. This risk is mitigated by encrypting the `_flowExecutionId`, but not entirely, and therefore needs to be considered.

- There is no way to track conversation invalidation after completion (for example, when a continuation reaches an end state). It is possible to "go back" after completing a flow and resubmit, completing a single logical application transaction more than once. Supporting conversation completion detection properly likely involves combining a client-based continuation strategy with some form of centralized storage, like a database-backed conversation table.

■Note Although the `_flowExecutionId` encryption can be customized, the default implementation is still open to attack. The default encoding algorithm is done by the Commons Codec package (`http://jakarta.apache.org/commons/codec`), with optional support for GZIP compression.

Conversation Invalidation After Completion

All but one of the `FlowExecutionRepository` implementations provide support for "conversation invalidation after completion." This ensures that after a logical conversation ends, it is not allowed to continue. In other words, once a flow execution has ended, you cannot resume it; you can only start a new, independent `FlowExecution`. This prevents the possibility of a duplicate submission.

This is accomplished by explicitly managing the duration of a logical conversation between a client and the server with the aforementioned `conversationId`. Once a `FlowExecution` associated with a conversation reaches an end state, the entire conversation will be invalidated. Any subsequent requests to continue that conversation will result in a `NoSuchConversationException` being thrown consistently each time.

■Note The exception to this is `ClientContinuationFlowExecutionRepository`, which does not yet provide support for conversation invalidation at the time of writing. This will likely be added in a future release of Spring Web Flow.

States and Transitions Revisited

In Chapter 11 we took a brief look at the various constructs within Spring Web Flow, such as the flow, states, and transition elements, and this section will explore them again in more detail. Table 12-7 recalls the different types of states.

Table 12-7. *Different States*

Name	Description
Action state	Executes your application code, typically delegating to a business service in the middle tier.
View state	Renders a view allowing the user to participate in the flow by entering data, viewing a message or making a decision.
Subflow state	Spawns another flow as a subflow. The parent flow is suspended until the subflow reaches an end state, at which point the subflow will end and the parent flow will resume.
Decision state	Evaluates a condition to drive a transition to a new state.
End state	Terminates a flow.

Action States

Action states are the primary way to execute your business logic within Spring Web Flow. They are comprised of `action` beans and transitions, but may also specify `action` beans to be executed whenever the state is entered or exited.

Chain of Responsibility

A common requirement is to chain a number of logical actions together, and this is easily achieved within Spring Web Flow. There are essentially two strategies:

- Create distinct action states for each of the logical steps in the chain, transitioning from state to state. This provides the most flexibility.

- Invoke multiple actions within a single action state by using named actions. This does not provide as much flexibility, but it is more concise.

Let's look at the first case in Listing 12-19, which shows two actions invoked in a chain using two distinct action states.

Listing 12-19. *Chaining Action States*

```
<action-state id="exposeFormObject">
    <action bean="formAction" method="exposeFormObject"/>
    <transition on="success" to="setupReferenceData"/>
</action-state>

<action-state id="setupReferenceData">
    <action bean="formAction" method="setupReferenceData"/>
    <transition on="success" to="setupDateChooser"/>
</action-state>

<action-state id="setupDateChooser">
    <action bean="formAction" method="setupDateChooser"/>
    <transition on="success" to="nextState"/>
</action-state>
```

Now let's look at an alternative, using named actions within one action state, as shown in Listing 12-20.

Listing 12-20. *Using Named Actions to Invoke Multiple Actions As Part of a Chain*

```
<action-state id="setupForm">
  <action name="exposeFormObject" bean=formAction" method="exposeFormObject"/>
  <action name="setupReferenceData" bean="formAction" method="setupReferenceData"/>
  <action name="setupDateChooser" bean="formAction" name=""setupDateChooser"/>
  <transition on="setupDateChooser.success" to="nextState"/>
</action-state>
```

The name attribute provides a namespace for the action event id, allowing you to distinguish the same event id from different actions. You may choose to transition on an event returned by any of the actions, but you are not required to provide a transition for each event. Essentially Spring Web Flow will execute all actions until a matching transition is found. If there is no transition that matches the result of the last action, a NoSuchTransitionException will be thrown.

FormAction

Form processing is a common requirement for many web applications, and Spring Web Flow provides the org.springframework.webflow.action.FormAction implementation to handle this. FormAction provides the following convenience methods, as listed in Table 12-8.

Table 12-8. *FormAction Methods*

Method	Purpose	Life Cycle
exposeFormObject()	Instantiate and expose the form object in the configured scope.	Before the form is displayed.
bind()	Update the form from the supplied properties.	After the form has been submitted.
validate()	Perform validation of the populated form.	After the form has been submitted and bound.

The SimpleFormController in Spring MVC may appear to be similar, but the appearance is deceiving. SimpleFormController implements a predefined work flow to manage a single-page form flow, and it allows you to customize that work flow by overriding template methods. FormAction does *not* implement such a predefined work flow; rather, it implements and exposes methods that *you* are responsible for calling.

This separation of command and controller logic is generally a good thing. One of the limitations of a template-based approach is that you are restricted to the work flow exposed by the superclass. If your work flow differs considerably from the template, things start to get complex. This is not an issue with Spring Web Flow, as you are in full control over the flow and when certain actions are executed.

For convenience, FormAction does provide some coarse-grained methods that implement the same functionality as methods in SimpleFormController, and we list these in Table 12-9.

Table 12-9. *FormAction Coarse-Grained Methods*

Method	Purpose	Life Cycle
setupForm()	Calls exposeFormObject, but also performs data binding (if bindOnSetupForm is true).	Before the form is displayed.
bindAndValidate()	Performs binding and validation of the form object.	After the form has been submitted.

As mentioned in Chapter 11, you would typically require these methods to be executed before and after a form view is displayed. Listing 12-21 shows how to do this.

Listing 12-21. *Spring Web Flow Fragment Showing Entry and Exit Actions on a View*

```
<view-state id="enterPurchaseInformation" view="purchaseForm">
  <entry-actions>
    <action bean="formAction" method="setupForm"/>
  </entry-actions>
  <transition on="submit" to="enterShippingInformation">
    <action bean="formAction" method="bindAndValidate"/>
  </transition>
  <transition on="cancel" to="cancel"/>
</view-state>
```

As in Listing 12-19, you could break up each of the steps into distinct states. This is a little more verbose, but more clearly demarcates the different steps. It also provides greater flexibility, allowing you to reenter a state definition from a different point within the flow. Listing 12-22 shows this approach.

Listing 12-22. *Spring Web Flow Fragment Showing Form Management in Explicit States*

```
<action-state id="setupForm">
    <action bean="formAction" method="setupForm"/>
    <transition on="success" to="enterPurchaseInformation"/>
</action-state>

<view-state id="enterPurchaseInformation" view="purchaseForm">
    <transition on="submit" to="processPurchasePostback">
    <transition on="cancel" to="cancel"/>
</view-state>

<action-state id="processPurchasePostback">
    <action bean="formAction" method="bindAndValidate"/>
    <transition on="success" to="enterShippingInformation"/>
</action-state>
```

POJO Actions

Chapter 11 defined the `Action` as the central construct for executing your application code from within a flow definition. It also stated that every `action` bean had to implement the `org.springframework.webflow.Action` interface. And this is true. Every Spring Web Flow action bean does need to implement the `Action` interface, but Spring Web Flow will do a bit of magic for you so you aren't forced into writing custom action glue code just to invoke methods on your business services.

When you reference a bean that doesn't implement the `Action` interface (a plain old Java object (POJO), `http://en.wikipedia.org/wiki/Plain_Old_Java_Object`), Spring Web Flow will create a new instance of `org.springframework.webflow.action.LocalBeanInvokingAction` to automatically adapt a method on your class to the `Action` interface. The purpose of `LocalBeanInvokingAction` is to be an *adapter* (`http://en.wikipedia.org/wiki/Adapter_pattern`) between the Spring Web Flow `Action` interface and a method on your class. Let's look again at the XML fragment that declares the POJO bean that will be used as an action:

Listing 12-23. *The placeOrder Action*

```
<action-state id="placeOrder">
    <action bean="orderClerk" method="placeOrder(${flowScope.purchase})"/>
    <transition on="success" to="showCostConfirmation"/>
</action-state>
```

When Spring Web Flow encounters this fragment, it will construct an instance of `LocalBeanInvokingAction` and pass it a reference to your bean (`orderClerk`), and the signature of the method you want invoked (`placeOrder(${flowScope.purchase})`. When Spring Web Flow executes the `action` bean (by calling `LocalBeanInvokingAction.doExecute()`), the method you specified will be invoked on the bean you provided.

■**Note** Spring Web Flow delegates the actual execution of your method to an instance of `org.spring framework.binding.method.MethodInvoker`, part of the Spring Framework method binding infrastructure.

In the XML fragment Spring Web Flow was instructed to pass in the value of the expression `${flowScope.purchase}` (i.e., the object stored under the name `purchase` in flow scope) to the `placeOrder` method.

The result of `MethodInvoker.invoke()` is a `java.lang.Object`. If your method signature was void, this will be `null`; if your method returned a primitive it will be automatically converted to the `java.lang.Object` equivalent (`boolean` to `java.lang.Boolean` and the like).

Exposing POJO Method Return Values

If you wish to have the return value of an invoked method exposed in either flow scope or request scope, you must set the property `resultName` to the name under which you want it stored and the `resultScope` property to either `flow` or `request` (the default is `request`). If you do not explicitly set the `resultName` property, the return value will not be stored in any scope. Refer to Listing 12-24.

Listing 12-24. *placeOrder Definition Exposing an orderConfirmation Return Value in Request Scope*

```
<action-state id="placeOrder">
  <action bean="orderClerk" method="placeOrder(${flowScope.purchase})"➥
resultName="orderConfirmation"/>
  <transition on="success" to="showCostConfirmation"/>
</action-state>
```

The preceding action-state definition reads: "When the `placeOrder` state is entered, invoke the `placeOrder` method.on the `orderClerk` bean, passing in the `purchase` object from flow scope as input. Expose the method return value in request scope under the name `orderConfirmation`. On success, transition to the `showCostConfirmation` state."

Customizing View Selection with View States and End States

Recall from Chapter 11 that view states instruct Spring Web Flow to pause the execution of a flow and render a view allowing the user to participate in the flow.

Spring Web Flow creates logical view selections (consisting of a view name and a set of model data), but the resolution of those view selections to a renderable `View` is the responsibility of the calling web framework. That said, Spring Web Flow allows you full control over view selection logic via the `org.springframework.webflow.ViewSelector` interface.

Listing 12-25. *org.springframework.webflow.ViewSelector*

```
public interface ViewSelector {
    ViewSelection makeSelection(RequestContext context);
}
```

This interface allows you to customize how the view name is calculated and/or what model data is available to the view.

The `ViewSelection` returned by the `ViewSelector` is then converted into a renderable artifact by the calling web framework (e.g., a Struts `ActionForward` or a Spring MVC `ModelAndView`). This conversion is performed by the appropriate Front Controller (`FlowAction` for Struts or `FlowController` for Spring MVC). Figure 12-3 illustrates this conversion.

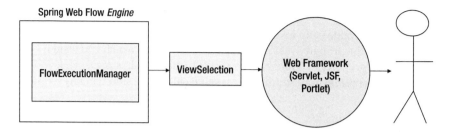

Figure 12-3. *Conversion of a ViewSelection to a View*

There are two implementations of `ViewSelector` provided out of the box, shown in Table 12-10.

Table 12-10. *ViewSelector Implementations*

Name	Behavior	Model Exposed
`org.springframework.webflow.support.RedirectViewSelector`	Represents a redirect view.	Only exposes parameters explicitly specified in the redirect Expression (e.g., `redirect:/url.htm?param0=${flowScope.foo}&param1=value1`).
`org.springframework.webflow.support.SimpleViewSelector`	Refers to a static view name.	Exposes all data in both flow and request scope data in the model.

The `FlowBuilder` decides which `ViewSelector` to use based upon the value of the `view` property. Table 12-11 describes the criteria Spring Web Flow uses to choose a `ViewSelector`.

Table 12-11. *ViewSelector Selection*

ViewSelector	Criteria
`RedirectViewSelector`	If the `viewName` contains a `redirect:` prefix.
`YourViewSelector`	If the `viewName` is `bean:YourViewSelector`.
`SimpleViewSelector`	If none of the other two conditions are met.

Indicating Transitions

When Spring Web Flow encounters a view state it will

1. render the view;

2. pause the `flowExecution`;

3. wait for a user-supplied `eventId` to resume.

The view can submit the eventId in one of two ways. The first way is to submit a request parameter whose name is FlowExecutionManagerParameterExtractor.getEventIdParameterName() (the default is _eventId) and whose *value* will be the actual user eventId (like submit).

Note For the sake of brevity and readability, FlowExecutionManagerParameterExtractor may be referred to as FEMPE.

Alternatively, the second way is to have the view submit a parameter whose name has the format FEMPE.getEventIdParameterName()FEMPE.getParameterDelimiter()*value* (the default value for FEMPE.getParameterDelimiter() is "_"). This form is primarily used with the name of an HTML input button to support multiple buttons per form without JavaScript. In this case, the eventId is derived fully from the parameter name, and the value of this parameter is ignored.

To illustrate these two approaches, to signal the submit event you may provide either of the following request parameters: _eventId=submit or _eventId_submit=ignored.

Note FlowExecutionManagerParameterExtractor will also support image buttons that submit parameters of type eventId.*x* or eventId.*y*.

Decision States

Although the example decision state in Chapter 11 defined a simple, single if/else expression, decision states can do more. As well as supporting multiple if conditions, the decision state can also delegate the criteria for the decision to Java application code.

If multiple if conditions are supplied, they are evaluated one by one. If none of the conditions evaluates to true, then a NoMatchingTransitionException is thrown. You can implement a chain of if conditions, but realize that any if condition that defines an else clause will *by definition* evaluate to true, and none of the remaining if conditions will be evaluated. For example, the fragment in Listing 12-26 will never evaluate the second condition.

Listing 12-26. *Badly Defined Decision State*

```
<decision-state>
  <if test="${flowScope.object.booleanProperty}" then="stateA" else="stateB"/>
  <if test="${this.will.never.be.called}" then="neverGetCalled"/>
</decision-state>
```

Listing 12-27 shows a chain of conditions that behaves as you would expect.

Listing 12-27. *Correctly Defined Decision State*

```
<decision-state>
  <if test="${flowScope.object.booleanProperty}" then="stateA" />
  <if test="${this is called if the above test evaluates to false}" then="stateB"/>
  <if test="${this is called if the above test evaluates to false}" then="stateC"➥
else ="stateD"/>
</decision-state>
```

■**Caution** It is generally wise to put an `else` branch on the last `if`; otherwise, you run the risk of Spring Web Flow not being able to find a matching transition.

Finally, a decision state can be used to invoke a single action that is used as the basis for the decision. In this case, the action's result event becomes the primary basis for the transition decision.

When combined with a POJO `action`, this allows you to call a method in application code that returns a single value that can be used as the basis for a routing decision. The decision state will automatically adapt the method return value to an appropriate action result event identifier according to a set of rules.

The rules are simple: for example, one rule is if a method return value is a `java.lang.Boolean` a yes or no result event will be returned. Table 12-12 details the exact behavior for adapting method return values of different types.

Table 12-12. *Behavior of POJO Return Values*

Return Value	Event Identifier
null	null
true	yes
false	no
Enum	The `String` representation of the `Enum`

This allows you to implement branching logic very conveniently. Assuming our backing object (`purchase`) has a method `boolean isTaxable(TaxationRule rule)`, in our web flow definition we can write the code shown in Listing 12-28.

Listing 12-28. *Listing of a POJO to Be Used As an Action*

```
<decision-state id="determineTaxable">
  <action bean="orderClerk" method="isTaxable(${flowScope.taxationRule})"/>
  <transition on="yes" to="enterTaxDetails"/>
  <transition on="no" to="lucky"/>
</action-state>
```

Exception Handling

Exceptions within Spring Web Flow are managed the same way that exceptions are handled within the rest of the Spring Framework. Exceptions from which you cannot recover are treated as unchecked exceptions.

Spring MVC provides org.springframework.web.servlet.HandlerExceptionResolver to handle exceptions, but they are common for the entire web application. Given that web flows are self-contained units of work, it would be inappropriate to allow web flow-specific exceptions to leak out of the web flow if the flow knows how to handle them.

Spring Web Flow defines a single interface, org.springframework.webflow. StateExceptionHandler (Listing 12-29) for handling exceptions thrown by the execution of a state.

Listing 12-29. *org.springframework.webflow.StateExceptionHandler*

```
public interface StateExceptionHandler {
    boolean handles(StateException exception);

    ViewSelection handle(
                            StateException exception,
                            FlowExecutionControlContext context);
}
```

■**Note** The exception handling within Spring Web Flow is for exceptions thrown by states within flows.

To register your own ExceptionHandler, simply define it within your web flow definition <exception-handler bean="myCustomHandler"/>.

Upon encountering an exception thrown by a state, Spring Web Flow will traverse all registered implementations of org.springframework.webflow.StateExceptionHandler, and if one can handle the exception, it will hand it off for processing.

■**Caution** This means that the order in which ExceptionHandlers are defined is important, Spring Web Flow will stop as soon as it finds a StateExceptionHandler that can handle the specified exception.

Table 12-13 lists the common exceptions that might be thrown by Spring Web Flow during normal runtime execution.

Table 12-13. *Spring Web Flow State Exceptions*

Class	Description	Thrown By
org.springframework. webflow.StateException	Common base class for all state exceptions.	This is a convenience class and is not thrown.
org.springframework.webflow. ActionExecutionException	Indicates an exception (checked or runtime) was thrown by an action. The exception may be from the action itself, or it may be an exception thrown by the target of the action (e.g., your business method).	ActionExecutor.execute
org.springframework.webflow. execution.EnterStateVetoException	Indicates that the requested state cannot be entered because of a constraint violation.	FlowExecutionListener. sessionStarting and FlowExecutionListener. stateEntering.
org.springframework.webflow. NoMatchingTransitionException	Thrown if there are no matching transitions that match the signaled event in the current state.	TransitionableState. getRequiredTransition.
org.springframework.webflow. execution.repository. NoSuchConversationException	Thrown if a request to resume an execution of a flow references a conversation that is invalid (i.e., a nonexistent conversation or an expired conversation).	FlowExecutionRepository implementations when loading a conversation.
org.springframework.webflow. execution.repository. InvalidConversationContinuationException	Thrown if a request to resume an execution of a flow references an invalid continuation (e.g., a nonexistent continuation or a continuation that has expired).	FlowExecutionRepository implementations when loading a continuation.

The default behavior is for Spring Web Flow to allow unhandled exceptions to trickle out of the flow and up the call stack, eventually to be handled by the calling web framework or ultimately the application container.

Spring Web Flow provides a default implementation of StateExceptionHandler: org. springframework.webflow.support.TransitionExecutingStateExceptionHandler, which allows you to catch an occurrence of a type of Exception and execute a transition to a error state. So for example, if you decided that you wanted to display a specific error page for DuplicatePurchaseException exceptions, you would modify your web flow definition to include <exception-handler class="purchase.domain.DuplicatePurchaseException" state="error"/>.

Whenever purchase.domain.DuplicatePurchaseException is thrown, this definition fragment instructs the flow to transition to the specified target state (error), which in this case would result in an error view being displayed.

State Scoped ExceptionHandlers

You may decide that you want exception handling to be implemented at a finer-grained level than that of a flow. You can also define ExceptionHandlers at the state level against any state type (action, decision, and so on). To achieve this, simply move the exception-handler declaration to within the definition of the state. Listing 12-30 demonstrates how to scope the ExceptionHandler.

Listing 12-30. *Spring Web Flow Fragment Registering a State-Level ExceptionHandler*

```
<action-state id="placeOrder">
  <action bean="orderClerk" method="placeOrder(${flowScope.purchase})"/>
  <transition on="success" to="showCostConfirmation"/>
  <exception-handler bean="myCustomHandler"/>
</action-state>
```

Exception Handling Summary

Exception handling within Spring Web Flow is simple yet powerful. Any number of state ExceptionHandlers can be registered at both the flow and state level. The default ExceptionHandler implementation is sufficient for most scenarios, allowing you to catch an exception and execute a recovery transition as part of the flow definition. Providing your own implementation is also possible by implementing a custom state ExceptionHandler.

Summary

Spring Web Flow is a powerful framework for defining and executing reusable, self-contained controller modules within a web application. However, no tool can cater for every possible use case. We've shown you that Spring Web Flow provides a number of extension points and implementations of key strategies that allow for customization. We've also shown how Spring Web Flow drives the execution of your business logic without tying you to Web Flow APIs. Finally, we've demonstrated how Spring Web Flow employs the concept of a continuation to solve many issues facing web application developers.

Documenting Your MVC Application

As your applications grow larger and more complex, the XML files used to define your beans can become more difficult to maintain, especially in multidiscipline teams where different people maintain the context files for different parts of the application. Documenting your application is as important as documenting your source code, and with Spring applications, that means documenting your context files.

BeanDoc

BeanDoc (`http://opensource2.atlassian.com/confluence/spring/display/BDOC/Home`) is an official Spring subproject, and it can help by producing a similar kind of documentation for your Spring beans that Javadoc produces for your Java classes. Beans that are wired together are cross-linked, their class names can be linked to the relevant Javadoc pages, and many disparate XML files can be managed and viewed as a logical application context. Beans are documented with their descriptions and class names (linked to Javadoc locations) and linked to their dependencies (references, parent-beans, lookup-methods). Best of all, in association with the open-source tool Graphviz (`http://www.graphviz.org`) you can visualize your application contexts as graphs.

Although BeanDoc is still early release software (version 0.7.0 was current at the time of writing) it should be stable enough for everyday use. It is highly configurable and skinnable in terms of its output and designed for extensibility if the basic functionality doesn't meet your needs. BeanDoc can be operated from the command line, programmatically, or via its own Ant task. Figure A-1 shows a sample of BeanDoc's output (based on the Spring JPetStore sample application).

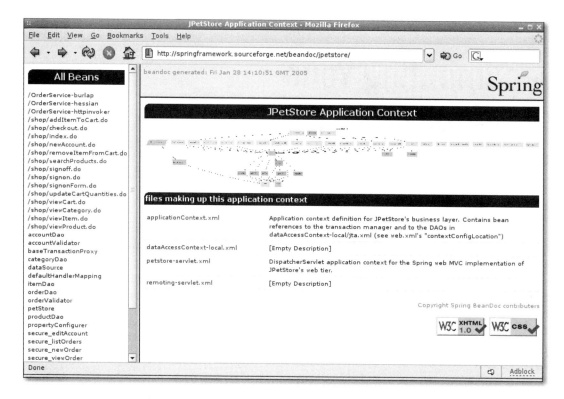

Figure A-1. *BeanDoc output of the JPetStore sample*

If your context consists of multiple XML files, as it usually will, BeanDoc will aggregate them into a consolidated graph (as shown in Figure A-1) and provide links to the documentation for each individual context file. The individual documentation pages have graphs of just the beans in that file. Clicking a graph will reveal it at full size, and each bean on the graph can be clicked to link to the documentation fragment for that bean.

Installing and Building BeanDoc

BeanDoc is a source-only download, so you'll have to compile and build it. For this, you will need Ant (which you will doubtless already have if you are a Java developer who has not been living on the moon for the last ten years) or Maven. From the main site for BeanDoc you can download the latest version and extract it to your hard drive. Alternatively, if you're comfortable with CVS, you can check out the sources from the main Spring repository at SourceForge under the module name `spring-beandoc`.

Having acquired a release version or CVS snapshot, the next task is to build the JAR file. BeanDoc is a small utility, so this doesn't take long. Using Ant, simply run the `dist` target from the root of the main `spring-beandoc` directory that you extracted the file to. If Maven is your thing, run `maven install:jar` from the project root instead.

If you want to enable the graphs you will additionally need to download and install a version of Graphviz suitable for your platform. Its website offers details, but this is a very straightforward procedure.

Running BeanDoc on Your Configuration Files

When you build BeanDoc, it places the `spring-beandoc.jar` file and all of its runtime dependencies in the `target/dist` directory under the project root. Whenever you use the tool, you must ensure that all of the runtime dependencies are available. Two of those are Spring JAR files, so if you already have a recent `spring.jar` file in your project, you probably don't need to duplicate them.

BeanDoc can be invoked from the command line, through Java code, or as an Ant task—which is supplied with BeanDoc and is in the `spring-beandoc.jar` file. Since using Ant is the most common way to interact with it, that's what we'll describe here. The Ant option is perfect for this type of task, since you need to set it up only once and can make the beandoc target a dependency of your main build target. That way, every time you build your code, the documentation and object graphs are up to date.

Listing A-1 shows a simple `build.xml` file defining the task and a target to run BeanDoc on your application.

Listing A-1. *build.xml File for BeanDoc*

```
<project name="spring-beandoc-sample" basedir="." default="beandoc">

  <!-- sets up BeanDoc classpath -->
  <path id="main-classpath">
    <fileset dir="${lib.dir}">
      <include name="**/*.jar"/>
    </fileset>
  </path>

  <target name="init">
    <taskdef name="beandoc"
      classname="org.springframework.beandoc.client.AntTask">
      <classpath refid="main-classpath"/>
    </taskdef>
    <mkdir dir="${output.dir}" />
  </target>

  <target name="beandoc" depends="init">
    <beandoc outputDir="${output.dir}">
      <fileset dir="${conf.dir}">
        <include name="*Context.xml"/>
        <include name="*-servlet.xml"/>
      </fileset>
    </beandoc>
  </target>

</project>
```

The Ant syntax should be familiar enough, so we'll concentrate on the key points. The classpath that is set up initially is there to ensure that BeanDoc has access to those JAR files we mentioned earlier. In this example, the runtime dependencies would all be located in ${lib.dir}. The BeanDoc task itself is declared in the init target (which the beandoc target depends on, so it's guaranteed to be ready for use). In the last section, we actually call the BeanDoc task.

To run successfully, BeanDoc only needs to know which files make up your application context and where you want to place the output. You can use one or more nested filesets to choose the input resources.

Other Options

With the setup described, BeanDoc will happily function and maintain a nicely formatted set of HTML documentation for your Spring project. But there are many ways in which you can customize the output should you so wish. Following is a brief overview of some of the more widely useful options. (For details of more advanced options, see the BeanDoc reference documentation linked from the main website.)

Most of BeanDoc's customizable attributes are managed through a properties file that you can locate anywhere. To tell the Ant task where to load them from, specify the beandocProps attribute on the task itself, as shown in Listing A-2.

Listing A-2. *Specifying beandoc Properties*

```
<beandoc outputDir="${output.dir}"
  beandocProps="/path/to/beandoc.properties">
  <fileset dir="${conf.dir}">
    <include name="*Context.xml"/>
    <include name="*-servlet.xml"/>
  </fileset>
</beandoc>
```

Tip The samples directory of the BeanDoc distribution contains a well-commented beandoc.properties file that will give you examples of most of the other properties you might be interested in.

Controlling the Output

Let's briefly look at the two most common options you want to set in the properties file to affect the documentation produced. First, if you've downloaded and installed Graphviz (and we highly recommend that you do), then you need to specify where the executable file is. Listing A-3 shows the relevant options. Modify your paths depending on where you chose to install to, of course.

Listing A-3. *Graphviz Executable Location*

```
# for Unix/Linux i.e.
compiler.dotExe=/usr/bin/dot

# OR for Windows..
compiler.dotExe=C:/Program Files/ATT/GraphViz/bin/dot.exe
```

The next important option is choosing JavaDoc locations. BeanDoc will by default link any classname attributes of your beans to their JavaDoc page for several well-known libraries. These include the standard Java API for your platform, Spring classes, and many others. You can override the locations for these (for example, if you have them installed locally) and add your own by setting one or more properties similar to those shown in Listing A-4.

Listing A-4. *Specifying JavaDoc Locations*

```
javadoc.locations[com.mycompany]=http://your.local.server/apidoc/
javadoc.locations[com.vendor]=http://www.vendor.com/javadoc/
```

The format of each line is the same: In brackets after the `javadoc.locations` part you place the prefix of the classnames that should link to the URL used as the property value. In the listing above, a classname of `com.mycompany.foo.Bar` will be linked to `http://your.local.server.com/apidoc/com/mycompany/foo/Bar.html`.

Summary

We've taken a brief look at BeanDoc and some of the basic options that you can take to customize the way it works. In fact, the tool has many more options for controlling graph layouts and colors that can be selected in `beandoc.properties`. It is quite extensible too, and you can switch out the XSLT stylesheets or add new components to it if you require something a bit out of the ordinary. BeanDoc's reference documentation contains all the information you need to delve beyond the basics.

■■■

Ajax and DWR

For a while, web application development has been a little stagnant. Developing for the browser has offered the option of creating simple HTML interfaces that work on any browser or operating system, or taking advantage of specific browser functionality to add more dynamic behavior at the cost of vendor lock-in or non-portability. The former type of application was more suited to an Internet audience and the latter more common in the intranet where organizations typically control the desktop software.

But things are changing for a variety of reasons. For one, browsers of all types now have more commonality in the standards that they implement than at any time in the past. Secondly, `XMLHttpRequest` was adopted as standard. Combined, they make cross-platform dynamic browser solutions a real possibility in the shape of *Ajax: Asynchronous JavaScript and XML*.

With Ajax, you retrieve from the server only the data that you actually need, and you don't have to load a whole page, much of which might be the same as was fetched before. That means we can post and retrieve data to and from the server *after* the page has loaded.

In the last 6 to 12 months, loads of toolkits, frameworks, utilities, and applications have sprung up, all based on Ajax. *DWR* (`http://www.getahead.ltd.uk/dwr`), which stands for *Direct Web Remoting*, is one such toolkit. It provides a bunch of commonly used functions that your web application will inevitably need anyway to be able to make use of Ajax, and therefore it saves you from a lot of typing. For all self-respecting coders, this is never a bad thing, of course.

Spring and DWR

What does this all have to do with Spring MVC, you might be wondering. Well, not a great deal directly, but this is such a popular technology right now that we thought it would be interesting to include a few pages on how you might enhance your Spring web applications through the use of DWR. It would even be possible, if you really wanted to try, to replace the majority of MVC functionality with Ajax/DWR, but we feel that a blend of the two offers the most promise.

DWR works, as the name suggests, by making server-side objects available to your client-side JavaScript functions. That means you have the ability to call methods on those objects from within your JavaScript functions and work with the results. DWR handles the conversion of the server-side objects by dynamically creating JavaScript objects that implement the same interface. When you call the methods on the JavaScript object, DWR proxies the call to the server and converts the returned object (if any).

Hopefully you're starting to see where this is leading now, and you've probably guessed correctly that DWR can expose the objects from your Spring ApplicationContext *directly* to the JavaScript functions in your web pages. In fact, DWR even has support for Spring built in—making this task even easier and one of the reasons we choose to highlight it.

A Practical Example

Enough of the history and theory; let's see some code! In order to demonstrate the concepts and a couple of the gotchas, we've taken one of the Spring sample applications (PetClinic, shipped with the Spring distribution) and enhanced it. We'll step through those changes that Ajax-enabled our application.

Tip If you'd like to hack along or prefer to just dive in, you can download a WAR file of the modified PetClinic application from the Spring wiki at http://opensource.atlassian.com/confluence/spring/x/Yws.

Configuration and Code Changes

First, we added dwr,jar from the DWR download to the WEB-INF/lib directory. We also created a new file called WEB-INF/dwr.xml. Listing B-1 shows the complete dwr.xml file.

Listing B-1. *WEB-INF/dwr.xml*

```
<?xml version="1.0" encoding="UTF-8"?>
<!DOCTYPE dwr PUBLIC
 "-//GetAhead Limited//DTD Direct Web Remoting 1.0//EN"
 "http://www.getahead.ltd.uk/dwr/dwr10.dtd">

<dwr>
  <allow>
    <create creator="spring" javascript="Clinic" scope="session">
      <param name="beanName" value="clinic"/>
    </create>
    <convert
      converter="bean"
      match="org.springframework.samples.petclinic.*"/>
    <convert
      converter="bean"
      match="org.springframework.samples.petclinic.jdbc.*"/>
  </allow>
</dwr>
```

The `dwr.xml` file is where we configure which objects are going to be exposed to the client-side scripts. In our example, we're exposing the main business object from PetClinic's service layer. DWR has several different types of creators. As you can see in the preceding listing, we're using a Spring creator. This type of creator knows how to obtain a bean by name from a `BeanFactory` or an `ApplicationContext`. Other types of creator that you might use are *scripted*—as with a Bean Scripting Framework–supported script language—and *new*, where the object is simply instantiated via reflection.

In the other half of the configuration file, you can see some `convert` elements too. Not only does the service object need to be understood by DWR, but any objects that its methods accept as parameters or objects that they return also have to be capable of conversion. For `Strings` and primitives, this is a simple 1:1 mapping to JavaScript equivalents, but for other objects this has to be specified in configuration. For the PetClinic demo, we simply allow all of the model beans and the concrete implementation of the service bean to be converted.

■**Note** It would be a security risk to automatically allow conversion of any object for JavaScript use, and that is the main reason you have to specifically allow conversion on a case-by-case basis in DWR.

DWR is servlet-based; it uses a servlet to dynamically generate much of the JavaScript code that the client will use. The servlet code is already in `dwr.jar`, so we just need a declaration and mapping in `web.xml`. Listing B-2 has the details.

Listing B-2. *Changes to WEB-INF/web.xml*

```
<servlet>
  <servlet-name>dwr-invoker</servlet-name>
    <display-name>DWR Servlet</display-name>
    <servlet-class>uk.ltd.getahead.dwr.DWRServlet</servlet-class>
    <init-param>
      <param-name>debug</param-name>
      <param-value>true</param-value>
    </init-param>
</servlet>

<servlet-mapping>
  <servlet-name>dwr-invoker</servlet-name>
  <url-pattern>/dwr/*</url-pattern>
</servlet-mapping>
```

We left the debug parameter, which enables a nifty test page to be called for each service object that you export. See Figure B-1 for an example.

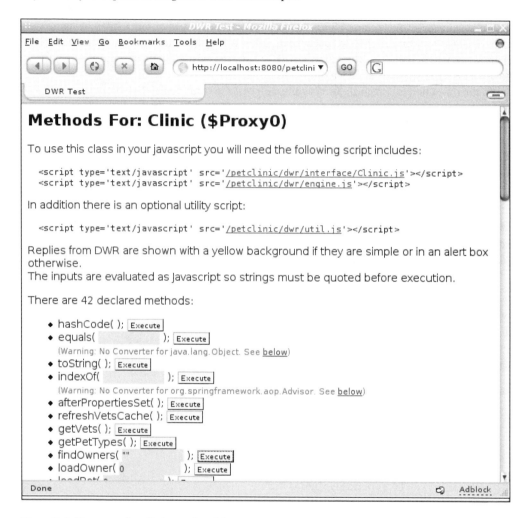

Figure B-1. *Test page for clinic service object*

The only other change to the server side of the operation was a method name that needed to be refactored. One of the DWR gotchas is that JavaScript is a little more picky about reserved names being used as methods than Java is. A common one is the method delete(), which would be illegal in JavaScript. In our case, we had to rename the isNew() method on the Entity class, as shown in Listing B-3.

Listing B-3. *The Refactored Entity Class*

```
package org.springframework.samples.petclinic;

public class Entity {

  private Integer id;

  public void setId(Integer id) {
    this.id = id;
  }

  public Integer getId() {
    return id;
  }

  public boolean isNewEntity() {
    return (this.id == null);
  }
}
```

Bean property names are converted to JavaScript properties by default, so isNew() would become just new() on the JavaScript object, which is a reserved name. Using an IDE such as Eclipse (with a little manual search and replace in the JSP files!), we were quickly able to manage all of the dependencies of such a change. That wraps it up for the configuration and code changes—all in all, a fairly simple exercise to set the application up for DWR.

Presentation File Changes

Now for the interesting bit: We added two files to the root of the PetClinic web application— index.html and local.js—which contain the application-specific functions to complement the DWR-provided ones. In the <head> section of the HTML file, we add references to all of the script libraries required, as shown in Listing B-4.

Listing B-4. *Script Library References*

```
<head>
  ...
  <script type='text/javascript' src='/petclinic/dwr/interface/Clinic.js'></script>
  <script type='text/javascript' src='/petclinic/dwr/engine.js'></script>
  <script type='text/javascript' src='/petclinic/dwr/util.js'></script>
  <script type='text/javascript' src='/petclinic/local.js'></script>
</head>
```

At the bottom is the file we code ourselves, which we'll look at shortly. The other three are supplied by DWR. engine.js and util.js are fairly static and contain the bulk of the DWR functionality. clinic.js is the interesting one: the JavaScript representation of the service object that we exported in our WEB-INF/dwr.xml file.

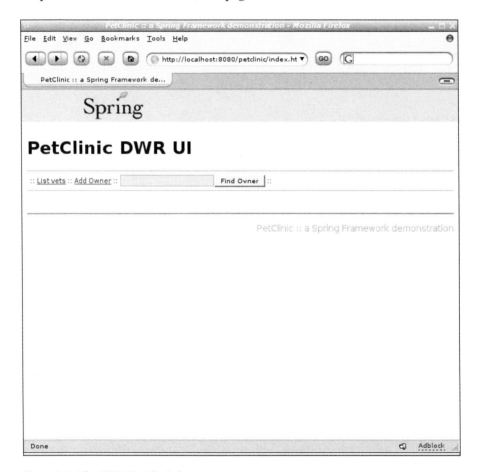

> **Note** Because all of the other JavaScript files have a /dwr/*-type URL, they will all be served up by the DWR servlet according to the web.xml mapping we looked at in Listing B-2.

Let's put all this together and show it in action (or at least as much as we can in the static pages of a book). Figure B-2 shows the index.html page loaded in the browser. It contains a couple of tables in the main area of the page that are hidden with CSS attributes.

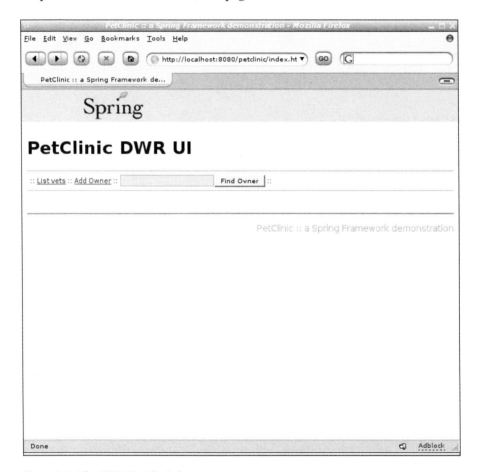

Figure B-2. *The DWR PetClinic home page*

Listing B-5 shows one of the hidden tables in the left half of the blank area of the screen. Note how the table body is given an id attribute, but is left empty.

Listing B-5. *Hidden Tables in index.html*

```
<div id="leftPanel" style="width:58%; float: left">
  <table id="vetlist" class="initHidden">
    <thead>
      <tr>
        <th>first name</th>
        <th>last name</th>
        <th>specialties</th>
      </tr>
    </thead>
    <tbody id="vets"/>
  </table>
```

When we click the List Vets link in the page, a JavaScript function called getVets() is called. It's this function, and the one it delegates to, that do the work of populating the table of vets. Both functions are in local.js and are shown in Listing B-6.

Listing B-6. *local.js Functions for List Vets*

```
function getVets() {
  Clinic.getVets(showVets)
}

function showVets(vetData) {
  document.getElementById("ownerlist").style.display = "none";
  document.getElementById("ownerForm").style.display = "none";
  document.getElementById("vetlist").style.display = "inline";
  DWRUtil.removeAllRows("vets");
  DWRUtil.addRows("vets", vetData, [ getFirstName, getLastName, getSpecialties ]);
}
```

Don't worry if you can't follow all the logic here. The key points are that the JavaScript version of the Clinic object is invoked with Clinic.getVets(). DWR handles the translation of the call to the real object in the ApplicationContext and marshals the returned Collection of vets for us. This is passed to the showVets() function for display, based on the parameter supplied to the getVets() method, where DWR utility methods are called to first clear and then repopulate all of the table rows. The addRows() method takes three parameters:

- The id of the element to update (vets), which as we saw in Listing B-5 was the <tbody> element.

- The collection of data to use (vetData). This was passed to the function by DWR and is the returned value from the Clinic.getVets() method.

- An array of method names to call on each element of the vetData collection. Each of the method names in the array will populate a column of the current table row.

There's a lot going on in those two methods, and the result is shown in Figure B-3.

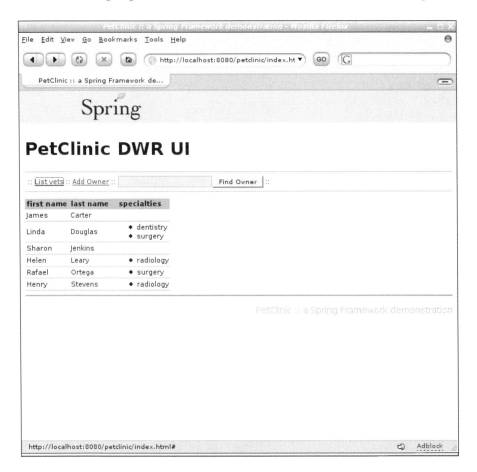

Figure B-3. *Populated vet table*

What we can't easily demonstrate in the book is that the call to the server-side `Clinic` object and the population of the table all took place asynchronously, without requiring a page reload in the browser. If the server-side operation is long running, the browser will still remain responsive for the user, but usually the page updates much faster than when reloading too.

POSTing Updates

We'll complete the lightning tour of functionality with a look at form posts. In Figure B-4, we see the same page again, this time after clicking the Find Owner button to bring up a table of all owners and then clicking the "edit" link for one of them. Both operations are handled by DWR and update the page very snappily (of course, you'll have to download the application and try it out for yourself to see).

The Submit button for the Edit Owner form is linked to another JavaScript function coded in the file `local.js`. In turn, it relies on yet more DWR utility functions (did we mention how much typing it saved you?). Listing B-7 shows the code for the form, and Listing B-8 describes the relevant JavaScript functions.

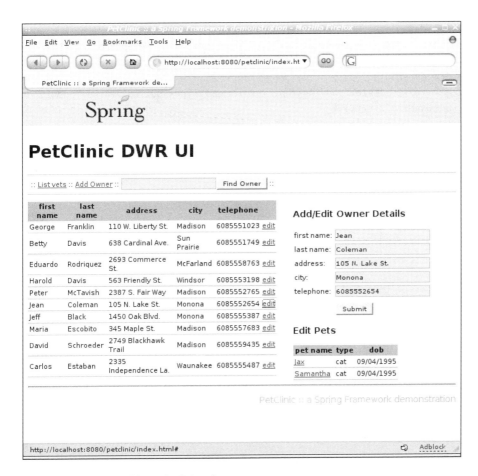

Figure B-4. *Owners table and editing form*

Listing B-7. *Form for Editing Owners*

```
<input type="hidden" id="id"/>
<table>
  <tr style="border-width: 0px">
    <td>first name: </td><td><input class="inp" type="text" id="firstName" /></td>
  </tr>
  <tr style="border-width: 0px">
    <td>last name: </td><td><input class="inp" type="text" id="lastName" /></td>
  </tr>
  <tr style="border-width: 0px">
    <td>address: </td><td><input class="inp" type="text" id="address" /></td>
  </tr>
  <tr style="border-width: 0px">
    <td>city: </td><td><input class="inp" type="text" id="city" /></td>
  </tr>
```

```
<tr style="border-width: 0px">
  <td>telephone: </td><td><input class="inp" type="text" id="telephone" /></td>
</tr>
<tr style="border-width: 0px">
  <td> </td><td style="padding-top: 7px"><input type="button" value="Submit"
onclick="updateOwner()"/></td>
</tr>
</table>
```

Listing B-8. *JavaScript Function for Updating Owners*

```
function updateOwner() {
  DWRUtil.getValues(currentPerson);
  Clinic.storeOwner(findOwners, currentPerson);
}

function findOwners() {
  var s = document.getElementById("owner").value;
  Clinic.findOwners(showOwners, s);
}

function showOwners(ownerData) {
  document.getElementById("vetlist").style.display = "none";
  document.getElementById("ownerlist").style.display = "inline";
  DWRUtil.removeAllRows("owners");
  DWRUtil.addRows(
    "owners",
    ownerData,
    [getFirstName, getLastName, getAddress, getCity,  getTelephone, getOwnerEdit ]
  );
}
```

What's going on here? First off, we need to explain that the value of the JavaScript variable currentPerson was initialized to the name/value pairs of the form when the form was populated. As the submit button calls the updateOwner function, we take advantage of another DWR utility method; getValues. Its input is any object that contains name-value pairs—currentPerson in our example. The names are assumed to be the ids of HTML elements, and the values are altered to reflect the contents of those ids.

Next, we invoke the storeOwner() method of the Clinic service object, instructing DWR to call findOwners immediately after the update returns and passing the currentPerson object holding the name-value pairs from the input fields as the parameter. In the findOwners() function, we make the call on the Clinic's findOwners() Java method and lastly pass control to the showOwners() function, which updates the display. The page, of course, updates just the values that were changed in the owner table with barely a flicker to look like the one in Figure B-5.

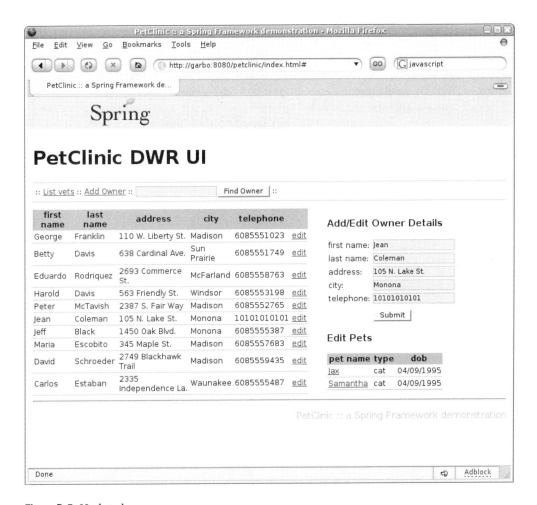

Figure B-5. *Updated owner*

Accessibility

Please remember your target audience when developing web content. If you are producing websites for a large organization, you are almost certainly aware of recent legislation in the U.S. and U.K. that is cracking down on companies that produce inaccessible sites. An over-abundance of JavaScript is a surefire way to make your site unusable for people with audio browsers, text-based browsers and possibly those unable to use a pointing device. Always check that whatever you do with JavaScript can be done another way if the user doesn't have JavaScript available to them.

Summary

We've taken a very brief look at a narrow section of the Ajax world. Our tour covered a quick look at Ajax technology and a practical example of applying Ajax to your Spring applications in the form of DWR. We would strongly encourage you to read up on some of the other Ajax-based technologies too and pick the ones that fit your needs best. In our opinion, it's brought a little more fun back in to the development of browser-based sites; we hope it does for you too.

Index

You Need the Companion eBook

Your purchase of this book entitles you to its companion eBook for only $10.

We believe this Apress title will prove so indispensable that you'll want to carry it with you everywhere, which is why we are offering the companion eBook for $10 to customers who purchase this book now. Convenient and fully searchable, the eBook version of any content-rich, page-heavy Apress book makes a valuable addition to your programming library. You can easily find, copy, and apply code—and then perform examples by quickly toggling between instructions and the application. Even simultaneously tackling a donut, diet soda, and complex code becomes simplified with hands-free eBooks!

Once you purchase this book, getting the $10 companion eBook is simple:

❶ Visit **www.apress.com/promo/tendollars/**.

❷ Complete a basic registration form to receive a randomly generated question about this title.

❸ Answer the question correctly in 60 seconds and you will receive a promotional code to redeem for the $10 eBook.

2560 Ninth Street • Suite 219 • Berkeley, CA 94710

Offer valid through 8/06.